SECOND EDITION

CANADIAN FAMILIES

Diversity, Conflict, and Change

▼

Nancy Mandell
DEPARTMENT OF SOCIOLOGY
YORK UNIVERSITY

Ann Duffy
DEPARTMENT OF SOCIOLOGY
BROCK UNIVERSITY

▲

NELSON
✦ TM
THOMSON LEARNING

Australia • Canada • Mexico • Singapore • Spain • United Kingdom • United States

For more information contact
Nelson Thomson Learning,
1120 Birchmount Road,
Scarborough, Ontario,
M1K 5G4.
Or you can visit our Internet site at
http://www.nelson.com

Canadian Cataloguing in Publication Data

Main entry under title:

Canadian families

2nd ed.
Includes bibliographical references and index.
ISBN 0-7747-3629-1

1. Family — Canada.   I. Mandell, Nancy.   II. Duffy, Ann.

HQ560.C3584   2000   306.85'0971   C98-932434-6

New Editions Editor: Megan Mueller
Senior Developmental Editor: Martina van de Velde
Production Editor: Stephanie Fysh
Production Coordinator: Cheryl Tiongson

Copy Editor: Beverley Beetham Endersby
Cover Design: Sonya V. Thursby, Opus House Incorporated
Interior Design: Brett Miller/Sonya V. Thursby, Opus House Incorporated
Typesetting and Assembly: Bookman Typesetting Co.
Printing and Binding: Transcontinental Printing Inc.

Cover Art: Kathy Ruttenberg, *They Brought Their Dog* (1992). Oil on linen. 60 × 60 inches. Image provided by Gallery Henoch, New York. Reproduced with permission of the artist.

This book was printed in Canada.

2 3 4 5 6   TC   04 03 02 01

To our mothers,

Margaret Louise Pennal

and

Elizabeth Matilda Kaiser

PREFACE

Canadian society and Canadian families are in flux. Global economic restructuring, continuing unemployment, and the downloading of state responsibilities onto individuals represent processes transforming a society that is at the same time wrestling with the effects of profound changes initiated by the disabled, post-colonial, feminist, gay, and racial/ethnic movements.

In this dynamic context, new avenues for understanding the personal and political content of Canadians' lives must be explored. *Canadian Families: Diversity, Conflict, and Change*, Second Edition, is intended as a contribution to this emerging perspective on our families and our lives. Each of the ten chapters, written specifically for this collection, challenges our traditional approaches to the sociology of the family and suggests new directions for analysis and research.

This collection addresses a variety of family-related concerns that until now have received little, if any, systematic attention in traditional family texts. For example, authors explore the proliferation and diversity of families and the critical effects of gender, race, class, age, sexual orientation, economics, and violence on public and private experiences. Societal issues, often on the front page of newspapers and in the forefront of changes in family law and public policy, are examined here in light of recent research findings and feminist activists' concerns. Considerations of woman abuse, single-parent families, poverty, racism, lesbian and gay rights, and aging present contemporary and historically based accounts of the diverse cultural forces affecting the ways people create family units.

The result is a text that seeks to be both accessible and challenging to students. As editors, we have encouraged contributors to present ideas and arguments in clear, well-organized, jargon-free language. While undergraduates will find the material easy to read and comprehend, they will also be confronted with challenging and refreshing perspectives. Their lives are reflected in the narrative accounts of minority families, lesbian and gay-male families, aging families, single-parent families, and poor families. "Learning Objectives," chapter summaries, and boxed inserts highlight important points. "Critical Thinking Questions," a glossary, and suggested further readings are included to stimulate both individual reflection and classroom debate.

Constructing this second edition has put us in contact, once again, with our excellent group of contributors, who continue to incorporate feminist struggles around race, class, economics, sexuality, and violence into everyday explanations of family lives. We remain dazzled by the truly fine work of

Canadian feminist academics and activists who enrich and broaden our understanding of our personal and political experiences.

ACKNOWLEDGEMENTS
▼

Sincere gratitude we extend to all those who have laboured over various chapters, providing critical insight: Heather McWhinney, Megan Mueller, Martina van de Velde, and Stephanie Fysh. We particularly want to acknowledge the enormous contribution of Julianne Momirov, who worked with Nancy Mandell and Tania Das Gupta in revising and incorporating changes into their chapters. Without Julianne's help, neither would have been able to meet her deadline as academic administration, in Mandell's case, and a new baby, in Das Gupta's, pulled them away from this book. We cannot thank her enough for pitching in at the last minute in such an effective, sophisticated, and efficient fashion. We continue to love and cherish the men and women in our lives: Lionel, Jeremy, Ben, Adam, Dusky, Hermana, and Mayra. Their presence sustains and enriches us.

Readers wishing further information on data provided through the co-operation of Statistics Canada may obtain copies of relevant publications by mail from Publication Sales, Statistics Canada, Ottawa, Ontario, Canada K1A 0T6, or by calling 1-613-951-7277 or toll-free 1-800-267-6677. Readers may also send their order by fax to 1-613-951-1584.

A NOTE FROM THE PUBLISHER
▼

Thank you for selecting *Canadian Families: Diversity, Conflict, and Change*, Second Edition, edited by Nancy Mandell and Ann Duffy. The authors and publisher have devoted considerable time to the careful development of this book. We appreciate your recognition of this effort and accomplishment.

We want to hear what you think about *Canadian Families: Diversity, Conflict, and Change*, Second Edition. Please take a few minutes to fill in the stamped reply card at the back of the book. Your comments, suggestions, and criticisms will be valuable to use as we prepare new editions and other books.

CONTRIBUTORS

Anne-Marie Ambert	*York University*
Dorothy E. Chunn	*Simon Fraser University*
Tania Das Gupta	*Atkinson College, York University*
Ann Duffy	*Brock University*
Ellen M. Gee	*Simon Fraser University*
Aviva Goldberg	*York University*
Carolyne A. Gorlick	*King's College, University of Western Ontario*
Lesley D. Harman	*King's College, University of Western Ontario*
Nancy Mandell	*York University*
Anne Martin-Matthews	*University of British Columbia*
Julianne Momirov	*McMaster University*
Carol-Anne O'Brien	*Wilfrid Laurier University*

CONTENTS

Introduction   1

INTRODUCTION

As we near the end of the twentieth century and approach the new millennium, Canadian society is experiencing a profound social and economic transformation every bit as wrenching and far-reaching as the one that occurred in the early nineteenth century: a total rearrangement of the links between families and the wider economy, along with a reorganization of work, gender roles, race relations, family structures, intergenerational expectations, and personal rights (Coontz, 1997). Clinging to old values and outdated behaviours merely prolongs what has been a century-long trek toward the liberation of individuals from traditional family forms and structures, that is, toward ones that offer more freedom to create families that fit the changing needs of individuals over the life course. Diversity, plurality, and individuality distinguish postmodern families of the 1990s. Today, multiple forms and structures — dual earner, never married, reconstituted, cohabitating, gay and lesbian — co-exist with more traditional units, making it almost impossible talk about "the" family. Definitions of what constitutes a family have enlarged, focussing more on what families do than on what they look like. These more expansive family definitions reflect the experience of individuals and their intimate relationships, and acknowledge that families evolve and change.

Feminist, postmodern, and post-colonial analyses of family reveal the contradictions contained within family life. They argue that past narratives or stories of family life have produced a kind of "foreign fiction" about family, inscribing our history within frames that have been largely Western, middle-class, and often arising from unquestioned heterosexist premises. These stories situate the non-powerful in Canadian history as deficient, as lacking, as "other." Feminists, postmodernists, and post-colonialists argue that knowledge about families is often androcentric and constructed from positions of privilege, thus resonating to experiences vastly different from those of most women. Relations of domination and subordination are presented as socially constructed and discursively produced through daily interactions. Systems of hierarchy privilege some family members over others, inscribing power and control through daily rituals, family traditions, and codes of conduct. Taking into account these elements of power, patriarchy, and privilege, a fresh approach reveals women's ambivalent relationship to family as chief family labourer, as principal victim of family violence, as embodiment of family sentimentality and romance. Through material and social discourses, families produce gendered subjectivities in which women and men learn quite different values and ways of behaving. Even though they understand that theoretically all roles are possible, for women the primary role offered and rewarded is wife and mother. Whatever else they do, most women continue to learn that their worth lies in being attractive and desirable to men, directing their emotional energy to men and children, and giving their sexuality to one man.

In the last half of this century, we have seen the erosion of traditional family forms, although family values and ideals seem more resistant to change. Diversity is now the norm. Constraints against homosexual unions have diminished, encouraging the more open acknowledgement of same-sex arrangements. Out of 100 heterosexual families in Canada, 48 are married with children, 29 are married without children, 13 are single-parent, 6 are common-law with children, and 4 are common-law without children. Of these family types, fewer than 13 percent of those married with children conform to the traditional model of the husband/father as the "good provider," the breadwinner, and the wife/mother as the "good" homemaker. This middle-class, mostly white, model existed as a statistical entity and ideological force for about 150 years, from the 1830s to around the 1980s (Bernard, 1972). As the numbers of married women who work full-time for their entire work lives increase, dual-earner families have become the norm, with 53 percent of all families in 1996 following this pattern. Married women now look forward to a lifelong combination of employment and family roles. Married men are increasingly likely to engage in domestic labour and child care as their part-ners' involvement in the labour force has shifted the load somewhat more equitably between spouses (Gerson, 1993). Marriage is a changed institution, and the power of the "good provider" role as a central defining image in our society is diminishing.

While marriage remains one of Canada's most important and valued institutions, fewer people are marrying. At the beginning of the century, more than 90 percent of men and women married once in their lives before the age of 50. Now, estimates suggest that between 63 percent of men and 67 percent of women will marry once before age 50. While marriage was once the pri-mary way of defining gender and age roles, of organizing work lives, of distributing resources, and of marking adulthood, there are now other arrange-ments for regulating sexual behaviour and gender roles, and raising children. Marriage has become an option, rather than a necessity, for women and men (Coontz, 1997). The average age at first marriage has risen to 28 for men and 26 for women. Canadian families continue to shrink in size, with the average family now containing 3.1 persons. Combining work and family responsibil-ities, the lack of affordable and reliable child care, and economic difficulties are some of the reasons that fertility rates among Canadians are depressed. Childlessness is on the rise, with estimates that 16 percent of women now of childbearing age will remain voluntarily or involuntarily childless. Extended families are rare.

We will never again live in a world where people are compelled to stay married (Goode, 1993). Around 30 percent of Canadian marriages end in divorce. Canada's rising divorce rates are the product of long-term social and economic changes, not a breakdown in family values. Canadian attitudes toward divorce have shifted considerably over the century: almost all Canadians believe one should not tolerate an abusive or disrespectful partner; more than one-third think constant argument about money or an unsatisfactory sex life is grounds for divorce; fewer than one-fifth think conflict over raising children, sharing household tasks, or fertility issues justify leaving a marriage; fewer than 50 percent would stay in an unhappy relationship because of the children. At the same time as we have more marital breakdown, we also have many more long marriages, with many people celebrating fortieth anniversaries. A new marital polarization is emerging between increasing numbers of long-lasting, and presumably high-quality, marriages and increasing numbers of short-lived, low-quality marriages (Oppenheimer, 1995).

The spread of diverse, inclusive family types has contributed to the shattering of long-held myths and ideologies. The myth of the family as a private haven, as an idyllic retreat from the harsh realities of modern life, has been largely shattered by revelations of child abuse, incest, and woman battering. Women more often and more brutally fall prey to violence, yet many male children, too, have felt the vulnerability and pain of assault at the hands of caretakers in orphanages and residential schools, and within their own nuclear enclaves. The myth of egalitarianism, of mutual and reciprocal interdependence between spouses, has been sharply criticized by women who point out that employment, while providing a measure of financial security and independence, has doubled their load, adding wage labour to domestic responsibilities. The myth of the family wage, of a wage earned by a male breadwinner sufficient to sustain dependent women and children, though never accurately descriptive of working-class situations, has been completely eroded by economic recessions (Ghalam, 1997).

Families have always been shock absorbers for larger economic trends taking place in Canadian society. Economic news for most Canadian families in the past twenty years has been negative. Most families have acutely felt the devastating consequences of unemployment, recession, and economic restructuring. Real wages, the amount a worker can actually buy with a pay cheque, have been declining since 1973. Most families need two earners, working longer hours, to maintain a family living standard that could be provided by one earner in the 1950s and 1960s. The amount left in a worker's pocket from her or his hourly wage, after taking out income taxes and adjusting for inflation, has fallen by nearly 1 percent each year since the early 1970s. This gradual economic decline has been borne by young families who increasingly cannot afford family life. A young man, under age 25, working full-time, in 1994 earned 31 percent less per week than his counterpart in 1973 (Gordon, 1996). This has meant a greatly lengthened period of "economic adolescence," the period when young adults are working full-time but not earning enough to support a family or be fully self-sufficient (Sum, Fogg, and Taggert, 1996). Permanent jobs with full-time benefits are hard to find. Companies have become more portable, and workers more easily thrown away. Insecure working conditions, low pay, long hours, and lack of control over work conditions are associated with significant increases in drug use, alcohol, accident-proneness, and displacement of anger onto family members (Coontz, 1997). Not everyone has fallen behind. Rising inequality between the rich and poor means that, in the 1990s, the top 20 percent of wealth holders received 99 percent of the total gain in marketable wealth, while the bottom 80 percent of the population received only 1 percent of the total. Unemployment, underemployment, and insecure employment widen the gap between the financially comfortable and the poor, undermining the economic status of individuals and families. Everyday understandings of what is just and fair, of what can and should be expected in a family lifetime, are disrupted.

Statistics and polls reveal that Canadians are bewildered by the myriad changes affecting families. Sociologists suggest that marriage has become deinstitutionalized, meaning that the family has a declining ability and a declining need to carry out its functions of procreation; socialization of its young; affective nurturance; social control of its members; and production, consumption, and distribution of goods and services. While Canadians agree that marriage and family are transformed, they disagree about the effects of this transformation on both individuals and society. Optimists view the family, not as declining, but as adapting and reshaping to meet new economic and cultural demands. Traditional family structures are deemed inappropriate, too restrictive, too male-dominated, and too lacking in resilience. Pessimists tend to frame their discussion of effects in an alarmist manner, warning that acceptance of diverse family forms signals the eventual demise of the family. They fail to recognize that change comes from factors few people would change, even though changing these factors would strengthen the institution of marriage. Who wants to shorten life spans? Who wants to lower the age of marriage or force young people to live at home or make marriage the only path for living a productive, fulfilling adult life (Wilson and Clarke, 1992)? Population changes, urbanization, marriages at younger ages, children living at home longer, fewer mortality crises, marriages based on mutual satisfaction, and the household need for lots of wage earners are all trends that have been brewing for centuries.

The essays in this book highlight many of these themes, conflicts, and contradictions. They point to the need for a discussion of family that acknowledges that historically families have always been diverse, that families have frequently experienced considerable economic pressure, and that families constantly challenge legal and social definitions of appropriate roles and relationships. This collection has been guided by a consideration of variables of gender, race, class, and sexuality as they alter and modify traditional forms and ideologies. As we leave behind old ideas from this century, we move into the new millennium with fresh perspectives from the traditions of feminism, post-modernism, and post-colonialism.

FAMILY HISTORIES
▼

The first chapter on the history of Canadian families conceptualizes change as a constant feature. By examining the past, we come to understand contemporary family forms and ideas. As Mandell and Momirov explain, the human odyssey starts in Canada with hunting-and-gathering societies. Here, family relations were mostly communal and co-operative. Starting around 800 B.C.E., some Native societies adopted a more settled, horticulture-based lifestyle. Despite vast differences in Native ways of life, beginning in the late 1400s and early 1500s European invasion initiated a long process of colonization aimed to destroy Native culture and subordinate its people. In the early days of the fur trade and the establishment of colonial settlements, women were in short supply and enjoyed considerable economic and cultural privilege. As populations grew, women's legal and religious status was subordinated to that of their husbands and fathers. Women's skills and labour, always crucial to the family's and community's survival, meant women and men shared a mutual dependency. Too often, this daily interdependency did not translate into economic or political equality.

With the growth of industrialization, family life was modified. Cities grew and were transformed as local and immigrant labour began to build the country. Families became dependent on wage labour as production moved out of the household into factories and shops. Ideas about appropriate behaviour for men and women altered. Increasingly, women were restricted to the domestic realm, while their employment options were eroded. When family production was replaced by family consumption, large families diminished as children became a financial liability. Family privacy, personal fulfilment, and individualism became more prominent concerns, especially among the well-to-do classes. The demands, routines, and standards of paid employment and the market economy intruded more and more into the lives of families, especially working-class and poor families. Economic stresses were further compounded for immigrant and visible-minority families, who also had to contend with the daily pressures of racism and discrimination.

The modern family, with all its diversity of structure and content, is the outgrowth of these various historical trends and forces. Present-day Canadians may feel caught up in a whirlwind of political, cultural, social, and economic change, yet such change has been integral to understanding the history of our family lives.

CHILDREN'S ROLE IN THE PARENT-CHILD RELATIONSHIP: AN INTERACTIVE PERSPECTIVE ON SOCIALIZATION
▼

What causes children's behaviour? Traditional theories of socialization posit a unidirectional, linear view of learning. In family terms, this view suggests that adults speak and children listen. In her provocative chapter, Anne-Marie Ambert reveals traditional socialization theories as deficient insofar as they ignore the significant role children play in determining parents' behaviour and fail to conceptualize socialization as an ongoing, interactive process. Traditional, causal perspectives deflect attention away from children's individual characteristics, their social locations, and their efficacy in shaping the behavioural responses they receive. Delinquency research, for example, often focusses on parents as the source of and solution to delinquent children's actions rather than seeing children as co-producing their own problems. Individual personality traits and environmental influences affect behaviour, with parents moderating practices accordingly. Children and adolescents may elicit coercive or rejecting behaviour from adults. Parents, for example, may become more controlling and harsh in parenting style once their children are apprehended for delinquent acts. Difficult children facilitate the disruption of their own environment, while compliant children are experienced as more easily socialized by parents. Ambert also discusses the effect of young adult children on their parents, noting the diminishing saliency of the "empty nest" syndrome. Young adults often fail to recognize that their mothers also experience relief when they leave home. The relationship between adult children and their parents remains underresearched, with the emphasis remaining on the children, not the parents. Research examines the effect on children of caring for parents, ignoring the effect on parents of the type of care they receive. Overall, parental influence has been waning throughout this century as children spend less and less time with them. In fact, new studies suggest that peers constitute the single most important influence on children's lives.

CONTEMPORARY DIVERSITIES
▼

Using mostly demographic data, Gee deconstructs the idea that the modern family is in decline or crisis. By examining long-term, empirical trends, she demonstrates the ways in which household and family structures have become more diverse and the ways in which they have remained the same. Underlying her explanation is an emphasis on the economic and institutional. Gee begins with the most common misconception, that families in the past were large, extended units with clearly defined roles for men and women. Historical evidence suggests that extended structures were never common; that death and desertion, not divorce, led to many single-parent units; and that working-class, and especially non-white, women have always contributed to family income. Moreover, state policies, such as the Oriental Exclusion Act, affected family formation. In fact, diversity — traditional, single-parent families, blended families, gay and lesbian partnerships, and other forms proliferate — has always been the norm in Canada, except during a brief period when stable marriages, husband-as-breadwinner, and wife-as-homemaker forms were commonplace. Gee points out how, in discussion of family life, diversification and normalization are often obscured by the illusion of change. For example, contrary to popular perceptions that marriages are now being delayed, age at first marriage has merely returned to its historically typical pattern. Similarly, it is still the case that most wives are younger than their husbands, which has important implications for family power relations. There has, however, been a dramatic increase in common-law relations, opening up a new route into marriage entry. There has also been a sharp increment in marital dissolution — estimates predict that 30 to 38 percent of first marriages will end in divorce — although more marriages still end in widowhood. Remarriages, ever popular, are even more likely to end in divorce than first marriages. Until the 1999 National Survey of Gays and Lesbians is analyzed, reliable statistics on the numbers of gay and lesbian partnerships remain unavailable. The overall decline in family fertility has eliminated earlier diversities in family size found among different social classes, religions, and rural areas. There exists now a two-child norm. Family responsibilities are shifting as well. Over the life course, we will now spend more time caring for our parents than raising our children. The drop in real family income, limited employment opportunities for young men and women, unemployment of fathers/husbands, women's unemployment, and reduced government spending on social programs are all economic trends with negative impacts on families. Family poverty and the stress women experience in managing both paid and unpaid work continue to be alarming trends.

LESBIANS AND GAY MEN INSIDE AND OUTSIDE FAMILIES
▼

O'Brien and Goldberg's revisionist chapter on the lived experiences of gay men and lesbians living inside and outside traditional family structures offers a much-needed corrective to family texts. They deconstruct monolithic ideas common in most family texts that tend to describe and evaluate all aspects of family life by unequal and heterosexist norms. Instead, they expand definitions of what constitutes a family, to embrace the range of diverse forms that have always existed. O'Brien and Goldberg identify numerous myths that continue to underlie family sociology. Family ideology that positions lesbians and gay men as outside of and a menace to families is exposed as homophobic in its artificial division of gay and non-gay families and as heterosexist in its treatment of heterosexual unions as the only legitimate family form. They also disrupt normally complacent family stories by privileging the role of gay men and lesbians in creating Canada. In the past, for example, in the settlement of the Canadian West, sex between men was common and tolerated in all-male logging, mining, and farming communities. In the present, lesbian and gay relationships are numerous, committed, enduring, and monogamous, with a breakup rate approximately equal to that of heterosexual partnerships. While partner abuse remains a problem, same-sex relationships more often contain two wage earners and are distinguished as more egalitarian in decision making, more likely to share power, and more likely to encourage individual self-esteem, than are heterosexual couples.

Living in a homophobic society means that lesbian and gay youth encounter physical and verbal harassment, social isolation, and rejection by their families and schools. Social and institutional assumptions of heterosexuality render invisible the experiences of homosexual youth. Youth and adults counter negative environments by creating supportive communities among peers and around common interests, such as religion. Extensive friendship and social support networks come into existence through people voluntarily caring for each other, providing material and emotional support. In addition, by establishing nurturing partnerships and by adding children, through birth, adoption, previous marriages, and artificial insemination, to these relationships, lesbians and gay men love and live in enduring arrangements.

FAMILIES OF NATIVE PEOPLE,
IMMIGRANTS, AND PEOPLE OF COLOUR
▼

Das Gupta provides an anti-racist perspective on Canadian family lives, providing a powerful description of the ways state policies affect family formation among Native people, immigrants, and people of colour. Focussing on Chinese, South Asian, Japanese, black, and Native histories, she outlines mechanisms the state has employed to deny these groups opportunities to create families of their own choice. Beginning with the fur trade, Das Gupta shows how Native women and men were forced to engage in colonial enterprises or face decimation through warfare. When their labour was no longer essential, they were disregarded and abandoned. White destruction of Native traditions continued through racist educational policies, sexual abuse, adoption of their children, and their sequestration on reserves. Native resilience and resistance to state genocidal policies led to their creation of alternative educational, work, and child-welfare practices, thus ensuring their cultural survival. Das Gupta also discusses the history of "sojourners," men from various Asian countries who migrated to Canada in the nineteenth century who were so called as it was assumed they would not permanently settle in Canada. Chinese men, for example, were originally subjected to a head tax that ensured a bachelor society for many years. Before 1908, the Japanese community consisted mostly of single males. The 1908 continuous-journey stipulation of Canadian immigration laws and stringent financial limitations restricted entry of South Asians. Once allowed to enter, visible-minority groups faced numerous racist policies. For a long time, immigration for Filipinos and Caribbeans favoured only women, who were encouraged to enter as domestics. Foreign domestic workers in Canada are denied basic citizenship rights as temporary workers who are vulnerable to economic exploitation. Canadian slavery also created a structure of cultural, economic, and political oppression that communities have struggled to overcome. Racist attitudes to families have resulted in numerous adaptations in form and relationships. Das Gupta's chapter highlights the effects of immigration policies, economic structures, educational systems, child welfare, and social-service initiatives in making it extremely difficult for families of Native people, people of colour, and immigrants to construct families of their own choosing.

FAMILY POVERTY AND ECONOMIC STRUGGLES
▼

Most discussions of family life ignore the impact of economic stress upon families. Yet, the significant and continuing drop in real family incomes, rising unemployment and underemployment, and the decline in government support for social services means that increasing numbers of families face daily stress as they struggle to "make ends meet." Beginning with definitions of poverty, Harman discusses the meaning of deprivation in our relatively wealthy country. Why is it that Canada, with one of the world's highest standards of living, has so many people relying on food banks, state contributions, school lunch programs, clothing donations, and subsidized housing? Why are our numbers of homeless people increasing? Harman points out that poverty has always been a persistent feature of Canadian society. The shift from an agrarian to a wage-labouring economy created a class of highly mobile, wage-dependent employees subject to irregular, seasonal, dangerous, unhealthy, and usually poorly paid work. Tenacious poverty grew alongside industrialization, giving rise to the new "working poor," a large group of full-time workers not earning enough money to support dependent partners and children. Today's poor are more likely to be found in cities, to include more young families than ever before, and to include more elderly and single-parent families. Structural inequality widens the gap between the "have" and "have not" portions of the population. Persistent poverty inflicts devastating consequences on families, shattering dreams, lowering self-esteem, and dashing future expectations. As a society, Canada also pays a price for impoverishment, with increased social-assistance costs, higher school drop-out rates, and decreased productivity. Harman's chapter provides a sobering reminder of the reality of many people's lives and forces us to rethink our social commitment to equity and justice.

"POLITICIZING THE PERSONAL": FEMINISM, LAW, AND PUBLIC POLICY
▼

Family law and policy have always privileged the traditional, nuclear-family form, assuming a male-breadwinner and female-homemaker norm. Legal reforms have thus had a contradictory effect on women's social status, sometimes maintaining the status quo and more recently promoting social equity. Canadian feminists began campaigning for legal and policy reforms in the late 1800s. First-wave, or maternal, feminists promoted legal reforms that would enable women to carry out their duties as wives and mothers. Second-wave feminists were more reformist or radical in their demands, assuming women and men were social equals who required legal enactment of their rights. Beginning in the 1960s, liberal feminists worked to achieve equality of opportunity in the public sphere for women, by accessing education, promoting divorce reforms, and advocating child- and family-welfare laws. By the 1970s, radical and socialist feminists mounted a more explicit critique of bourgeois family ideology, marking the family as a site of personal and social oppression for women. More recent decades have seen challenges from disabled women, visible-minority women, and lesbian women who challenge legal scholars to examine middle-class, white, heterosexist, and able-bodied presumptions and solutions. Using a series of historical cases, Chunn provides a detailed analysis of the efficacy and effects of first- and second-wave initiatives. Too often, feminist-inspired legal changes have not achieved equality, but instead have increased women's structural dependency on marriage and male wages. The discourse of "individual rights" fails to contextualize difference insofar as it assumes that monolithic change affects all women everywhere in the same way. Chunn concludes that legislation aimed to promote greater equality in family relationships and structures needs to theorize difference and promote substantive, rather than only formal, equality.

DIVORCE: OPTIONS AVAILABLE, CONSTRAINTS FORCED, PATHWAYS TAKEN

▼

The recent rapid rise in the divorce rate focusses attention on both the process and the consequences of divorce. As around 30 to 35 percent of the married population experience divorce, Gorlick alerts us to significant patterns: female single-parent families are far more prevalent than their male equivalents, and almost 45 percent of Canadian children can expect to experience divorce before age 18. What are some of the effects on family relationships, children's behaviour, and family involvement with the state? For a long time, the deviance model of divorce pathologized divorce as profoundly negative for everyone involved. More recently, the opportunity model positions divorce as a chance for personal growth. Both models tend to ignore economic, ethnic, and gender differences in experience.

Gorlick reviews some of the common myths of divorce emerging from both these models, and counters previous misconceptions: the belief that divorce always has long-term negative effects on children; that divorced fathers provide sufficient and consistent alimony and child support; that custodial mothers can choose whether to take on paid employment; that mothers who do not seek custody are either immoral or unfit; that divorce legislation reforms eliminate gender inequities; and that divorce mediation and joint custody provide more equitable solutions for women. Having reviewed divorce literature, Gorlick turns to a longitudinal study of 150 single mothers on social assistance. The continued increase and impoverishment of female-headed single-parent families alarms social planners. Yet still, Gorlick's study provides some sites of optimism. For most single mothers, time spent on social assistance is short, not lengthy as the myth suggests. Despite their enormous burdens, single mothers fight constantly to stabilize income, devising innovative cost-saving measures that ensure their children's welfare and happiness. Social policy and practices — low welfare payments; negative practices of social-service agencies; and misleading myths about the poor that constrain, rather than facilitate, options for single mothers — need to be abandoned if we as a society are going to work to improve the lives of single mothers.

FAMILY VIOLENCE: ISSUES AND ADVANCES
AT THE END OF THE TWENTIETH CENTURY
▼

This chapter explores one of our most troubling areas of life, family violence. Duffy and Momirov's subtitle phrase, "at the end of the twentieth century" reminds us that, far from being resolved, family violence continues to permeate the daily lives of many. Despite receiving constant media attention and being addressed in numerous academic studies and policy initiatives, family violence remains routine and widespread. The 1993 Canadian national survey of violence against women estimates that assaults on wives occur with alarming frequency and severity. In half of all violent relationships, a weapon has been used. Similar data on child abuse are not available, although estimates suggest that a substantial amount of physical abuse and neglect occurs. These devastating reports of fairly common experiences of family violence have motivated studies investigating both individual and social effects. Social costs are quite staggering as one tallies direct costs such as lost income, welfare payments, and housing subsidies, as well as individual costs, including abandoned careers, destroyed self-esteem, and pervasive anxiety. Duffy and Momirov insist that our belief in myths of family harmony, peace, and prosperity blind us to current reality and hamper our ability to make change. Historical accounts demonstrate that Canadian women have long experienced violence, including rape of young women, physical and sexual abuse of children, elder and sibling abuse, and woman assault. Historical and global evidence helps explain the current normalization of everyday violence despite efforts by sociologists and feminists to identify systemic causes. Theories of socialization, exchange, materialism, and feminism provide frameworks within which studies explore this continued problem. More recent attempts to integrate diversity into analyses reveal the complex intersection of economics, sexuality, racism, and colonialism in violent acts that move beyond a simple gender-based explanation. Despite this attention to context and control, we remain handicapped by an incomplete understanding of and willingness to act against family violence. Success in articulating and enacting effective policy solutions continues to elude too many Canadians.

CHANGE AND DIVERSITY IN AGING FAMILIES
AND INTERGENERATIONAL RELATIONS
▼

In her chapter on aging families, Martin-Matthews discusses the changing context of aging and families in Canada. Throughout the twentieth century, the proportion of elderly people in Canada has increased from about 6 percent of the population in the early 1960s to 12 percent in 1996. The number of elderly has more than doubled since the 1970s. By 2001, the proportion of people over 65 years of age is projected to be about 4 million. By 2010, when the oldest baby boomers begin to retire, the impact of population aging will be most pronounced. As life expectancy has increased, ideas and attitudes toward aging and the elderly have altered. For the most part, the world of the elderly is a world of women, as women continue to live about seven years longer than men. Increased longevity has led to longer family ties across generations, with parents and children often sharing 50 years together. Couples stay married longer, with many reporting increased marital satisfaction as time passes. Martin-Matthews discusses how aging is a social process influenced by health, economic, and social changes. In particular, she demonstrates how values, norms, and social-structural features, such as gender, race and ethnicity, religion, and social class, affect aging experiences. Well-educated, wealthy elderly are likely to experience greater independence and social support than those who reach old age with lower levels of income. Intergenerational caregiving, especially serial caregiving, has emerged as a major issue in the past twenty years. Most adult children continue to live within an hour's travel of their elderly parents. Daughters, more than sons, provide emotional kin care and are more likely to take days off work to meet family obligations. Lesbian women report high levels of social support. Almost one-quarter of the aged speak neither English nor French, reflecting the ethnic diversity of the elderly. Language barriers, religious and cultural differences, and economic dependency may reduce access to social services. As the population ages, social-policy considerations take on special urgency.

CONCLUDING REMARKS
▼

The ten chapters in *Canadian Families: Diversity, Conflict, and Change,* Second Edition, are organized into three major sections: (1) the historic and social context of change; (2) diversities in Canadian families; and (3) family issues on the edge of change. Each chapter challenges myths and stereotypes by drawing on historical and diverse comparisons. Ideas of the family as a harmonious and peaceful enclave are contradicted by the growing evidence of daily conflicts over power and control, some resulting in serious violence. Ideas of the family as separate from society at large, a space where we may shut out the cares of the world, are contradicted by the intrusion into family life of economic instability, restructuring, racism, heterosexism, and other expressions of cultural conflict. Finally, we have seen that it never did make sense to talk of the family as a two-parent, two-children, father-breadwinner and mother-homemaker unit. Family diversity characterizes our past and present arrangements. Acknowledging diversity enables us to recognize the dynamic nature of families, interacting as they do with the ever-changing social, political, cultural, and economic contexts that surround and shape daily life. Postmodern families embrace change, celebrate diversity, revel in contradiction, and work to demolish violence.

REFERENCES
▼

Bernard, Jessie. 1972. *The Future of Marriage*. New York: Bantam.

Cootnz, Stephanie. 1997. *The Way We Really Are: Coming to Terms with America's Changing Families*. New York: Basic Books.

Gerson, Kathleen. 1993. *No Man's Land: Men's Changing Commitments to Family and Work*. New York: Basic Books.

Ghalam, Nancy Zukewich. 1997. "Attitudes Toward Women, Work and Family." *Canadian Social Trends*. Ottawa: Statistics Canada, Autumn.

Goode, William. 1993. *World Changes in Divorce Patterns*. New Haven, CT: Yale University Press.

Gordon, David. 1996. *Fat and Mean: The Corporate Squeeze of Working America and the Myth of Managerial "Downsizing."* New York: Martin Kessler Books/The Free Press.

Oppenheimer, Valerie. 1995. "Women's Economic Independence and Men's Career Maturity: Their Impact on Marriage Formation in the 1980s." *Mathematical Social Sciences* 30: 95–96.

Sum, Andrew, Neal Fogg, and Robert Taggert. 1996. "The Economics of Despair." *American Prospect* 27: 83–84.

Wilson, Barbara, and Sally Clarke. 1992. "Remarriages: A Demographic Profile." *Journal of Family Issues* 13: 41–63.

▼

PART ONE

FAMILIES IN HISTORICAL AND SOCIAL CONTEXT

▼

FAMILY HISTORIES

NANCY MANDELL AND JULIANNE MOMIROV

LEARNING OBJECTIVES

In this chapter, you will learn that:

- gender, race, and class shape family histories;
- Canada's history has been told from multiple perspectives, some of which are better known than others;
- the status of women, children, and men varies according to the economic context in which they live;
- assumptions about women's and men's responsibilities for wage and domestic labour differ over time;
- historical accounts tend to idealize the past.

INTRODUCTION

This chapter sketches the histories of Canadian families, beginning with those belonging to hunting-and-gathering societies, briefly considering families in fur-trading and agrarian settlements, and concentrating largely on family changes brought about by industrialization. Its purposes are threefold: to correct previous historical accounts, which have uncritically superimposed a European framework onto the Canadian past; to assess the classed, raced, gendered, and sexed nature of **family** structures and relationships; and to stress the diversity and multiplicity of family histories. Canadian historical writing, for instance, almost completely ignores the presence of a black community here, despite their 350-year history. Yet, to overlook black, Native, immigrant, or working-class history is to distort our image of ourselves as Canadians and the forces that have made us what we are.

An effort has been made in this chapter to devote attention to our early history, as the rest of this book concentrates on contemporary roles, relationships, and issues. As this book makes clear, many of our current family patterns emerge from our unique Canadian background.

HUNTING AND GATHERING
▼

Compared with that of other countries, Canada's human prehistory is recent. Until the last ice age ended, Canada's landscape was largely inhospitable for human settlement (Price, 1979). Humans first entered Canada about 30 000 years ago. Approximately 10 000 years ago, the first people moved into the far north of what is now the Yukon. Information gathered during the establishment of the new Canadian territory of Nunavut[1] in 1999 indicates that, from pre-contact times, the Inuit have used and occupied virtually all of the land north of the tree line and used most of the northern ocean (Bryan, 1986; Elliott, 1983; Stout, 1997).

The aboriginal population was and remains ethnically diverse. Historically, some tribes engaged in a sedentary way of life in Southern Ontario; others took up a migratory, buffalo-oriented life on the prairies (Ponting, 1986). Some groups were considered affluent, acquiring more food than needed to meet group needs, while others remained impoverished (Ray, 1996, p. 84). Despite their many differences, aboriginal groups successfully adapted to their environmental situations, and because of those differences they developed distinct economies, oral cultures, art forms, and philosophies (Bryan, 1986).

For 99 percent of human history, hunting and gathering has been the major means of subsistence.[2] Today, hunters and gatherers constitute only about 0.01 percent of the world's population. The Inuit and Indians of Canada are among them (Nett, 1988, p. 40). In the past, Canadian hunters and gatherers regularly moved with each season, following available food supplies. Hunting groups of between 6 and 30 people (1 to 5 families), lived by hunting and trapping wild game — caribou, moose, beaver, bear, hare, porcupine, and waterfowl — by fishing, by hunting small animals, and by gathering wild berries and vegetation (Leacock, 1991). Like most hunting people, the Inuit lived frugally, travelled lightly, and seldom intentionally recorded their accomplishments (Bryan, 1986). Hunting-and-gathering groups developed shared economies and leadership based on residence, gender, age, and ability. Life expectancy was short (Druke, 1986).

In hunting-and-gathering societies, family structure and organization has certain general features. First Nations groups valued the family as the fundamental unit of the community. Most families were characterized by interdependent and extensive kinship ties. Intragroup marriage resulted in large, extended families and multiple obligations. Many families were matrilineal, wherein mothers, daughters, and sisters worked together. Although hierarchies of status, gender, and authority existed, family members were interdependent, as they relied upon the work of others for their survival.

Within families and communities, a gendered division of labour appeared. Women and men lived in separate but mostly reciprocal spheres, each of them responsible for certain tasks (Leacock, 1991). Among the Iroquoian- and Algonquian-speaking people, men were associated with forests, and women with clearings. Men were primarily responsible for hunting large game, fishing, warfare, councils, religion, politics, building, manufacturing implements for hunting and fishing, and, among those groups involved in horticulture, clearing the fields (Druke, 1986). Men also made wooden devices such as toboggans, sleds, snowshoe frames, and spoons. Men butchered animals and skinned them for pelts, and repaired lanterns, canoes, fish nets, and clothes. Men often cut and hauled wood.

Women, aided by children, did most of the agricultural work and gathering of fruits, vegetable foods, and firewood (Druke, 1986). Women's foraging took place close to home, with children in tow. Men's hunting and fishing took them away from the campsite for long periods and was not always successful. So, women's fishing, hunting of small animals, and gathering of roots, herbs, fruits, berries, insects, birds, and eggs, supplied the band's basic caloric and protein requirements (Leacock, 1991). Women were generally restricted from participating in certain activities, such as making war, hunting of large animals, and ruling the tribe, but enjoyed a fair degree of autonomy and control over their own work. Group recognition of the essential nature of women's work meant women had some control over their sexuality and exercised some authority in local politics (Bourgeault, 1988; Bradbury, 1996; Van Kirk, 1992).

Women also managed the household: they bore and reared children, prepared food, made clothing, repaired household items, as well as developing a wide range of domestic equipment such as wooden utensils, basketry, pottery, and the mortar and pestle. Native women had knowledge of medicinal herbs, midwifery, and some surgery. Some authors suggest that women were pregnant or nursing most of their brief lives (Price, 1979); others suggest that the small family size indicates women's knowledge of birth control and abortifacients (McLaren, 1977). Still others suggest that a nomadic lifestyle, irregular diet, and taboos restricting sexual relations depressed women's fertility (Van Kirk, 1992).

Hunting cultures survived in Canada well into the 1800s. In 1850, there were about 30 bands in Quebec and Labrador. In the West, a Native population of 150 000 people was harvesting herds of millions of buffalo. It was not until the mid-1800s that the first major wave of white migration settled the Canadian West. The Native people, as described by the Europeans between 1830 and 1880, had the most highly developed hunting culture in the world.

HORTICULTURE AND AGRICULTURE
▼

Agriculture swept through North America after 1500 B.C.E., but the short Southern Ontario growing season precluded the cultivation of decent corn crops. In fact, corn agriculture did not take hold in Southern Ontario until 800 C.E., making agriculture a recent phase in Canadian history. For most of Canadian history, hunting predominated and was supplemented by other food sources: fish in coastal British Columbia, agriculture in Southern Ontario and in the St. Lawrence River valley, shellfish on Prince Edward Island, and wild rice around the Great Lakes.[3]

By the 1500s, there were two cultures in Ontario: hunter–gatherer bands in the north, and horticultural, tribally organized Native people in the south. Permanent Iroquois settlements appeared in the St. Lawrence River valley and the Great Lakes region, while those speakers of the Algonquian language family remained hunter–gatherers, inhabiting what is now Quebec and the forests bordering the Atlantic (Morrison and Wilson, 1986; Price, 1979).

Plant-gathering, shellfish-gathering, and fishing societies tended to be more sedentary than hunting societies. Societies that relied on domesticated plants cultivated with hand tools provided a more reliable food supply and set the stage for more sedentary communities, an increased population, and more complex social and political arrangements (Nett, 1988). The Maritime Mi'kmaq, whose language is part of the Algonquian language family, for instance, were a solidly maritime group, with extended families living in villages stretched along the Atlantic coast (Miller, 1986).

Since women gathered most of the plants in tribal societies, they took responsibility for agriculture. After marriage, women stayed with and worked co-operatively with their mothers and sisters, planting corn, beans, and squash. The increased protein provided by crops rendered meat protein less important. This steady supply of nutrients led to a population expansion. Gradually, large villages were built, with rows of multifamily longhouses (Druke, 1986). The collective family existed as the primary unit of production. Within these, the **nuclear family** functioned as an integral part of each band, on which all individuals depended (Leacock, 1991).

THE EUROPEAN CONQUEST: 1500s–1700s
▼

Despite vast differences among aboriginal peoples, all share a historical resistance to corporate and government policies of cultural genocide, of what

Ponting (1986) calls "the deliberate extinction of Indians as Indians." Colonization of aboriginal peoples, the process of bringing territory and people under new and more stringent forms of control, began with the establishment of English and French settlements. European colonizers drained resources from Native lands and transferred wealth to England and France; in the process, they destroyed numerous Native cultures (Bolaria and Li, 1988).

Fur trading early in the 1400s and 1500s led to the establishment of trading posts and provided Native people with a stable food supply in exchange for furs. Eventually, economic dependence was fostered when European goods replaced traditional ones; when alcohol came into use; when new tools of work such as guns, knives, and axes were introduced; and when Native labour activities became largely controlled by Europeans (Bourgeault, 1988). When English and French explorers entered Canada in the 1500s, Native people were thriving (Druke, 1986). Europeans brought disease, destruction, and defeat. Smallpox and other infectious illnesses decimated populations, as did the warfare central to the fur trade (Druke, 1986). Smallpox epidemics of the 1630s decreased the Huron population from 20 000 to 9000 (Druke, 1986). Devastating wars broke out among tribes who were backed by rival French, Dutch, and English powers. Intense hostilities between warring nations over the immensely profitable fur trade led to atrocities. In the 1700s, the 50-year English campaign of genocide against all Mi'kmaq peoples, who supported the French, included such vile acts as the English serving poisoned food at a feast in 1812; trading contaminated cloth in 1745; and employing Mohawks, Algonquians, and soldiers to track and kill Mi'kmaqs (Miller, 1986). Native warfare led then to disease, famine, and fierce competition over trade routes. The Huron population, for example, was reduced from between 60 000 and 80 000 in the late 1500s to 24 000 in 1640, and finally to a mere 1500 in 1651.

Colonial fur trading demanded changes in Native lifestyles that depleted their populations. Among the Mi'kmaq, for example, diets were affected, food stores became inadequate and nutritionally deficient, miscellaneous accidents and injuries increased, and life expectancy dropped dramatically (Miller, 1986). Since colonizers were interested only in the production and circulation of fur as a commodity in the world market, Indian communal society had to be transformed from subsistence to producing goods for exchange (Bourgeault, 1988). For other tribes, further trading demanded their specialization in trapping and reduced reliance on traditional subsistence practices. By the time Champlain landed in what were to be Montreal and Quebec City, in 1603, those prospering villages had been abandoned.

NATIVE SENSE OF FAMILY
▼

For 200 years, from the 1500s to the 1700s, mostly white men and Native people engaged in fur trading, hunting, gathering, horticulture, and agriculture. Colonial accounts of Native life, while paternalistic, describe cultural conflicts. Once the Christian conversion of Native people began in earnest in 1632, in Quebec, Jesuit priests were forced to confront the vast differences between European and Native family lives. Native spouses were said to enjoy easy relations, as "women know what they are to do and the men also; and One never meddles with the work of the other" (Leacock, 1991, p. 13). Many Native family relationships and practices baffled Europeans: personal autonomy; lack of hierarchy; spousal interdependence; abundant love for their children; abhorrence of inflicting corporal punishment, fear, or humiliation on children; easy divorce by consent; flexible residential choice; polygamy; and sexual freedom after marriage for both women and men.

In contrast, European marriages of the 1600s subscribed to the **patriarchal theory of the family**, as men's superiority was enshrined in law and religion. Wives, especially bourgeois ones, were enjoined to be obedient, pious, and dependent decision-makers in deference to their husbands. Frequently, husbands were physically abusive and enjoyed the legal right to beat their wives and children. Divorce was virtually unobtainable. Husbands' adultery was sanctioned, whereas wives' was severely punished (Zinn and Eitzen, 1993).

Inevitably, Native women clashed with Catholic priests. Used to consultative and co-operative decision making, Native women found European demands for unquestioned obedience to men ludicrous and demeaning. Most Native people never accepted European family ideals of unequal spousal relationships, premarital chastity, marital fidelity, monogamy, male courtship, and male dominance.

Despite their resistance to European and Christian mores, Native women played such a vital role in fur trading that interracial unions were sanctioned by an indigenous rite known as **customary marriages** with "les femmes du pays" (country wives).

Women's skills in hunting, gathering, skinning animals, and preserving furs, their abilities in trade and diplomacy, and their knowledge of several Native languages made their services invaluable to their voyageur husbands (Jamieson, 1986). Many European traders survived harsh Canadian winters by supplementing their unreliable meat diets with the small game, berries, and wild rice their Native wives gathered (Van Kirk, 1992).

For most of the 1700s, Native people were treated with the cautious respect accorded allies in war and partners in trade (Jamieson, 1986). However,

---

BOX 1.1
▼
MÉTIS WOMEN IN THE 1800s

Studies on Aboriginal women are few. Diane Payment (1996) interviewed eighteen Métis women elders born between 1886 and 1910 about their personal experiences and those of their ancestors as members of Batoche society.

Around 1805, a Métis settlement emerged at Red River, Manitoba. Métis women, with their voyageur husbands, entered a world where Christian marriages, social and economic dependence, racial prejudice, French-Canadian traditions, and Catholic beliefs dominated. Some married into high social classes, while others had husbands who were employed as labourers by the Hudson's Bay Company, or who were primarily hunters and freighters.

Attitudes toward Métis women were mixed. In the early 1800s, Abbé Provencher wrote of them as inferior, calling them "le sexe," implying a tainted sexual role. He also commented on the moral depravity and cruelty of many French-Canadian voyageurs who abused their wives. But Provencher also saw Métis women as generous, hardworking, enterprising; as skilled weavers and spinners; and as family agents of civilization and Christianization.

By the 1850s, with the arrival of more French-Canadian women in the community, Métis women were encouraged to emulate French-Canadian dress and behaviour. By 1870, the year of the Métis resistance and the negotiation of Manitoba's entry into Confederation, Métissage was viewed positively as part of the dual Métis-Canadien heritage in the early years of Manitoba. Following Louis Riel's execution in 1885, hundreds of Métis families left the area to maintain their ethnic identity and to seek new economic opportunities (Payment, 1996).

---

after 1812, Native people were no longer regarded as useful allies, and customary marriages were rejected once the fur trade was replaced by agriculture as the main economic base. As Jamieson (1986) tells us, with this economic change Europeans increasingly came to ascribe importance to French and British class and ethnic codes. European–Native marriages declined once the fur-trade society produced a new pool of acceptable women — Métis, or mixed-blood, daughters. Métis, not Native, wives became fashionable while trading posts were being established across the North and West. In the early 1800s, the North West Company, an agent of British imperial interests, outlawed marriages with full-blooded Native women. Missionaries who arrived with the Hudson's Bay Company in the 1820s, company officials, and government representatives denounced interracial marriages in an effort to prescribe strict racial segregation and to eschew efforts at assimilation characteristic of the earlier French regime (Jamieson, 1986). White women, heretofore unknown in the fur trade, began slowly to settle in trading posts.

As the agrarian frontier developed in the mid-1800s, Native and Métis women's status declined precipitously as they moved from being wives to becoming domestics; today, their essential role in opening the Canadian West and the fur trade is largely forgotten (Anderson, 1987; Van Kirk, 1992). By the 1830s, 20 percent of the contracted servants were Métis, and by the 1850s, 50 percent of the Métis were engaged in seasonal labour in transportation and as general labourers around the posts (Frideres, 1998).

Racist work and marriage patterns were encouraged by the state, which implemented an ethnocentric ideology of "civilizing" the Indians, a policy that replaced previous military and economic alliances (Jamieson, 1986). Government policy set out to achieve assimilation, to absorb the Native people into the mainstream by forcing them to shed their languages, customs, religious beliefs, and traditional structures (Ponting, 1986). A series of acts, culminating with the Indian Act of 1876, was thought of by the government as an incentive and mechanism to encourage assimilation. Native people were offered enfranchisement, forcibly Christianized through residential schools, and separated from their children as ways of encouraging assimilation. (See Chapter 5 in this volume for more on contemporary Native life.)

PREINDUSTRIAL FAMILIES: 1600s–1700s
▼

In the 1600s, European settlement, as well as marriage and family patterns, varied considerably in what is now Ontario, Quebec, and the Maritimes. Quebec settlements were characterized by the clash between fur traders and colonists, the pervasive involvement of religious orders, and the introduction in 1628 of the seigneurial system, which controlled immigration and land distribution.

The first French family arrived in Quebec in 1617 and was virtually the only family to live there and own a house until 1634, the official beginning of settlement. Before this time, there were no white European women in New France. For a long time, Quebec was populated mostly by male soldiers, sailors, merchants, indentured labourers, interpreters, and Native people (Dumont et al., 1987).

When settlement began to increase, the rang system, a secular, French-Canadian creation, provided uniformly sized river lots for peasant-status settlers. Immigrants centred family and community life around the parish, a religious institution pioneers brought with them. Village life developed on the class-based seigneurial system and was bound by traditional religion, two forces that historians suggest impeded the development of early agriculture and industrialization in Quebec (Queen, Habenstein, and Quadagno, 1985). **Romantic love** was not the basis for marriage in the 1600s and 1700s. Marriage in New France was a family and kinship matter rather than an individual arrangement, and it took place by contract, with dowries. Families could withhold dowries or disinherit couples when they disapproved of their marriage (Krull, 1996, p. 374). In middle- and upper-class families — those of merchants, administrators, and seigneurs — children usually married only with their parents' consent, in a religious ceremony, someone known in the community who had some financial security. Rural families were particularly patriarchal, with fathers exercising legal, religious, and civil authority. Farmers and peasants cherished hardworking, healthy spouses who could contribute long and successfully to the family enterprise (Landry and Legare, 1987).

New France in the 1600s profited enormously from the non-traditional, heroic, and enterprising activities of women. One such group consisted of the nearly 800 "King's Daughters," les *filles du roi*, so named because their transport and keep were paid for by the king of France. These women originated from the Paris Hôpital-Général, an institution for the disadvantaged, the poor, the sick, prostitutes, and the insane, as well as abandoned children and orphans. These women were recruited between 1663 and 1673 and sent to New France as prospective brides for male settlers. New France offered opportunities not possible for them in France (Landry, 1992).

The other notable category of emigrating women comprised those who were extremely well born, had generous dowries, and were often religiously dedicated (Noel, 1991). These women founded charities; undertook missionary work; and began monasteries, hospitals, and schools. In fact, in 1663, Montreal had a school for girls but none for boys, meaning that, for a time, Montreal women surpassed men in literacy.

During the early period of settlement, ideas about women's roles were surprisingly flexible, a result of the complex set of responsibilities they undertook within the fur-trading and military economy. Although, in law, men had authority over their wives and were responsible for their misdemeanours, husbands did not always exercise their control in economic and domestic life (Noel, 1991). Harsh economic and military conditions demanded the labour and intelligence of women as well as men.

In the preindustrial economy, many families barely eked out a living. Providing food, clothing, and shelter proved arduous. Families regularly confronted death, women being widowed, and children orphaned. Precarious lifestyles meant that many female-headed households, just like today, were poor (Bradbury, 1992). Often the only families enjoying financial security were those with access to male earnings, who lived in towns, on French-Canadian seigneurial manors, or on Southern Ontario estates.

Public and private life were undifferentiated. Agricultural and commercial pursuits were usually domestic industries or family affairs. Men and women worked the fields together; women kept the farm accounts and managed purchases and sales. Women as well as men were tavern owners, storekeepers, grocers, moneylenders, peddlers, and bonesetters (Noel, 1991).

Spousal interdependence made marriage an economic necessity for both women and men. While, in Europe, women were slowly losing their status in guilds and professions, in New France women tended to be equal partners to their husbands. Women's work was recognized as being as indispensable as that of men. On farms, women generally were responsible for the stables, the hen-houses, and the vegetable gardens; for preparing food; for making clothes; and for tending the sick. Women's farm tasks were enormously time-consuming and arduous. Hours every day were spent in food production. Cooking was accomplished with only rudimentary tools and using hearths and fireplaces. Game and fowl had to be preserved in root cellars, ice pits, or cold attics. Sometimes women worked alongside their husbands and children in the fields, and, when husbands went off logging, women performed the farm work themselves (Noel, 1991).

Housework as we think of it today was not a major preoccupation for preindustrial wives. Houses were small. Often everyone lived in one big room that functioned as a bedroom and kitchen. Except among the affluent, furniture was sparse, consisting of a few chairs, a table, a trunk, a large bed, a cupboard, and a few straw mattresses. Cleanliness was superficial; floors were rarely washed, bed linen and clothing rarely laundered, and furniture rarely dusted (Dumont et al., 1987).

In the towns, women engaged in a variety of commercial enterprises, taking in boarders, sewing or washing clothes, and minding children. Throughout the 1600s and 1700s, women worked alongside men, operating businesses and supervising apprentices, and they worked for wages as maids, laundresses, and nurses. Family resources dictated whether a woman participated (for free) in her husband's activities or brought in extra income, but all women, of all classes and ethnic groups, contributed to the family economy.

Women's activities were closely linked to the military machine, as publicans, as prostitutes, and as nurses. Women engaged in fur trading, shipping, and selling imported goods. Still others began commercial enterprises. Widows acquired the right to manage the family's assets until the children reached age 25; in this way, by 1663, women held the majority of seigneurial land. In New France, the rules governing inheritance and marriage were then generous to

BOX 1.2
▼
WOMEN IN NEW FRANCE

Women in the early days of New France were a highly select group of immigrants, small in number and in an excellent position to participate widely in society in roles not allowed in France. As Jan Noel (1991) tells us, two major immigrant groups of women — the *religieuses* and the *filles du roi* — largely account for the superior education and "cultivation" attributed to the women in New France.

The first *religieuses* to arrive were extremely well born, well endowed, and highly dedicated religious figures, the Ursulines and Hospitallers, who landed in Quebec in 1639. Nuns undertook missionary work that gave them an active role in the colony, supplying money, publicity, skills, and settlers. These women conducted schools, recruited settlers, and raised money for hospitals and charities, thus playing an important role in supplying leadership, funding, publicity, recruits, and social services for the colony.

The second distinct group of female immigrants to New France was the famous *filles du roi*, women sent out by the French government as brides in order to boost the colony's permanent settlement. More than 800 arrived between 1663 and 1673.

Colonial economy enhanced the position of women. Inhabitants engaged in either military activity or the fur trade, both of which removed men physically for long periods of time, thus freeing women to assume a wide range of economic roles. Some women actually fought, while others made a good living by providing goods and services to armies. Still others managed family farms and directed commercial enterprises such as iron forging; tile making; sturgeon fishing; sealing; contract building; operating sawmills, tanneries, and flour mills. The following describes one particularly enterprising woman and her mother, both of whom took on numerous economic activities:

> Louise de Ramezay, the daughter of the governor of Montreal, operated the large Richelieu lumbering enterprise. Louise, who remained single, lost her father in 1724. Her mother continued to operate the sawmill on the family's Chambly seigneury but suffered a disastrous reverse due to a combination of flooding, theft, and shipwreck in 1725. The daughter, however, went into partnership with the Seigneuress de Rouville in 1745 and successfully developed the sawmill. Louise then opened a flour mill, a Montreal tannery, and another sawmill. By the 1750s, the trade was flourishing. In 1753, she expanded her leather business, associating with a group of Montreal tanners to open new workshops. (Noel, 1991, p. 44)

women, protective of their rights and property (Dumont et al., 1987). The opposite was found in English Canada, where English common law dictated that men legally held all power and property in families. Upon marriage, women lost all legal status: they could not control their property, start businesses, initiate legal actions, or administrate family assets without their husband's approval.

Throughout the 1600s and 1700s, North America was a colonial battlefield. Both the British and the French maintained military bases in Canada from which to fight their innumerable battles for control of the highly lucrative fur trade. By the late 1600s, the French war machine employed one-quarter of the Quebec population.

The vagaries of war altered Canada. After the defeat of the French on the Plains of Abraham in 1759, Canada was handed over to the British in 1763 under the Treaty of Paris. Quebec City was bombarded and besieged, and hundreds of farms were burned and destroyed (Dumont et al., 1987). With British rule came waves of English and Scottish immigration along with the United Empire Loyalists fleeing the 1776 American Revolution. Many Irish Protestants and Catholics emigrated. Initially, most British immigrants stayed on the Atlantic coast, so that, during the 1600s, Atlantic coast populations increased 25 times more rapidly than did the population of New France. By the 1700s, most Canadian families lived in rural settings clustered in Quebec, Ontario, and the Maritimes. Generally, the 1700s were economically prosperous. Families continued to produce most of the articles needed, land was available, and harvests were plentiful (Dumont et al., 1987).

As agricultural settlements grew and gradually replaced the fur trade during the 1700s, women's position in the Québécois family began to take a more traditional and less egalitarian cast. Once the colonial population stabilized, marriageable girls were no longer in short supply. Social institutions were established, seigneuries filled up, social classes became more readily distinguishable, and women began to be relegated to the domestic sphere of the family. One of the most discouraging European imports was shelters for the destitute, which opened in Montreal and Quebec in the late 1600s. As is the case today, two-thirds of the poor in Montreal shelters were women. The difficulty of earning a living meant that single women lived in poverty. Women's average salaries were half those earned by men, and most lucrative professional jobs were closed to women, who lacked specialized training and education (Bradbury, 1992).

Throughout the 1700s, identities were spun entirely around families (Dumont et al., 1987). All domestic, economic, and social activities centred around the family. Men and women relied on each other to keep their **family-**

based economy functioning. Yet spousal interdependence did not translate into spousal equality.

Children were an economic necessity in preindustrial family economies. Family tasks were differentiated by sex. Girls imitated their mothers' work, and boys followed male household pursuits. Schooling was not institutionalized in the 1600s and 1700s, except through religious communities. Girls received instruction from the first days of colonial establishment, but education was not widespread and extended to little more than the teaching of basic literacy. Still, convents ensured that working-class girls often had far more access to education than did boys. In Ontario, the Maritimes, and Quebec, upper-class boys were far more likely to receive formal instruction, more sophisticated teaching, and more specialized and professional training than were girls. The only jobs for which young girls were apprenticed were housekeeping tasks. However, boys of 9 or 10 apprenticed in a range of jobs — as carpenters, coopers, blacksmiths, accountants, doctors, and lawyers. Domestic contracts usually began for girls around the age of 10 and lasted until they were married or could be financially self-sufficient. Apprenticeship as a seamstress often began at the age of 19 and lasted one year. Young adults married when their parents could spare their labour (Conrad, 1991).

Sexual harassment and assault in workplaces were common practices against which women had little protection. Family life was often violent for women and children. Women who retaliated in self-defence were harshly punished. Marie-Josephte Corriveau is still a legend in Quebec. At her trial in 1783, she admitted to killing her abusive husband with an axe while he slept. British authorities hanged her and left her body hanging for public display for more than a month (Dumont et al., 1987, p. 98).

CANADIAN SLAVERY
▼

At the time slavery was introduced in Canada, there was no assumption that the condition attached to a single race (Winks, 1971, p. 17). The majority of slaves were Native people, either Pawnees or members of closely related tribes. The first written record of a person of African descent in Nova Scotia is from 1605, when Matthew da Costa arrived with the Champlain expedition (Williams, 1983). The first known black slave arrived in Canada in 1628 as a boy of 7 or 8; he was brought from Madagascar and sold to a Quebec resident (Walker, 1980, p. 19). From the late 1600s until the early 1800s, black slaves were held in Quebec, Nova Scotia, New Brunswick, and Ontario, making slavery a constituent feature of pioneer life in colonial society (Calliste, 1996b).

Through a series of French laws, slavery was given legal foundation in New France. The 1685 Code Noir, which regulated the practice of slavery in the West Indies, was assumed to have legal application in France's North American colony. The code was actually designed to protect owners, not slaves, from slaves' violence and escape (Thomson, 1979). By 1762, the colony recognized slavery as an acceptable institution. Whereas initially the fur trade had little need for slave labour, beginning in 1663 the demand for cheap labour escalated so much that colonists petitioned their governors for the right to import black slaves to supplement scarce labour (Winks, 1971).

Both the necessity of slave labour in the development of Canada and slaves' resistance to their servitude were evident in the 1709 fining law instituted in New France. Despite reports of "humane and familial treatment," slaves obviously did not find the terms so agreeable, as evidenced by their numerous attempts to escape (Winks, 1971, p. 14). Those assisting slaves to escape were fined, and colonial newspapers were full of notices regarding runaways. Despite these punishments, free Blacks sheltered runaways, petitioned governments to abolish slavery, and frequently brought cases to court when they believed that Blacks, especially children, were being mistreated or illegally detained.

In 1749, when the English settled in Halifax, they evidently brought slaves with them (Williams, 1983). The first recorded slave sales in Halifax occurred in 1752. In 1767, Nova Scotia, which then included New Brunswick, had a population of 3022, of which 104 were slaves living mostly in Halifax (Walker, 1980). By the time of the British conquest of New France in 1759, local records revealed 3604 slaves, of which 1132 were black and the rest were Pawnee. Half of the Blacks lived in or near Montreal, working mostly as domestic servants. Few worked in the fields or mines. Many were held at the French fortress of Louisbourg (Walker, 1980; Winks, 1971). The exploitation of black labour in commercial enterprises and on farms was essential to Canada's economic development. Free Blacks received about one-quarter the prevailing wage rate for whites for day work and were especially vulnerable to exploitation because they were desperate for work (Walker, 1980). Slave women worked mostly as domestics. In 1744, 5 percent of all female servants in Quebec City were black slaves and 10 percent were Native people (Dumont et al., 1987, p. 97).

The treatment of black slaves ranged from paternalistic to outright exploitative. Some authors suggest that slavery in New France was benevolent, compared with slavery in the United States (Thomson, 1979; Walker, 1980; Winks, 1971). The family life of slaves was severely restricted by their legal status. Slaves could marry only with their owner's permission. Children became the property of the mother's owner, so female slaves were prized for their reproductive capacity. Some writers suggest **gender roles** among slaves were not as differentiated as those of white people, as males and females often performed the same types of work (Calliste, 1996a, p. 248).

Canadian Blacks were socially, economically, and legally excluded. They were without rights, could not vote, could not associate with white people as equals, could not marry interracially, were not welcome in white churches, and were segregated in black schools (Thomson, 1979). Social Darwinism described Blacks as fun-loving, imitative, and "naturally" obsequious, thus academically instituting a racist theory of social inequality that many academics and journalists supported (Thomson, 1979). Given these policies, it is not surprising that Blacks were thought of as unlikely to assimilate and unsuited to the northern climate.

The arrival of Loyalists in 1783, following the American Revolution, brought another 2000 or more Blacks into Canada. About 1232 arrived in Nova Scotia, 300 in Lower Canada, and about 500 in Upper Canada. Loyalist-owned slaves were also found in Prince Edward Island, Cape Breton Island, and Newfoundland. By the end of 1783, Blacks were found in virtually every white settlement in Canada (Clairmont and Magill, 1974, p. 40). With the Loyalist influx, black slaves supplanted Pawnee slaves, even in Quebec (Winks, 1971).

Britain freed many American **black Loyalists**, offering them free land and free provisions while they prepared their farms for harvest (Clairmont and Magill, 1974, p. 41). However, only about a third of black Loyalists in Nova Scotia and New Brunswick received any land at all, and their farms were considerably smaller and usually in less fertile or more remote regions than those of white Loyalists. Usually, Blacks failed to receive any provisions and found that they were economically dependent. Groups of Loyalists, black and white, were settled together. Three separate black settlements were created in Nova Scotia. The largest one, Birchtown, consisted of 649 male family heads; the one at Preston contained 100 families (Walker, 1980; Winks, 1971).

Most white and black Loyalists arriving in Nova Scotia in the late 1700s were wretchedly destitute. Blacks were even more deprived. They were disproportionately represented in sharecropping, domestic service, and indentured occupations. A number of free Blacks were forced to sell themselves, or their children, into slavery or long-term indenture. Conditions were so desperate that, when an agent of the Sierra Leone Company came recruiting among Nova Scotia Blacks in 1792, offering free land and full equality, about 1200 accepted his company's offer and sailed to the British colony in West Africa. Additional migration took place in 1800 to Sierra Leone, and in 1821 to Trinidad, leaving 2500 Blacks in North America, more slaves than free (Clairmont and Magill, 1974, p. 42).

BOX 1.3
▼
BLACK CANADIANS

Writers have only recently admitted that the recording of Canadian history is often racist, erasing the history of black Canadians. Adrienne Shadd (1987) relates the history of blacks in Canada, a history too seldom taught in schools. Blacks, first brought as slaves in the 1600s and 1700s, were among the earliest to settle on Canadian soil. Ten percent of the Loyalists who migrated to Canada after the American Revolution were black. Their descendants, particularly in the Maritimes, have been living in quasi-segregated communities for over 200 years. Between 1815 and 1860, Blacks were one of the largest groups to enter Canada, when between 40 000 and 60 000 fugitive slaves and free people "of colour" sought refuge in Ontario (Shadd, 1987, p. 4).

These settlers enriched the culture of the country, yet their many contributions are often neglected. Founder of the Queen Victoria Benevolent Society in 1840, the first organization to offer aid to black women, indigents, and fugitive slaves, was Mrs. Wilson Abbot. Founder of the Anti-Slavery Society and the first newspaperwoman in Canada was Mary Ann Shadd, who edited a paper for fugitives between 1853 and 1859 in Toronto, and later in Chatham, Ontario. In 1883, Elizabeth Shadd Shreve, a black preacher, established the Women's Home Missionary Society in Ontario. Joe Fortes, a Barbadian-born sailor, came to British Columbia in 1885 and, as a lifeguard, taught three generations of people to swim at English Bay. The term "the real McCoy" was coined after the inventions of a black man, Elijah McCoy, born in Harrow, Ontario, in 1840 (Whitla, 1995, pp. 321–49; Shadd, 1987, p. 3).

As Violet Blackman tells us, the lives of black Canadians continued to be difficult far into this century. In Toronto, immigration was restrictive, work was scarce, and societal discrimination was rampant. Yet, individuals prevailed and succeeded:

> You couldn't get any position, regardless who you were and how educated you were, other than housework, because even if the employer would employ you, those that you had to work with would not work with you.
>
> It was a man here — Donald Moore. He saw the conditions, he formed a committee, and we used to go to different churches and hold different rallies. It was the '30s. Later, with this committee, he went to Ottawa with a brief and presented it — of allowing the coloured people from the different islands to come in. Then, after that, the government permit that so many could come in each year from different islands. But you had to come in as a domestic: you had to go and serve a year with some lady up in Rosedale or up in the upper section, and then when you're satisfactory — took a year — you get your landing, and you're free to go and do anything that you want to do. That was how coloured people start coming into this country. (Brand, 1991, pp. 37–38)

By 1815, another 2000 free Blacks arrived in Nova Scotia, having been offered freedom by the British during the War of 1812. Those hardworking refugee Blacks came in search of a new life, bringing with them numerous skills. They built homes, petitioned for schools and churches, and used their skills to farm and do other jobs (Williams, 1983). They settled on small lots of rocky soil and scrubby forest, politically free but physically starving. Their condition of subsistence poverty, begun in the early 1800s, continues today. A number of Blacks moved to Victoria, British Columbia, in 1859 from California. They worked on farms, in shops, and on wharves; owned farms; became teachers and businessmen; and achieved community success, as they had in other parts of Canada.

Slavery as a system was accepted and supported by many prominent and respectable Canadians for about a hundred years, from the early 1700s, when it was first authorized, until 1834, when it was abolished throughout the British Empire. Ontario was the first British territory to legislate against slavery, in 1793. The abolition bill faced severe opposition from large landowners concerned about the scarcity of cheap labour. The heroes of Canadian abolition were the judges who, by judicial legislation, moved against an institution that retained sufficient public support in Nova Scotia, New Brunswick, and Lower Canada to prevent popularly elected assemblies from abolishing slavery (Winks, 1971, p. 110). By 1800, the chief justices of Lower Canada and the Maritimes felt slavery was illegal and refused to use state power to retrieve runaways, instead insisting that owners produce the almost unobtainable proof of ownership. Any slave who quit could do so without fearing a return to enslavement by the courts or state officials (Walker, 1980).

THE SHIFT TO INDUSTRIALIZATION
▼

At the beginning of the 1800s, Canada was still a sparsely populated colony whose economy was based primarily on farming, fishing, lumbering, and some fur trading (Wilson, 1991, p. 14). The major cities of Montreal, Quebec, Toronto, Hamilton, and Kingston were slowly transforming from ports to primarily administrative and manufacturing, commercial centres. The preindustrial economy of the time was small-scale, labour-intensive, and domestically focussed. Daily life was centred on the land, production was based in the **household**, age and gender roles were fixed by custom, and few people lacked useful work (Gaffield, 1990).

In the first half of the 1800s, wage labour and an emerging capitalist economy co-existed with domestic production. Handicrafts and homemade goods could be found alongside goods manufactured in small factories. Two major economic changes occurred. Small-scale subsistence farming declined and was gradually replaced with large-scale, high-volume commercial agriculture, and employment based at or near the home was replaced by work at central locations like shops and factories (Zinn and Eitzen, 1993). The Canadian economy was slowly transformed from one based on agriculture to one determined by industrial capital. Cities grew rapidly, immigration exploded, and the frontier was expanded to include profound social and economic transformation. Gradually, economic life evolved from a farm- to a cash-based economy as urban centres expanded and factories increased from 2.4 million in 1851 to 5.4 million in 1901 (Katz, 1975).

With the advent of commercial and industrial enterprise in the nineteenth century, work and family life became increasingly separate. Men and women no longer worked side by side in family businesses; the land could no longer support all members of a family, so people migrated to cities in search of work for wages, often in one of the new factories being established. New immigrants also followed this model. An urban, industrialized working class began to grow in great numbers. Women in some cases had greater difficulty finding work in factories, with the notable exception of Paris, Ontario, where the Penman knitting company employed mostly women. In Paris, women were less likely to marry and more likely to establish their own homes and work most of their lives, making family life unique in that town (Parr, 1990).

Large numbers of young women moved to cities during the mid-nineteenth century to work for wages. Their appearance in the public sphere alarmed many people who fretted that these young women might not be willing to retreat into the domestic realm after experiencing independence. They also worried that these young women would fall prey to all kinds of licentious and immoral temptations, as they lacked supervision. The emergence of new forms of entertainment, such as dance halls, vaudeville, and amusement parks, raised more concerns among staid Torontonians (Strange, 1997).

In most working-class families, men rarely earned enough money to support a dependent wife and children, despite the ideology of a "**family wage**," adequate for a male worker to support himself, a dependent wife, and children. Moreover, industrial accidents, sudden layoffs, and illnesses meant that working-class jobs were mostly irregular, seasonal, and unhealthy. In order to stay above the poverty line, family members pooled their resources. Children's wages were turned over to parents, and often children dropped out of school to work to supplement their parents' earnings (Palmer, 1983).

Economic opportunities for women outside the home were limited. When women did find work, the domestic ideal glorifying women as homemakers whose income was seen as supplemental to that of their husbands was used by employers as justification for paying women one-third less than men.

The lack of stable, well-paying work plunged single, widowed, and deserted women into poverty.

When they did work, both working-class and middle-class women were concentrated in gender-specific occupations in textile and garment industries, in shoe factories, in the tobacco industry, in domestic service, and in teaching (Bullen, 1992). Few women laboured at middle-class jobs as innkeepers, grocers, clerks, or tax collectors (Bloomfield and Bloomfield, 1991; Katz, 1975). Testimony to the 1889 Royal Commission on the Relations of Labour and Capital revealed that women and children were economically exploited, often brutalized, and frequently dismissed without cause. Jobs did not necessarily offer security or protection (Bullen, 1992; Katz, 1975; Parr, 1990).

Only about 5 percent of married women took up labour, and then only because of dire economic necessity, such as was caused by desertion or widowhood. Wage-labouring by women was considered a demeaning, low-status activity, compromising the husband's position as household head and dangerous for children's moral and cognitive development (Wilson, 1991). When extra money was required, wives tended to take in washing or sewing, clean homes for other people, or raise animals or vegetables (Bradbury, 1996).

Some women were inventive, adhering to traditional ideas about women's "proper" roles as wives and mothers while earning money. The story of middle-class Halifax resident Annie Hamilton illustrates prevailing domestic ideology. Annie took herself and her children to stay with relatives in the country whenever her husband's business was not doing well. In this way, Annie's husband did not have to support her and their children, and could redirect his funds into the business. In another Halifax case, Maria Morris Miller, whose father died when she was only 3, began her own drawing school and worked as an artist when she was 23. She married and had five children but lived apart from her husband for most of the year. Thanks to her ability to produce an income, Maria was able to assist her mother and gain a certain amount of independence when her married life did not turn out to be what she expected (Guildford, 1997). Both Maria and Annie perpetuated their middle-class status by finding creative ways to earn money.

CHANGES IN MEN'S, WOMEN'S, AND CHILDREN'S ROLES
▼

With the move to industrialization, there gradually emerged a shift in both functions and values attributed to the home and its members. Rather than operating as a combined mini-manufacturing workshop, agent of religious indoctrination, or apprenticeship training site, the family became more specialized in procreation, child rearing, consumption, and affection (Hareven,

1977, p. 198). The "modern" family became expert in moulding personality development and satisfying emotional needs. This specialization created a new quality of family life by opening up a space within which individual and group self-actualization could take place. Today, some critics contend that such self-scrutiny has degenerated into individualized narcissism, with the family often functioning as an encounter group (Lasch, 1977). Structurally, household size and composition altered to accomplish the family's new industrial functions. Over time, families are becoming smaller, as birth rates continue to decline, marriages are delayed, and the incidence of living alone as a lifestyle option increases. Canadians in 1871 resided in households averaging 5.9 people (Darroch and Ornstein, 1984, p. 163). Husbands, wives, and children shared their quarters with dependent elderly relations and maintained labour-market networks. Fifty years later, households were smaller, more specialized, more isolated, and more urbanized.

The emergence of a wage-labouring economy had different effects on family values. For the working class, kin were sources of social and economic family support. Working-class families lacked savings, pensions, social security, and social assistance. When widowed, women often discovered that their domestic talents of cooking and caring did not easily translate into marketable skills; nor were they welcomed into scarce jobs reserved for male heads of households (Bradbury, 1992). Thus, kin were forced to rely on one another to get through rough economic times, and work continued to be considered a family enterprise, even if it did not take place in the home.

For the middle class, the physical separation of the home from the workplace led to a new articulation of family privacy as the home was glorified as a domestic retreat, as a haven of intimacy against the harsh realities of the workplace. Unlike the working-class home, the middle-class home was defined as a non-work domain in which family members experienced personal intimacy unachievable, undesirable, and unsuitable in workplace environments (Smith, 1985).

The transformation of the household from a busy workplace and social centre to a private enclosure widened the division between men's and women's tasks. Husbands became responsible for breadwinning, and wives for homemaking and child rearing. Children existed as sentimental love objects, offering an opportunity for intimacy not experienced in other relationships.

This new family **ideology** emphasized strong feelings of affection as an essential ingredient in marriage. Sentimental love replaced economic considerations in bringing couples together; individual self-development and personal happiness replaced property and lineage as criteria for choosing a spouse. The role of parents as matchmakers virtually disappeared. The ideal marriage was thought to be based on mutual love, affection, attraction, and respect.

These new demands for everlasting and exciting companionship brought new strains to marital life. While both spouses were expected to contribute to mutual matrimonial bliss, wives were considered more responsible than husbands for nourishing and maintaining the sentimental and romantic qualities of a couple's relationship. Women were thought to possess characteristics more attuned to child care, emotional nurturing, and tension management — namely, gentleness, patience, sweetness, and a comforting demeanour (Smith, 1985).

For men, the gradual separation of the private and the public led to a new emphasis on masculinity as measured by the "breadwinner" role. This role involved the size of a man's pay cheque, especially for working-class men for whom earning a living (or family) wage meant that their wives (like the wives of middle-class men) did not have to work outside the home. For instance, Cape Breton coal miners during the 1920s were considered to be "real" men if they maintained solidarity with fellow workers in opposing management (Penfold, 1996). Positive male attributes were those associated with successful workers: aggressiveness, perseverance, toughness, and competitiveness were valued. These male qualities were in a sharp contrast to the presumed female traits. The ideological **cult of domesticity**, with its clear division of family roles and responsibilities, was dominant until the 1970s.

This new ideology of domesticity was built on women's homemaking skills and legal dependence on men. Middle-class women were glorified for their domestic pursuits, for their childbearing skills, and for their "natural abilities" as emotional nurturers of their wage-labouring husbands. So constraining were these domestic demands that, by the beginning of the 1900s, some Canadian writers were describing marriage as the legal death of women (Dumont et al., 1987). Husbands were legally the uncontested heads of families; they controlled the family's resources. Wives' income, resources, and legal rights were subject to their husbands' authority.

As women's roles altered, there followed a repositioning of children within the family. New ideas about children grew alongside the cult of domesticity. A gradual combination of restrictive child-labour laws, compulsory education in 1871, and declining employment opportunities pushed children out of the labour market. The 1891 census records 13.8 percent of Canadian children between the ages of 11 and 14 were gainfully employed. By 1921, this number had declined to 3.2 percent. Middle-class parents relinquished their children's wages and subsidized their spending through allowances. By 1893, child labour had declined so dramatically that giving an allowance was a routine middle-class practice. Slowly, children, especially middle-class ones, became defined as economically useless but emotionally priceless (Penfold, 1996; Zelizer, 1985).

Once children had been defined as incomplete adults in need of special cognitive and emotional protection and development, women, as mothers and teachers, were designated to provide this special treatment. Middle-class mothers were seen as economically unproductive but emotionally and morally superior in child rearing. In contrast, working-class women were characterized as economically productive wives but incompetent mothers in need of scientific and school guidance (Smith, 1985).

IMMIGRATION AND FAMILY LIVES
▼

As industrialization progressed, Canada populated its cities and recruited the bulk of its working class through immigration. Immigrant families faced particular circumstances and thus responded with special family coping strategies and structures. For example, the Chinese workers who first arrived in Canada from China and San Francisco in the 1860s and 1870s were men. Women were specifically excluded on the grounds that Chinese men were merely temporary workers, and by a federal head tax, a substantial fee only the Chinese had to pay to enter the country. This tax was sufficiently burdensome to make it difficult for men to bring their wives or female relatives into the country. The first Chinese women who came to Canada were merchants' wives, who were excluded from the head tax, prostitutes bought and sold by men, and "slave girls" or female servants imported to Canada to work as unpaid labourers. Slave girls performed domestic labour, freeing Chinese women to engage in piecework sewing and as general labourers or clerks, or in family-run businesses such as tailor shops, laundries, restaurants, and small grocery stores. Women's labour, both unpaid and poorly paid, enabled Chinese businesses to succeed (Adilman, 1984).

Family life was often solitary, arduous, and lonely for early immigrants. Early twentieth-century Greek and Japanese immigrants followed a pattern that subsequent groups experienced. First, the young men emigrated to Canada, seeking economic opportunity and fleeing political restrictions. They lived in boarding houses and married as soon as financially feasible. Their wives, often Greek and Japanese immigrants, found married life lonely and isolating, and missed the warmth and familiarity of their former communities (Ayukawa, 1995; Pizanias, 1996).

Frequently, immigrant families found that discrimination restricted the work experiences of both men and women. Chinese women were not accepted into the teaching or nursing professions as late as the 1940s, forcing women to remain in working-class positions in mostly Chinese-run businesses (Nipp, 1986; Yee, 1992).

BOX 1.4
▼
JAPANESE PICTURE BRIDES

From about 1908 to 1928, many single Japanese Canadian men sought wives by travelling to Japan for arranged marriages. Men unable to travel to Japan and meet prospective brides before marriage relied on photographs from Japanese catalogues, and held marriages by proxy. In traditional arranged marriages, the parents selected a bride for her ability to preserve family traditions, her domestic abilities, and her intelligence and accomplishments. However, once they arrived in Canada, many Japanese picture brides did not adhere strictly to their traditional gender roles because of what was required of them in their married lives. Still, few rebelled to the extent of Mrs. Kiyoko Tanaka-Goto.

In 1914, Kiyoko was 19 years old. She came to Canada as a picture bride. She married Mr. Tanaka and worked on someone else's farm with him on Salt Spring Island. She also cleaned chicken coops and did hand-laundry for a hotel. After four years, she had managed to save $2000. At that point, for whatever reason, she left her husband and went to Vancouver, where she purchased a bawdy house with three other Japanese women. They turned their premises into a very successful restaurant-bar. Contracting venereal disease, Kiyoko went to Kamloops, where a Mr. Goto paid for her medical care. She stayed with him for some years, cooking and doing laundry for his crew of railway workers. She went back to Vancouver and ran a bawdy house for a number of years.

In 1942, when the Canadian government evacuated the Japanese from coastal regions, Kiyoko refused to go. She was arrested and imprisoned, but apparently escaped and went back to Vancouver, where she lived as a Chinese woman in Chinatown (Ayukawa, 1995).

Asian Indian male and female immigrants suffered similar racism. South Asian men began to arrive in the mid-1800s after the imposition of the Chinese head tax temporarily limited immigration. Like the first Chinese settlers, Asian Indian men left behind their families and friends. Racist immigration laws banned Indian women from entering Canada until the 1917–19 Imperial War Conference agreement legislated their entry (Doman, 1984).

Government assessment of available industrial work shaped immigration policies. Between 1900 and 1930, more than 170 000 British women came to Canada as domestics. In the 1920s, the Ontario government, encouraged by affluent women's groups, actively recruited English, Welsh, Irish, and Scottish girls by advertising "Sunny Ontario for British Girls" on posters across Britain (Barber, 1986).

Black women, forced immigrants from Africa and the West Indies, worked largely on farms, in domestic service, and at home. Until the 1940s, 80 percent of black women worked as domestics, as mother's helpers, as housekeepers, as general helpers, and as laundresses. It was not until World War II that labour shortages forced employers to hire black women to work in areas that formerly employed only white females. When white females moved into essential war-industry jobs, black women took up their spaces in hospitals, restaurants, hotels, laundries, dry cleaners, and in non-essential companies making candy, tobacco, and soft drinks (Brand, 1991, p. 15).

Institutionalized racism directed at Canada's visible-minority immigrants greatly affected family strategies. Girls from immigrant families started work and left home earlier. Immigrant families had consistently higher fertility rates, higher rates of child labour, and lower rates of non-kin living with them than did non-immigrants. Like working-class families in general, black men could rarely earn enough money to support their families, so the income of women and children was essential.

Even wage-labouring showed certain trends. Irish women tended to withdraw more completely from paid employment than did Germans. Italian mothers chose cannery and field work over factory employment because it permitted them to work alongside their children. Polish women preferred domestic work to factory work, whereas Jewish women avoided domestic work and sought industrial employment at home or in factories (Coontz, 1988; Draper and Karlinsky, 1986; Iacovetta and Valverde, 1992).

Low rates of pay, seasonal layoffs, and lack of trade unionization and social-security measures meant working-class and immigrant families had to organize themselves as economic units, closely co-ordinating their reproductive and domestic strategies with their wage earning. High fertility made economic sense as long as children's wages boosted total family income. But a full-time wage-earning wife did not make good economic sense, given the low wages paid to women, the lack of household technology, and the lack of help caring for children and the elderly. Unless the family was living substantially below the subsistence level, the family was better off having a wife to prepare food and engage in income-generating schemes such as doing piecework at home or taking in boarders or laundry (Katz, 1975).

Throughout most of the 1800s and early 1900s, homemaking was a full-time, labour-intensive job. Most working-class households kept livestock and grew their own vegetables, made their own bread, lacked indoor plumbing, washed clothes by hand, and spent hours tending wood and coal stoves (Bradbury, 1996). A 1910 study of working-class families in a U.S. steel town revealed that most families existed on a surplus of $0.02 a day (Coontz, 1988,

p. 296). Hence, many working-class married women would actually have cost the family money by engaging in wage labour. These families managed better if mothers devoted themselves full-time to **domestic labour** and the production of the necessities of life (Smith, 1985).

CONCLUSION
▼

Today, collective actions and definitions of family needs have been replaced by an emphasis on individual priorities and preferences. Yet, modern families retain a mixture of collective and individual features. Economic recessions, for example, may force young adults to remain at home for longer periods and to delay marriage and childbearing. Still, their individual needs and aspirations are accepted as legitimate bases for separation and decision making.

Women are now as committed to full-time wage-labouring as men, yet elements of traditional family ideology remain. Romantic love as the basis of courtship and marriage continues to glue couples together, at least temporarily. Many young women spend their adolescence planning and waiting for a Prince Charming with whom to fall in love, only to discover the emotional insolvency of such arrangements. By wrapping their futures around the plans of their male partners, young women limit their own financial stability. By taking on the emotional work of family relationships, women suppress their own needs and desires and become the recipients of others' frustrations. By accepting too much of the responsibility for wage and domestic labour, women have difficulty balancing the demands of home and work. Men miss out on the delight, intimacy, and frustration that child rearing brings. As we move into the next century, it may well be that the next generation will actively reshape family roles and realign family priorities to achieve equilibrium between wage and domestic demands.

SUMMARY
▼

- Ethnically diverse aboriginal populations have developed economies suitable to their environment.
- For First Nations communities, the family has been a fundamental unit of organization, structuring kinship relations, assigning roles and responsibilities, and shaping intimate relations.
- In hunting-and-gathering societies, women, aided by children, performed most of the daily food gathering, while men's hunting and fishing, not always successful, took them away from the campsite for long periods of time.

- European colonization attempted to destroy Native culture.
- Public and private life were undifferentiated in the preindustrial family-wage economy.
- Blacks were socially, economically, and politically excluded from mainstream activities throughout Canadian history.
- The shift to industrialization separated private and public life, with men increasingly associated with public activities, and women relegated to the private domain.

NOTES
▼

1. As of April 1, 1999, Canada has a new northern territory; what was previously the Northwest Territories has been divided in two. The eastern two-thirds of the existing Northwest Territories is now known as Nunavut, meaning "our land" in the Inuktitut language of the Innu. The western region has yet to be named. Names being considered include "Northwest Territories," "Denendeh," meaning "home of the people" in the Athapaskan language of the Dene people, and "Nunakput," meaning "our land" in the western arctic Inuktitut dialect. The current Northwest Territories was once part of a larger area known as "Rupert's Land and the Northwest Territory." The province of Manitoba was separated from this territory in 1870, the Yukon Territory in 1898, and the provinces of Alberta and Saskatchewan in 1905. In 1912, following the northward extension of Manitoba, Ontario, and Quebec, the current boundaries of the Northwest Territories were established (Stout, 1997).

2. Anthropologists date the first occurrence of hunting-and-gathering societies involving the use of tools, language, cooking, and a sex-based division of labour to between 200 000 and 500 000 years ago. By 10 000 to 15 000 years ago, hunting-and-gathering societies were widespread. These arrangements were gradually replaced by horticultural-and-agricultural settlements about 12 000 years ago. Industrial society is only about 200 years old (Nett, 1988).

3. The west coast was home to the most dense pre-agricultural fishing society in Canada, with an aboriginal population of about 50 000 extending along 2400 kilometres (Morrison and Wilson, 1986; Price, 1979).

CRITICAL THINKING QUESTIONS
▼

1. Trace the changing material, social, and family relationships between Native and non-Native Canadians from the early days of the colonial fur trade through to today.

2. Some historians argue that family relations reflect the economic context in which families live. Explore this link by examining the roles and responsibilities of family members in two different social classes in one historical period.

3. To what extent do men and women enjoy equality in family life? Define "equality." Discuss the power and privilege of men and women by examining their domestic, emotional, and wage-labouring responsibilities.

4. The Canadian government is often viewed as implementing and enforcing racist policies. In what ways has government policy toward Native people, Blacks, and immigrants been discriminatory?

5. "The past is said to be a window into the future." Discuss this statement by focussing on two aspects of family life, such as family history, gender roles, authority patterns, income earning, or social policy.

SUGGESTED READING
▼

Bettina Bradbury, ed. 1992. *Canadian Family History: Selected Readings*. Toronto: Copp Clark Pitman.

> A wonderful collection of essays on Canadian family life, paying particular attention to the struggles encountered by the more disadvantaged.

Dionne Brand. 1991. *No Burden to Carry: Narratives of Black Women Working in Ontario, 1920s to 1950s*. Toronto: Women's Press.

> This moving collection of narratives recounts the lives of African-Canadian women who have struggled to adapt to the barriers of gender, race, and class found in Canadian society.

Ken S. Coates and Robin Fisher, eds. 1996. *Out of the Background: Readings on Canadian Native History*, 2nd ed. Toronto: Copp Clark.

> A far-reaching collection of essays on Native life, past and present.

Micheline Dumont, Michele Jean, Marie Lavigne, and Jennifer Stoddart (The Clio Collective). 1987. *Quebec Women: A History*. Translation by Roger Gannon and Rosalind Gill. Toronto: Women's Press.

> An in-depth account of the history of Quebec women from the earliest days of settlement to more recent times.

Marion Lynn, ed. 1996. *Voices: Essays on Canadian Families*. Scarborough, ON: Nelson Canada.

> An extensive and inclusive collection of narratives on many different ethnocultural groups in Canada.

Joy Parr and Mark Rosenfeld, eds. 1996. *Gender and History in Canada*. Toronto: Copp Clark.

> A fascinating collection of articles written about various groups across Canada and their particular histories.

Geoffrey York. 1990. *The Dispossessed: Life and Death in Native Canada*. London: Vintage. A chilling portrait of the lives of Native people across Canada on different reserves, ranging from those fighting poverty and addiction to those that represent remarkable models of economic success.

REFERENCES
▼

Adilman, Tamura. 1984. "A Preliminary Sketch of Chinese Women and Work in British Columbia, 1858–1950." In Barbara Latham and Roberta Pazdro, eds., *Not Just Pin Money: Selected Essays on the History of Women's Work in British Columbia*. Victoria: Camosun College.

Anderson, Karen. 1987. "A Gendered World: Women, Men, and the Political Economy of the 17th-Century Hurons." In Heather Jon Maroney and Meg Luxton, eds., *Feminism and Political Economy: Women's Work, Women's Struggles*. Toronto: Methuen.

Ayukawa, Midge. 1995. "Good Wives and Wise Mothers: Japanese Picture Brides in Early Twentieth-Century British Columbia." *B.C. Studies* 105/106 (Spring/ Summer): 103–18.

Barber, Marilyn. 1986. "Sunny Ontario for British Girls, 1900–30." In Jean Burnet, ed., *Looking into My Sister's Eyes: An Exploration in Women's History*. Toronto: Multicultural History Society of Ontario.

Bloomfield, Elizabeth, and G.T. Bloomfield. 1991. *Canadian Women in Workshops, Mills, and Factories: The Evidence of the 1871 Census Manuscripts*. Department of Geography, Research Report 11. Guelph: University of Guelph.

Bolaria, B. Singh, and Peter S. Li, eds. 1988. *Racial Oppression in Canada,* 2nd ed. Toronto: Garamond.

Bourgeault, Ron. 1988. "Race and Class under Mercantilism: Indigenous People in Nineteenth-Century Canada." In B. Singh Bolaria and Peter S. Li, eds., *Racial Oppression in Canada,* 2nd ed. Toronto: Garamond.

Bradbury, Bettina. 1992. "Gender at Work at Home: Family Decisions, the Labour Market, and Girls' Contributions to the Family Economy." In Bettina Bradbury, ed., *Canadian Family History: Selected Readings*. Toronto: Copp Clark Pitman.

———. 1996. "The Social and Economic Origins of Contemporary Families." In Maureen Baker, ed., *Families: Changing Trends in Canada,* 3rd ed. Toronto: McGraw-Hill.

Brand, Dionne. 1991. *No Burden to Carry: Narratives of Black Working Women in Ontario, 1920s to 1950s*. Toronto: Women's Press.

Bryan, Alan Lyle. 1986. "The Prehistory of Canadian Indians." In R. Bruce Morrison and C. Roderick Wilson, eds., *Native Peoples: The Canadian Experience*. Toronto: McClelland & Stewart.

Bullen, John. 1992. "Hidden Workers: Child Labour and the Family Economy in Late Nineteenth-Century Urban Ontario." In Bettina Bradbury, ed., *Canadian Family History: Selected Readings*. Toronto: Copp Clark Pitman.

Calliste, Agnes. 1996a. "Black Families in Canada: Exploring the Interconnections of Race, Class, and Gender." In Marion Lynn, ed., *Voices: Essays on Canadian Families*. Toronto: Nelson Canada.

———. 1996b. "Race, Gender and Canadian Immigration Policy: Blacks from the Caribbean, 1900–1932." In Joy Parr and Mark Rosenfeld, eds., *Gender and History in Canada*. Toronto: Copp Clark.

Clairmont, Donald, and Dennis Magill. 1974. *Africville: The Life and Death of a Canadian Black Community*. Toronto: McClelland & Stewart.

Conrad, Margaret. 1991. "Sundays Always Make Me Think of Home: Time and Place in Canadian Women's History." In Veronica Strong-Boag and Anita Clair Fellman, eds., *Rethinking Canada: The Promise of Women's History*, 2nd ed. Toronto: Copp Clark Pitman.

Coontz, Stephanie. 1988. *The Social Origins of Private Life*. London: Verso.

Darroch, Gordon, and Michael Ornstein. 1984. "Family and Household in Nineteenth-Century Canada: Regional Patterns and Regional Economies." *Journal of Family History* 9/2: 158–77.

Doman, Mahinder. 1984. "A Note on Asian Indian Women in British Columbia, 1900–1935." In Barbara Latham and Roberta Pazdro, eds., *Not Just Pin Money: Selected Essays on the History of Women's Work in British Columbia*. Victoria: Camosun College.

Draper, Paula J., and Janice B. Karlinsky. 1986. "Abraham's Daughters: Women, Charity and Power in the Canadian Jewish Community." In Jean Burnet, ed., *Looking into My Sister's Eyes: An Exploration in Women's History*. Toronto: Multicultural History Society of Ontario.

Druke, Mary A. 1986. "Iroquois and Iroquoian in Canada." In R. Bruce Morrison and C. Roderick Wilson, eds., *Native Peoples: The Canadian Experience*. Toronto: McClelland & Stewart.

Dumont, Micheline, Michele Jean, Marie Lavigne, and Jennifer Stoddart (The Clio Collective). 1987. *Quebec Women: A History*. Trans. Roger Gannon and Rosalind Gill. Toronto: Women's Press.

Elliott, Jean, ed. 1983. *Two Nations, Many Cultures*. Toronto: Prentice-Hall.

Frideres, James S. 1998. *Native Peoples in Canada: Contemporary Conflicts,* 5th ed. Toronto: Prentice-Hall.

Gaffield, Chad. 1990. "The Social and Economic Origins of Contemporary Families." In Maureen Baker, ed., *Families: Changing Trends in Canada,* 2nd ed. Toronto: McGraw-Hill Ryerson.

Guildford, Janet. 1997. "'Whate'er the duty of the hour demands'": The Work of Middle-Class Women in Halifax, 1840–1880." *Social History* 30/59 (May): 1–20.

Hareven, Tamura. 1977. "Family Time and Industrial Time." *Daedalus* 106: 57–70.

Iacovetta, Franca, and Marianna Valverde, eds. 1992. *Gender Conflicts: New Essays in Women's History*. Toronto: Women's Press.

Jamieson, Kathleen. 1986. "Sex Discrimination and the Indian Act." In J. Rick Ponting, ed., *Arduous Journey: Canadian Indians and Decolonization*. Toronto: McClelland & Stewart.

Katz, Michael. 1975. *The People of Hamilton, Canada West: Family and Class in a Mid-Nineteenth-Century City*. Cambridge, MA: Harvard University Press.

Krull, Catherine D. 1996. "From the King's Daughters to the Quiet Revolution: A Historical Overview of Family Structures and the Role of Women in Quebec." In Marion Lynn, ed., *Voices: Essays on Canadian Families*. Toronto: Nelson Canada.

Landry, Yves. 1992. "Gender Imbalance, *Les Filles du Roi*, and Choice of Spouse in New France." In Bettina Bradbury, ed., *Canadian Family History*. Toronto: Copp Clark Pitman.

Landry, Yves, and Jacques Legare. 1987. "The Life Course of Seventeenth-Century Immigrants to Canada." In Tamara Harevan and Andrejs Plakans, eds., *Family History at the Crossroads*. Princeton, NJ: Princeton University Press.

Lasch, Christopher. 1977. *Haven in a Heartless World: The Family Besieged*. New York: Basic Books.

Leacock, Eleanor. 1991. "Montagnais Women and the Jesuit Program for Colonization." In Veronica Strong-Boag and Anita Clair Fellman, eds., *Rethinking Canada: The Promise of Women's History*, 2nd ed. Toronto: Copp Clark Pitman.

McLaren, Angus. 1977. "Women's Work and Regulation of Family Size." *History Workshop Journal* 4 (Autumn): 70–73.

Miller, Virginia. 1986. "The Micmac: A Maritime Woodland Group." In R. Bruce Morrison and C. Roderick Wilson, eds., *Native Peoples: The Canadian Experience*. Toronto: McClelland & Stewart.

Morrison, R. Bruce, and C. Roderick Wilson, eds. 1986. *Native Peoples: The Canadian Experience*. Toronto: McClelland & Stewart.

Nett, Emily. 1988. *Canadian Families: Past and Present*. Toronto: Butterworths.

Nipp, Dora. 1986. "But Women Did Come: Working Chinese Women in the Inter-War Years." In Jean Burnet, ed., *Looking into My Sister's Eyes: An Exploration in Women's History*. Toronto: Multicultural History Society of Ontario.

Noel, Jan. 1991. "New France: *Les Femmes Favorisées*." In Veronica Strong-Boag and Anita Clair Fellman, eds., *Rethinking Canada: The Promise of Women's History*, 2nd ed. Toronto: Copp Clark Pitman.

Palmer, Bryan D. 1983. *Working Class Struggle: The Rise and Reconstitution of Canadian Labour, 1800–1980*. Toronto: Butterworths.

Parr, Joy. 1990. *The Gender of Breadwinners: Women, Men and Change in Two Industrial Towns, 1880–1950*. Toronto: University of Toronto Press.

Payment, Diane P. 1996. "*La Vie en Rose*? Metis Women at Batoche, 1870 to 1920." In Christine Miller and Patricia Chuchryk, eds., *Women of the First Nations: Power, Wisdom and Strength*. Winnipeg: University of Manitoba Press.

Penfold, Steven. 1996. "'Have You No Manhood in You?': Gender and Class in the Cape Breton Coal Towns, 1920–26." In Joy Parr and Mark Rosenfeld, eds., *Gender and History in Canada*. Toronto: Copp Clark.

Pizanias, Caterina. 1996. "Greek Families in Canada: Fragile Truths, Fragmented Stories." In Marion Lynn, ed., *Voices: Essays on Canadian Families*. Toronto: Nelson Canada.

Ponting, Rick, ed. 1986. *Arduous Journey: Canadian Indians and Decolonization.* Toronto: McClelland & Stewart.

Price, John A. 1979. *Indians of Canada: Cultural Dynamics.* Toronto: Prentice-Hall.

Queen, Stuart A., Robert W. Habenstein, and Jill S. Quadagno. 1985. *The Family in Various Cultures,* 5th ed. New York: Harper and Row.

Ray, Arthur J. 1996. "Periodic Shortages, Native Welfare, and the Hudson's Bay Company, 1670–1930." In Ken S. Coates and Robin Fisher, eds., *Out of the Background: Readings on Canadian Native History,* 2nd ed. Toronto: Copp Clark.

Shadd, Adrienne. 1987. "300 Years of Black Women in Canadian History: Circa 1700–1980." *Tiger Lily* 1/2: 4–13.

Smith, Dorothy E. 1985. "Women, Class and Family." In Varda Burstyn and Dorothy E. Smith, *Women, Class, Family and the State.* Toronto: Garamond.

Strange, Carolyn. 1997. "'Sin or Salvation?' Protecting Toronto's Working Girls." *The Beaver* 77/3 (June/July): 8–13.

Stout, Cameron. 1997. "Canada's Newest Territory in 1999." *Canadian Social Trends.* Catalogue no. 11-008-XPE, Statistics Canada (Spring).

Thomson, Colin A. 1979. *Blacks in Deep Snow: Black Pioneers in Canada.* Toronto: J.M. Dent.

Van Kirk, Sylvia. 1992. "The Custom of the Country: An Examination of Fur Trade Marriage Practices." In Bettina Bradbury, ed., *Canadian Family History.* Toronto: Copp Clark Pitman.

Walker, James W. 1980. *A History of Blacks in Canada: A Study Guide for Teachers and Students.* Hull, PQ: Minister of State for Multiculturalism and Supply and Services Canada.

Whitla, William. 1995. "A Chronology of Women in Canada." In Nancy Mandell, ed., *Feminist Issues: Race, Class and Sexuality.* Toronto: Prentice-Hall.

Williams, Savanah E. 1983. "Two Hundred Years in the Development of the Afro-Canadians in Nova Scotia, 1782–1982." In Jean Elliott, ed., *Two Nations, Many Cultures.* Toronto: Prentice-Hall.

Wilson, S.J. 1991. *Women, Families, and Work.* Toronto: McGraw-Hill Ryerson.

Winks, Robert W. 1971. *The Blacks in Canada: A History.* Montreal: McGill-Queen's University Press.

Yee, May. 1992. "Chinese Canadian Women: Our Common Struggle." In Gillian Creese and Veronica Strong-Boag, eds., *British Columbia Reconsidered: Essays on Women.* Vancouver: Press Gang.

Zelizer, Viviana. 1985. *Pricing the Priceless Child: The Changing Social Value of Children.* New York: Basic Books.

Zinn, Maxine, and D. Stanley Eitzen. 1993. *Diversity in Families,* 3rd ed. New York: HarperCollins.

2

▼

CHILDREN'S ROLE IN THE PARENT–CHILD RELATIONSHIP: AN INTERACTIVE PERSPECTIVE ON SOCIALIZATION

ANNE-MARIE AMBERT

LEARNING OBJECTIVES

In this chapter, you will learn that:

- traditional theories of socialization have failed to consider the role that children play in their own socialization;
- traditional theories have also failed to understand how children affect their parents;
- interactive theories of socialization, in contrast, emphasize children's active role and the reality that children and parents react to each other from the children's day of birth;
- parents adapt to their children's personalities and behaviours, so that whereas a child who is easygoing requires less parental adaptation, in contrast, a child who suffers from emotional or behavioural problems may tax parental adaptive abilities as well as child-rearing effectiveness;
- difficult children can contribute to the disruption of parenting skills and to the deterioration of their familial environment, with the consequence that their socialization outcomes or results are less positive;
- mothers are particularly affected by problematic children and traditionally have been blamed for children's pathologies and maladaptive social functioning;
- children (and adults) who are problematic often have perceptual and cognitive biases that make it difficult for them to appreciate their parents' efforts, to identify with their parents, and to recognize their parents' positive feedback;
- children's effects on parents, both positive and negative, continue throughout the life course;
- in our current sociocultural context, parents are less influential in their children's lives than in the past.

INTRODUCTION

The goal of this chapter is to introduce the interactive perspective in relation to child socialization and the parent–child relationship. We accomplish this by focussing on the effect that children themselves have on the way their parents raise them and on their parents' lives. This chapter addresses, and even redresses, the excesses of past theories on child rearing. We begin by critiquing the traditional socialization model in light of interactive theories. Other sections examine, respectively, the beginning of the parent–child relationship at the neonate stage; parental adaptation to children with pathologies; parental adaptation to **conduct disorders**; the disruption of parenting skills; mothers and problematic children; children's cognitive biases; the effect of young-adult children on parents; adult children's effect on elderly parents; and the waning of parental influence. The chapter concludes with a presentation of the implications of this perspective for theory and research as well as for the family and society.

TRADITIONAL VERSUS INTERACTIVE THEORIES

▼

Up to a decade ago, most research on the parent–child relationship was carried out by psychologists from a developmental perspective, while sociologists were mainly interested in the topic of **socialization**. The concept of socialization broadly refers to children's learning how to think and behave according to the norms of their society, or even of their subgroup. Parents are considered to be the primary agents of socialization. However, peers and the media have become extremely influential in this respect and may even supplant parents. Schools also contribute to child socialization and, in the past, various churches were also prime agents and supported parents' role in this domain.

Since World War II, a purely environmental, or nurture, model has held sway in both psychology and sociology. This model explains the results of child socialization, and even adults' emotional balance, by their parents' characteristics or behaviours. Parental characteristics favoured by sociologists are mainly demographic; they include marital status, gender, and socio-economic status. For their part, psychologists have focussed on parents' mental states (maternal depression is heavily emphasized) and on their child-rearing practices (warmth, control, consistency, types of punishment, and so on). The end result has been **unidirectional**. That is, the causality, in the end result, flows from parents to children. The main questions asked have been: What do parents do *to* their children? What kinds of parents produce such-and-such type of child? How do parents raise their children to produce offspring with problems?

Such a causality model stems from **social constructs,** or definitions, of children as passive entities, victims, **non-agentic** little persons, clean slates upon which parents indelibly put their prints to children's advantage or disadvantage. With these constructs, children are deprived of **agency** and are not seen as social actors. Moreover, this causality model disregards the fact that children are also biological or genetic entities: children are born with certain characteristics or attributes that are in part genetic and that affect their development, their relationship with their parents, and how their parents raise them.

In the past two decades, a new and better balanced perspective on the parent–child relationship and child socialization has begun to view and study children as social actors (Corsaro, 1997) who co-produce their own development, who co-create their social environments, and, even as early as 1969, who socialize their parents (Rheingold, 1969), and affect them in general (Bell and Harper, 1977). Sociologists also recognize children as proactive actors. This theoretical perspective directs our attention to the interactive nature between child effect and parental effect and was recognized as early as 1928 by the psychologist A. Gesell — but this theoretical advance was soon buried under Freudian influences prevailing at the time.

Furthermore, this perspective is not reflected in the empirical or research literature and is not yet well known among laypersons, or even accepted by clinicians, physicians, and other concerned professionals. For instance, although a few researchers in the area of conduct disorders or behaviour problems have emphasized interactive, or **bidirectional,** effects between parents and problematic youngsters, this theoretical orientation *is rarely utilized in research.* Even the extensive literature on juvenile delinquency contains no work focussing directly on the interactional perspective or on the impact of juvenile delinquency on delinquents' *parents.* The unidirectional question generally asked is: What kinds of parents do juvenile delinquents have? What child-rearing styles lead to conduct disorder and delinquency? Parents are studied as one of the main, and often the key, background variables. But researchers fail to ask how children's delinquency affects parents. The role that these youths play in their parents' adult development and lives is ignored (Lefley, 1997, p. 445).

This gap between theory and empirical research is particularly damaging in the area of delinquency because delinquent adolescents' actions carry many unpleasant consequences, including being arrested, labelled, prosecuted, penalized, treated, and even institutionalized. It is important, therefore, to move away from the focus on parents as the source of their children's problems, and to begin discussing the overlooked fact that children in general, and problematic children in particular, affect their parents as well as their own outcomes and life course (Russell and Russell, 1992). The interactional perspective focusses on the mutual effects between persons — in this instance, on the reciprocal effects between parents and children. It also emphasizes the fact that children co-produce the development of many of their problems. Parents are not the all-powerful moulders they were once believed to be (Miller, 1993). For instance, the more antisocial children are, the more they tend to choose an environment that maintains, and even increases, their aggressiveness (Patterson, 1982). They gravitate toward peers similar to them, they resist their parents' attempts to socialize them, and they in effect teach their parents to abandon their duties. In contrast, prosocial children tend to gravitate toward peers who are similar to them, choose activities that enhance their positive outcomes in life, and are generally close to their parents and supportive of their efforts to socialize or raise them.

THE BEGINNING OF THE PARENT–CHILD RELATIONSHIP
▼

At birth, depending on genetic inheritance and intrauterine influences, each newborn is different. If you visit the nursery of a hospital maternity ward, you may see one newborn, Lucia, who cries constantly, even when picked up, and who is agitated and difficult to feed. Baby Roberto in the next crib may be a total contrast: he sleeps contentedly, nurses avidly, cries momentarily but stops when fed, changed, or picked up. A third baby, Latitia, is small, quiet, does not cry, sleeps most of the time, and drinks little milk. Each baby requires different types of care or approaches on the part of the nursing staff, and from parents.

Baby Lucia requires more attention because she *calls* for more of it with her cries. In contrast, Baby Roberto demands little attention and is actually easy to care for; all that his parents have to do is feed, change, and cuddle him. That baby allows his caretakers more free time and makes his parents feel competent because it seems to them that everything they do for him is rewarded with success. Unless something drastic occurs in his environment, Baby Roberto is already poised to have good behavioural outcomes later on because he will adapt easily and will not be a source of stress for his parents (Lerner and Lerner, 1994).

Baby Lucia's temperament presents at the outset the potential for problems. Her parents may feel less competent and more tense, especially if she is their first child and if she is very different from what they had expected. If her parents are preoccupied with problems of their own, Baby Lucia may simply be an additional cause of concern. As a result, she may not elicit parental reactions that are always positive. She may then grow up with less positive interactions and may not find interpersonal relationships as rewarding as will Roberto. As can be seen, poor little Lucia unwittingly initiates a chain of negative life events. Belsky and Rovine (1990) have even found that babies such as Lucia may contribute to a decrease in their parents' marital happiness. One could also presume that a baby such as Roberto would enhance his parents' marital happiness or, at the very least, allow them to stabilize their relationship.

For her part, Baby Latitia will arouse her parents' concern because of low birthweight and minimal appetite. At the same time, her parents are likely to feel comfortable because she is an easy baby. If fed regularly, she will eventually thrive and will not make too many demands on her parents. However, in a deprived environment and with a mother who does not know much about baby care, tiny Latitia may deteriorate, waste away, and even die because she may not cry enough to draw adult attention to her hunger. In times of famine, food may go to her more demanding siblings, a situation observed in Africa by de Vries (1987). Infant demandingness or difficultness may be particularly well suited for survival in the harsh Masai environment. But it may not be so well suited for positive outcome in our society.

Parents' perception that their baby is difficult or easy depends in part on their own characteristics and level of tolerance. Nevertheless, several studies indicate that the frequency and intensity of a baby's crying or fussiness can be objectively assessed by detached observers, who rate infants on a scale of difficultness. For instance, Lounsbury and Bates (1982) taped the hunger cries of infants who had already been described by their mothers as being difficult, average, or easy. The tapes were played to unrelated mothers who were unaware of the ratings. They still judged the cries of the more difficult infants to be more irritating. The **correlations** between the biological mothers' judgement of their baby's difficultness and the observers' rating were quite substantial. This indicates that each society evolves norms as to what constitutes child and infant difficultness. A child who exhibits difficult characteristics will elicit less positive reactions from his or her caretaker. When the caretaker is very mature and much in control of herself, the negative reactions may be merely mental and stressful, but may not affect how the parent treats the child. When the caretaker is less mature and more irritable, for instance, the negative reaction may be directly expressed in the form of relative neglect and, in cases of problematic parents, child abuse.

What emerges from our discussion so far is a perspective of interaction occurring on two levels. First, each baby has a personality to which parents react, depending on their own personalities and life circumstances. The infant initiates many of the parental gestures that form the cornerstone of the relationship. Second, in discussing the parent–infant relationship, we enter into yet another level of interaction: that between nature and nurture, or between genetics and environment. The environment resides not only in the hospital, the home, and the parental personalities, but also in the parental reactions babies elicit because of their predispositions. Babies evoke reactions (being fed, changed, caressed, or discouragingly ignored) and these reactions become part of their environment; hence, the close relationship between genetics and environment. Parental reactions also mark the beginning of the parent–child relationship. When the infant is a bit older, a favourable child temperament (that is, low on impulsivity, good attention span, and easily soothed) is a factor that may foster self-regulation and compliance to socialization requests. This child will internalize family norms more easily and require less supervision, as we will see later. Such children may form stronger attachments to their parents.

PARENTAL ADAPTATION TO CHILDREN WITH PATHOLOGIES
▼

Most parents adapt their child-rearing practices to fit their children's behaviours and personalities; hence, children affect their own socialization. For instance, when hyperactive children are successfully treated with the drug Ritalin, their hyperactivity diminishes substantially. Longitudinal research has shown that mothers modify their parenting style accordingly and become less controlling because their children create a lesser need for monitoring and are less disruptive (Tarver-Behring and Barkley, 1985). The same maternal adaptations have been observed in experiments for which child **confederates** were trained to behave in a compliant or in an oppositional manner by researchers. In these experiments, mothers of oppositional children and mothers of co-operative children of their own were chosen to see how they would react to the child confederates who were not their own children. The idea was that, if mothers really "cause" their children to be oppositional or hyperactive because of their inadequate mothering practices, they would not adapt to a child confederate's behaviour, but would instead react similarly to a child confederate who is oppositional and one who is co-operative. Therefore, a sample of these mothers were paired with the child confederate acting the oppositional role, while the others were paired with the child confederate acting the prosocial role.

What did the researchers find? Their results indicated that both groups of mothers exhibited more controlling and intrusive behaviour with the oppositional child confederate than with the co-operative one (Brunk and Hengeller, 1984). In other words, mothers were simply reacting to the child's cues. Several other experiments have also supported the concept of children having an effect on their parents' reactions. Hence, as we see, children not only affect their parents, but in so doing contribute to the quality of their parents' child-rearing practices toward them.

In a similar vein, but in a different field, researchers have established that the presence of a **schizophrenic** child in an experimental situation hinders parents' ability to perform cognitive tasks (Tompson et al., 1990). The child's presence disrupts parents' cognitive skills during a simple experiment. One can only infer that these parents' ability to perform their daily tasks in real life are seriously affected when their child is severely emotionally or behaviourally disturbed. ("It consumes me," as one mother put it.) In contrast, children who are easy, prosocial, and reasonably successful at their tasks probably enhance their parents' ability to cope, even within their work context. Parents are not constantly worried over and distressed by their successful children. Research has also shown that parents of schizophrenic children do not differ in their behaviour from parents of non-schizophrenic children when experimentally paired with a normal, and then a schizophrenic, child. This again implies that parents adapt to a child's attributes rather than "cause" these attributes. Moreover, Cook and colleagues (1990) observe that mothers of schizophrenic children try to de-escalate negative interactions. This certainly contradicts past literature, which presumed that schizophrenic children's mothers initiated negative interactions and created their children's emotional problems.

These studies taken together indicate that emotionally disturbed offspring do contribute to the disruption of family relationships and parental child-rearing activities. There is a complementary body of literature describing the deleterious effects on parents of adult children who are psychiatrically ill, especially when the child resides with the parents, or when there is a great deal of contact (Cook, 1988; Hatfield, 1987). Thus, emotionally disturbed children can exert a powerful influence on their parents' life all the way into the parents' last years (Greenberg, Siltzer, and Greenlay, 1993).

PARENTAL ADAPTATION TO CONDUCT DISORDERS
▼

As we begin to realize, children and adolescents can influence their parents to become coercive or rejecting, even if they do so unconsciously (Patterson, 1986). They may disobey, talk back, threaten to run away, fail to return home, and be disrespectful — as well illustrated by Andrea's behaviour (see Box 2.1). These behaviours can lead parents to become more forceful. Other parents may simply avoid contradicting their youngsters, who will then be the recipients of a permissive parenting style. This sequence of interactions has been initiated by the adolescents, not by the parents. In some cases, these types of interactions with parents appear during the early part of adolescence, while, in other cases, they are set up early in childhood. From this perspective, it can be said that adolescents co-produce the parental child-rearing practices of which they are the beneficiaries or the victims, as well as the scores that their parents receive on measures of child-rearing practices (**authoritative** versus **authoritarian**). For instance, studies find that parents who tend to be controlling or authoritarian have children with more behavioural and emotional

BOX 2.1
▼
ANDREA: A CASE STUDY

From the time Andrea was small, she has always needed more attention from her parents and her teachers than her two siblings did because she tended to disobey at home, whine a lot, talk back, and, at school, she disrupted classes constantly and was frequently sent to the principal's office. By age 14, she started arriving late at school in order to smoke cigarettes, and then skipped classes to meet with her boyfriend. Her parents felt stressed around her, as they did not know when she would "have a screaming fit." At home, they tried to stay away from her.

Six months ago, Andrea abruptly moved out and went to live with her same-age boyfriend at his parents' home. The boy's parents did not inform her parents, who frantically searched for her. After the long weekend, Andrea returned home. Her parents grounded her, but she threatened to run away, and returned to the boy's home. The two sets of parents met, but Andrea's parents were simply told that she was welcome to live there. Three weeks later, after a verbally heated quarrel with the boy's mother, who had grown tired of her intrusive guest, Andrea left for the streets in downtown Toronto. This led her parents to another round of searching, after which they subsequently learned that she was using drugs and engaging in prostitution. A social worker came to their home after a contact at a shelter in order to investigate the possibility that she had been physically and sexually abused. The parents, who were already devastated at this point, felt totally betrayed both by their daughter and by the "system." Currently (at the time of the interview with the parents), the daughter has returned home after treatment for drug addiction. She receives counselling. But she resents her parents, bristles at the slightest request, and then threatens to leave again. The mother, who has never suffered any emotional problems before, is now taking Prozac and has joined a parent support group. She had to leave her job as a financial analyst because of family burdens and stress. Both parents are particularly concerned about the effect of Andrea's example on their younger daughter.

problems. The conclusion drawn by previous studies has been that parents' controlling child rearing causes their children's negative outcomes. This certainly happens in some families and for some situations. But it is as realistic to assume a reverse causality; that is, in families in which children are very difficult, they provoke their parents into becoming more controlling and harsh. The studies discussed above would seem to support this.

In my own research on middle-class juvenile delinquents' parents, I have found that these parents tend to change their parenting practices after their child is first apprehended. Some become so discouraged that they give up, particularly when the adolescent returns home in an even more rebellious state. Others supervise their youth more closely than before (some, but not all, of these parents had been too permissive). This higher level of supervision is often rejected by the adolescents, who may run away or threaten to do so, further undermining parental resolve. Other adolescents, however, do welcome the greater level of structure, and life returns to normal. Thus, parents *react* to their adolescents' behaviours. How they react depends in part on what the children have done and in part on parents' personalities. Parents who are more passive and easily defeated may simply give up or pretend that everything is in order. Parents who are more agentic may become more supervisory, spend more time with the adolescent (if the adolescent allows it!), or seek external help.

All in all, children can turn off positive parental gestures just as adults can turn off positive spousal behaviours. Indeed, Simons and colleagues (1994, p. 359) point out that "rebellious, antisocial children often punish parental efforts to monitor and discipline while reinforcing parental withdrawal and deviance." Even normal adolescents do this occasionally. Patterson, Reid, and Dishion (1992, p. 11) observe that it is difficult to monitor the whereabouts of an adolescent who is extremely oppositional. Unfortunately, the end result of this chain of events often is that social agencies (police, courts, social workers) may deem these parents to be responsible for the child's behaviour and label them "bad" parents. Or, yet, parents may try to find some symptoms of mental illness or deviance to account for their children's behaviours. These are regressive rather than progressive social measures.

DISRUPTION OF PARENTING SKILLS

Difficult boys engage in aversive–coercive behaviours with their mothers practically every minute. As these children's conduct disorders become more entrenched, not only the rate, but also the severity, of aversive behaviours increases. Attempts to control these behaviours often result in an escalation of parent–child adversity until the conflict spills outside at school or in delinquent acts (Patterson, 1982). In extreme forms of parenting breakdown, the child controls the house. Mothers of difficult children often become so used to their situation that they are desensitized to misbehaviour and accept it as normal. They are less able than mothers of non-problematic children to distinguish misbehaviour from acceptable behaviour as they become unfamiliar with the latter. In effect, their expectation level plummets. This means that they become less competent at teaching their children better coping skills. Loeber (1982) reports a similar phenomenon occurring among college students who are experimentally exposed to coercive child behaviour in a laboratory setting. They become less apt to differentiate coercive from normative behaviour.

While adults' inappropriate parenting skills contribute to a child's conduct disorder in many families, as children gain the upper hand they may cause a further disruption of parenting practices. The causality becomes interactive and bidirectional. At the same time, such children may also contribute to the deterioration of their parents' marital relationship, particularly when the relationship was already precarious. In other words, *difficult children facilitate the disruption of their own environment* "by eliciting maladaptive parental behaviour, or increasing the strain on a marginally good marriage" (Earls, 1994, p. 316). Patterson, Bank, and Stoolmiller (1990) show that, when a child has an extreme antisocial score on personality tests in Grade 4, parenting practices are much more disrupted when the same child is assessed again in Grade 6 than when a child had been more prosocial in Grade 4. They hypothesize that, in any environment, the person who is the most coercive has control of the situation. Children who are hostile, conflictual, and even aggressive also impair a family's ability to solve problems that are relevant to its good functioning.

When the oppositional behaviour becomes chronic, parents lose control over family life and over their children. "Some children ultimately 'win' when they perform in such a way as to stop virtually all parental behaviours aimed at changing the misbehaviour" (Loeber and Stouthamer-Loeber, 1986, p. 110). Brown and colleagues (1988, p. 126) add that parents of children who suffer from **ADD, or attention deficit disorder,** score significantly higher on depression scales than do other parents. "ADD children often have a way of disrupting activities, wherever they may be." The authors conclude that "these parents become discouraged, demoralized, and depressed." In contrast, the traditional literature would turn the causality around and proclaim that depressed parents have caused their children to have ADD. This is why longitudinal studies are important: they allow researchers to test parents and children at a particular time and to establish how both parents and children are. When they return some months or years later, they then test parents and children again and are able to see what came first: the children's problems or the parents' disrupted practices. Depending on the type of family, both often occur simultaneously and reinforce each other. In other families, children's problems arrive first and parents' negative reactions follow. In still other families, highly problematic parents can create an atmosphere that leads to difficult child behaviours, particularly when the parents are antisocial or aggressive.

MOTHERS OF PROBLEMATIC CHILDREN

Mothers are children's primary caretakers in an unequal household division of labour. They are socially constructed as the nurturing parent, and many previous theories have blamed them for all the ills affecting their children (Ambert, 1997). Thus, Patterson (1980, p. 10) has pertinently remarked that "the role of mother is structured in such a manner as to almost guarantee higher rates of aversive events than does the role of the father." Coercive boys actually *target their mothers rather than their fathers as victims of conflict*, perhaps because mothers "are more likely to reinforce coercive attacks" (Patterson et al., 1992, p. 49). Mothers try harder to please and to accommodate, while fathers engage more in play interactions with their children, which allows them to attract less coercive behaviour from their conduct-disordered children than the mothers who have to take care of their daily needs and routine. As a result, fathers may not sympathize with the child's mother when she complains about the misbehaviour, hence increasing the mother's isolation and feelings of self-blame. Fathers of difficult children are little different from fathers of normal children in terms of stress reactions, while the opposite occurs among mothers. Patterson (1982, p. 24) remarks that "this leads to the conclusion that the role label most appropriate for fathers might be that of 'guest'!"

Families with disruptive children are marked by conflictual mutuality between mother and child (Johnston and Pelham, 1990). Mothers usually prevail with normal children, but with difficult boys in particular, it is the children who do — as is well illustrated in the vignette in Box 2.2. Hence there is a role reversal and the parent–child relationship becomes dysfunctional. Effective child socialization stops. At some point in the escalation of parent–child conflict, the mother may become afraid of disciplining, or even contradicting, the child, whether male or female. Patterson (1980, pp. 32–33) also notes that "mothers tend not to provide an aversive antecedent for these chains" of behaviours and desperately try "to avoid/escape from confrontations with a practiced aggressor." We have seen that the same maternal reaction occurs with children who suffer from schizophrenia. In fact, a mother's positive behaviour toward a usually disruptive boy may unwittingly encourage the son to take advantage of her (Lavigueur, Tremblay, and Saucier, 1995). Boys are not much afraid of mothers who have a lower status in society, at any rate; this is why, after divorce, single mothers often have a very difficult time with their adolescent sons.

Not surprisingly, research indicates that maternal satisfaction and mother–child harmony correlate with child compliance. *A compliant child is more easily socialized*, thus providing the mother with a higher sense of parenting success. A compliant or co-operative child does not force his or her mother to

---

BOX 2.2
▼
CHILD AGGRESSES MOTHER

I recently observed the following scene in a subway train in Toronto. A well-dressed mother, aged between 25 and 30, walked in the train with an equally well-groomed little boy, aged 4 or 5. The little boy was screaming at his mother at the top of his lungs.

B: You hurt my feelings!
M: (bending down to soothe him): I'm so sorry, honey. I apologize.

B: I hate you, I hate you! (He was red in the face with rage and was hitting his mother with his fists.)
M: (softly): Again, I'm sorry honey, it won't happen again.

B: You're stupid: (He kicked her with his booted foot.)

The mother had tears in her eyes and was very troubled by the child's behaviour but did not put an effective stop to it. Neither did she notice that, by now, everyone was looking at her and felt sorry for her. Although, the boy noticed us staring, it did not deter him in the least bit as he continued punching and yelling.

---

repeat the same requests over again and may be perfectly happy to be well behaved. Mike is a case in point (see Box 2.3). As a result, the mother is less stressed and her life evolves more smoothly. She can more easily attend to other tasks and, when gainfully employed, can better balance family life and work life. One likely effect of difficult child behaviour, at least on the mother, is an increasing tendency on her part to issue directives, commands, and threats in an effort to reduce the negative behaviour. But this is usually futile because, although parental reprimands do lower negative child behaviour in *normative* children, they do not generally affect the behaviour of problem children. Quite the opposite often occurs, and children may simply increase the frequency and severity of their coercive and oppositional episodes. When things get out of hand, certain parents are fortunate to encounter a competent professional or to join a parent support group with whom they learn techniques that will help reduce their children's negative episodes. But once parents already have a difficult child, "parent-effectiveness training" can be a long and painful road. At the slightest parental error, the difficult child will once again gain the upper hand. These parents always have to be vigilant — which is not exactly a normal state.

BOX 2.3
▼
MIKE: A CASE STUDY

Mike, 14, is a good student, does his homework without being prompted, and is very active in sports and music. In addition, each weekend, he accompanies one of his parents, who alternate volunteering for recreational activities for physically challenged children. His biological father died when he was 6, and his mother remarried when he was 12. His stepfather had no children from a previous marriage and adopted both his wife's children. Mike's mother talks warmly of how easy it is to raise her children, particularly Mike, compared with other parents: "I ask him to do something and explain why and that's it. It's as good as done." She also appreciates his affectionate personality. He hugs her daily, asks about her day when she returns home (she's a nurse), and does the same to his father a little later on (he has a small business). "He's really interested in what we do and it's so nice." He brings friends home and proudly introduces his parents to them. He gets along well with his sister, "more because he is good-natured honestly than because she's all that interested. She thinks he's a bit of a sissy," the mother says, with a shrug. By the end of the interview, Mike had returned home and came to sit with us, ready with questions about the study.

Note: This family had been introduced to me by Andrea's mother.

CHILDREN'S COGNITIVE BIASES
▼

There is a vast literature that has studied parental perceptions of their children, and of their role and how these attributions affect their parenting. In this section, we instead investigate children's perceptions, because children's perceptions of their parents' motives are key factors in the parent–child relationship (Rohner, Bourque, and Elordi, 1996). Researchers indicate that aggressive or difficult children are often biased in how they process information. Children with conduct disorders may be difficult in part because their cognition and perceptions are faulty, including the ones they maintain concerning their parents and other authority figures. For instance, they may misconstrue authority figures as people who do not care for them or "gang up" on them, or as people who have to be resisted. As Tein, Roosa, and Michaels (1994, p. 343) put it, "children's symptomatology affects their perceptions of parental behaviours."

It often leads them to view their parents more negatively than do average children. In turn, problematic behaviours and their consequences reinforce, and even heighten, the level of bias in the children's cognitions: their poor behaviours evoke negative social and parental reactions that they cannot accept — such as scoldings, disapproval, or punishment. Studies indicate that children with low self-esteem have a tendency to emphasize their parents' negative behaviours toward them and to *downplay* parents' positive behaviours (Stafford and Bayer, 1993). Small wonder that studies which give questionnaires or interviews to children, asking them to describe themselves and their parents, find that children with low self-esteem have parents who treat them poorly! There is no question that bad parenting can lower a child's self-esteem. However, there are indications that self-esteem in great part derives from other attributes of the child, such as his or her level of intelligence, as well as personality characteristics, such as shyness or low impulse control. Moreover, nowadays, low self-esteem is more likely to be caused by how children are treated by their peers (Ambert, 1997). Girls are particularly vulnerable to negative peer treatment, and their self-esteem often plummets in early adolescence.

Bates (1987, p. 1132) has hypothesized that infants and children who are difficult may learn less about their parents' attitudes and feelings than do more easygoing children. They may have an attention bias that orients them to ignore their parents and to focus on other areas of concerns to them, such as delinquent peers. Similar attention biases are observed among adults who suffer from emotional problems. Difficult children may be less able or willing than others to learn social cues and to "read" other people, perhaps due to high levels of impulsivity or of self-centredness. This deficit may, in turn, contribute to friction between the parents, as well as between child and parents, further reinforcing the negative child behaviour. Moreover, difficult children are less prosocial, and may identify less with parents who try to teach them prosocial skills. There are children who not only disobey their parents and turn against them, but identify with a deviant peer group. Moreover, as early as 1982, Patterson began discussing the possibility that some children may be genetically predisposed to be less responsive to social reinforcers such as praise or punishment; this predisposition would understandably make it more difficult to raise them properly as they would have more difficulty learning to distinguish right from wrong.

THE EFFECT OF YOUNG ADULT CHILDREN
▼

In the recent past, parents, and particularly mothers, suffered from the "empty-nest syndrome." That is, after their children had gone, parents were lonely, did not know what to do with their free time, and sharply felt the pain of the loss of their parental role. Researchers even used to find that this empty-nest stage led to depression among mothers, who were losing their primary, "natural" role in life — that of motherhood. Needless to say, feminism and the burgeoning participation of women in the labour force have cast a shadow on the validity of this perspective for current times. Parents generally look forward to seeing their young adults settle down with a good job, and later on with a family of their own. Other parents look forward to becoming grandparents since it generally is an easier role to play. There are strong indications that adult children's departure is related to an improvement in the parents' marital relationship.

Still, myths die hard: according to an American study, university students usually believe that their parents will be very lonely without them (Shehan and Dwyer, 1989). These students focus on problems that co-residence has for *them* rather than for their parents. They emphasize their lack of autonomy and freedom (perhaps failing to note that their parents may have the same problem). The data are inconsistent, and even contradictory, when it comes to evaluating parental satisfaction concerning co-residence with their children. Parental stress is higher when the children are financially dependent, and lower when the interaction is positive and there is little conflict (Aquilino and Supple, 1991). There may also be differences according to social class and race. There are indications that black mothers perceive their children to be less supportive than do white mothers (Umberson, 1992), possibly a question of income and resource differentials between the two groups, a fact that would prevent a young black adult from helping his or her mother and, instead, obligates her to help her child.

There are unfortunate young persons who are or become emotionally disturbed or who have a disability that forces them to remain under parental care, or at least under the parents' roof. They fail to reach the independence we expect with the passage into adulthood. In terms of the life course, they are "off time" and will remain so. Parental expectations of maturity are shattered. These children cannot emancipate themselves from their parents or hold a job successfully. They may be unable to form intimate relationships with others, and even to make friendships. The end result is that their parents have to fulfil many roles for them. In other cases, these young persons live in a group home or by themselves, but parents remain their main lifeline. Parents, especially as they age, may find their predicament not only difficult to bear, however devoted they may be, but worrisome. Some are concerned that their child is unhappy, or is being taken advantage of by unscrupulous persons; others have to live with the ever-present threat of the adult child's suicide or dangerous behaviour. But, above all, the question that such parents ask themselves is: "What will happen to him [or her] when we get really old and after we die? Who will be responsible for our child?"

THE ADULT CHILD'S EFFECT ON ELDERLY PARENTS
▼

Pillemer and Suitor (1991a) pointedly remark that the research on the relationship between adult children and their aging parents resembles the unidirectional parental causality model of the traditional child-development literature: the focus in gerontology is on the impact, often negative, *on* children of caring for their elderly parents, just like the focus of the child-socialization literature has been on the negative impact *on* children of various parental characteristics. In other words, it seems that researchers hound parents as culprits, both when their children are small and at the other end of parents' lives, when their offspring may be 40 to 75 years old.

As parents reach their eightieth year and onward, a number of them fall prey to either illnesses from which they recover, or to illnesses that are chronic, such as arthritis or heart disease. Other parents experience problems such as osteoporosis or poor eyesight that can reduce their activity level and their mobility. Still others become frail or can no longer walk far without help. Others become mentally incompetent. Therefore, each year the relationship between many elderly parents and at least some of their children is altered in some respects because of these fluctuations in parents' health. Adult children become the key instrumental and social-support resources for their elderly parents. Some children begin to take full responsibility for their care, either in person or by supervising tasks that they have delegated to paid caretakers or retirement homes (Chappell, Strain, and Blandford, 1986). However, as Logan and Spitze (1996) document it, very few adult children become caretakers of their parents in the true sense of this word and/or for a long period of time. As they point out, most elderly remain independent until their last years, and, of those who are incapacitated, very few become the entire responsibility of one of their children.

Although elderly adults who are childless are not less happy or in poorer health than those who have living children, adults receive more help when they have children. What seems to count for the well-being of our senior citizens is not whether they have children, but the quality of the relationship between them and their children. Silverstein and Bengtson (1991) find that a warm relationship with adult children may increase parental longevity after widowhood. Hence, a "good" child can have a lifelong positive impact on his or her parents.

Actually, elderly parents are happier when they give more than they receive, and they accept help more readily when they can contribute something in return. In fact, when parents require a great deal of support from their children, they are less satisfied with the relationship (Chappell, 1985). In part, this can be explained by the fact that contact with the child is necessitated by the parent's needs rather than by the child's desire to see the parent or by the spontaneity of a visit just to chat. When the entire family, and not just the parents, have always valued reciprocity, elders may be satisfied that their earlier parental efforts were appreciated and they may not be negatively affected if they are unable to reciprocate in their later years. Lee, Netzer, and Coward (1995) find that older parents who receive more help are more depressed. As they point out, American elders value their independence, and dependence on children may be troublesome. But they also suggest the possibility of reversed causality, where children respond to their parents' depression by helping them more. It is not surprising, therefore, that when older parents are in better health, they report a more positive relationship with their children.

Da Vanzo and Goldscheider (1990) show that male children, whether single or married, are more likely to return home than are female children; moreover, males are found to do 20 percent less housework than females when they live with their parents. *Hence, co-residence is more likely to benefit the adult child than the parents.* As parents age, they often do not or cannot disengage from the joys and problems experienced by their adult children. As Pillemer and Suitor (1991b) report, 26 percent of senior parents mention that at least one of their children is experiencing serious physical or mental health problems or a high level of stress. These children's problems correlate significantly with depression in the older parents, and some studies report that older parents who have to help their children a lot feel more depressed (Mutran and Reitzes, 1984). In addition, when children have problems, they may receive advice that is not wanted. One can see that, at the very least, the potential for intergenerational conflict is high when adult children have problems — as is the case with adolescent offspring.

There are indications that the elderly are often abused by a dependent relative who lives with them, even if the elderly themselves are self-sufficient (Wolf and Pillemer, 1989). In that case, it generally is the adult child who depends on the parent financially or for shelter because he or she is unemployed, or may be mentally delayed, physically incompetent, or emotionally disturbed. Indeed, after discharge from hospital care, 85 percent of adult unmarried children who are mentally ill are sheltered by their aged parents (Greenberg et al., 1993). Hence, Pillemer (1985) believes that we may have placed too much emphasis on the dependence of the elderly as a source of abuse from their caretakers and that we should refocus our attention to include those elderly who have a dependent and physically stronger spouse or child living with them.

It is difficult to know whether adult daughters abuse their elderly parents more than sons do. As we have seen, as daughters are more frequently caretakers, they have more opportunities to do so and also more frustration to vent. On the other hand, more sons live with their elderly parents because they are dependent. In addition, males are more aggressive than females and may not be as emotionally attached to their parents as are adult females. These factors could contribute to more parental abuse by sons. Complicating the issue is the existence of covert forms of abuse, such as siphoning off revenues or controlling the house that belongs to the aged parents (Korbin, Anetzberger, and Austin, 1995). Abuse of elderly parents is a relatively easy act to commit and can have even less social visibility than abuse of school-age children. Consequently, it is possible that today's abused elderly parents are less likely to report the abuse than would be a maltreated adolescent. Moreover, an abused child can grow up to denounce the parents, whereas the elderly parent will carry the secret to his or her grave.

THE WANING OF PARENTAL INFLUENCE
▼

The influence of parents on child/adolescent development is historically and ecologically grounded, and changes with the societal contexts. The parent–child relationship and child development are realities that are very sensitive to cultural, social, and economic changes. Indeed, family relationships and human development take place within a given cultural context (Bronfenbrenner, 1988; Elder, 1995), at a given period of social change or stability, and under specific economic conditions. The contexts in which children live have changed drastically within the past 30 years, and continue to evolve with spiralling technologization. The result has been a decrease in parental influence on children. To begin with, research indicates that children spend far less time with their parents than was the case just over a decade ago, in part because both parents tend to be employed. Single mothers also have to be gainfully employed. Therefore, parents have less time to influence their children. Second, children react to their parents according to the expectations of their environment, including peer-group pressure (which can be positive or negative) and the messages they receive from professionals, and particularly from the media. Hence, children's receptivity to parenting efforts and influence may be simultaneously waning because external factors have an enormous impact upon them.

There are periods in a society's history when it is easier for parents to influence their youngsters, and others when it is far more difficult to do so. First, social changes usher in new influences on children's lives and diminish other influences. Fifty years ago, there was no television, but that medium has long since become a prime agent of socialization. In contrast, religion, which supported parents, was then a more powerful influence than is currently the case. Therefore, certain childhood and adolescent outcomes may be less strongly affected by parents than was the case 50, or even 10, years ago, because of the presence or absence, strength or weakness, of a variety of other influences. Thus, parents may have less of an impact now than before on their children's moral development, manners, and even character.

Furthermore, as our society evolves, it places a premium on certain specific child characteristics that become highly valued (Alwin, 1990). For instance, mainstream anglophone culture currently values high self-esteem, educational achievement, and individual autonomy. While these outcomes may be affected by parents, they are also subject to the impact of peers and school, as well as by partly genetic factors such as cognitive ability and hyperactivity. For instance, children who are less well endowed intellectually and are less persistent by nature do not do well in school, often develop a low self-esteem, and may seek peers who are less school-oriented — all of this despite parents' efforts to the contrary. A few decades ago, more importance was given in child rearing to politeness, obedience, conformity, or patriotism. Parents were more influential in the development of these outcomes because these outcomes *require direct teaching or example*. In contrast, outcomes that are more *personality-driven*, such as self-esteem and independence, fall more under the influence of genetic predispositions and the situation outside of the home sphere. Therefore, as one can see, the social context in which parenting is embedded has changed drastically and has reduced parents' ability to influence their children. Hence, parents are generally less responsible than before when their children "go wrong." Similarly, they may be less responsible for their children's successes than before.

IMPLICATIONS
▼

In this section, we examine implications of the effect of children on parents, of the interactive perspective, and of the consequently lesser influence of parents on their children, particularly in view of recent sociocultural changes. We first focus on theoretical implications; we then turn to implications for the family and society, and then finally for research.

THEORETICAL IMPLICATIONS

We saw earlier how traditional theories of socialization and social constructs of children have evolved this century along lines of parental responsibility, and even mother blaming. We have also explained how the new interactive theoretical orientation offers a better balanced perspective on the reality of children as active members of their family and of their society; children are not a mere blank slate for their parents, but are actually co-producers of their own development and affect their parents' lives very deeply, both positively and negatively.

Not only is this perspective more realistic, particularly within our current sociocultural environment, but it meshes with feminist and **behaviour genetics** theories. The framework that we use here also takes into consideration the structure of the maternal role as defined by society. Mothers are their children's main caretakers and nurturers, even when most are gainfully employed. This means that mothers are far more vulnerable than fathers to child effect. They have to accommodate their schedule to their children's needs, and, more than fathers, have to adapt their child-rearing practices, generally unconsciously so, to the requisites of their children's personalities, abilities, behaviours, attitudes, and health.

An important contribution of this perspective is that it allows for a closer examination of mother blaming, not only in society at large, but in clinical practice in particular (Ambert, 1992, 1997). Until very recently, parents, but particularly mothers, were overtly blamed for their children's negative outcomes such as mental illness, juvenile delinquency, behavioural problems, and school failure; they were even held responsible for the development of male homosexuality. In the past two decades, the blame has become more subdued and more covert — more "subdued" because research results no longer support parental responsibility as the main factor in children's mental illnesses. Consequently, researchers have had to search for more adequate theories and, in turn, it is fair to say that the interactive perspective itself has had much to do with researchers' change of orientation in their explanatory models. But mother blaming has also become more covert because it is a myth that dies hard, and the new theories and research have not yet trickled down adequately enough to laypersons, clinicians, and even social workers. The end result is that parent blaming often goes "underground" and becomes insidious, shrouded in euphemisms such as maternal employment and single mothering. Family therapy, may then be used to urge parents to adapt to their children.

This chapter's perspective also meshes very well with behaviour genetics theories at the micro level of analysis. Behaviour genetics is a science that focuses on finding and explaining similarities and differences among siblings and between parents and children in the same family. It explains that individuals' personalities and abilities are a result of the interaction between their genetic predispositions and their environment, both familial and non-familial (Plomin, 1994). In order to both disentangle genetic and environmental effects and to look at their co-ordination in producing human development, scientists in this field compare identical twins (who have the same genes) and fraternal twins (who share only 50 percent of their genes), both adopted separately (different familial environments) and living together with their biological parents (same familial environment). They also compare adopted and non-adopted siblings, as well as offspring and parents, both adopted and non-adopted.

This line of inquiry has allowed behaviour geneticists to establish that parents affect their children both genetically (in the sense that children inherit 50 percent of their genes from each parent — a totally overlooked matter in sociology) and environmentally; second, that parents' environmental influence wanes as children are exposed to the external environment; third, that children tend to choose aspects of their environment that suit their own personalities; and, fourth, as a result, as children grow into adults, their parents' influence becomes less salient and their genetic predispositions predominate in the sense that, left to their own devices, adults choose a line of behaviour, peers, friends, work, and leisure activities that suit their predispositions rather than necessarily what their parents have taught them.

From our perspective, and even from a feminist perspective, there are profound implications to these theoretically inspired behaviour genetics results. First, perhaps most of the correlations that have been found to exist between parental behaviours and children's behaviours and personalities are best explained by children's genetic link to their biological parents. This genetic link accounts both for what children might have biologically inherited that they thus share with their parents in terms of similarities, and for the fact that some parental child-rearing practices are linked to the personalities of both parents and children. Therefore, perhaps as many as 50 percent of the correlations between parenting practices and child outcomes that have been explained solely on the basis of parental behaviours can be explained by genetics instead. For instance, when an irritable parent reacts harshly to a 10-year-old's yelling or disobedience, two things are happening. First, it is likely that both parent and child are irritable in great part because of a common genetic inheritance (or the child's similarity to the other parent). Thus, the child is difficult and does not obey, while the parent reacts in a less than mature way because of the shared negative temperaments involved. Second, unfortunately, the less-than-reasonable parental reaction, which becomes part of the child's familial environment (an example of genes indirectly affecting familial environment), may worsen the child's irritable predisposition.

BOX 2.4
▼
SCHIZOPHRENIA IN FAMILIES

The lifetime risk for schizophrenia in the general population is 1 percent. But this risk increases when close relatives are similarly affected. Identical twins (who are the closest relatives genetically) have a 17 to 60 percent **concordance,** or similarity. Children with one schizophrenic parent or sibling have a 7 to 13 percent risk, and with two schizophrenic parents the risk jumps to 40 or 50 percent, with perhaps an additional risk for other emotional problems. Children of a mother with schizophrenia who are adopted away retain approximately a 7 percent risk even though their adoptive environment is normal. Children of mentally healthy biological parents who are adopted by a family in which one of the adoptive parents eventually develops schizophrenia have about the same 1 percent risk as the rest of the population. (For a review of this research, see Ambert, 1997.)

Moreover, behaviour genetic studies also clearly indicate that the major mental disorders, such as schizophrenia and manic depression, "run in families" along blood lines — not by adoption. The more severe the mental illness, the more likely it is that an identical twin shares the disease or that someone in the family (a grandparent, an uncle) also has it or has another severe mental illness (see Box 2.4). Again, it is difficult to accept traditional theories of maternal blaming in the face of these realities. When mothers' children are very difficult temperamentally, mothers basically have to "fight nature." This is not easy. When these mothers are similarly afflicted and their own mothers have not been able to temper their nature, then the mother–child interaction and child socialization is less than optimal. Nature can be tempered, but not necessarily vanquished, by a good environment — particularly an optimal familial environment — and, in extreme cases, proper medication. This is where mothers are so vulnerable: they have to be very vigilant when raising a problematic child, the more so because external influences, in the guise of violence, individualism, and materialism, do not provide support for the maternal and paternal roles.

FAMILIAL AND SOCIAL IMPLICATIONS

The concluding statement above leads to the discussion of the familial and social implications of the interactive perspective. There are currently legislative changes being considered in some provinces, and others that have been enacted, that can be seen as regressive in light of this chapter. At least one province now has a law allowing a citizen to sue parents for up to $5000 in damages when their children have committed acts of vandalism, crashed a stolen car, or assaulted another child, among other delinquent acts. This law is anti-parent. Why? Because, as we have seen in the section on the waning of parental influence, parents have far less authority over their children than in the past. Actually, parental authority is no longer valued or supported by adolescents, professionals, clinicians, the media, and even courts. Therefore, it is illogical and unfair to make parents responsible and financially liable for their adolescents' delinquent acts under these circumstances. Moreover, parents (unless they are themselves criminogenic) discourage "bad" behaviour. When their children shoplift, steal a car, assault a peer, they do it *behind their parents' back*.

A more realistic and progressive law would make the adolescents themselves responsible for their acts by garnisheeing their wages (a majority of Canadian adolescents work part-time to support their consumer habits), or putting a lien on their future salaries when they reach adulthood, or, giving them a paid job and then garnisheeing their wages. At the same time, these adolescents could be counselled. But this counselling should reinforce, and not undermine, their parents' attempts at raising them or, at the very least, at monitoring their activities.

In view of the fact that children affect their parents, courses on family life in high school might include at least one section on this topic. Such discussions might be very timely in the lives of adolescents. I also submit the immodest proposal that both children and parents should be made more responsible toward each other. Currently, rights are emphasized. While rights are individualistic, responsibilities are more familial, altruistic, and collectivistic. Furthermore, parents whose children are emotionally disturbed or who exhibit disruptive behaviours should be given social, moral, and instrumental support — rather than being blamed or simply abandoned to their fate. Parenting would then become more effective and less emotionally costly. (It would also become less financially costly to society and governments.) Children would benefit as their lives would be more adequately structured; society would gain in terms of lower rates of behaviour problems, teen pregnancy, and juvenile delinquency.

RESEARCH IMPLICATIONS

The major research implication is that studies should be designed to reflect the realities of children's effect on parents, of the interactive nature of the relationship, and of the effect of children on their own socialization. Besides asking what parents do to raise their children, we should also ask what children do in the production of their parents' child-rearing practices. How do children's behaviours affect their parents' reactions to them? How do children facilitate or hinder their parents' socialization practices? What cognitive or perceptual biases do some children maintain vis-à-vis their parents, and what role do these biases play in children's reactions to their parents and in their own socialization outcomes.

When a birth occurs to a "high-risk" mother (that is, a disadvantaged, or teenage, or emotionally fragile mother), child characteristics should become one of the bases for intervention. Currently, there are only two related neonatal child characteristics that are included in research designs on high-risk mothers: pre-term and low-birthweight infants. These infants are vulnerable to illnesses and neurological deficits, and they tend to do particularly poorly when their parents are very young, uneducated, and disadvantaged, or even depressed. But research should also include a baby's fussiness and reactivity. These are only two of the very few temperamental characteristics that are manifest at the outset of life. We have seen earlier that mothers were negatively affected by babies who cry a great deal, do not sleep or eat on a schedule, and appear inconsolable. Less mature mothers react more negatively and inappropriately to such infants, which may lead to child neglect, and even abuse, lack of maternal enthusiasm, maternal exhaustion, and, consequently, depression. Nevertheless, whatever their age, their maturity level, or their education, mothers of such infants need more social support than mothers of easygoing and predictable infants.

In the literature on adoption, there is a tendency to emphasize research results that show negative "consequences" of adoption. That is, most studies find that adopted children have a few more problems than non-adopted children. The focus is placed on this disadvantage, despite the fact that, in a majority of adoptions, the outcomes are as positive as those in biological families. But it is noteworthy that the research on adoption fails to consider children's and parents' personal characteristics, particularly the match between the two. It is possible that, more often, adoption unites a child with parents from whom he or she is too temperamentally different than is the case among biological families. When the fit between parents' and children's personalities is poor, whether the families are adoptive or biological, it is logical to assume that the parent–child interaction will be less successful, that attachment may come less easily, and that mutual understanding and identification may flounder.

Hence, it would be particularly important to study parent–child fit, comparing families where a "target" child (i.e., the child chosen by the researcher) is well adjusted with families where the child has achievement, behavioural, or emotional problems. One would want to know the processes that might be involved in the development of child problems and child effect on parents in cases of familial homogeneity compared with familial dissimilarity, both in biological and in adoptive families. These are only three examples of changes that could occur in the micro-level research on parents and children or on socialization were the interactive paradigm utilized as a theoretical basis.

SUMMARY
▼

- Children play a role in their socialization process: children, by their personality characteristics, attitudes, behaviours, and abilities, contribute to shaping the environment in which they are raised and in which they grow up.
- The most obvious aspect of children's environment resides in their parents, and particularly in their mothers, who are the first observers and recipients of children's behaviours.
- As children interact with their parents, the latter adapt to them according to their own personalities and their social situation.
- The negative impact on parents and on their child-rearing practices of children who suffer from various forms of emotional problems and others who are very difficult has been emphasized. This emphasis is necessary because mothers, in particular, have been blamed for their children's emotional and behavioural problems.
- In terms of children's effect on their parents and on their socialization, one domain that has not sufficiently been considered is that of their perceptual and attributional modes — the interactive role of children and parents has also been placed within the context of the waning of parental influence in the recent decades due to a wide variety of interconnected sociocultural changes.
- The interactive perspective has implications for theory, particularly its complementariness to feminist and behaviour-genetic theories.
- The fact that our society does not grant parents sufficient moral authority has familial and social implications and renders it questionable whether parents can be held responsible for their children's misbehaviours outside the home.
- Researchers should place a greater emphasis on children's characteristics and on the fit between parents' and children's personalities.

CRITICAL THINKING QUESTIONS
▼

1. What may be wrong or biased in studies that establish a causality between parental behaviours and adolescent negative outcomes as reported by adoles-

cents in a questionnaire? (There are at least two problems involved in this approach.)

2. Suppose that you are a child therapist and a mother brings in her 10-year-old son because she finds him out of control, disobedient, aggressive, and generally ill-tempered.
   a. What would you say or do as a traditional therapist who believes in parental causality?
   b. What would you do or say as a therapist guided by an interactive model?

3. Design a brief research proposal to test the hypothesis that boys and girls who are prosocial identify more closely with their parents than those who are oppositional and difficult. Provide an explanatory framework.

4. Use the example of schizophrenia to establish a link between interactive and behaviour genetics theories. Explain the link.

5. Discuss how another theoretical framework presented in another chapter of this volume complements the interactive perspective discussed here.

6. Using the case of Andrea, how would you analyze this situation using a behaviour-modification approach, an interactionist approach, or a social-learning approach?

SUGGESTED READING
▼

Anne-Marie Ambert. 1997. *Parents, Children, and Adolescents: Interactive Relationships and Development in Context.* Binghamton, NY: Haworth Press.

This book studies the parent–child relationship throughout the life course and within different familial and social contexts. It utilizes a perspective that combines interactionist, behaviour genetics, and environmental theories.

William A. Corsaro. 1997. *The Sociology of Childhood.* Thousand Oaks, CA: Pine Forge Press.

This short introductory textbook differs from others in that the author focusses on children as social actors, on peer cultures, as well as on historical and cultural perspectives of childhood.

James Garbarino. 1995. *Raising Children in a Socially Toxic Environment.* San Francisco: Jossey-Bass.

A provocative book, easy to read, that details the negative influence on children of the "nastiness" present in our current sociocultural environment.

Reed Larson, and Maryse H. Richards. 1994. *Divergent Realities: The Emotional Lives of Mothers, Fathers, and Adolescents.* New York: Basic Books.

This book is the result of a creative research project whereby both parents and one adolescent in a number of families wore a pager. When it beeped, at different times of the day, all three respondents filled out a form on their current activity and their mood. Questionnaires and interviews were also used.

Harriet P. Lefley. 1996. *Family Caregiving in Mental Illness.* Thousand Oaks, CA: Sage.

>Lefley specializes mainly in the care of mentally ill adult children by their parents. Her work challenges many myths and uses a perspective congruent with this chapter.

Gerald R. Patterson, John B. Reid, and Thomas J. Dishion. 1992. *Antisocial Boys.* Eugene, OR: Castalia.

>Patterson and his team report on their interactive theories and research results based on studies of families, particularly single mothers, who have one very difficult boy.

Robert Plomin. 1994. *Genetics and Experience: The Interplay between Nature and Nurture.* Thousand Oaks, CA: Sage.

>For those who are interested in further exploring the contribution of behaviour genetics in our understanding of human development.

REFERENCES
▼

Alwin, D.F. 1990. "Cohort Replacement and Changes in Parental Socialization Values." *Journal of Marriage and the Family* 52: 347–60.

Ambert, A.-M. 1992. *The Effect of Children on Parents.* New York: Haworth Press.

———. 1997. *Parents, Children, and Adolescents: Interactive Relationships and Development in Context.* New York: Haworth Press.

Aquilino, W.S., and K.R. Supple. 1991. "Parent–Child Relations and Parents' Satisfaction with Living Arrangements When Adult Children Live at Home." *Journal of Marriage and the Family* 53: 13–28.

Bates, J.E. 1987. "Temperament in Infancy." In J.D. Osofsky, ed., *Handbook of Infant Development*, 2nd ed. New York: Wiley.

Bell, R.Q., and L.V. Harper. 1977. *Child Effect on Adults.* Hillsdale, NJ: Lawrence Erlbaum.

Belsky, J., and M. Rovine. 1990. "Patterns of Marital Change Across the Transition to Parenthood: Pregnancy to Three Years Postpartum." *Journal of Marriage and the Family* 52: 5–19.

Bronfenbrenner, U. 1988. "Interacting Systems in Human Development: Research Paradigms: Present and Future." In N. Bolger, A. Caspi, and M. Moorehouse, eds., *Persons in Context: Development Processes.* New York: Cambridge University Press.

Brown, B.B., K.A. Borden, S.R. Clingerman, and P. Jenkins. 1988. "Depression in Attention Deficit–Disordered and Normal Children and Their Parents." *Child Psychiatry and Human Development* 18: 119–32.

Brunk, M.A., and S.W. Hengeller. 1984. "Child Influences on Adult Controls: An Experimental Investigation." *Developmental Psychology* 20: 1074–81.

Chappell, N.L. 1985. "Social Support and the Receipt of Home Care Services." *The Gerontologist* 25: 47–54.

Chappell, N.L., L.A. Strain, and A.A. Blandford. 1986. *Aging and Health Care. A Social Perspective.* Toronto: Holt, Reinhart and Winston.

Cook, J. 1988. "Who 'Mothers' the Chronically Mentally Ill?" *Family Relations* 37: 42–49.

Cook, William, Joan R. Asarnow, Michael J. Goldstein, Valerie G. Marshall, and Edith Weber. 1990. "Mother–Child Dynamics in Early-Onset Depression and Childhood Schizophrenic Spectrum Disorders." *Development and Psychopathology* 2: 71–84.

Corsaro, W.A. 1997. *The Sociology of Childhood.* Thousand Oaks, CA: Pine Forge Press.

Da Vanzo, J., and F.K. Goldscheider. 1990. "Coming Home Again: Returns to the Parental Home of Young Adults." *Population Studies* 44: 241–55.

de Vries, M.W. 1987. "Cry Babies, Culture, and Catastrophe: Infant Temperament Among the Masai." In N. Scheper-Hughes, ed., *Child Survival.* Dordrecht: D. Reidel.

Earls, F. 1994. "Oppositional-Defiant and Conduct Disorders." In M. Rutter, E. Taylor, and L. Hersov, eds., *Child and Adolescent Psychiatry*, 3rd ed. Oxford: Blackwell.

Elder, G.H., Jr. 1995. "The Life Course Paradigm and Social Change: Historical and Developmental Perspectives." In P. Moen, G.H. Elder, Jr., and K. Luscher, eds., *Perspectives on the Ecology of Human Development.* Washington, DC: American Psychological Association.

Gesell, A. 1928. *Infancy and Human Growth.* New York: Macmillan.

Greenberg, J.S., M.M. Siltzer, and J.R. Greenlay. 1993. "Aging Parents of Adults with Disabilities: The Gratification and Frustration of Later-Life Caregiving." *The Gerontologist* 33: 542–49.

Hatfield, A.B. 1987. "Families as Caregivers: A Historical Perspective." In A.B. Hatfield and H.B. Lefley, eds., *Families of the Mentally Ill.* New York: Guilford.

Johnston, C., and W.E. Pelham. 1990. "Maternal Characteristics, Ratings of Child Behaviour, and Mother–Child Interactions in Families of Children with Externalizing Disorders." *Journal of Abnormal Child Psychology* 18: 407–17.

Korbin, J.E., G. Anetzberger, and C. Austin. 1995. "The Intergenerational Cycle of Violence in Child and Elder Abuse." *Journal of Elder Abuse and Neglect* 7: 1–15.

Lavigueur, S., R.E. Tremblay, and J.-F. Saucier. 1995. "Interactional Processes in Families with Disruptive Boys: Patterns of Direct and Indirect Influence." *Journal of Abnormal Child Psychology* 23: 359–78.

Lee, G.R., J.K. Netzer, and R.T. Coward. 1995. "Depression among Older Parents: The Role of Intergenerational Exchange." *Journal of Marriage and the Family* 57: 823–33.

Lefley, H.P. 1997. "Synthesizing the Family Caregiving Studies: Implications for Service Planning, Social Policy, and Further Research." *Family Relations* 46: 443–50.

Lerner, J.V., and R.M. Lerner. 1994. "Explorations of the Goodness-of-Fit Model in Early Adolescence." In W.B. Carey and S.C. McDevitt, eds., *Prevention and Early Intervention: Individual Differences as Risk Factors for the Mental Health of Children*. New York: Brunner Mazel.

Loeber, R. 1982. "The Stability of Antisocial and Delinquent Child Behaviour: A Review." *Child Development* 53: 1431–46.

Loeber, R., and M. Stouthamer-Loeber. 1986. "Family Factors as Correlates and Predictors of Juvenile Conduct Problems and Delinquency." In M. Tonry and N. Morris, eds., *Crime and Justice*, vol. 7. Chicago: University of Chicago Press.

Logan, J.R., and G.D. Spitze. 1996. *Family Ties*. Philadelphia: Temple University Press.

Lounsbury, M.L., and J.E. Bates. 1982. "The Cries of Infants of Differing Levels of Perceived Temperamental Difficultness: Acoustic Properties and Effects on Listeners." *Child Development* 53: 677–86.

Miller, B.C. 1993. "Families, Science, and Values: Alternative Views on Parenting Effects and Adolescent Pregnancy." *Journal of Marriage and the Family* 55: 7–21.

Mutran, E., and D.G. Reitzes. 1984. "Intergenerational Support Activities and Well-Being among the Elderly: A Convergence of Exchange and Symbolic Interaction Perspectives. *American Sociological Review* 49: 117–30.

Patterson, G.R. 1981. *Mothers: The Unacknowledged Victims*. Chicago: University of Chicago Press for the Society for Research in Child Development.

———. 1982. *Coercive Family Process*. Eugene, OR: Castalia.

———. 1986. "Maternal Rejection: Determinant or Product of Deviant Behaviour?" In W.W. Hartup and Z. Rubin, eds., *Relationships and Development*. Hillsdale, NJ: Lawrence Erlbaum.

Patterson, G.R., L. Bank, and M. Stoolmiller. 1990. "The Preadolescent's Contributions to Disrupted Family Process." In R. Montemayor, G.R. Adams, and T.P. Gullotta, eds., *From Childhood to Adolescence*. Newburry Park, CA: Sage.

Patterson, G.R., J.R. Reid, and T.J. Dishion. 1992. *Antisocial Boys*. Eugene, OR: Castalia.

Pillemer, K. 1985. "The Dangers of Dependency: New Findings on Domestic Violence Against the Elderly." *Social Problems* 33: 147–58.

Pillemer, K., and J.J. Suitor. 1991a. "Relationship with Children and Distress in the Elderly." In K. Pillemer and K. McCartney, eds., *Parent–Child Relations Throughout Life*. Hillsdale, NJ: Lawrence Erlbaum.

———. 1991b. "'Will I Ever Escape My Child's Problems?' Effects of Adult Children's Problems on Elderly Parents." *Journal of Marriage and the Family* 53: 585–94.

Plomin, R. 1994. *Genetics and Experience: The Interplay between Nature and Nurture*. Thousand Oaks, CA: Sage.

Rheingold, H.L. 1969. "The Social and Socializing Infant." In D.A. Goslin, ed., *Handbook of Socialization Theory and Research*. Chicago: Rand McNally.

Rohner, R.P., S.L. Bourque, and C.A. Elordi. 1996. "Children's Perceptions of Corporal Punishment, Caretaker Acceptance, and Psychological Adjustment in a Poor, Biracial, Southern Community." *Journal of Marriage and the Family* 58: 842–52.

Russell, A., and G. Russell. 1992. "Child Effect on Socialization Research: Some Conceptual and Analysis Issues." *Social Development* 1: 163–84.

Shehan, C.L., and J.W. Dwyer. 1989. "Parent–Child Exchanges in the Middle Years: Attachment and Autonomy in the Transition to Adulthood." In J.A. Mancini, ed., *Aging Parents and Adult Children*. Lexington, MA: Lexington Press.

Silverstein, M., and V.G. Bengtson. 1991. "Do Close Parent–Child Relationships Reduce the Mortality Risk of Older Parents?" *Journal of Health and Social Behaviour* 32: 382–95.

Simons, R.L., L.B. Whitbeck, J. Beaman, and R.D. Conger. 1994. "The Impact of Mothers' Parenting, Involvement by Non-Residential Fathers, and Parental Conflict on the Adjustment of Adolescent Children." *Journal of Marriage and the Family* 56: 356–74.

Stafford, L., and C.L. Bayer. 1993. *Interaction between Parents and Children*. Beverly Hills, CA: Sage.

Tarver-Behring, S., and R.A. Barkley. 1985. "The Mother–Child Interactions of Hyperactive Boys and Their Normal Siblings." *American Journal of Orthopsychiatry* 55: 202–209.

Tein, J.-Y., M.W. Roosa, and M. Michaels. 1994. "Agreement between Parent and Child Reports on Parental Behaviours." *Journal of Marriage and the Family* 56: 341–55.

Tompson, M.C., J.R. Asarnow, M.J. Goldstein, and D.J. Micklowitz. 1990. "Thought Disorders and Communication Problems in Children with Schizophrenic Spectrum and Depressive Disorders and Their Parents." *Journal of Clinical Child Psychology* 19: 159–68.

Umberson, D. 1992. "Relationship between Adult Children and Their Parents: Psychological Consequences for Both Generations." *Journal of Marriage and the Family* 54: 664–74.

Wolf, R., and K. Pillemer. 1989. *Helping Elderly Victims: The Reality of Elder Abuse*. New York: Columbia University Press.

CONTEMPORARY DIVERSITIES

ELLEN M. GEE

LEARNING OBJECTIVES

In this chapter, you will learn that:

- beliefs and assumptions about what families were like in the past and what families should be like now cloud our understanding about family change and family diversity. Diversity has always been a characteristic of Canadian family life, with the exception of one period of history — the "baby boom" years, *circa* 1946–62;
- considerable diversity in household structure exists. Fewer than one-third of households consist of the cultural "ideal" of a (legally) married couple with children. Nearly one-quarter of households consist of one person only, and 14.5 percent contain lone-parent families;
- certain aspects of family life have undergone significant long-term changes, such as increases in divorce, cohabitation, and one-person households; and fertility decline. Other aspects have changed very little over the long haul, such as the continued universality of marriage; age at first marriage; the age difference between wives and husbands; and the percentage of lone-parent families. Many of the changes that have occurred have had negative economic impacts for women;
- average family income after taxes (and adjusted for inflation) has decreased over the past fifteen or so years. Decreasing family income — and its associated factors — have a number of adverse consequences for families, illustrating the interpenetration of family and work;
- family poverty is structured along social lines. Families most likely to be poor are those whose head is a woman, a single parent, and a recent immigrant. Approximately one-half of female-headed lone-parent families live in poverty;
- the organization of work and family life do not "mesh." It is women who attempt to accommodate the contradictions, usually by private (personal) strategies.

INTRODUCTION

This chapter examines aspects of diversity in Canadian family life, using demographic data for the most part. In order to contextualize contemporary family patterns, a temporal approach is needed. Depending on data availability, our starting point is around 1930 for the analysis of household and family structure. We will be looking at ways in which Canadian families have become more diverse, but *also* at some dimensions of family life in which there is less, or no more, diversity now. As Cheal (1991a) points out, there are elements of increased uniformity embedded in a pattern of increasing diversification in contemporary family life and family organization. We will see that there are many complexities in family change. These complexities illustrate the contribution of a sociological approach to the examination of family life and highlight the errors that can be made when unexamined assumptions dominate our thinking about families.

Also, this chapter relates family patterns to economic factors and state structures. This is not to say that ideology and values (for example, individualism) are unimportant in family change/diversity; however, it is often the case that value transformation follows (and reinforces) family change, rather than directly causing it. In addition, economic and state structures create conditions that either encourage or impede the expression of individualism as it relates to family life, that is, diversity in family structure and organization. If people establish more and different types of family/living arrangements than before, an examination of changing material conditions of life and social-policy measures is more useful than a blanket explanation that focussed upon individualistic expression.

Throughout this chapter, there is a particular focus on women in families. This is not because family is seen as the special purview of women, but rather because women experience family life in ways that are unique to them, and which have been ignored in standard treatments of family that use demographic data.

A PERSPECTIVE ON FAMILY CHANGE AND DIVERSITY
▼

Views concerning contemporary families and family change are conditioned by beliefs about what families used to be like, as well as an ideology of the modern "ideal family." Let us first examine these two (related) sets of beliefs.

It is assumed that families in the past — at some unspecified time — were large and harmonious units, with an extended structure, to which women and men made clearly defined and clearly different contributions.[1] Coupled with this is the assumption that virtually *all* families fit the same description; that is, families were homogeneous or "monolithic." Against this backdrop, families are viewed as having become small, rather isolated units ("the rise of the **nuclear family**"), wracked by disharmony (to which increasing divorce rates are pointed as proof), and characterized by gender normlessness, as women's and men' lives become more similar.

This set of assumptions about "traditional" families — the starting point, as it were — is overly simplistic and contains elements that are not empirically valid. An extended family structure was never common in Canada.[2] Also, historical mortality levels created family "disorganization"; high mortality robbed families of children (especially infants and young children) and "broke up" families as a result of the not-infrequent occurrence of death of a parent/spouse. Remarriage might follow, particularly if the wife/mother died (Gee, 1993). Further, stringent legal prohibitions against divorce, coupled with social stigma, rendered marital disharmony invisible; however, invisibility should not be taken as proof of non-existence. In addition, women were not necessarily economic dependants; the roles of husbands and wives varied with social class and economic circumstances. Apart from paid labour tied to the home (e.g., out-work, domestic tasks for others, farm work), in certain economic contexts married women worked outside the home in the "modern" sense (see Parr, 1990, for a discussion of working women and their husbands, and the domestic adaptations made to accommodate lifelong female wage work, among the mill workers of Paris, Ontario, from the late 1800s to 1950). Indeed, as Fox and Luxton (1991) note, in the earlier stages of capitalist development, women and children were the first to be drawn into paid labour; it was not until the end of the nineteenth century that women were effectively removed from formal work. Finally, this model of the past ignores family variations by class and race/ethnicity, which were sometimes structured by relations with the state. For example, the Oriental Exclusion Act had a devastating impact on the family life of Asians in Canada in the first half of the twentieth century.

With reference to the modern family ideal, it is assumed that families consist (or should consist) of a closely knit, emotionally caring, nuclear unit of husband/father (as head), wife/mother, and children — no more and no less. This is viewed as a natural arrangement, based on biological relatedness and on heterosexual relations. Further, the ideology assumes a separation of public and private arenas of life, which buttresses a gendered division of labour whereby men are primarily breadwinners and women are primarily engaged in domestic activity and nurturance (Andersen, 1991). Any movement away from this ideal family structure and organization is viewed as deviance from a cultural "good" (although feminist scholars are quick to point to the underlying fallacies and falsities of the ideal).

Together, these assumptions about past and present family life create distorted views about family change. Starting from an assumption of past family homogeneity, it is postulated that families have become more diverse (e.g., Burke, 1986); this diversity (or deviation from the universal standard of the modern family ideal) is often taken as indicating that Canadian families are in "decline" or "crisis" (Conway, 1997; Dumas and Péron, 1992; Légaré, Balakrishnan, and Beaujot, 1989; Ram, 1990). In turn, family decline/crisis is viewed as the result of increasing individualism and "hedonism" (Ambert, 1990; Bumpass, 1990; Romaniuc, 1989).

Family diversity is the norm in Canadian society, past and present. Only for a short period of history — the post–World War II "baby boom" years (*circa* 1946–62) — did Canadian (and U.S.) families approach uniformity, centred around near-universal marriage and parenthood, family "intactness," and highly differentiated gender roles. This period was anomalous in terms of family life (Gee, 1986); a time when the gap between "actual" and "ideal" narrowed to an unprecedented degree. This was due, in part, to improved mortality levels (deaths contributed less to family breakup) and also to substantial economic growth (men's wages alone could support a family).[3] It is no coincidence that the then pre-eminent U.S sociologist Talcott Parsons's conceptualization of the homogeneous modern nuclear family model was developed at this time in history (Parsons and Bales, 1955). It is very important *not* to examine today's families in the light of that period; to do so is to overestimate familial change and trends related to diversity. Hence, whenever possible we will be looking at data that commence around 1930.

FAMILY AND HOUSEHOLD STRUCTURE
▼

In this section, we examine current family and **household** structure in the light of variables, such as marriage (legal and consensual), marital dissolution, fertility, and family life course, that have an impact on such structures. The section concludes with a summary of the presented material, with an emphasis on the theme of diversity.

OVERALL STRUCTURE

Table 3.1 provides a "snapshot" of the composition of households in 1996. A (legally) married couple with children — the ideal model, by cultural definition — makes up 45 percent of census families and less than one-third of households in Canada today (although this household type is the largest single category in Table 3.1). If the "deviant" household types with children — that is, cohabiting couples with children and **lone-parent families** — are aggregated with the

---

BOX 3.1
▼
A NOTE ON DATA

The data used in this chapter are drawn from secondary sources such as the *Census of Canada*, *Vital Statistics*, and various Statistics Canada surveys. **Secondary data** are collected by persons other than the researcher, often by government statistical agencies. They are a rich source of information about certain aspects of families. For example, they can provide a broad picture of family structure, family formation and dissolution, and the social and economic characteristics of different types of families. However, secondary data have limitations:

1. They cannot — nor are they meant to — tell us about the interactive context of family life; for example, the ways that people interpret or negotiate their family lives and how varying family structures affect that interpretation and negotiation.
2. These data are often not provided to researchers in a form that allows for analyses by race and sexual orientation.*
3. These data are embedded in conceptual and operational definitions that we cannot alter. For example, the (Canadian) census definition of family ("**census family**") is a husband and wife (either legally married or in a common-law union) with or without children who are never-married, regardless of age, or a lone parent with one or more children who are never-married, regardless of age. This definition is restrictive — it limits relationships among co-resident family members to husband/wife and to parent/never-married child(ren). Other related persons (e.g., a divorced child, a widowed parent of a husband or wife) are not considered part of the "family," even if they are co-resident.

* Various methodological problems are involved with the variables of race and sexual orientation from secondary data sources. Some data on race are available (census data, mostly), but small cell sizes make analyses unreliable. Data on sexual orientation are not available at all, as discussed later in this chapter.

"married with children"[4] category, the total still falls short of a majority (46.9 percent) of Canadian households. The reason for this lies in the large number of households consisting of one person only; nearly one-quarter of all households. (We discuss one-person households later in this chapter.)

Census family structure is somewhat more uniform; (legally) married couples, either with or without children, comprise approximately three-quarters of families (see Table 3.1 and endnote 4). Nevertheless, categorization bro-

TABLE 3.1
▼
HOUSEHOLD STRUCTURE, CANADA, 1996

TYPE OF HOUSEHOLD	Number*	Percentage
CENSUS FAMILY** HOUSEHOLDS	7 837 865	71.9
MARRIED COUPLES	5 779 720	(73.7)***
With children	3 535 630	[61.2]
Without children	2 244 085	[38.8]
COHABITING COUPLES	920 635	(11.7)
With children	434 950	[47.2]
Without children	485 690	[52.8]
LONE-PARENT FAMILIES	1 138 000	(14.5)
Female parent	945 230	[83.1]
Male parent	192 275	[16.9]
OTHER HOUSEHOLDS	3 061 560	28.1
One-person households	2 622 180	24.1
Two- (or more) person households****	439 380	4.0
TOTAL HOUSEHOLDS	10 899 425	100.0

* Numbers do not add exactly due to Statistics Canada's procedure of "random rounding."
** For census definition of family, see Box 3.1 (on page 82) and the glossary.
*** Numbers in parentheses represent the percentage distribution of different type of census families. Numbers in square brackets refer to the percentages of families within the category of the immediately preceding family type.
**** Includes private households containing unrelated individuals as well as households containing individuals who are related, but not in terms of the census definition of family.

Source: Based on *1996 Census of Canada*; http://www.statcan.ca/Daily/English/971012 and http://www.statcan.ca/Daily/English/970415.

ken down by both couple status and presence/absence of children reveals that no one type makes up a majority of families.

Overall, these data show that Canadian households and families are indeed dispersed into a number of different types, diverging along various combinations of dimensions, such as presence/absence of spouse, legal status of marital union, presence/absence of children, and number of persons. Let us now turn to marriage, marital dissolution, and fertility — social-demographic processes that play a determining role in family structure. Then we will look in more detail at some selected family/household types — lone-parent families, cohabiting couples, one-person households, and same-sex unions.

MARRIAGE

The majority of Canadians (legally) marry at least once. As shown in Figure 3.1, the percentages of persons never married at ages 45–49 (after which the likelihood of a first marriage is rare) is low, and has been decreasing over time. Of course, these data do not relate to young people today, and we do not know what percentage of them will never marry. However, the fact that approximately 60 percent of women aged 25–29 in 1996 had already legally married suggests that there has not been a large-scale movement away from marriage.

The percentage of never-married women and men at ages 25–29 has increased rather substantially over the last two decades. However, one could interpret this increase as a return to pre–baby boom "traditional" marriage patterns (corresponding to "ordinary" [cf. boom] economic times) rather than the emergence of new marriage behaviour.

The data relating to never-marrieds at ages 25–29 reflect trends in average age at first marriage, which are presented in Table 3.2. From a temporal viewpoint, current ages at first marriage are not atypical. The 1995 ages at marriage are only a bit higher than those for the pre–World War II period, although there is more of an increase for women than for men. *The idea that we are witnessing an era of delayed marriage is a direct result of comparison with an unusual period in the history of family, and economic, life — the two decades after World War II.* If we consider persons who are never-married (legally) but who are living in **consensual unions** (or have lived in them), then the ages at entry into a first union are younger, for the last decade or so, than the data in Table 3.2 suggest.

While we discuss common-law unions in a later subsection of this chapter, it is important to note here that there are now *two* routes to a sexual, co-residential relationship — namely, legal marriage and cohabitation. The opening up of a second (more or less) socially sanctioned route to a marital relationship represents a major change in family behaviour; a change reflecting diversity in "marriage entry." At the same time, it hides, in official data such as in Table 3.2, the extent of continued early initiation into marital unions.

While the data on never-marrieds at ages 45–49 and on average age at first marriage suggest no significant departure from "typical" patterns, common-law marriage is a recent marital pattern (and one that makes the interpretation of official marriage data problematic). Yet there are two other aspects of marriage patterns that are not undergoing significant change/diversity.

First, women continue to marry at younger ages than men — a pattern that has important implications for women. The younger spouse (the wife)

FIGURE 3.1
▼
PERCENTAGES NEVER-MARRIED AT AGES 25–29 AND 45–49, BY SEX: CANADA, 1931–1996

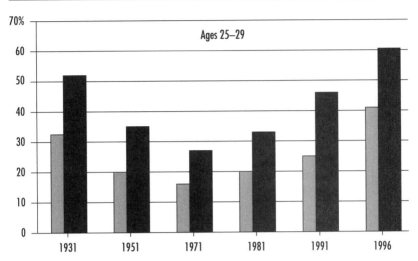

Ages 25–29

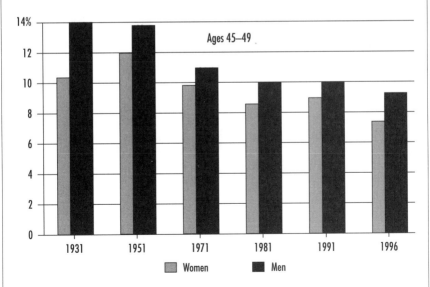

Ages 45–49

▨ Women   ■ Men

Source: *Censuses of Canada: 1931* (vol. 3); *1951* (vol. 3); *1971* (Catalogue no. 92-730); *1981* (Catalogue no. 92-901); *1991* (Catalogue no. 93-310); *Annual Demographic Statistics, 1996* (Catalogue no. 91-311); *1996*, http://www.statcan.ca/ Daily/English/971012 and 970415.

TABLE 3.2
▼
AVERAGE AGE AT FIRST MARRIAGE, BY SEX: CANADA, 1921–1995

| YEAR | Average Age at First Marriage | |
	Women	Men
1921	24.3	28.0
1931	25.1	28.5
1941	24.4	27.6
1951	23.8	26.6
1961	22.9	25.8
1971	22.6	24.9
1981	23.5	25.7
1990	26.0	27.9
1995	27.1	29.0

Source: Ellen M. Gee, *Fertility and Marriage Patterns in Canada, 1851–1971*. (Unpublished Ph.D. dissertation, University of British Columbia, 1978); Dominion Bureau of Statistics, *Vital Statistics, 1961* (Catalogue no. 84-202); Statistics Canada, *Health Reports, Marriages, 1990*, Supplement 16 (Catalogue no. 82-0003516); Statistics Canada, *Marriages, 1995* (Catalogue no. 84-212) (Ottawa: Minister of Industry, 1996), Table 1.2, p. 3.

begins marriage with fewer social assets — less schooling, less job experience, lower income, for example. The disadvantage cumulates over time; the husband's job will be given priority because it is more important to the overall economic situation of the family. For example, the husband's job may dictate that the family must move; the wife, if working outside the home, will have to start over wherever they relocate. The wife will usually be the one who quits her paying job to care for small children. Over time, the initially small economic difference between husband and wife becomes a substantial gap — this is termed the "**mating gradient**." Of course, there are other factors that create economic inequalities between husband and wife, such as women's lower salaries and the segregation of jobs by gender. However, the point here is that women's "choice" to marry older men contributes to their economic dependency. That women face more pressure to marry and to marry early illustrates a way in which gendered experience has economic implications that operate in rather subtle ways.

Second, Canadian women have internalized a "**social clock**" — a set of expectations and beliefs about the "proper" time to undergo important family life events/transitions. For example, they believe that there is a "best age" to marry (24), and to have a (first) child (25). (Gee, 1990b). As these "best ages" are young — preceding by many years any consideration of an unwinding "biological clock" — they illustrate the role of gender socialization in exacerbating women's low economic status.

MARITAL DISSOLUTION

Marriages dissolve as a result of either separation/divorce or the death of one of the spouses. In Canada, the rate of divorce has increased markedly over the last 30 years; it is now estimated that 30–38 percent of first marriages will end in divorce (Adams, 1990; Wolfson, 1990). Thus, it remains the case that *more marriages end in widowhood than in divorce.*

Fundamental to the increasing divorce rate is legal change that has made divorce easier to obtain. (Cross-cultural research has shown that, in general, the level of divorce in a society or social group is related to its accessibility.) Prior to the 1968 Divorce Act, the only grounds for divorce was proven adultery. In 1968, there was a substantial expansion in allowable grounds for divorce, including, among other others, a provision that three years of marital separation was sufficient for a divorce to be granted. (In the 1985 Divorce Act, the required period of separation was reduced from three years to one.) A large increase in divorces occurred in the years immediately after 1968, indicating that numerous unsatisfactory marriages existed prior to 1968 but had remained "intact" because of the stringent divorce laws of the time.

Yet, the divorce rate continued to increase, long after any "backlog" of unsatisfactory marriages had been dealt with. Thus, factors other than a changing legal context have operated to increase divorce. The work of Balakrishnan and colleagues (1987) provides clues as to what factors have been responsible in the Canadian case; it also provides a basis for speculations about the future level of divorce in Canada. The strongest predictor of divorce is young age at marriage; the above-noted trend toward later marriage in the last two decades has the potential to lower our divorce rate in the future. However, Balakrishnan and colleagues (1987) report other variables predictive of divorce that could counterbalance the dampening effect of delayed marriage. They include low religiosity, premarital birth, and economic crises such as unemployment. Other factors reported in the research literature include female labour-force participation (which lessens women's economic dependence and makes departure from an unsatisfactory marriage more possible for women); changing views of what marriage should be (i.e., a relationship that is intimate, expressive, and mutually gratifying), and increased individualism (i.e., less willingness to sacrifice one's own interests for the sake of collective [family/kin] interests) (Ambert, 1990; Bumpass, 1990; Michael, 1988).

Remarriages are more prone to divorce than first marriages, particularly the remarriages of divorced women. While the remarriage rate of the divorced has declined markedly — by more than 50 percent in the last twenty years (Ram, 1990) — at the current time at least one of the partners has been previously married (in most cases, divorced) in approximately one-quarter of marriages.

The consequences of divorce can be examined along several dimensions. Divorce contributes to diversity in family and household structure. It is one route by which lone-parent families are established. Also, divorce followed by marriage can lead, if children are present,[5] to blended (or reconstituted) families. These families face special problems — related to more complex interactive environments, financial pressure, and the lack of social norms to guide behaviour toward step-relations — and are more prone to break up than families that do not have the legacy of an earlier marriage to deal with. In addition, stepchildren leave home earlier than children residing with their own parents (Mitchell, Wister, and Burch, 1989), which contributes to the increase in one-person households. Another implication for family structure is the creation of an "invisible" type of family — the bi-nuclear family — in which the children of divorce continue to have two parents, but in separate households (Eichler, 1988).

FERTILITY

With the exception of the baby-boom years, the overall trend of fertility in Canada (and in all other industrialized countries) has been one of decline (see Table 3.3). Declines in fertility result from a complex combination of factors, including urbanization (which lowers the economic utility of children), women's outside-the-home employment (which increases the opportunity costs of child rearing as well as women's autonomy), declining religiosity, increases in women's educational attainments, and improvements in contraceptive technology.

With fertility decline, much of the diversity surrounding fertility has disappeared. Previous fertility differentials by education, income, type of religion, rural/urban place of residence, region, anglophone or francophone origin, and so on have all but gone — so much so that a former preoccupation of demographers (i.e., explaining differentials in number of children born) has had to be abandoned. Furthermore, much of the dispersion in number of children born no longer exists, as we have converged to a two-child norm. For example, 1991 census data (the latest such information we have) show that in the twenty year period represented by women aged 60–64 and aged 40–44 (in 1991), the average number of children born per woman declined from 3.4 to 2.1 (McVey and Kalbach, 1995, p. 272).

TABLE 3.3
▼
TOTAL FERTILITY RATES: CANADA, 1921–1995

Year	Total Fertility Rate*
1921	3536
1931	3200
1941	2832
1951	3503
1956	3858
1961	3840
1966	2812
1971	2187
1976	1825
1981	1704
1986	1672
1991	1700
1995	1640

*Number of children that 1000 women will bear in their lifetime, based on certain assumptions about the age structure of fertility behaviour.

Source: Based on Statistics Canada, *Vital Statistics* (various years); Statistics Canada, *Report on the Demographic Situation in Canada, 1996* (Catalogue no. 91-209-XPE) (Ottawa: Minister of Industry, 1997), Table A5, p. 107.

Delayed child bearing has received much media coverage. Time-series data, however, show that the average age at first birth is only slightly higher now than in the mid-1940s. Does this mean that the trend toward "old" first-time motherhood is a myth? No, there is evidence that *some* women (with high levels of education, better jobs, social "visibility") are postponing child bearing to quite late ages. But, the percentage of births to unmarried women has increased to about one-quarter of all births (compared with approximately 4 percent in 1960); these unmarried women tend to be young — 65 percent are under the age of 25 (Eichler, 1988). More than three-quarters of the births to women under age 20 are "out-of-wedlock" births.

Thus, the *diversity in fertility now involves the timing of child bearing*, and appears to be related to social class in two ways. Age at first birth is both predicted by social and economic resources and has consequences for economic status. More privileged women bear children later, with minimal impact on their already established careers. Less privileged women have children earlier and are more likely to be unmarried and face the economic hardships associated with lone-parenting.

An obvious impact of fertility trends is to lower family size. Another less obvious effect relates to the fact that declining fertility is the major cause of population aging. An older population creates pressures for three-generational living (although this has not yet surfaced at the behavioural level) and an escalation in one-person households resulting from widowhood (Nett, 1988). An aging population is also one in which the likelihood of joint adult child–parent survival is increased, with implications — especially for women — regarding caregiving to frail parents (Gee, 1990a). And, finally, the escalation in fertility to unmarried women has implications for family structure by increasing lone-parent families.

LONE-PARENT FAMILIES

As shown in Table 3.4, 14.5 percent of families in 1996 were lone-parent families (i.e., families consisting of a parent and one or more children who have never married). While this represents a substantial upswing over the last 25 years, the current level is not much higher than it was in 1931. Thus, once again, our perspective is dependent upon our starting point. Nevertheless, while today's level is comparable to that of the pre–World War II period, the factors accounting for lone-parent families have radically changed. In the past, the main reason was death of spouse/parent. That reason was gradually replaced by separation/divorce. Marital breakup (separation/divorce) remains the chief factor accounting for single parents, but, over the last two decades,

TABLE 3.4
▼
PERCENTAGE OF LONE-PARENT FAMILIES IN CANADA, 1931–1996

Year	Percentage
1931	13.4
1941	10.5
1951	9.9
1961	8.4
1971	6.8
1981	6.0
1991	13.0
1996	14.5

Source: *Censuses of Canada: 1931* (vol. 5); *1941* (vol. 5); *1951* (vol. 3); *1961* (Catalogue no. 93-516); *1971* (Catalogue no. 93-703); *1981* (Catalogue no. 93-937); *1991* (Catalogue no. 93-311); *1996* (http://www.statcan.ca/Daily/971014).

the non-marriage of the mother has become increasingly important. In 1991, nearly 20 percent of female lone parents had never been married (Vanier Institute of the Family, 1996).

Probably the most striking characteristic of single-parent families is their low economic status — an issue that will be discussed later in the chapter. Related to the poverty of (many) lone-parent families is the non-involvement of fathers. This is clearest in evidence related to divorce and settlements. Children continue to be "awarded" to mothers, despite a belief that courts are more now likely to grant custody to fathers. Non-custodial fathers have a poor record of support and contact with children (Richardson, 1992; Teachman, 1991); Richardson reports that, even among fathers ordered to pay child support, approximately one-third fail to do so at all or are irregular supporters with regard to timing or amount, and Teachman finds that 20 percent of divorced fathers do not provide any type of assistance to their children.

In the light of information that shows paternal non-involvement associated with divorce and non-marriage, Dumas and Péron (1992, pp. 107–108) speak of "the pre-eminence of the mother–child bond over the father–child bond" and the emergence of a "new and unexpected kind of matriarchy." Apart from the fact that it is unclear how much paternal involvement there ever was, this interpretation misses a fundamental point. Rather than an end to patriarchy, there has been a shift in power from individual men to the state. Women and children are increasingly being directly linked to the state, rather than via the male head of the family. In the process, the state has become more involved in family life, through, for example, legislation relating to the best interests of the child and parental fitness (Arnup, 1987).[6] This shift has been variously termed a move from familial **patriarchy** to state patriarchy (Ursel, 1986) and from family patriarchalism to state paternalism (Bardaglio, 1981). Whatever the terminology, it is important to recognize the continuation of patriarchal control, albeit in a different guise.

COHABITING COUPLES

In 1996, 11.7 percent of Canadian families were formed through cohabitation,[7] with provincial variation, ranging from 7.7 percent in Prince Edward Island to 20.5 percent in Quebec (Statistics Canada, 1997). The earliest Canadian data are for 1981,[8] when 6 percent of couples were living in a consensual union (that is, in a self-defined co-resident [hetero]sexual relationship). The increase in cohabitation over the past decade or so is quite substantial; and it is likely there were low levels of cohabitation earlier in the twentieth century. We are probably safe in assuming that some amount of cohabitation has always occurred, but was masked as legal marriage. However, at present, the "line" separating legal marriage and common-law marriage is not at all clear. This lack of clarity, which Eichler (1997, p. 51) terms *rapprochement* is illustrated in the various provincial definitions of "legal" common-law marriage. For example, in Manitoba, a common-law union is deemed to exist if a man and woman have lived together as husband and wife for five years, or for one year if there is a child of the union; Ontario and Saskatchewan require three years and a child; Newfoundland requires one year and a child; British Columbia requires not less than two years; Alberta and Quebec do not have legal definitions; and Prince Edward Island does not recognize common-law couples in its Family Law Reform Act, but does in its Worker's Compensation Act (Eichler, 1997, p. 209). It should be noted that our data on the incidence of common-law unions in Canada are based on self-identification and not legal definition.

A recent study, based on 1995 Canadian data, reveals a number of factors that appear to play a role in determining which women will form their first union as common-law spouses (Turcotte and Bélanger, 1997). Probabilities are higher for women who are younger; are born in Canada; are living in Quebec with French as their mother tongue; are employed; never attend religious services; have parents who divorced/separated; and have had a child outside of any union. Interestingly, educational level does not make a difference — the stereotype of university women being more likely to live common-law is not true. Indeed, women who are currently enrolled at school are less likely to form first common-law unions than are women not at school (Turcotte and Bélanger, 1997).

Many people who live in a common-law union view it as a "trial run" to marriage (although Milan [1998] finds that a portion of cohabitors are "marriage resistors"). (Among never-married persons who entered common-law unions in the 1970s, three-quarters were married by the end of the 1980s, often to their first partner [Dumas and Péron, 1992].)[9] In times of high divorce rates, this may seem like a wise choice. However, Canadian (and U.S.) research consistently shows that marriages preceded by a common-law union are more likely to end in divorce than marriages that are not so preceded (e.g., Balakrishnan et al., 1987). While this finding is unambiguous, it is not clear whether the explanation lies in the common-law experience itself, the characteristics of the persons who choose this option, or both. What is clear, though, is that women who live in common-law unions run a greater risk than other women of ending up economically needy — in the aftermath of divorce.

ONE-PERSON HOUSEHOLDS

One-person households are a new phenomenon in Canadian household structure; rapidly increasing, especially since 1961, to account for nearly one-quarter of all households in 1996 (see Figure 3.2). This is not to say that "unattached individuals" — in Statistics Canada's terminology — are a (relatively) new occurrence. For example, Canadian censuses up to 1961 included a "lodgers" category in data on household structure.[10] Thus, what is particularly distinctive in the last 30 years is the increased likelihood that unattached persons establish their own separate households.

The age and sex characteristics of persons living alone reveal much about the phenomenon. First, women are about one and one-half times more likely than men to live by themselves. Second, of the women who live alone, nearly one-half are aged 65 and over. Thus, to a substantial degree, the increase in one-person households reflects population aging and growth in terms of the

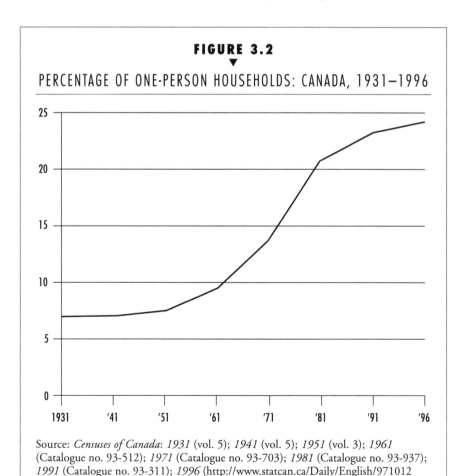

FIGURE 3.2
▼
PERCENTAGE OF ONE-PERSON HOUSEHOLDS: CANADA, 1931–1996

Source: *Censuses of Canada: 1931* (vol. 5); *1941* (vol. 5); *1951* (vol. 3); *1961* (Catalogue no. 93-512); *1971* (Catalogue no. 93-703); *1981* (Catalogue no. 93-937); *1991* (Catalogue no. 93-311); *1996* (http://www.statcan.ca/Daily/English/971012 and 970415).

number of widows — many of whom will live very meagrely or in poverty in order to maintain their independence and not be a burden to their children (Gee and Kimball, 1987). Third, of the men who live alone, about one-half are in the age group 30–54. They represent the "fallout" from divorce, given that child custody is typically granted to women. Fourth, fewer than 10 percent of young adults (ages 20–24) live alone. This small percentage reflects the **cluttered nest** (Boyd and Pryor, 1989; Gee, Mitchell, and Wister, 1995) — the phenomenon of adult children remaining at home longer and/or returning home — related to economic recession, unemployment, high housing costs, and so on. Thus, the increase in one-person households is largely the result of demographic, family, and economic factors that do not necessarily imply a major change in living-arrangement preference.

SAME-SEX UNIONS

One dimension of diversity in household/family structure is the increased numbers of acknowledged homosexual unions. Unfortunately, there are no data regarding the numbers and the social, economic, and demographic characteristics of gay or lesbian couples living together as spouses. These couples are included in the "Other Households: Two- (or more) person households" category in Table 3.1 on page 83. As the census definition (and most definitions) of family specifies that couples must be of differing sexes, gay or lesbian couples (and their children) are not considered to comprise family units.

While the 1996 census asked no direct question on homosexual couples, "write-in responses" (i.e., volunteered information) in the "household" question were permitted. However, same-sex unions were not provided as an example, and it is reported that the response by gay or lesbian couples was quite low (Fischer, 1998). Statistics Canada has retained this information — unlike in the 1981 and 1986 censuses, in which same-sex couple information was "corrected" by Statistics Canada either by changing the reported relationship of individuals or by changing the reported sex of either of the partners. However, while the 1996 data have been retained, it is not clear when, and if, they will be released. Nevertheless, the collection of data (albeit incomplete) is a sign that we will eventually have data on same-sex unions as part of the Canadian census — sooner or later. Indeed, a National Survey of Gays and Lesbians was launched in 1998, with funding from various federal departments (Statistics Canada was not involved).

By the time we have these national data, the legal definition of "family" may have changed to include gay and lesbian partners living together as spouses. In a landmark decision in September 1992, the Ontario Supreme Court ruled that the Ontario government must pay survivor pensions to partners of their gay and lesbian employees. British Columbia is the only juris-diction in North America in which gay and lesbian couples have the same child-support obligations as heterosexual parents. In B.C., same-sex couples can adopt and are defined as equal to heterosexual couples in its Family Relations Act (*Vancouver Sun,* 1998b). (However, in neighbouring Alberta, a 1998 Canadian Supreme Court decision was needed to strike down a provin-cial human rights code that excluded gays and lesbians.) In an ongoing fed-eral Supreme Court case (*M.* v. *H.*), it will be decided whether lesbian and gay families have recognition across the country. In this case, M. is seeking spousal support from her lesbian partner of nine years (*Vancouver Sun,* 1998a). If the Supreme Court decides in favour of M., laws that define spouses solely to be of the opposite sex will be invalidated.[11] At the 1998 Liberal Party National Convention, a resolution to recognize same-sex couples in the same way that opposite-sex couples are recognized in the distribution of federal benefits (such as pensions) was endorsed by approximately three-quarters of the delegates (*Vancouver Sun,* 1998c).

The inclusion of homosexual partners in census figures will have little numerical impact on overall household structure in Canada. However, the way gay and lesbian partnerships will be categorized has immense social and the-oretical implications. If co-residing gay and lesbian couples are considered to be families, then, as a society, our way of thinking about family, always tied — however implicitly — to heterosexual relations and their product (chil-dren), will be fundamentally transformed. Similarly, sociological theorizing on the family will have to undergo revision. If same-sex unions are deemed to be non-family units, one dimension of increased familial diversity will be sub-merged — at least officially and temporarily. Indeed, research on gay and les-bian families is starting to surface in Canada (e.g., Epstein, 1996; Miller, 1996) despite the lack of general legal or official recognition, and in the face of wide provincial differences in approach and legislation.

FAMILIES OVER THE LIFE COURSE
▼

Families, of course, are not static entities: they change over time — through marriage, divorce, fertility (new entrants), and mortality. One way to assess family change is to look at how these demographic processes have shaped the family life course over time. While we often think that changes in marriage and divorce have been the major factors responsible for family change, declines in fertility and mortality have played a far more critical role. In the nineteenth century, children were often not planned; infant and child mortality was not uncommon. Women, if they did not die in childbirth, would be widowed before their last child was grown up. Men would typically not live to see their youngest child reach adulthood (Gee, 1986). People were very much at the mercy of the forces of fertility and mortality. With this century's fertility and mortality declines have come "middle-aged" and "elderly families." These families have not been studied very much, although this situation is starting to change for a number of reasons. One reason is simply that the magnitude of fertility and mortality decline has made older families much more common. Another reason is a growing appreciation within sociology as a whole of the dynamics and fluidity of social life. A third, and more ominous, reason is the growing importance of family for social policy, with family care (sometimes euphemistically termed "community care") becoming increasingly called upon in the face of shrinking social dollars for formal care (McDaniel, 1996).

We have already seen some of the ways in which "younger families" have changed, for example, greater likelihood of cohabitation, greater likelihood of divorce, fewer children. These families will age, having experiences unlike those of earlier generations, for whom "living together" was unheard of, and divorce a highly stigmatized event.

At the same time, as these families age, they will be less likely to have experienced what earlier generations found all too common — death of young children, continuous child bearing and child rearing, and the early death of a spouse.

Declines in fertility and mortality have fundamentally changed intergenerational relations. One important change lies in the increased amount of time that adult children and their parents will be jointly alive (Gee, 1990a). Indeed, it has been estimated that we will spend more time caring for our parents than raising our children (McDaniel, 1992). This has major implications for social policy dealing with elder care. It has been suggested that we are facing a "caregiving crunch," given that increases in the frail elderly population are occurring alongside women's increasing labour-force participation (Myles, 1991).

FAMILY/HOUSEHOLD DIVERSITY: AN OVERVIEW
▼

The current heterogeneity in family and household structure results from the play of a complex set of factors. Some aspects of family life reveal a significant departure from the past. However, there is no substantial change, especially when the postwar baby-boom years are not used as a departure point, in other dimensions of families/households. Box 3.2 provides a graphic overview of areas of significant and minimal change.

Many of the family patterns that exist or have emerged recently have negative implications for the economic situation of women. The age difference between husband and wife creates a mating gradient that works to the economic

---

BOX 3.2
▼
DEGREE OF LONG-TERM CHANGE IN ASPECTS
OF FAMILY/HOUSEHOLD STRUCTURE

Significant Change
- increase in divorce
- increase in cohabitation
- fertility decline (diversity now is in timing of children)
- increase in one-person households
- apparent increase in same-sex families
- increased period of joint survivorship of adult children and their parents

Minimal Change
- universality of marriage
- age at first marriage
- age difference between wife and husband (mating gradient)
- percentage of lone-parent families

---

disadvantage of women; women who live common-law are, if and when married, more prone to divorce and subsequent economic hardship; the economic implications of divorce are felt acutely by women (and children) especially in lone-parent family situations; lone-parent families, likely to be female-headed, face the brunt of state patriarchal mechanisms of social control; and older women who live alone, mostly widows, run a high risk of poverty.

Changes in family and household structure have created, for the most part, more heterogeneity. This heterogeneity has, as mentioned above, been attributed to increased individualism and freedom of choice. From the experience of women, though, this freedom has an illusory element. While they may be freer from the dictates of individual men, in many cases women must pay the price of economic deprivation and the substitution of state prescriptions. In the following section, we examine in more detail some aspects of current family life in relation to economic and state structures.

FAMILIES IN RELATION TO ECONOMY AND STATE
▼

ECONOMIC STRESSORS

Average family income has been relatively stagnant over the past fifteen years. In fact, average family income after taxes (and adjusted for inflation) has decreased (see Table 3.5). This is so despite the contribution stemming from increases in married women's employment, as shown in Figure 3.4 on page 103. A major factor accounting for deteriorating income is taxes, which increased approximately 28 percent between 1980 and 1994. The drop in income over the last decade — and underlying and associated factors (e.g., domestic and global economic restructuring, free trade, rising unemployment, government debt and deficit) — have numerous consequences for families. Only a few will be dealt with here.

1. Limited employment opportunities for young men and women, coupled with decreases in the likelihood of enrolment at a post-secondary institution (related to reductions in federal government transfer payments for higher education) mean that many young people are "trapped." Their continued presence in the parental home — the "cluttered nest" phe-

---

TABLE 3.5
▼
AVERAGE FAMILY MONEY INCOME, AND AVERAGE FAMILY INCOME AFTER TAX, IN CONSTANT (1994) DOLLARS: CANADA, 1980–1994

YEAR	Average Money Income ($)*	Average Income After Tax ($)
1980	53 877	45 552
1981	53 049	44 849
1982	51 733	43 668
1983	51 180	42 995
1984	51 014	42 872
1985	53 323	43 712
1986	53 292	43 979
1987	53 970	43 938
1988	55 154	44 902
1989	56 777	45 821
1990	55 905	44 849
1991	54 572	43 749
1992	54 273	43 812
1993	53 157	42 935
1994	54 153	43 486

* Refers to income plus transfer payments

Source: Based on Statistics Canada, *Income After Tax, Distributions by Size in Canada, 1994* (Catalogue no. 13-210-XPB) (Ottawa: Minister of Industry, 1996), Table IX, p. 41.

nomenon alluded to earlier — and the uncertainties surrounding their economic situation can create tension for them and their families, although a recent study shows that mothers are more satisfied than fathers with this arrangement (Mitchell, 1998).

2. Unemployment of fathers/husbands has a very negative impact on family standard of living; their income usually contributes the "lion's share" to family livelihood (Grindstaff and Trovato, 1990), due to women's lower wages and greater likelihood of part-time employment. Apart from economic effects per se, male unemployment is associated with reduced quality of interaction between father and children (McLoyd, 1989), spousal conflict that can lead to separation/divorce (Balakrishnan et al., 1987), and a heightened risk of domestic violence (Armstrong, 1990).

3. Women's unemployment has similar consequences, depending in part on the size and importance of their income to the family. Both public-sector employment reductions (Armstrong, 1989) and free-trade initiatives (Cohen, 1987) place women's jobs in particular jeopardy; even the threat of unemployment creates stresses on individuals and families.

4. Government debt/deficit and the subsequent reduction in funding for social programs affects families. For example, families are adversely affected — in varying degrees[12] — by the recent abandonment of plans for a federal child-care policy, the termination of family allowances, our lean maternity leaves (and the scarcity of paternity leaves), reductions in transfer payments for health and higher education, the lack of progressive reforms in the public pension system (which affects women in particular, as they are less likely to be covered by private pensions), and so on.

These four examples illustrate the interpenetration of family and work. *That formal work and family life are physically apart (for most of us) — in "separate spheres" — disguises their connectedness.* The image of separate spheres may have approached reality for men at a certain point in history; it never rang true for women, and it is less valid for men as this century nears an end.

FAMILY POVERTY
▼

So far, we have been discussing economic stressors on families in general. We now turn to poor families, which face economic stress as an ongoing part of life. As shown in Figure 3.3, the incidence of poverty among families is socially structured; families headed by women and by recent immigrants (who are increasingly non-white) are more likely to be poor than other families. The highest rate of poverty occurs in female-headed lone-parent families;

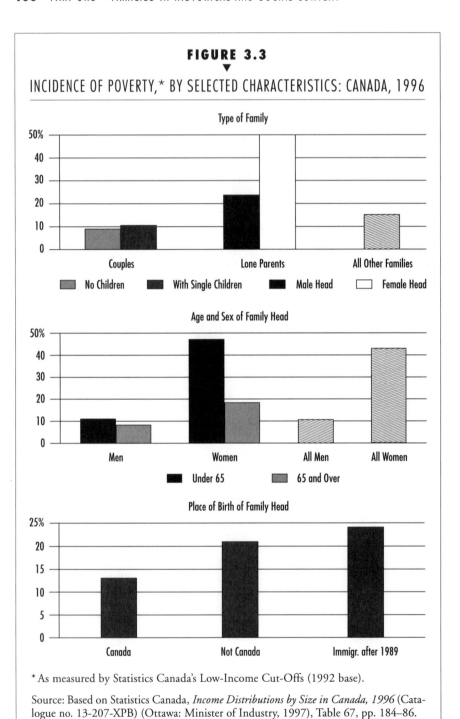

FIGURE 3.3
▼
INCIDENCE OF POVERTY,* BY SELECTED CHARACTERISTICS: CANADA, 1996

* As measured by Statistics Canada's Low-Income Cut-Offs (1992 base).

Source: Based on Statistics Canada, *Income Distributions by Size in Canada, 1996* (Catalogue no. 13-207-XPB) (Ottawa: Minister of Industry, 1997), Table 67, pp. 184–86.

approximately one-half are poor. It should be noted that female-headed lone-parent families and recent-immigrant families are distinct groups, which tend not to contain overlapping members (McKie, 1993). Therefore, poverty is structured along discrete dimensions; ascribed characteristics — sex and race — have been constructed into socially relevant attributes.

The type of family — female-headed lone-parent families — most likely to be poor and with substantial numerical importance (involving nearly 1.5 million children in 1996) will be our focus here. The average income of female-headed lone-parent families has been declining somewhat, in constant dollars, over the last decade. Perhaps even more telling, female-headed lone-parent families in which the mother earned income are increasingly likely to be poor (McKie, 1993). Thus, the poverty in these families is not due to non-involvement in the labour force. These mothers are much more likely to be part of the "working poor" than are their male counterparts or couples with children (Gunderson and Muszynski, 1990). This is partly due to the lack of resources that lone-mothers bring to jobs, for example, inexperience associated with youth, low levels of educational attainment (22 percent have less than Grade 9) (McKie, 1993). However, structural factors are extremely important. One is provincially set minimum wage rates, which are so low that, for example, for a single parent with one child, minimum wages are more than 55 percent below the poverty line (Gunderson and Muszynski, 1990). Also the prevailing gender segregation of jobs and lower pay of women contribute to the high rate of poverty among lone-mother families, as do low levels of child support from fathers and meagre public assistance. With regard to social assistance/social policy and lone-parent family incomes, Hunsley (1997) shows that Canada's approach to reducing poverty is less successful than that in many European countries. In Canada (and the United States, Britain, and Australia), we "target" welfare expenditures to the poor. However, the countries that have been most successful in reducing poverty among lone-parent families (and other families) have focussed more on creating equality and on supporting family life for all. However, it is true that social-security measures in all industrialized countries have been more successful in dealing with work transitions — such as a job loss or retirement — than with family-related events such as divorce (McDaniel, 1995).

The effects of living in lone-mother families seem to be long-term — even if the arrangement is not necessarily permanent (Moore, 1991). For mothers, there is a cumulative effect, in that pension-plan entitlements and other forms of equity are not built up (McKie, 1993). For children, this type of living arrangement is associated with lower levels of educational attainment, lower income in adulthood, and a greater risk of divorce (among females only) (Gee, 1993). A good deal of the negative outcomes associated with lone-mother families are a result of economic deprivation, rather than paternal absence or this type of family structure per se.

How do we deal with the problem of economic deprivation? On one level, it is representative of women's low status and a gendered division of labour regarding child care, which reduces women's earnings and economic independence. But the economic problems of mother-led families are too pressing to wait for a general social "overhaul." In the meantime, a combination of public and private policies could be put into place. Private solutions, such as improved child support, carry a risk of increased dependency on men; direct state support may foster welfare dependency (McLanahan and Booth, 1991). It is clear that the problems of female-headed lone-parent families are embedded in a broader set of issues concerning women's position in society and the relationship between family and state.

FAMILY AND WORK CONTRADICTIONS
▼

The labour-force participation rate of women, particularly married women, has increased quite dramatically over the past 35 years (see Figure 3.4). As a result, the most common family type, in relation to the employment status of spouses, is now the "dual earner" family — comprising 63 percent of husband–wife families (in which there is at least one earner) in 1994 (Charette, 1995). The descriptor "dual earner" is something of a misnomer, as it implies an equality in earnings and in spousal power relationships that does not exist. With regard to the former, Grindstaff and Trovato (1990) report that married women who work in paid labour contribute only one-third to family income; with regard to the latter, Cheal's (1991b) research indicates substantial differences in family financial decision making within marital units in which both spouses are engaged in paid labour. Nevertheless, women's paid employment is crucial to family income level; indeed, about 40 percent of Canadian families would be poor if both parents did not work (Duxbury and Higgins, 1994).

This discussion focusses on families, and the women in them, in which both spouses are working in the formal economy. (However, one must not forget the family situations, which are not inconsequential in numbers, where only one spouse works for pay — usually the husband, but not always — and where neither works.) The main argument here is that *the organization of work in modern society and family life do not "mesh"; it is women who attempt private (personal) accommodations to two social institutions who do not "fit."* Despite the increase in women in the paid labour force, both the workplace and the family are structured on a one-earner (male) model. Evidence that this is true in the family setting is the continued expectation, and the continued reality, that

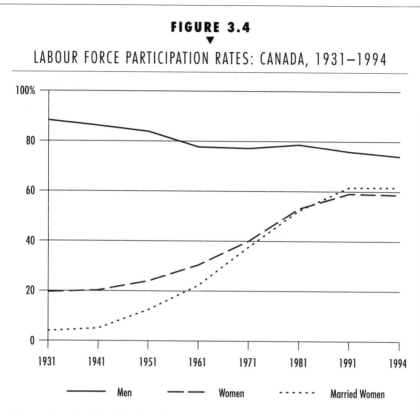

FIGURE 3.4
▼
LABOUR FORCE PARTICIPATION RATES: CANADA, 1931–1994

Source: Based on Statistics Canada, *Women in Canada: A Statistical Portrait,* 2nd ed. (Catalogue no. 89-503E); Statistics Canada, *Labour Force Annual Averages, 1989–1994* (Catalogue no. 71-529) (Ottawa: Ministry of Industry, 1995), Table 3, pp. B-40, B-43.

women — regardless of their labour force status — are responsible for child (and elder) care and for domestic chores. Research confirms the continuing gendered division of labour in the household (Baker and Lero, 1996). For women working full-time, this "double day" creates demands that cannot all be met; therefore, they work out various individualistic (cf. social) coping strategies (Mandell, 1989). These strategies may be either home-centred (e.g., reduction in number of children, lowering household-cleaning standards) or work-centred (e.g., refusing promotions). One of the most common accommodations is to choose part-time work (nearly one-quarter of women work part-time).[13] While this choice is an understandable one, it has immense implications: for individual women, it increases the likelihood that they will not receive fringe benefits, such as acces to a private pension plan; for women as a whole, it reinforces beliefs that women are not "really serious" workers and justifies low pay, occupational segregation, and marginalized treatment.

Work is structured in ways that are not "user-friendly" for family life, and for its chief managers — women (Duffy and Pupo, 1996). Inflexible hours conflict with the impossible-to-schedule needs of children and/or frail parents. The expected career timetable, particularly in professional jobs, is such that the age when one has to "make it" (i.e., twenties and thirties) conflicts with the time of most onerous child-rearing duties. Most workplaces do not have child-care facilities (and the operating hours of child-care facilities, regardless of their location, do not correspond to the non–"9 to 5" working hours of a service-based economy). Some employers, recognizing that the organization of work conflicts with family needs, are beginning to provide child care, family-related leave, and flexible working hours (Conference Board of Canada, 1990). However, it must be kept in mind that the motivation behind these changes is the improvement of worker productivity and that only employees in certain work settings, typically large firms, would have access to such supportive arrangements. Public-policy measures to alleviate family–work contradictions seem very far off. If anything, cutbacks in social-program funding reinforce women's obligation to provide unpaid care to children and the aged, as well as any family members with disabilities — at the expense of their contribution to the economy through pay.

SUMMARY
▼

This chapter has provided an overview of contemporary family diversity in Canada, in the light of historical trends and material conditions. Specific points that you should take away with you include the following:

- Families in Canada have always exhibited diversity, although for a brief period of time in the post–World War II years diversity was mimimal.
- Beliefs and assumptions about families can easily create a distorted picture of change and diversity.
- While there has been a trend of increasing diversity along many dimensions of family life, there are also elements of continuity.
- Contemporary families can be viewed as adapting to change in historical and economic conditions, rather than being in crisis or decline. Nevertheless, many of the changes have detrimental implications for women.
- Work and family are not "separate spheres": they are interconnected and contain contradictions. Women often find themselves trying to accommodate the contradictions, using personal strategies.

- Many challenges lie ahead. While these challenges appear to be different (e.g., the elimination of family poverty, an equitable distribution of child care and household labour, the meshing together of the institutions of family and work), they have a common denominator — the construction of a society in which gender equality prevails.

NOTES
▼

1. As Gaffield (1992) points out, assumptions regarding past French-Canadian and English-Canadian families vary somewhat, with the former assumed to be larger, more extended, and more cohesive than the latter.
2. This comment excludes First Nations groups. Also, there is historical evidence that some Québécois families took on a stem-family structure (Verdon, 1980), which is a variant of family extension.
3. Parenthetically, it is probably no coincidence that this period of ideological and behavioural conformity to highly differentiated gender roles spawned a feminist movement. The status quo is dependent upon a certain amount of "give" in relation to cultural ideals; when behavioural variability is reduced, the weight of constraint leads to social and cultural change.
4. It should be noted that the "married with children" category includes families with stepchildren. The Canadian census has yet to collect data on the number, or characteristics, of blended families. However, recently released data from the National Longitudinal Survey of Children and Youth indicate that, of children under the age of 12, 78 percent live with their biological parents (including children born into stepfamilies), 16 percent live in lone-parent households, 4 percent live in stepfamilies, and 1 percent live in other types of arrangements. In total, 9 percent of children under the age of 12 live in blended families — about one-half are actual stepchildren and about one half are born into or adopted into stepfamilies (*Canadian Social Trends*, 1997).
5. More than one-half of all divorces involve at least one dependent child.
6. Ursel (1986) also discusses the ways that the state and employers increasingly control women's labour.
7. The following terms are used synonymously: "common-law unions," "cohabitation," and "consensual unions." In French, the term is *union libre*.
8. The 1976 Canadian census collected data on common-law unions; however, the issue was considered to be too politically sensitive for data release.
9. However, a team of U.S. sociologists has recently argued that cohabitation should no longer be viewed as a precursor to legal marriage but, rather, as an alternative to remaining single (Rindfuss and VandenHuevel, 1990).
10. In the nineteenth century and earlier parts of the twentieth century, women took in lodgers/boarders as a way to augment family income.
11. While this book was in press, the Supreme Court decided the case of *M.* v. *H.* in favour of M.

12. As pointed out by Eichler (1988), social policies and programs have very different implications for different types of families and for different family members.
13. It must be kept in mind, however, that not all women who work part-time choose this work option; it may be the only work available.

CRITICAL THINKING QUESTIONS
▼

1. It is common to hear that the Canadian family is in "crisis" or "decline." How and why is this view perpetuated? In what ways is it inaccurate?
2. In what ways are work and the family interconnected?
3. Why and in what ways have recent changes in families led to negative consequences for women? How could these negative consequences be ameliorated?
4. If you could design the next Canadian census, what questions on family would you include, and why?
5. How have the economy and the state produced changes in family life? Have these changes been positive or negative, or a combination?

SUGGESTED READING
▼

Maureen Baker, ed. 1994. *Canada's Changing Families: Challenges to Public Policy.* Ottawa: Vanier Institute of the Family.

This volume consists of ten chapters that deal with policy issues that emanate from the changes in Canadian families that have been discussed in this chapter.

Roderic Beaujot, Ellen M. Gee, Fernando Rajulton, and Zenaida R. Ravanera. 1995. *Family Over the Life Course.* Ottawa: Statistics Canada, Catalogue no. 91-543E.

Using a combination of census and other Statistics Canada survey data, these authors examine the ways in which the family life of young adults, midlife persons, and the elderly are changing. The final chapter examines the changing family life course over this century, using cohort analysis.

Canadian Council on Social Development. 1994. *Family Security in Insecure Times: The National Forum on Family Security,* vols. 1–3. Ottawa: Canadian Council on Social Development.

Prepared for the International Year of the Family (1994), volume 1 provides individually authored chapters that examine the extent, nature, and causes of family economic/social insecurity; volume 2 includes chapters offering new perspectives for resolving family insecurity; and volume 3 focusses on building a partnership of responsibility among families, workplaces, communities, and governments.

Canadian Families on the Eve of the Year 2000. (In press). Nelson Canada and Statistics Canada.

Part of the 1991 Census Monograph Series, this volume provides an exhaustive quantitative analysis of Canadian families, based on 1991 census data.

Marion Lynn, ed. 1996. *Voices: Essays on Canadian Families.* Toronto: Nelson Canada. A collection of sixteen chapters, each focussing on giving a "voice" (hence, the title of this volume) to diverse family types that have generally been neglected in mainstream sociological research. The family types examined include: single-parent families; stepfamilies; lesbian families; families with a parent with a disability; a number of "ethnic" families in Canada (Nedut'en, Black, Chinese, Hindu, and Greek); and families in different regions (Quebec, Cape Breton, rural Saskatchewan).

Susan A. McDaniel. 1994. *Family and Friends.* Ottawa: Statistics Canada, Catalogue no. 11-612E, No. 9.
Using data from the 1990 General Social Survey (which had a special focus on families), this publication provides a thorough analysis of the family life of Canadians.

REFERENCES
▼

Adams, Owen. 1990. "Divorces in Canada, 1988." *Health Reports* 2/1. Ottawa: Statistics Canada, Catalogue no. 82-003.

Ambert, Anne-Marie. 1990. "Marital Dissolution: Structural and Ideological Changes." In Maureen Baker, ed., *Families: Changing Trends in Canada,* 2nd ed. Toronto: McGraw-Hill Ryerson.

Andersen, Margaret L. 1991. "Feminism and the American Family Ideal." *Journal of Comparative Family Studies* 22: 235–46.

Armstrong, Pat. 1989. "Work and Family Life: Changing Patterns." In G.N. Ramu, ed., *Marriage and Family in Canada Today.* Scarborough, ON: Prentice-Hall.

———. 1990. "Economic Conditions and Family Structures." In Maureen Baker, ed., *Families: Changing Trends in Canada,* 2nd ed. Toronto: McGraw-Hill Ryerson.

Arnup, Katherine. 1987. "Lesbian Mothers and Child Custody." In Heather Jon Maroney and Meg Luxton, eds., *Feminism and Political Economy: Women's Work, Women's Struggles.* Toronto: Methuen.

Baker, Maureen, and Donna Lero. 1996. "Division of Labour: Paid Work and Family Structure." In Maureen Baker, ed., *Families: Changing Trends in Canada,* 3rd. ed. Toronto: McGraw-Hill Ryerson.

Balakrishnan, T.R., T.K. Burch, K.V. Rao, E. Lapierre-Adamcyk, and K.J. Krotki. 1987. "A Hazard Model Analysis of the Covariates of Marriage Dissolution in Canada." *Demography* 24: 395–406.

Bardaglio, Peter. 1981. "Paternalism, Family Law, and the State: A Study of Child Custody Law in the Nineteenth Century South." Paper presented at the Berkshire Conference on the History of Women, June. (Cited in Arnup, 1987).

Boyd, Monica, and Edward T. Prior. 1989. "The Cluttered Nest: The Living Arrangements of Young Canadian Adults." *Canadian Journal of Sociology* 14: 461–77.

Bumpass, Larry L. 1990. "What's Happening to the Family? Interactions between Demographic and Institutional Change." *Demography* 27: 483–98.

Burke, Mary Anne. 1986. "Families: Diversity the New Norm." *Canadian Social Trends* 3 (Summer): 6–9.

Canadian Social Trends. 1997. "Canadian Children in the 90s: Selected Findings of the Longitudinal Survey of Children and Youth." *Canadian Social Trends* 44 (Spring): 2–9.

Charette, Dan. 1995. "Hours of Working Couples." *Perspectives on Labour and Income* (Statistics Canada Catalogue no. 75-001E) 7/2: 9–11.

Cheal, David. 1991a. *Family and the State of Theory.* Toronto: University of Toronto Press.

———. 1991b. *Financial Resource Management in Couples: Breadwinner Families and Double Income Families.* Report prepared for the Review of Demography and Its Social and Economic Implications, Health and Welfare Canada.

Cohen, Marjorie Griffin. 1987. *Free Trade and the Future of Women's Work: Manufacturing and Service Industries.* Toronto: Garamond Press and the Canadian Centre for Policy Alternatives.

Conference Board of Canada. 1990. "Work and Family: Employment Challenges of the '90s." *Synopsis,* Report 59-90. Ottawa: Conference Board of Canada.

Conway, John F. 1997. *The Canadian Family in Crisis.* Toronto: James Lorimer.

Duffy, Ann, and Norene Pupo. 1996. "Family-Friendly Organizations and Beyond: Proposals for Policy Directions with Women in Mind." In Canadian Council on Social Development, *Family Security in Insecure Times: National Forum on Income Security,* vol. 2. Ottawa: Canadian Council on Social Development.

Dumas, Jean, and Yves Péron. 1992. *Marriage and Conjugal Life in Canada.* Ottawa: Statistics Canada, Catalogue No. 91-534E.

Duxbury, Linda, and Christopher Higgins. 1994. "Families in the Economy." In Maureen Baker, ed., *Canada's Changing Families: Challenges to Public Policy.* Ottawa: Vanier Institute of the Family.

Eichler, Margrit. 1988. *Families in Canada Today: Recent Changes and Their Policy Implications,* 2nd ed. Toronto: Gage.

———. 1997. *Family Shifts: Families, Policies, and Gender Equality.* Toronto: Oxford University Press.

Epstein, Rachel. 1996. "Lesbian Families." In Marion Lynn, ed., *Voices: Essays on Canadian Families.* Toronto: Nelson Canada.

Fischer, John. 1998. Personal communication.

Fox, Bonnie, and Meg Luxton. 1991. "Conceptualizing Family: A Research Project on Conceptualization and Historical Development." Report prepared for the Review of Demography and Its Social and Economic Implications, Health and Welfare Canada.

Gaffield, Chad. 1992. "Canadian Families in Cultural Context: Hypotheses from the Mid-Nineteenth Century." In Bettina Bradbury, ed., *Canadian Family History: Selected Readings*. Toronto: Copp Clark Pitman.

Gee, Ellen M. 1978. "Fertility and Marriage Patterns in Canada, 1851–1971." Unpublished Ph.D. dissertation, University of British Columbia.

———. 1986. "The Life Course of Canadian Women: An Historical and Demographic Analysis." *Social Indicators Research* 18: 263–83.

———. 1990a. "Demographic Change and Intergenerational Relations in Canadian Families: Findings and Social Policy Implications." *Canadian Public Policy* 16: 191–99.

———. 1990b. "Preferred Timing of Women's Life Events: A Canadian Study." *International Journal of Aging and Human Development* 31: 279–94.

———. 1993. "Adult Outcomes Associated with Childhood Family Structures: An Appraisal of Research and an Examination of Canadian Data." In Burt Galaway and Joe Hudson, eds., *Single Parent Families in Canada: Perspectives on Research and Policy*. Toronto: Thompson Educational.

Gee, Ellen M., and Meredith M. Kimball. 1987. *Women and Aging*. Toronto: Butterworths.

Gee, Ellen M., Barbara A. Mitchell, and Andrew V. Wister. 1995. "Returning to the Parental 'Nest':Exploring a Changing Canadian Life Course." *Canadian Studies in Population* 22: 121–44.

Grindstaff, Carl, and Frank Trovato. 1990. "Junior Partners: Women's Contribution to Family Income in Canada." *Social Indicators Research* 22: 229–53.

Gunderson, Morley, and Leon Muszynski. 1990. *Women and Labour Market Poverty*. Ottawa: Canadian Advisory Council on the Status of Women.

Hunsley, Terrance. 1997. *Lone Parent Incomes and Social Policy Outcomes: Canada in International Perspective*. Kingston, ON: Queen's University School of Policy Studies.

Légaré, Jacques, T.R. Balakrishnan, and Roderic P. Beaujot, eds. 1989. *The Family in Crisis: A Population Crisis?* Ottawa: Royal Society of Canada.

Mandell, Nancy. 1989. "Juggling the Load: Employed Mothers Who Work Full-Time for Pay." In Ann Duffy, Nancy Mandell, and Norene Pupo, *Few Choices: Women, Work and Family*. Toronto: Garamond.

McDaniel, Susan A. 1992. "Life Rhythms and Caring: Aging, Family, and the State." Annual Sorokin Lecture. Saskatoon: University of Saskatchewan Sorokin Lecture Series.

———. 1995. "Serial Employment and Skinny Government: Reforming Caring and Sharing in Canada at the Millennium." In Canadian Federation of Demographers, *Towards the XXIst Century: Emerging Socio-Demographic Trends and Policy Issues in Canada*. Ottawa: Canadian Federation of Demographers.

———. 1996. "The Family Lives of the Middle-Aged and Elderly in Canada." In Maureen Baker, ed., *Families: Changing Trends in Canada,* 3rd ed. Toronto: McGraw-Hill Ryerson.

McKie, Craig. 1993. "An Overview of Lone Parenthood in Canada." In Burt Galaway and Joe Hudson, eds., *Single Parent Families in Canada: Perspectives on Research and Policy*. Toronto: Thompson Educational.

McLanahan, Sara, and Karen Booth. 1991. "Mother-Only Families: Problems, Prospects, and Politics." In Alan Booth, ed., *Contemporary Families: Looking Forward, Looking Back*. Minneapolis: National Council on Family Relations.

McLoyd, V.C. 1989. "Socialization and Development in a Changing Economy." *American Psychologist* 44: 393–402.

McVey, Wayne W., Jr., and Warren E. Kalbach. 1995. *Canadian Population*. Toronto: Nelson Canada.

Michael, R.T. 1988. "Why Did the U.S. Divorce Rate Double within a Decade?" In T.P. Schultz, ed., *Research in Population Economics*, vol. 6. Greenwich, CT: JAI Press.

Milan, Anne M. 1998. "The Characteristics and Experience of Cohabitors as a Heterogeneous Group." Unpublished Ph.D dissertation, University of New Brunswick.

Miller, James. 1996. "Out Family Values." In Marion Lynn, ed., *Voices: Essays on Canadian Families*. Toronto: Nelson Canada.

Mitchell, Barbara A. 1998. "Too Close for Comfort? Parental Assessments of 'Boomerang Kid' Living Arrangements." *Canadian Journal of Sociology* 23: 21–46.

Mitchell, Barbara A., Andrew Wister, and Thomas K. Burch. 1989. "The Family Environment and Leaving the Parental Home." *Journal of Marriage and the Family* 51: 605–13.

Moore, Maureen. 1991. "How Long Alone? The Duration of Female Lone Parenthood in Canada." In Jean E. Veevers, ed., *Continuity and Change in Marriage and the Family*. Toronto: Holt, Rinehart and Winston.

Myles, John. 1991. "Editorial: Women, the Welfare State, and Caregiving." *Canadian Journal on Aging* 10: 82–85.

Nett, Emily. 1988. *Canadian Families: Past and Present*. Toronto: Butterworths.

Parr, Joy. 1990. *The Gender of Breadwinners: Women, Men and Change in Two Industrial Towns, 1880–1950*. Toronto: University of Toronto Press.

Parsons, Talcott, and Robert F. Bales, eds. 1955. *Family Socialization and Interaction Process*. Glencoe, IL: Free Press.

Ram, Bali. 1990. *New Trends in the Family: Demographic Facts and Features*. Ottawa: Statistics Canada, Catalogue no. 91-535E.

Richardson, C. James. 1992. "The Implications of Separation and Divorce for Family Structure." Report prepared for the Review of Demography and Its Social and Economic Implications, Health and Welfare Canada.

Rindfuss, Ronald, and A. VandenHuevel. 1990. "Cohabitation: A Precursor to Marriage or an Alternative to Being Single?" *Population and Development Review* 16: 703–26.

Romaniuc, Anatole. 1989. "Fertility in Canada: A Long View — A Contribution to the Debates on Population." In Jacques Légaré, T.R. Balakrishnan, and Roderic

P. Beaujot, eds., *The Family in Crisis: A Population Crisis?* Ottawa: Royal Society of Canada.

Statistics Canada. 1997. *The Daily.* http://www.statcan.ca/Daily/English/971014.

Teachman, Jay. 1991. "Contributions to Children by Divorced Fathers." *Social Problems* 38: 358–72.

Turcotte, Pierre, and Alain Bélanger. 1997. "Moving In Together: The Formation of First Common-Law Unions." *Canadian Social Trends* 47 (Winter): 7–10.

Ursel, Jane. 1986. "The State and the Maintenance of Patriarchy: A Case Study of Family, Labour and Welfare Legislation in Canada." In James Dickinson and Bob Russell, eds., *Family, Economy and State: The Social Reproduction Process under Capitalism.* Toronto: Garamond.

Vancouver Sun. 1998a. "Editorial: Today Judges Define the Canadian Family." April 4, p. A22.

———. 1998b. "Latest Gay Rights Ruling Finally Defines Equality Before the Law, Lawyer Writes." (Barbara Findlay). April 4, p. A23.

———. 1998c. "With Deficit under Control, Liberals Shift to Left with Focus on Social Justice." (Joan Bryden). March 23, p. A10.

Vanier Institute of the Family. 1996. *Canada's Families — They Count.* Ottawa: Vanier Institute of the Family.

Verdon, Michel. 1980. "The Quebec Stem Family Revisited." In K. Ishwaran, ed., *Canadian Families: Ethnic Variations.* Toronto: McGraw-Hill Ryerson.

Wolfson, Michael. 1990. "Perceptions, Facts and Expectations on the Standard of Living." In Roderic Beaujot, ed., *Facing the Demographic Future.* Ottawa: Royal Society of Canada and the Canadian Federation of Demographers.

PART TWO

▼

WELCOMING FAMILY DIVERSITY

▼

LESBIANS AND GAY MEN INSIDE AND OUTSIDE FAMILIES

CAROL-ANNE O'BRIEN AND AVIVA GOLDBERG

LEARNING OBJECTIVES

In this chapter, you will learn that:

- lesbians and gay men are found within Canadian families;
- lesbians and gay men compose family units, parenting and **co-parenting** their children;
- rather than being a menace to the family, lesbians and gay men find themselves in fact menaced by family;
- systemic homophobia is detrimental to the lives and well-being of lesbian and gay youths;
- lesbians and gay men are confronting the Canadian state, challenging and changing legal interpretations of family;
- sociological research must focus its attention on the diversity of family, including the experiences of lesbians and gay men.

INTRODUCTION

> *AHEA [American Home Economics Association], defines the family unit as two or more persons who share resources, share responsibility for decisions, share values and goals and have commitment to one another over time. The family is the climate that one "comes home to" and it is this network of sharing and commitments that most accurately describes the family unit, regardless of blood, legalities, adoption or marriage. (cited in Butler, 1997, p. 52)*

Lesbians and gay men are found within Canadian families. This simple and obvious statement contradicts the popular misconception that lesbian and gay male lives exist entirely outside family relations. Most of us who have lesbian/gay relatives are aware of it, or, being lesbian/gay ourselves, realize that we are part of families since we have sisters and brothers, mothers and fathers, partners and children. Lesbians and gay men grow up in families, establish relationships that are of similar duration and have the same emotional significance as those of heterosexual couples, and sometimes become parents.

The relationship between heterosexual family members and their lesbian/gay relatives is often problematic as many heterosexual people feel discomfort around and fear and hostility toward gay men and lesbians, whether or not they are aware of the sexual orientation of particular individuals. Familial prejudice and societal discrimination against lesbians and gay men has an especially harsh impact on lesbian and gay youth in their families of origin and in the school system, leading to disproportionately high secondary school dropout rates and incidence of street youth among gay/lesbian teenagers. Social researchers and other observers have noted the reliance of lesbians and gay men on non-familial intimate relations, linking this to marginalization from the kinship system (Weeks, 1991). While lesbians and gay men are located within the **family/household** system, their relationship to it is not the same as that of heterosexual people due to the stigmatization of same-gender sex by families, the law, and the **state**.

In this chapter, we provide evidence that a socially systemic and homophobic ideology is dividing lesbians and gay men from families (Weston, 1991, pp. 22–29). This ideology creates the widespread social misperception that lesbians and gay men are destined to lead lonely and unhappy lives. We examine how sociology has reproduced this opposition between "family" and "homosexuality" and suggest an alternative basis for research. This chapter discusses lesbian and gay youth, relationships, parenting, progressive changes in the Canadian legal system regarding lesbian and gay rights, and non-familial forms of intimate relations. In examining these issues, we highlight the complexity of the relations between families and lesbians and gay men in Canada — relations of inclusion and of tension.

LESBIANS, GAY MEN, AND FAMILIAL IDEOLOGY
▼

Women and men have formed sexual relationships with people of their own gender for centuries in Canada. Some aboriginal peoples had complex systems of sex and gender in which some people were thought to combine the spirits of female and male. These "two-spirited" people, who had sex with people of the same gender, were regarded as fortunate and associated with spiritual power, generosity, and luck (Gunn Allen, 1991, pp. 113–19; Williams, 1992, pp. 264–69). Conversion to Christianity and centuries of foreign rule brought the sexual and gender practices of aboriginal peoples closer to those of white settlers, administrators, and missionaries, but respect for "two-spirited" people is found among some First Nations to this day (Williams, 1992).

In contrast to aboriginal peoples, the European colonists, and subsequently both English and French Canadians, adopted punitive and hostile positions with respect to same-gender sexuality. Tellingly, the first known recorded instance of same-gender sex in Canada occurred in the context of a young man's prosecution by a church court in 1648 (Kinsman, 1987, p. 77). The historian Terry Chapman (cited in Kinsman, 1987, p. 77) has established that, in the Canadian West at the end of the nineteenth and beginning of the twentieth century, sex between men was common and tolerated in the all-male communities that mined, logged, threshed, and worked on the railways.

Even though women have had sex with women, and men with men, likely as long as there have been people in Canada, it would be wrong to say that there have always been "homosexuals" and "heterosexuals" in Canada. Christian churches, for instance, prosecuted people for being "sodomites," that is, engaging in non-reproductive sexual practices, but this crime applied as much to female–male sex as to male–male or female–female sex. Until the term "homosexual" was popularized in the second half of the nineteenth century, people who had sex with others of the same gender were not thought of as having exclusive same-gender attractions. Today, our sexual ideology leads us to think of homosexuality, heterosexuality, and bisexuality as absolute categories, likely fixed from birth and unchangeable. This is inaccurate. People may change their sexual orientation over the course of time, or they may be involved with both men and women, or define themselves as heterosexual or gay and still have occasional sex or relationships with people of a gender they do not usually desire. In the words of psychologist Carla Golden, "sexuality may be an aspect of identity that is fluid and dynamic as opposed to fixed and invariant" (1987, p. 19). Same-gender sex has changed in meaning over the course of history, and sexual attraction to those of the same gender has changed experientially as well.

Since the late 1960s in Canada, lesbians and gay men have formed a social movement dedicated to fighting, minimally, for civil rights and public acceptance and, maximally, for a complete reorganization of sexuality and gender (Adam, 1987; Herman, 1994; Kinsman, 1987, pp. 179–98). Heterosexual people commonly speak and write about lesbians and gay men as outside relationships, hedonistic, unhappy, and alone: objects of pity and fear. "Family" thus comes to mean just the opposite of homosexuality — a site of stability, caring, responsibility, and happiness amid a sea of social change. This characterization of families is ridiculously wrong. Families are sites of violence, of massive change and instability, as well as of comfort.

Defenders of family values generally attack populations — typically single mothers, women who have had abortions, and homosexuals — who supposedly undermine families. Lesbian and gay men advancing equality claims have been portrayed as menacing "the family" in recent Canadian history. In 1992, proposed amendments adding sexual orientation as a prohibited ground of discrimination to the Canadian Human Rights Code were opposed by a so-called Family Caucus in the Progressive Conservative party, a caucus that had not previously existed. Indeed, in Britain, during the 1988 passage of Section 28 of the Local Government Act, aimed to cut off government funds to any local governments or schools that dealt positively with homosexuals, "the family" was used to act in opposition to lesbians and gay men. In the debates about Section 28, families were portrayed as happy and heterosexual, contrasting with the purported unhappy lot of lesbians and gay men who, at best, had only "pretended family relationships" (Weeks, 1991).

Meanings given to "the family" have often undermined the claims of lesbians, gay men, and bisexuals for greater measures of social justice. This ideological use of "the family" against lesbians and gay men is homophobic; it spreads irrational fear and hatred of people who are not heterosexual. Deploying family and family values in opposition to homosexuality is also heterosexist: it treats heterosexuality as the only valid form of sexual behaviour, thus supporting the treatment of gay men, lesbians, and bisexuals as inferior to heterosexual people. Families can be talked about and lived (see "Lesbian and Gay Male Relationships" later in this chapter) in ways that do not reproduce these kinds of rigid social and sexual norms, but here we are writing specifically about one particular familial ideology that has marked negative outcomes for lesbians and gay men.

SOCIOLOGY FOR LESBIANS AND GAY MEN
▼

Canadian sociology, with the exception of a handful of sources, has done nothing to alleviate the ideology that places gay men and lesbians outside of and as hazardous to family relations. Instead, it has tended to reproduce this imaginary division. For the most part, lesbian and gay topics have fallen under the sociology of deviance (Adam, 1986, pp. 400–401). In his review of Canadian sociology textbooks, Barry Adam argued that, in these texts, "homosexuality remains dissociated from interpersonal relations, love, intimacy, **cohabitation**, mateship and even sexual relations" (1986, p. 401). The separation of lesbians and gay men from these topics has helped to reproduce the ideological division between family and homosexuality. However, as lesbian and gay rights movements have moved from criminal to human-rights law reform, new sociological expertise and paradigms are challenging traditional definitions of "family" and "spouse" (Herman, 1994, pp. 30–31).

Though outright **homophobia** has become less frequent in recent years (Watters, 1986), sociology has had a pronounced heterosexist bias. Heterosexual bias, as Helen Lensky (1991) demonstrates, shows up at many levels of the research process, from the formulation of research questions to the use of exclusionary language and methodology. Thus, for instance, much of the literature on domestic labour (the unpaid work, such as cooking and cleaning, done within households mostly by women) and dual-worker households is theorized on the basis of research performed on male–female households on the assumption that all households consist of partnerships between men and women. The resulting theories generalize lesbian and gay male households, indicating an underlying heterosexist bias in the research questions and selections of the population sampled. This leads to problems of overgeneralizing from unrepresentative samples that do not include lesbians or gay men — or many other social groups.

We would like to draw attention to the fact that little original sociological research has been done on the contemporary situation of Canadian lesbians and gay men. Over the past decade or so, some studies in Canadian lesbian and gay history and historical sociology have appeared (Chamberland, 1991; Adam, 1987; Kinsman, 1987; Ross, 1995), but a sociology of the present is urgently required in order to assist the liberation of lesbians, gay men, and bisexuals. Studies of the kind and magnitude of violence against gay men, lesbians, and bisexuals should be undertaken and compared with existing U.S. sources (Berrill, 1990; Comstock, 1991). The health needs of people living with AIDS need documenting, as do the experiences of lesbian and gay men at high school and university (Anderson and Nieberding, 1989; Khayatt, 1992). Research into gay parenting and children of same-sex parents must be initiated (Epstein, 1996).

Potential projects are numberless, but we would suggest that researchers begin from the everyday experiences recounted by lesbians and gay men, not from searches of the sociological literature. In Canada today, research questions derived from published sociological sources would often simply duplicate the framework found in the sociology of deviance. Work that begins from the standpoint of lesbians and gay men will be of interest and use to lesbian and gay organizations and will help in the long run to liberate lesbians and gay men. Beginning from the perspective of sociological theory would simply assist the growth of professional knowledge for administering and managing lesbian and gay people (Kinsman, 1992; Smith, 1988, pp. 163–69; Smith, 1990, pp. 629–35). Such research efforts as those by Rachel Epstein (1996) on lesbian mothering, and Miriam Kaufman and Susan Dundas (1995) on research directions regarding lesbian families, provide more positive guidelines for such projects.

It is crucial that research on gay men and lesbians be sensitive to gender, race, and class. There are significant social differences among lesbians and gay men organized through these forms of social inequality. Feminist work over the past generation has established the need for gender sensitivity in sociological research. Simply put, gender differences structure all forms of social action and social organization. One can, for example, predict that lesbians will have significantly lower incomes than gay men, since Canadian women in the 1990s earn on average roughly two-thirds of what men do. Grouping both sexes together under the heading "homosexuals" or "gay people" therefore can hide significant differences between lesbians and gay men. Racism is also an important determinant of the lives of lesbians and gay men of colour, who report experiencing racism within the white-majority lesbian and gay population, and homophobia within non-white communities. Moreover, the social consequences of being a member of a non-white group do not end when someone has sex with another person of the same gender: the low life expectancy and high mortality rates of aboriginal people may be predicted to also hold true for aboriginal gay men and lesbians. Little is known in the sociological literature about class differences among gay men and lesbians, but historians have documented distinctions in the use of leisure time among lesbians of differing classes (Chamberland, 1991). Feminist sociologists are increasingly aware of the importance of including race and class awareness in their research questions and research methods, and sociologists working within gay and lesbian studies should follow in recognizing the social differences among gay men and lesbians.

LESBIAN AND GAY YOUTH
▼

> Young gays live with families. We live with families who do not know we are gay. We live with families who know because they "discovered" through some incident or because we've told them. We live with families who beat us up for being gay; who will not allow "queer" friends to come over to the house, call on the phone, or go out with their daughters. These are families who will listen in on our phone conversations ... interrogate callers ... open and throw away mail, go through drawers, taking zealous measures to root this "evil" out of our lives. We also live with families who coerce us into seeing psychiatrists, who threaten and do hospitalize us and incarcerate us — "If we don't straighten up." Many of us live with families who totally ignore our gayness, thinking "it's just a phase." Nothing like wholesale invalidation. Young gays also don't live with families, for all of the above reasons. (Young lesbian quoted in Saperstein, 1981, p. 61)

Relations between families and lesbians and gay men are fraught with enormous difficulties and tensions. In this section, we examine relations between lesbians and gay men and their families of origin by focussing upon the situation of lesbian and gay youth. Since the 1960s, with the advent of a political culture radicalized by many social movements, especially the movements for lesbian and gay liberation, increasing numbers of lesbian and gay youth are coming out (acknowledging their homosexuality) at an earlier age and challenging their families of origin for acceptance (Gibson, 1989). There is growing visibility of lesbian and gay youth in cities across Canada as they form support groups, put their issues on the agendas of lesbian and gay organizations, and make demands of institutions such as schools and social services. Unfortunately, most lesbian and gay youth, particularly those who do not live in major urban centres in Canada, do not have access to the celebratory and supportive atmosphere of these groups. Instead, they experience social isolation, verbal and physical harassment, suicide, and rejection by their families. Coming out while they are still living with their parents and attending school puts them "in conflict with all the traditional childrearing institutions and support systems of our society" (Gibson, 1989, p. 112).

The vulnerability of lesbian and gay youth in relation to their families of origin should be put in the general context of understanding the status of youth in our society. Most young people are dependent upon their parents to provide them with shelter, food, and other necessities of life. In combination with their legally subordinate status, this means that minors are not free to make independent decisions about their lives. Youth, especially females, are particularly constrained in their sexual activities. Laws aimed at preventing child sexual abuse can also be used to control teenage sexuality; for example, federal legislation prohibits those under age 18 from engaging in anal intercourse (Sullivan, 1992).

This context has a particular influence on lesbian and gay youth. Most are still living in their parental homes, and economic dependence forces them to deny or hide their sexual and romantic needs in order not to jeopardize their material needs or their education. Running away from home or being pushed out usually means dropping out of high school with few employable skills (McCullagh and Greco, 1990). And many lesbian and gay youths, like other young people, are not socially and emotionally independent; they lack the skills and emotional resources to live on their own (Khayatt, 1991; Saperstein, 1981).

Families not only reflect societal homophobia, but are also institutions in which the dominance of heterosexuality is reproduced in different ways, depending upon class, race, and ethnicity. Young people are exposed to homophobic slurs, expressions of disgust, and demeaning jokes from peers, the media, and family members. The prevalent assumption that everyone is heterosexual means that parents, siblings, and friends may be unwittingly subjecting lesbian and gay youths to incessant verbal abuse. In contrast, young women are confronted by silence regarding the existence of lesbians (Khayatt,

1991). This environment has a devastating effect on lesbian, bisexual, or gay youths' attempts to come to terms with their sexual orientation and often leads to shame and self-hatred (Prairie Research Associates and Gay and Lesbian Youth Services Network, 1989; Remafedi, 1987; Sears, 1989).

In this environment young people may react to the desire for same-gender relationships in different ways, including acceptance, misunderstanding, denial, or attempts to change. Gay and lesbian young people who are forced "into the closet," forced to hide their homosexuality and pressured not to reveal their feelings, are caused serious psychological damage. They adopt a number of self-protective strategies, such as taking on a public heterosexual identity in the hope of changing themselves or deceiving others, rigorously monitoring their behaviour or dress for fear of discovery (Martin, 1982), suppressing their feelings with drugs and alcohol (Sears, 1989), and emotionally distancing themselves from other family members. Martin suggests that it is not homosexuality that is a danger to families; on the contrary, it is the closet.

Because of the limitations on autonomous female sexuality in our society, young women who are sexually attracted to other women often fail to understand their feelings or else deny them. For lesbians, more frequently than for gay male youths, this experience of being in the closet means making desperate efforts to conform by having heterosexual relationships; lesbians may become pregnant in an effort to prove they are heterosexual (Sears, 1989; Uribe and Harbeck, 1992).

Staying closeted is partially forced upon lesbian and gay youth by their economic dependence upon their parents and by their lack of autonomy. Studies show that young people's fears of the loss of family affection are also significant (Martin, 1982). These fears are realistic, for lesbian and gay youth face the real risk of total rejection (Gibson, 1989; Hunter, 1990; Prairie Research Associates ..., 1989). For non-white lesbian and gay youth, revealing their sexual orientation may also jeopardize the extended-family relations and communities that provide support in racist societies (Gibson, 1989).

When gay and lesbian youths come out to their families or their sexual orientation is discovered, responses frequently include a lack of support (Saperstein, 1981); misinformation, such as being told they are condemned to lead an unhappy life (Heron, 1983); anger; verbal harassment; the disruption of home life (Uribe and Harbeck, 1992); and restrictions or control of activities (Heron, 1983). Parents may also attempt to deny their child's sexual orientation, arguing that it is "just a phase," especially for lesbian youth (Uribe and Harbeck, 1992), or they may insist that the youth is "too young to decide" (Heron, 1983).

Families from a variety of cultures and classes may be places of danger for lesbian and gay youth. Parental and sibling verbal, sexual, and physical abuse of lesbian and gay youth who are open to their families about their sexuality has been well documented (Heron, 1983; Hunter, 1990; Martin, 1982; Saperstein, 1981; Uribe and Harbeck, 1992).

Suicide has been documented as a serious problem among lesbian and gay youth. A research paper by Paul Gibson, commissioned by the U.S. Department of Health and Human Services and then suppressed by the Bush Administration, suggested that lesbian, bisexual, and gay youths are two to three times more likely than heterosexual youths to attempt suicide, and that they account for 30 percent of completed suicides each year (Gibson, 1989, p. 111). Another study of gay and bisexual male youth found that 30 percent of the subjects had attempted suicide at least once, and almost half of the attempters reported more than one attempt (Remafedi, Farrow, and Deisher, 1991, p. 871). Bell and Weinberg found that 35 percent of gay males and 38 percent of lesbians in their study had either seriously considered or attempted suicide (Gibson, 1989). The only available Canadian figures are from a Winnipeg study, which found that, of the 45 young gay males and lesbians who were interviewed, one-third had attempted suicide and two-thirds had suicidal feelings, largely related to their sexual orientation (Prairie Research Associates ..., 1989, p. 19). Research indicates that the causes of such high percentages of gay and lesbian youth attempting suicide include family rejection and harassment at school (Khayatt, 1991; Kournay, 1987).

The most common problem of lesbian and gay youth is isolation (Martin, 1982). This results from the need to remain closeted at home and the dearth of accurate information about homosexuality. Another form of isolation is the absence of contact with gay and lesbian communities; young lesbians and gay men who grow up with heterosexual parents and relatives are deprived of opportunities to learn from older generations. Restrictions upon links between young people and adult gays and lesbians are strongly entrenched in school, recreational, social service, and other settings. Teachers and youth workers, for example, face powerful institutional pressures to pass for heterosexual with their students and clients (Khayatt, 1991; O'Brien, 1992; Smith, 1991). These professional practices are socially organized by the homophobic myth that gay and lesbian adults sexually abuse young people in order to "recruit" them to homosexuality. This belief contributes to the denial of widespread sexual abuse of children by heterosexual male relatives and caregivers (Committee on Sexual Offenses Against Children and Youths [Canada], 1984).

Gay and lesbian youth are also isolated, silenced, and harassed in their school lives, leading some to drop out (Khayatt, 1991; Smith, 1991; Uribe and Harbeck, 1992). Since they are largely closeted or rejected at home, lesbian and gay youths cannot turn to their families for support in dealing with the school system. The failure of parents of lesbian and gay young people to intervene in schools in defence of their children perpetuates these abusive and dangerous environments.

Evidence of the devastating impact of family rejection of lesbian and gay youth can also be found in the extremely high proportion of gay men, lesbians, and bisexuals among homeless and street youth. Canadian figures are not available, but in the United States estimates range from 25 to 50 percent in various cities (Kruks, 1991; Seattle Commission on Children and Youth, 1988; Green, 1991). Studies show that this overrepresentation is largely due to family rejection; these young people are mostly "pushaways" or "throwaways" rather than runaways (Gibson, 1989; Green, 1991; Uribe and Harbeck, 1992). Once on the streets they are at increased risk for prostitution, substance abuse, hunger, and ill health, including HIV infection. The threat of homelessness is one of the means through which lesbian and gay youths are subordinated and kept in the closet within their families.

Some gay and lesbian youth are placed in group homes or treatment centres when their families discover their sexual orientation (Mirken, 1992). In these settings, gay male youths are not protected from widespread verbal and physical abuse. Lesbian youths are silenced and controlled in the expression of their sexuality. Both are wrongly treated by social workers and other caregivers, who view their sexual orientation as a product of childhood sexual abuse or a mental illness (Gibson, 1989; O'Brien, 1992).

There is also evidence of families forcing lesbian and gay youths to undergo psychiatric or other forms of "treatment" aimed at suppressing their homosexual desires (Heron, 1983; Mirken, 1992). Although involuntary psychiatric "treatment" of gay men and lesbians at the behest of their families is less prevalent now than it was in previous decades, the legally subordinate status of minors continues to make them vulnerable to this form of abuse.

In sum, it is clear that the evidence bears out Paul Gibson's (1989) claim that families are a hazard for lesbian and gay youth, rather than the reverse. But **heterosexism** and homophobia are not totally dominant. They are contested in a number of ways. Many more young people are acknowledging their same-sex desires, often deciding to delay disclosure to their parents while secretly making links with lesbian and gay communities. Organizations such as Central Toronto Youth Services are sensitized to these youths' specific needs and in 1997 published a comprehensive book for teachers, doctors, therapists, and counsellors who work with lesbian, gay, and bisexual adolescents. This book, *Pride and Prejudice: Working with Lesbian, Gay and Bisexual Youth* (Schneider, 1997), includes articles by experts involved with gay and lesbian street youth, gay and lesbian youth and the welfare system, and youth who are victimized as a result of their coming out. The antihomophobic and antiracist policies and guidelines which the authors of this book provide have been initiated by such community groups as Youthlink Inner City in Toronto with positive results. As one South Asian queer youth stated, "I feel accepted there for who I am ... I don't have to justify my South Asianness or check it at the door" (as quoted in Ferren, 1997, p. 253).

Although there is very little current material published on lesbian and gay youths' experiences coming out in the latter part of this decade, the National Film Board of Canada has produced two films on the topic. The first film, *Out: Stories of Lesbian and Gay Youth* (1993; Director: David Adkin), presents a series of interviews with gay and lesbian youth from a variety of cultural and racial backgrounds. As the production notes state, the film "delves into the emotional, social and familial conflicts lesbian and gay youth often face. ..." The second documentary, *School's Out!* (1996; Director: Lynne Fernie), also deals honestly with the experiences of gay and lesbian youth. In this film, five Canadian young people talk about their lives as gay individuals and their experiences in confronting homophobia in high school. According to the producers, the film should be used in Canadian high schools and colleges as a resource and to provoke discussion about sexuality, sexual orientation, homophobia, and sexism.[1]

Lesbian and gay adults are also forming organizations to raise awareness about the situation of lesbian and gay youth and to advocate on their behalf. One such organization is Toronto's Coalition for Lesbian, Gay, and Bisexual Youth, created in 1991. This is a coalition of more than 100 service providers, educators, activists, and adult and youth members concerned with issues related to lesbian, gay, and bisexual youth. In the past few years, they have organized several province-wide conferences celebrating lesbian and gay accomplishments and focussing on needs and gaps in services for lesbian and gay youth. As well, their new project, "Supporting Our Youth," funded by the Trillium Foundation, aims at increasing "adult mentoring, education bursary programs, linking youth to supportive employment, education, and housing opportunities" (Coalition for Lesbian and Gay Rights in Ontario, 1998). Similarly, Rainbow Enterprises, an employment-development initiative funded by Human Resources Development Canada, has been established as the first entrepreneurial program in Canada designed to support and develop skills training for unemployed lesbians and gays who are looking to establish their own small businesses (Rainbow Enterprises, 1998).

Finally, in acknowledging the extent to which families of origin are places of danger for lesbian and gay youth, we should consider some of the ways this is socially organized. Families are one of the most influential locations in our society for the enforcement of heterosexuality, but many parents' behaviours and beliefs are socially produced by dominant ideologies about homosexuality as deviant. In a study of parents of gays and lesbians, Neisen (1987) found that parents needed more information and education about homosexuality from various sources (and, we would add, in different languages). They asked for positive role models for gay youth and for their parents, more support groups, and more knowledgeable professionals. These parents of lesbians and gay males spoke of the importance of meeting each other and discovering that they were all "normal." They wished that they had known more gay people throughout their lives, and they revealed that they experienced a tremendous "fear of the unknown" when they discovered their children's sexuality.

When this situation is combined with the subordination of children and youth to their parents and an ideology that blames parents for their children's "problems," we have a potent mixture that puts young people's lives in danger. However, an encouraging sign of the possibilities of change is the small but growing number of parents who are developing affirmative responses to their gay children, as witnessed by the growth of the organization Parents and Friends of Lesbians and Gays (PFLAG), which has chapters in several Canadian cities. PFLAG works to educate parents about homosexuality, to calm their fears about their role in "causing" their children's sexual orientation, and to help gay youth build closer relationships with their families.

It should be noted, as well, that there have been positive advances in Christian and Jewish faith communities toward acceptance of lesbians and gays. According to Johanna Stuckey, though most Christian traditions still consider homosexuality a sin, there are several liberal churches sympathetic to gays and lesbians. In larger Canadian cities, there are gay and lesbian churches, such as the Metropolitan Community Church. In Judaism, there are lesbian and gay synagogues affiliated with the Reform movement, and both the liberal Reform and Reconstructionist movements ordain openly gay and lesbian candidates for the rabbinate (Stuckey, 1998). This is a welcoming signal to lesbian and gay individuals and their families. In these churches and synagogues, gay and lesbian individuals can participate fully with their families without fear of discrimination or recrimination. In particular, lesbian and gay youth are introduced to positive role models in "out" gay and lesbian ministers and rabbis.

LESBIAN AND GAY-MALE RELATIONSHIPS
▼

Differences in cohabitation and gender are a reality to be equitably acknowledged, not an indulgence to be economically penalized. There is less to fear from acknowledging conjugal diversity than from tolerating exclusionary prejudice. (Rosenberg v. Canada (Attorney General), 1998, para. 48, per Abella, J.A., as cited in Gavigan, [In press a])

The dominant ideological positioning of gay men and lesbians in opposition to "the family" produces the stereotype that gay men and lesbians lead lonely lives characterized by casual sexual encounters. Although many heterosexual marriages do not conform to the ideal of permanent, monogamous unions, this is the standard against which a whole range of other relationships are judged, including those of heterosexual single parents, lesbians and gays, and non-nuclear or non-biological families described by people of colour.

The research literature on gay and lesbian relationships is small compared with that on topics such as the origins and development of homosexual identity, and the vast majority of studies have been of younger, urban, and primarily white participants (Peplau, 1991). Studies of same-gender relationships are hampered because homophobia and heterosexism render it impossible to find a random sample of gay men and lesbians. However, the literature shows that, contrary to the stereotypes, lesbians and gay men, like heterosexuals, form a variety of relationships, shaped by their age, by their class and ethnicity, and by whether or not they care for children.

Many gays and lesbians have committed and enduring relationships. Studies have found that serial monogamy is the dominant pattern, with 40 to 60 percent of gay men and 45 to 80 percent of lesbians engaged in live-in **couple** relationships, the others being single or in short-term relationships (Larson, 1982, p. 223; Peplau, 1991, p. 179; Raphael and Robinson, 1984). These figures also point to a pattern of gender differences in relationships. The breakup rates of married and cohabiting heterosexual couples, and lesbian and gay couples, have been found to be approximately equal (Blumstein and Schwartz, 1983), and research on older gay men and lesbians shows that relationships lasting twenty years or more are not uncommon (Peplau, 1991).

Many lesbian and gay couples participate in active social networks. Studies of predominantly white couples show that they receive the same levels of social support as non-gay couples, although, unlike the latter, their sources of support are more likely to be friends than family members (Kurdeck, 1988; Raphael and Robinson, 1984). Among aboriginal people and people of colour, family, kin, and racial or ethnic communities are often seen as vital cultural resources (Lorde, 1991; Gomez and Smith, 1991). However, a 1991 study with racially diverse participants indicated that, despite popular theories that families among people of colour offer "unconditional love" to their gay and lesbian members, many lesbians and gays of colour have experienced rejection by their families (Weston, 1991).

One study on heterosexual bias regarding lesbian and gay relationships has documented the ways heterosexuals perceive lesbian and gay couples as "less satisfied with their relationship" and "less in love" than heterosexual couples (Testa, Kinder, and Ironson, 1987). Research has shown the falsity of these myths. Despite the stresses of life in a heterosexist society, most gay men and lesbians are satisfied with their relationships, which are no more prone to problems than are non-gay relationships (Peplau, 1991). Nonetheless, as in heterosexual relationships, partner abuse is a problem in some same-sex relationships. Because of the involvement of lesbians in the feminist movement against violence against women, however, lesbian work on this issue is more advanced than that of gay men.

The research literature shows that lesbian and gay relationships provide many contrasts to heterosexual relationships that are organized around inequality. Studies have found that lesbian and gay relationships are more egalitarian than heterosexual relationships (Eldridge and Gilbert, 1990; Larson, 1982; Sang, 1984); for example, finances and decision making are characterized by a high degree of equality (Lynch and Reilly, 1986) and high levels of self-esteem (Eldridge and Gilbert, 1990).

Implicated in the greater degree of equality within lesbian and gay couples is the finding that, in virtually all lesbian and gay-male relationships, both partners are wage earners (Eldridge and Gilbert, 1990; Blumstein and Schwartz, 1983) and that gay men and lesbians are often characterized by a high level of "material self-sufficiency" (Weston, 1991, p. 148). Indeed, lack of institutional support and social subordination has also led to the development of greater pluralism in the forms of gay and lesbian relationships, and being single is less marginalized and stigmatized than it is for heterosexuals, especially heterosexual women. In fact, research indicates that single, older lesbians show a higher degree of sexual interest and have "realistic expectations" of finding sexual partners in the future (Raphael and Robinson, 1984). Also relevant are the findings in the scant number of studies that have examined housework and the division of labour in gay and lesbian households. Unlike heterosexual relationships in which each gender is automatically given duties and rights, lesbian and gay couples most commonly negotiate a division of labour based upon skill, preference, and energy related to age and ability (Desaulniers, 1990; Lynch and Reilly, 1986; Blumstein and Schwartz, 1983; Sang, 1984).

Although lesbians and gay men have successfully fought for the inclusion of sexual orientation as a prohibited ground of discrimination in the human rights codes of all the provinces, including the Yukon Territory (as of this writing, the Northwest Territories is the only jurisdiction that does not guarantee human rights protection to lesbians and gay men), Canada is a patchwork of gay rights regarding equal pension benefits available to lesbian and gay employees, child- and spousal-support provisions extended to same-sex couples, and equal workplace benefits to same-sex partners of government employees (see Table 4.1). In contrast, heterosexual couples have the exclusive

TABLE 4.1
▼
GAY RIGHTS ACROSS CANADA

	Discrimination against gays and lesbians prohibited in human rights legislation	Equal work-place benefits available to same-sex partners of government employees	Equal pension benefits available to lesbian and gay employees	Medical decisions on behalf of same-sex partner who is incapacitated	Adoption by same-sex couples allowed	Child- and spousal-support provisions extended to same-sex couples
Federal	✓	✓	x*	n/a	n/a	n/a
Alberta	✓	x	x	x	x	x
British Columbia	✓	✓	✓**	✓	✓	✓
Manitoba	✓	✓	x	x	x	x
New Brunswick	✓	✓	x	x	x	x
Newfoundland	✓	x	x	x	x	x
Nova Scotia	✓	✓	✓	x	x	x
Ontario	✓	✓	✓	✓	✓	✓***
Prince Edward Island	✓	x	x	x	x	x
Québec	✓	x	x	x	x	x
Saskatchewan	✓	✓	x	x	x	x
Yukon Territory	✓	✓	x	x	x	x
Nunavut	x	✓	x	x	x	x
Northwest Territories	x	✓	x	x	x	x

* The federal government has accepted an Ontario court ruling requiring it to accept for registration pension plans which offer equal pension benefits, but has not yet extended equal pension benefits to federal employees.

** British Columbia has introduced, but not yet enacted, legislation to extend equal pension benefits to those in same-sex relationships.

*** Support rights extended by the Ontario Court of Appeal; decision currently under appeal to the Supreme Court of Canada.

Source: Eleanor Brown, "Queer Fear," *The Globe and Mail*, October 24, 1998, p. D3. Used by permission of Equality for Gays and Lesbians Everywhere.

right to marry, jointly adopt children, receive spousal benefits and survivors' pensions, sponsor their partners' immigration to Canada, and sue for damages as a result of death or injury. Lesbians and gay men are not permitted to submit income tax reports based on their joint financial arrangements, and in many cases are denied equal access to "family rates" offered to consumers (Bell, 1991). Through such official and unofficial practices, the dominance of heterosexuality is enforced.

The lack of legal and social recognition of same-sex relationships can have grave implications. For example, gay men with AIDS want their partners to receive survivors' pensions and they need protection against potential efforts on the part of their birth-families to contest wills that leave property to their surviving partners. There have also been cases in which hospitals have permitted the families of origin of gay and lesbian patients — rather than their same-sex partners — to make decisions about medical care or the release of bodies for funerals (Larson, 1982). A particularly infamous case occurred in the United States, where for eight years the parents of Sharon Kowalski fought to prevent her lover, Karen Thompson, from having custody or visiting her after Kowalski was severly disabled in an automobile accident (Thompson and Andrzejewski, 1988). In December 1991, a Minnesota appeal court judge finally ruled that Kowalski and Thompson constituted a family, and that Thompson was suitable to care for Kowalski.

As the Kowalski case demonstrates, gay men and lesbians have successfully challenged official forms of discrimination in a number of different ways. The following summary[2] of the most recent cases brought before the courts in Canada illustrates not only the increasing battle by lesbians and gay men against the privileges and rights accorded only to heterosexual relationships and families, but also how the discourse of "homosexuality" is divided from the discourse of "the family."

In 1992, two lesbian couples in British Columbia and the Yukon launched suits against Canadian immigration regulations that excluded the sponsorship of same-gender partners. After many delays, Canadian Immigration granted residency to the non-Canadian partners, but insisted that the cases be handled as individual applications. Since 1994, hundreds of individuals have gained residency in Canada on the basis of their same-sex relationships with Canadians. However, the applications are discretionary in a way that the applications of heterosexuals are not. Same-sex couples in these dual-national relationships cannot invoke "family class" sponsorship; instead, each case is reviewed on "humanitarian and compassionate" grounds.

In 1995, the Supreme Court of Canada decided on the case of a gay man in a long-term relationship who sought "spousal allowance" under the tax-funded government old age security pension system. The Court unanimously held that the equality clause in the constitution applied to homosexuals. In the Ontario courts, in 1995, a landmark decision upheld adoption rights for same-sex couples. Four lesbian couples applied for joint adoption of a total of seven children. The judge ruled that "there was no evidence that families with heterosexual parents are better able to meet the physical, psychological, emotional or intellectual needs of children than families with homosexual parents" (*Re. K.*, p. 708). In 1996, the government amended the Canadian Human Rights Code, adding sexual orientation as a prohibited grounds of discrimination. In response to human-rights tribunals, Canada extended health benefits to same-sex partners and, in July 1997, the federal Treasury Board ordered all directors of personnel and chiefs of staff to interpret the definition of "**common-law** spouse" in collective agreements to include same-sex couples, ignoring any language which specifies that the parties are to be of the opposite sex.

In February 1998, British Columbia amended the Family Relations Act, extending the provisions of the law to same-sex couples and redefining the term "spouse" to include an individual in a same-sex relationship. British Columbia is the first jurisdiction in North America to give same-sex couples the same privileges and obligations as opposite-sex couples, including **custody**, **access**, and **child support**. In April 1998, Judges Abella, McKinlay, and Roudge ruled in the Ontario Court of Appeal that the heterosexual definition of "spouse" in the Income Tax Act is unconstitutional (*CUPE/Rosenberg* case: pension plans must now pay out survivor benefits to same-sex couples). Finally, the most recent decision of the courts (*Kane* v. *Ontario,* in November 1998) ruled that a lesbian was entitled to claim a death benefit of her same-sex spouse.

Though these victories are important to the lesbian and gay community, many activists have charged that winning, for example, the right to marry for same-sex couples, or the right to receive spousal employment benefits, will entrench the existing privileging of permanent monogamous couples at the expense of other forms of relationships, and will offer greater benefits to white, male, and higher-income sectors of gay communities (Bell, 1991; Ross, 1990). An interesting example of how some of these concerns may be addressed can be found in a "family protection" bill proposed to Boston City Council. This bill would permit the registration of two types of families: "domestic partnerships," including gay and non-gay relationships, and "extended family" relationships, which would recognize the right of any two or more people to be considered a family unit (Boyce, 1991).

Lack of recognition for same-sex relationships by state or social institutions, in concert with other forms of heterosexism, places unique stresses upon gay and lesbian couples. Large numbers of gay people are not able to come out at their workplace, requiring them to pass for heterosexual by denying their partner's existence, censoring their conversations about family and recreational activities, and silencing their pain and grief when a partner is ill or has died or when a significant relationship has broken up (Eldridge and Gilbert, 1990; Raphael and Robinson, 1984). Many lesbians and gay men from a variety of racial, ethnic, and class backgrounds are not able to disclose their sexual orientation to their families of origin, or are not affirmed by them and must bear the pain and stress of separation from their lovers during holidays or family events, or must censor their verbal and physical expressions of affection in the presence of family members (Blumstein and Schwartz, 1983; Weston, 1991). These experiences offer further evidence of the tensions and oppositions between gay men and lesbians and families.

LESBIAN- AND GAY-HEADED FAMILIES
▼

I've always wanted to have a child. In terms of being real tied up with being gay, it was one of the reasons that for a long time I was hesitant to call myself a lesbian. I thought that automatically assumed you had nothing to do with children ... I felt, well, if you don't say you're a lesbian, you can still work with children, you can still have a kid, you can have relationships with men. But once I put this label on myself, [it would] all [be] over. (Lesbian mother quoted in Lewin, 1994, p. 338)

Lesbian and gay men form families in which they parent children. The idea that lesbians and gay men may be parents is frequently perceived as impossible, contradictory, and simply wrong or immoral. Lesbians and gay men are seen as excluded from having children because sexual reproduction occurs only between men and women, or, in an age of in vitro fertilization and alternative methods of insemination, between eggs and sperm. If homosexuals are people who by definition do not have reproductive sex, then, so many infer, lesbian mothers and gay fathers simply do not exist. Human sexuality, however, is neither so unchanging (at a social or individual level) nor so uninventive.

Family formation among gay men and lesbians occurs in a variety of ways also found among heterosexuals. Lesbian mothers and gay fathers may have children by a previous marriage; households in these cases may be either lone-parent or dual-parent (if a new partner is willing to parent the children), or the parent may be non-custodial, that is, have visiting rights but lack live-in, permanent custody of the children. The majority of gay fathers become non-custodial parents to their children upon separation from their women partners; this situation parallels that of heterosexual fathers who infrequently retain child custody after the dissolution of a relationship. Unlike those heterosexual families in which the mother and father may both have genetic links to the children, gay and lesbian dual-parent households always contain a non-biological parent; that is, they formally are defined as stepfamilies (Baptiste, 1987). The children in lesbian- and gay-headed families are not all from prior heterosexual relationships; lesbians, single or with partners, may decide to become pregnant. During the 1980s, there was what is often called a lesbian baby boom, with many women becoming pregnant through alternative methods of insemination. Under these conditions of family formation, the identity of the sperm donor may be known or unknown, depending on the kind of relationship the mother foresaw she, her partner, and her child would have with the sperm donor (Pies, 1987; Weston, 1991). Lastly, lesbian mothers and gay fathers may form families through fostering or adoption. Occasionally, Canadian child-welfare agencies will place lesbian and gay youths with lesbian and gay men, particularly when these youths have been emotionally or physically abused in their heterosexual families of origin or in previous foster families. Private child adoptions to known lesbians and gay-male couples have taken place under particular circumstances and, as noted in the previous section, in British Columbia and Ontario, adoption by same-sex couples is allowed.

Lesbian- and gay-headed households may thus take a variety of family forms, but there is no valid reason for refusing to call them families. They fall under every conceivable sociological criterion for identifying families. They are groups of co-resident kin providing jointly through income-pooling for one another's survival needs of food and shelter. They socialize children, engage in emotional and physical support, and make up part of a larger kin network. The lack of recognition given to lesbian and gay-male couples does have a negative outcome for many non-biological gay and lesbian parents raising children with partners who are biological parents. Non-biological parents may not be regarded as parents socially by, for instance, schools and health-care systems. Moreover, their kin (mothers, father, brothers, sisters, grandparents, aunts, uncles) may not recognize the child of a non-biological parent as part of their family (Baptiste, 1987).

Homophobic ideology separating "homosexuality" and "the family" holds that lesbians and gay men should not be responsible for children, whether as teachers, hockey coaches, or parents. When child custody is contested, the courts have not been as favourable to granting custody to lesbian mothers and gay fathers when their homosexuality has been known and at issue. Until recently, the homosexuality of a parent was sufficient evidence for the courts to deem a person as "unfit" and deny him or her child custody. With the re-emergence of the lesbian, gay and feminist movements since the late 1960s, gay and lesbian parents have increasingly fought custody cases in the courts, seeing their parenting as equal to heterosexual parenting in the context of a larger political struggle for social equality (Gavigan, In press b;

Arnup, 1991, pp. 101–102). However, according to law professor Shelley Gavigan, "lesbian and gay parents are at risk in the courtroom if they do not conform to dominant notions of appropriate gay sexual behaviour: quiet and apolitical" (In press b). Nonetheless, there is a shift in which "judges now not only say that the mother's sexual orientation is not determinative of the issue in custody, some of them actually seem to mean it" (Gavigan, In press b).

Inside and outside the legal system, lesbian and gay fathers continually deal with a series of negative stereotypes that social-science evidence has completely discredited. Negative stereotypes include:

1. The accusation that gay men are child molesters. In Canada, the overwhelming majority of child sexual abusers are heterosexual men, who abuse both girls and boys (Committee on Sexual Offenses Against Children and Youths [Canada], 1984). Children are thus most at risk from heterosexual men, whose sexuality is never theorized as diseased. The sexual abuse of children is a problem involving masculine sexuality, overwhelmingly heterosexual and only secondarily gay.

2. The fear that children of lesbian or gay parents will become lesbian or gay. Studies indicate that the sexual orientation of parents has no effect whatsoever on the sexual orientation of youths. This may be readily surmised from the fact that gay men and lesbians originate in heterosexual-headed families. Research done on lesbian- and gay-headed families indicates that the proportion of children in these families who become lesbian/gay is the same as in the population as a whole (Kirkpatrick, Smith, and Roy, 1981; Golombok, Spencer, and Rutter, 1983).

3. The concern that the children of gay- and lesbian-headed families will not develop so-called appropriate **gender identity** (the subjective sense of being female or male) or **gender behaviour** (activities socially typical of male and female). Studies again show that when these children are compared with children of heterosexual-headed families and control groups, no significant differences emerge in their development of gender-role identities and gender-role behaviours (Golombok et al., 1983; Green, 1978, 1982; Hoeffer, 1981).

4. The fear that emotional damage will be done to children coping with the stigma of having lesbian/gay parents. The general psychological well-being of children in gay and lesbian households matches that of heterosexual and control match groups (Bozett, 1987; Gibbs, 1989; Golombok et al., 1983; Kirkpatrick et al., 1981). Moreover, this argument suggests that only people from powerful social groups should have children, for only their children would be socially accepted — a racist, anti-immigrant, and class-biased argument.

Much of the literature on gay- and lesbian-headed families has been aimed at eventual use in the courts. Although the findings are reliable and valid, they tend to emphasize the ways in which gay and lesbian families are the same as families headed by heterosexuals (Pollack, 1987; Polikoff, 1987). Ailsa Steckel's (1985) work has been unusual in investigating potential differences between the families of lesbian couples and those of heterosexual couples. She found that the children of heterosexual couples tended to be more aggressive, bossy, and engaged in power struggles than the children of lesbians. Lesbians' children were more open in expressing vulnerability and helplessness, corresponding to a more lovable sense of self; their parents and teachers considered them more affectionate, responsive, and caring toward younger children. Steckel uses a psychoanalytic model to explain differences, relating them to differences in the separation process between mother and child, the phase in which the infant develops a sense of self independent of the mother. The presence of the father makes, she argues, for a more aggressive role model, and fathers tend also to spend less time with their children than lesbian co-parents. Steckel theorizes that these children have a "more intense oedipal rivalry with fathers than with female coparents" (1987, p. 81). Clearly, psychology and psychoanalysis would be enriched by a closer theoretical attention to comparisons between heterosexual and lesbian/gay family dynamics.

The stigmatization of homosexuals, especially gay men, as dangerous to children has been disproved by social-scientific evidence, but it prevails in school systems, child-welfare systems, and the courts. Lesbian and gay men are popularly thought to have a negative influence on children. The societal hostility to lesbian and gay-male involvement with children puts lesbian- and gay-headed families at risk for harassment by neighbours, children's schoolmates and friends, school personnel, social-service agencies, and the state. The homophobic ideology that places "homosexuality" and "the family" in contradiction places strains on lesbian- and gay-headed families.

FRIENDSHIP NETWORKS AND SOCIAL SUPPORT
▼

During the early 1990s a slogan became popular in the gay and lesbian press and in lesbian and gay organizations: "We are family." This slogan is an emphatic counter-assertion to the homophobic ideology that poses gay men and lesbians as detrimental to family. The slogan is related to political efforts by lesbian and gay organizations to gain recognition for relationships: the power to marry, to obtain spousal benefits and privileges, to retain custody of children. "We are family" also proclaims the ongoing relations of social support that lesbian and gay men create, and the political, social-service, and commercial institutions that serve gay men and lesbians as a kind of family. A similar position has been put forward by the anthropologist Kath Weston in her book *Families We Choose* (1991), in which she argues that lesbian and gay families come into existence voluntarily through the actions of people caring for each other, providing material and emotional support, and developing shared histories.

What limited research exists on the subject of friendship among gay and lesbians tends to confirm that those without children rely on friends for social support to a greater degree than do heterosexuals. Kurdeck (1988) and Kurdek and Schmitt (1987) have shown that cohabiting lesbians and gay men received roughly the same social support as heterosexual couples, but that lesbian/gay couples received markedly more support from friends and less from their family of origin than did heterosexual couples. However, these studies used all-white samples, and there are serious questions as to whether they would generalize to other populations such as Asian Canadians or aboriginal Canadians.

Studies attribute the differences in the distribution of social support based on sexual orientation to the social distance that families take from known gay male/lesbian family members, or that lesbians and gay men take from their families if they have not disclosed their sexual orientation. Aura (1985), in her comparative study of social support from personal relationships available to heterosexual women and coupled lesbians, found that lesbian couples relied more on partners and friends, and less on families, than did the heterosexual women. Thus, among gay men and lesbians, friends may play a greater role than family members in providing support than is the case among heterosexuals.

But is it appropriate to call these networks of friends "family"? We think not. When people are born into families, their positions in kin relations — daughter, nephew, granddaughter, brother — are assigned to them; they are not something chosen or acquired. These are examples of what is called "ascribed social status." There are many kinship systems and many ways of ascribing differing kin statuses to people. This means that kin ascription is determined not by procreation, but by social practices. The kind of relations Weston and others would like to call family is not an ascribed social status; it is voluntary/elective. Status ascription is one of the reasons that family relations tend to be enduring, whereas friendships change over time, especially when significant changes take place in a person's life. It can be predicted that the friendship networks Weston and others call family will be highly changeable over time. The personal support networks that are being called families consist of people falling into the same range of age, income, education, and class. These networks are quite unlike families, which may vary a lot along all these parameters, yet are very like friends, a relation built on social similarities between pairs. It is, for instance, unusual to have wide age differences among friends, but this is common in families, which link generations. What Weston and others are calling families would thus better be called "friendship networks," given the kind of social relations involved. Networks need not be impersonal, contra Weston (1991, p. 69). In its broadest usage, "network" refers to the set of people known by someone; people in the set may or may not know each other (Willmott, 1987). There is no reason why some networks cannot be composed of friends who know, like, and support each other. For analytical reasons, the kinds of gay/lesbian social groups now sometimes being called "families" are more appropriately called "friendship networks." But lesbians and gay men do form families, as we have seen, and are members of their families of origin.

Distinguishing between friendship networks and families is not solely a matter of sociological theory. It is also a political question. We agree with Jeffrey Weeks that not all intimate and socially supportive relations should be called family. As Weeks says, "there exists a plurality of relational forms which are regarded by many as both legitimate and desirable and which are different from any recognizably familial pattern" (1991, p. 150). To expand the meaning of "family" to encompass all these forms would render family meaningless, and it would also leave intact the notion that the only social groups not dominated by a logic of individual gain are families. This would deny that forms of social support exist outside families.

We are asked to equate social solidarity with the familial, and all non-familial transactions with instrumentality. It would be better to begin recognizing the existence of social solidarity outside families: the kind of social support that brings volunteers, friends, and social-service workers together to help those dying of AIDS, or the strong friendship ties that often exist between lesbian ex-partners. Sociologists have done little work in the area of friendship and other kinds of non-familial social support. This positive area needs exploring, not least because it gives us glimmerings of what a society based more on ties of social solidarity would be like rather than one, like our present, that is structured principally on relations of social antagonism.

CONCLUSION
▼

Lesbian and gay men are consistently portrayed in politics, law, and the educational and child-welfare systems as menacing "the family." Lesbian and gay organizations, in co-operation with other social groups — unions, feminist organizations, antiracist groups — are resisting the ideology that sets same-sex relationships and families in opposition. Court cases and work with political parties may have cumulative, positive effects in altering discriminatory state legislation. Secondary-school systems are being pressured to provide gay-positive sex education. The negative experience of gay youth in elementary and high school can then be addressed through changes in school board policy, better teacher training, and more responsible management. In many regions of Canada, substantial progress toward these gains could be made over the next generation.

But it will be much more difficult to change lesbian and gay youths' experiences with social isolation and with verbal and physical harassment in their families of origin. Because families are not institutions with formal rules and public accountability in the same way that state institutions are, their form of social organization makes them resistant to quick intervention by social movements. Important work is now taking place among social-service workers to improve service to gay and lesbian youth, and organizations by and for gay and lesbian youth provide valuable support.

The homophobic ideology that views lesbians and gay men as outside of and menacing to families is being taken apart by multiple initiatives, many of them involving pressure on the Canadian state. Families will likely become less dangerous for gay and lesbian youth — and generally less homophobic overall — reactively, when they have been surrounded by massive social and cultural changes in other key institutions.

SUMMARY
▼

- Meanings given to "family" have undermined the claims and realities of lesbians and gay men for social justice.
- Until recently Canadian sociological research has been weak in addressing and alleviating the imaginary divisions between gays/lesbians and family relations.
- Research on family has been overgeneralizing and unrepresentative of lesbians and gay males and other social groups.
- Homophobia in the family, in the school system, and in social organizations is detrimental to lesbians and gay youth, creating an atmosphere of harassment, rejection, and fear.
- As such, young gays and lesbians often are alienated within their homes and schools: this results in higher instances of suicide, alcoholism, and isolation, particularly for those who willingly (or unwillingly) choose to "come out."
- Contrary to the societal mythology that lesbian and gay-male relationships are unsatisfactory, lesbians and gay males do create long-term, committed, and positive relationships.
- In this regard, lesbians and gay men since the 1960s have been fighting for and making gains in the recognition of their same-sex relationships within Canada's legal and social systems.

- It is necessary to destigmatize the negative stereotypes that accompany discussion of gay- and lesbian-headed families.
- Lesbian- and gay-headed families fall under every conceivable sociological criterion for identifying family.

NOTES
▼

1. The National Film Board's Web site provided material for the summaries of these films. Rina Fraticelli and Great Jane Productions Ltd. are the producers and co-producers of *School's Out!* Silva Basmajian and Dennis Murphy produced *Out: Stories of Lesbian and Gay Youth.*
2. The source materials for this summary are Sander (1997) and Coalition for Lesbian and Gay Rights in Ontario (1998).

CRITICAL THINKING QUESTIONS
▼

1. Trace the legal changes of the past five years that have affected both the economic and the social circumstances of lesbian and gay relationships in Canada.
2. Compare the legal recognition and economic benefits accorded heterosexual relationships and parenting with those accorded to lesbian and gay relationships and parenting.
3. What are some strategies for change that you would recommend for overcoming the social problems of lesbian and gay youth in their families of origin?
4. Discuss the claim that there is a pervasive ideological opposition set up between lesbians and gays and "the family."
5. What research topics would be useful contributions to a sociology for lesbians and gay men that would originate from their respective experiences rather than from the sociological literature.
6. What do you know about the sexual orientation of your relatives? How does the knowledge you have about your heterosexual relatives compare with your information about gay, lesbian, or bisexual relatives?

SUGGESTED READING
▼

Henry Abelove, Michele Barale, and David Halperin. 1993. *The Lesbian and Gay Studies Reader.* New York: Routledge.
> This text provides an introduction to a range of scholarship on lesbian and gay studies, including 42 essays on philosophy, classics, history, anthropology, sociology, ethics, and literary and cultural studies.

Katherine Arnup, ed. 1991. *Lesbian Parenting: Living with Pride and Prejudice*. Charlottetown: Gynergy.

> Arnup's book gives many first-person accounts of lesbian parenting, plus the voices of children in lesbian homes, and reflections on indentity, the law, and mothering.

Paul Gibson. 1989. "Gay Male and Lesbian Youth Suicide." In M.R. Feinleib, ed., *Report of the Secretary's Task Force on Youth Suicide*. Vol. 3: *Preventions and Intervention in Youth Suicide*. Washington, DC: U.S. Department of Health and Human Services.

> This is an in-depth report presented to the U.S. government on issues central to lesbian and gay youth, particularly the extent of and prevention of youth suicide.

Didi Herman. 1994. *Rights of Passage: Struggles for Lesbian and Gay Legal Equality*. Toronto: University of Toronto Press.

> This text explores the legal system and the struggles of lesbians and gays versus the New Christian Right regarding legal and social issues.

Fiona Nelson. 1996. *Lesbian Motherhood: An Exploration of Canadian Lesbian Families*. Toronto: University of Toronto Press.

> This work is composed of 30 personal interviews with lesbian women from Calgary, Edmonton, and other parts of Alberta regarding issues of blended families, reproduction, and motherhood.

Makeda Silvera, ed. 1991. *Piece of My Heart: A Lesbians of Colour Anthology*. Toronto: Sister Vision.

> Silvera's book is separated into eight sections of poetry and prose by lesbians of various cultural, racial, and class backgrounds on such issues as homophobia, eroticism, acceptance in the community, and coming out.

Margaret S. Schneider, ed. 1997. *Pride and Prejudice: Working with Lesbian, Gay and Bisexual Youth*. Toronto: Central Toronto Youth Services.

> This book provides a needed a guide for teachers, social workers, and social-service workers to assist in strategies to help lesbian, gay, and bisexual youths access services in schools and in social-service institutions.

Jeffrey Weeks. 1991. *Against Nature*. London: Rivers Oram.

> This book provides a thorough discussion of the history of sexuality and sexual identity in the West.

Kath Weston. 1991. *Families We Choose: Lesbians, Gays and Kinship*. New York: Columbia University Press.

> This book presents a thorough discussion of issues facing gay couples, such as family relationships. The book's focus is on issues in the United States.

REFERENCES
▼

Adam, Barry D. 1986. "The Construction of a Sociological 'Homosexual' in Canadian Textbooks." *Canadian Review of Sociology and Anthropology* 23/3: 399–409.

————. 1987. *The Rise of a Lesbian and Gay Movement.* Boston: Twayne.

Anderson, James D., and Ronald Nieberding. 1989. *In Every Classroom: The Report of the President's Select Committee for Lesbian and Gay Concerns.* New Brunswick, NJ: Rutgers University, Office of Student Life Policy and Services.

Arnup, Katherine. 1991. "We Are Family: Lesbian Mothers in Canada." *Resources for Feminist Research* 20 (3–4): 101–107.

Aura, J. 1985. "Women's Social Support: A Comparison of Lesbians and Heterosexuals." Ph.D. dissertation, University of California, Los Angeles.

Baptiste, David A. 1987. "The Gay and Lesbian Stepparent Family." In Frederick Bozett, ed., *Gay and Lesbian Parents.* New York: Praeger.

Bell, Laurie. 1991. *On Our Own Terms: A Practical Guide for Lesbian and Gay Relationships.* Toronto: Coalition for Lesbian and Gay Rights.

Berrill, Kevin T. 1990. "Anti-Gay Violence and Victimization in the United States: An Overview." *Journal of Interpersonal Violence* 5/3: 274–94.

Blumstein, P., and P. Schwartz. 1983. *American Couples: Money, Work, Sex.* New York: William Morrow.

Boyce, Ed. 1991. "Family Protection Act Introduced in Boston." *Gay Community News,* April 9–15, p. 1.

Bozett, Frederick, 1987. "Children of Gay Fathers." In Frederick Bozett, ed., *Gay and Lesbian Parents.* New York: Praeger.

Brown, Eleanor. 1998. "Despised for Being Gay." *Globe and Mail,* October 24, p. D3.

Butler, Becky, ed. 1997. *Ceremonies of the Heart: Celebrating Lesbian Unions.* Seattle: Seal Press.

Chamberland, Line. 1991. "Social Class and Integration in the Lesbian Subculture, Montreal: 1950s." In Sandra Kirby, Danya Daniels, Kate McKenna, Michèle Pujol, and Michele Valiquette, eds., *Women Changing Academe/Les femmes changent l'académie.* Proceedings of the 1990 Canadian Women's Studies Association Conference. Winnipeg: Sororal.

Coalition for Lesbian and Gay Rights in Ontario. 1998. *Spousal Collection.* Toronto: Coalition for Lesbian and Gay Rights in Ontario, October.

Committee on Sexual Offences Against Children and Youths (Canada). 1984. *Sexual Offences Against Children: Report of the Committee on Sexual Offences Against Children and Youths.* Ottawa: Minister of Supply and Services Canada.

Comstock, Gary David. 1991. *Violence against Lesbians and Gay Men.* New York: Columbia University Press.

Desaulniers. Suzanne. 1990. "The Organization of Housework in Lesbian Households." Unpublished paper, Carleton University, Ottawa.

Eldridge, N.S., and L.A. Gilbert. 1990. "Correlates of Relationship Satisfaction in Lesbian Couples." *Psychology of Women Quarterly* 14: 43–62.

Epstein, Rachel. 1996. "Lesbian Families." In Marion Lynn, ed., *Voices: Essays on Canadian Families.* Toronto: Nelson Canada.

Ferren, Don. 1997. "Making Services Accessible to Lesbian, Gay and Bisexual Youth." In Margaret S. Schneider, ed., *Pride and Prejudice: Working with Lesbian, Gay and Bisexual Youth.* Toronto: Central Toronto Youth Services.

Gavigan, Shelley A.M. In press a. "Legal Forms, Family Forms, Gender Norms: What Is a Spouse?" In Marie-Andrée Bertrand, ed., *The Gender and Colour of Legal and Other Normative Systems*. International Orati Series on the Sociology of Law. Halifax: Dartmouth Publishing.

———. In press b. "Mothers, Other Mothers, and Others: The Challenges and Contradictions of Lesbian Parents." In Dorothy E. Chunn and Dany Lacombe, eds., *Engendering Justice*. Toronto: Oxford University Press.

Gibbs, Elizabeth D. 1989. "Psychosocial Development of Children Raised by Lesbian Mothers: A Review of Research." In Esther D. Rothblum and Ellen Cole, eds., *Lesbianism: Affirming Nontraditional Roles*. New York: Haworth.

Gibson, Paul. 1989. "Gay Male and Lesbian Youth Suicide." In M.R. Feinleib, ed., *Report of the Secretary's Task Force on Youth Suicide*. Vol. 3: *Preventions and Interventions in Youth Suicide*. Washington, DC: United States Department of Health and Human Services.

Golden, Carla. 1987. "Diversity and Variability in Women's Sexual Identities." In Boston Lesbian Psychologies Collective, ed., *Lesbian Psychologies*. Urbana: University of Illinois Press.

Golombok, S., A. Spencer, and M. Rutter. 1983. "Children in Lesbian and Single-Parent Households: Psychosexual and Psychiatric Appraisal." *Journal of Child Psychology and Psychiatry* 24: 551–72.

Gomez, Jewelle, and Barbara Smith. 1991. "Taking the Home Out of Homophobia: Black Lesbian Health." In Makeda Silvera, ed., *Piece of My Heart*. Toronto: Sister Vision.

Green, Jesse. 1978. "Sexual Identity of 37 Children Raised by Homosexual or Transsexual Parents." *American Journal of Psychiatry* 135: 692–97.

———. 1982. "The Best Interests of the Child with a Lesbian Mother." *American Academy of Psychiatry and the Law* 10: 7–15.

———. 1991. "This School Is Out." *New York Times Magazine*, October 13, pp. 32–36.

Gunn Allen, Paula. 1991. "Lesbians in American Indian Cultures." In Martin Duberman, Martha Vicinus, and George Chauncey, Jr., eds., *Hidden from History: Reclaiming the Gay and Lesbian Past*. Harmondsworth: Penguin.

Herman, Didi. 1994. *Rights of Passage: Struggles for Lesbian and Gay Equality*. Toronto: University of Toronto Press.

Heron, Ann, ed. 1983. *One Teenager in Ten: Writings by Gay and Lesbian Youth*. Boston: Alyson.

Hoeffer B. 1981. "Child's Acquisition of Sex-Role in Lesbian-Mother Families." *American Journal of Orthopsychiatry* 51: 536–44.

Hunter, Joyce. 1990. "Violence against Lesbian and Gay Male Youths." *Journal of Interpersonal Violence* 5/3: 295–300.

Kaufman, Miriam, and Susan Dundas. 1995. "Directions for Research about Lesbian Families." In K. Arnup, ed., *Lesbian Parenting: Living with Pride and Prejudice*. Charlottetown: Gynergy.

Khayatt, Didi. 1991. "Proper Schooling for Teenage Lesbians." Paper presented at the annual meeting of the Canadian Sociology and Anthropology Association, June, at Kingston, ON.

———. 1992. *Lesbian Teachers: An Invisible Presence.* Albany: State University of New York Press.

Kinsman, Gary. 1987. *The Regulation of Desire: Sexuality in Canada.* Montreal: Black Rose.

———. 1992. "Managing AIDS Organizing: 'Consultation' 'Partnership,' the National AIDS Strategy." In William K. Carroll, ed., *Organizing Dissent: Contemporary Movements in Theory and Practice.* Toronto: Garamond.

Kirkpatrick, M., C. Smith, and R. Roy. 1981. "Lesbian Mothers and Their Children." *American Journal of Orthopsychiatry* 51: 545–51.

Kournay, R.F.C. 1987. "Suicide among Homosexual Adolescents." *Journal of Homosexuality* 13/4: 111–17.

Kruks, Gabe. 1991. "Gay and Lesbian Homeless/Street Youth: Special Issues and Concerns." *Journal of Adolescent Health* 12: 515–18.

Kurdek, Lawrence A. 1988. "Perceived Social Support in Gays and Lesbians in Cohabiting Relationships." *Journal of Personality and Social Psychology* 5/3: 504–509.

Kurdek, Lawrence A., and J.P. Schmitt. 1987. "Perceived Emotional Support from Family and Friends in Members of Gay, Lesbian and Heterosexual Cohabiting Couples." *Journal of Homosexuality* 14: 57–68.

Larson, P.C. 1982. "Gay Male Relationships." In W. Paul, J.D. Weinrich, J.C. Gonsiorek, and M.E. Horvedt, eds., *Homosexuality: Social, Psychological and Biological Issues.* Beverly Hills, CA: Sage.

Lensky, Helen. 1991. "The Treatment of the Sexualities in Research." *Resources for Feminist Research* 19(3–4): 91–93.

Lewin, Ellen. 1994. "Negotiating Lesbian Motherhood: The Dialectics of Resistance and Accommodation." In Evelyn Nakano Glenn, Grace Chang, and Linda Rennie Forcey, eds., *Mothering: Ideology, Experience and Agency.* New York: Routledge.

Lorde, Audre. 1991. "I Am Your Sister: Black Women Organizing across Sexualities." In Makeda Silvera, ed., *Piece of My Heart.* Toronto: Sister Vision.

Lynch, J.M., and M.E. Reilly. 1986. "Role Relationships: Lesbian Perspectives." *Journal of Homosexuality* 12/2: 53–69.

Martin, A. Damian. 1982. "Learning to Hide: The Socialization of the Gay Adolescent." In S.C. Feinstein, J.G. Looney, A. Schwartzberg, and A. Scrosky, eds., *Adolescent Psychiatry: Developmental and Clinical Studies,* vol. 10. Chicago: University of Chicago Press.

McCullagh, John, and Mary Greco. 1990. *Servicing Street Youth: A Feasibility Study.* Toronto: Children's Aid Society of Metropolitan Toronto.

Mirken, Bruce. 1992. "A Child's Worst Nightmare." *The Advocate,* March 6, pp. 56–57.

Neisen, Joseph. 1987. "Resources for Families with a Gay/Lesbian Member." *Journal of Homosexuality* 14: 239–51.

O'Brien, Carol-Anne. 1992. "The Social Organization of the Treatment of Lesbian and Gay Youth in Group Homes and Youth Shelters." Paper, School of Social Work, Carleton University, Ottawa.

Peplau, Letitia Anne. 1991. "Lesbian and Gay Relationships." In John C. Gonsiorek and James D. Weinrich, eds., *Homosexuality: Research Implications for Public Policy*. Newbury Park, CA: Sage.

Pies, Cheri. 1987. "Considering Parenthood: Psychosocial Issues for Gay Men and Lesbians Choosing Alternative Fertilization." In Frederick Bozett, ed., *Gay and Lesbian Parents*. New York: Praeger.

Polikoff, Nancy D. 1987. "Lesbian Mothers, Lesbian Families: Legal Obstacles, Legal Challenges." In Sandra Pollack and Jeanne Vaughan, eds., *Politics of the Heart*. Ithaca, NY: Firebrand.

Pollack, Sandra. 1987. "Lesbian Mothers: A Lesbian Feminist Perspective on Research." In Sandra Pollack and Jeanne Vaughan, eds., *Politics of the Heart*. Ithaca, NY: Firebrand.

Prairie Research Associates and Gay and Lesbian Youth Services Network. 1989. *Survey of Lesbians and Gay Youth and Professionals Who Work with Youth*. Winnipeg: Prairie Research Associates and Gay and Lesbian Youth Services Network.

Rainbow Enterprises. 1998. Press Release. November 11. Paula Miles, Project Manager; Philip Shaw, Media Relations Coordinator. Toronto.

Raphael, S., and M. Robinson. 1984. "The Older Lesbians, Love Relationships and Friendship Patterns." In Trudy Darty and Sandy Potter, eds., *Women-Identified Women*. Palo Alto, CA: Mayfield.

Re. K. (1995) 23 *Ontario Reports* (3d).

Remafedi, G. 1987. "Male Homosexuality: The Adolescent's Perspective." *Pediatrics* 79/3: 326–30.

Remafedi, G., J.A. Farrow, and R.W. Deisher. 1991. "Risk Factors for Attempted Suicide in Gay and Bisexual Youth." *Pediatrics* 87/6: 869–75.

Ross, Becki L. 1990. "Sexual Dis/Orientation or Playing House: To Be or Not to Be Coded Human." In Sharon Dale Stone, ed., *Lesbians in Canada*. Toronto: Between the Lines.

———. 1995. *The House that Jill Built: A Lesbian Nation in Formation*. Toronto: University of Toronto Press.

Sander, Douglas. 1997. *Same-Sex Partner Immigration: Does Canadian Law Support Us?* Vancouver: Lesbian and Gay Immigration Task Force.

Sang, B. 1984. "Lesbian Relationships: A Struggle toward Partner Equality." In Trudy Darty and Sandy Potter, eds., *Women-Identified Women*. Palo Alto, CA: Mayfield.

Saperstein, S. 1981. "Lesbian and Gay Adolescents. The Need for Family Support." *Catalyst* 3/4: 61–70.

Schneider, Margaret S., ed. 1997. *Pride and Prejudice: Working with Lesbian, Gay and Bisexual Youth*. Toronto: Central Toronto Youth Services.

Sears, James. 1989. "The Impact of Gender and Race on Growing Up Lesbian and Gay in the South." *National Women's Studies Association Journal* 1/3: 422–57.

Seattle Commission on Children and Youth. 1988. *Report on Gay and Lesbian Youth in Seattle*. Seattle: City of Seattle Department of Human Resources.

Smith, George W. 1988. "Policing the Gay Community: An Inquiry into Textually-Mediated Social Relations." *International Journal of Sociology* 16: 163–83.

———. 1990. "Politics Activist as Ethnographer." *Social Problems* 37/4: 629–48.

———. 1991. "The Ideology of 'Fag': Barriers to Education for Gay Students." Paper presented at the annual meetings of the Canadian Sociology and Anthropology Association at Kingston, Ontario, and the Society for the Study of Social Problems, at Cincinnati, Ohio.

Steckel, Ailsa. 1985. "Separation-Individuation in Children of Lesbian and Heterosexual Couples." Unpublished Ph.D. thesis, Wright Institute, Berkeley, CA.

———. 1987. "Psychosocial Development of Children of Lesbian Mothers." In Frederick Bozett, ed., *Gay and Lesbian Parents*. New York: Praeger.

Stuckey, Johanna H. 1998. *Feminist Spirituality: An Introduction to Feminist Theology in Judaism, Christianity, Islam and Feminist Goddess Worship*. Toronto: York University, Centre for Feminist Research.

Sullivan, Terrence. 1992. *Sexual Abuse and the Rights of Children: Reforming Canadian Law*. Toronto: University of Toronto Press.

Testa, R.J., B.N. Kinder, and G. Ironson. 1987. "Heterosexual Bias in the Perception of Loving Relationships of Gay Males and Lesbians." *Journal of Sex Research* 23/2: 163–72.

Thompson, K., and J. Andrzejewski. 1988. *Why Can't Sharon Kowalski Come Home?* San Francisco: Spinsters/Aunt Lute.

Uribe, Virginia, and Karen M. Harbeck. 1992. "Addressing the Needs of Lesbian, Gay and Bisexual Youth: The Origins of Project 10 and School-Based Intervention" In K.M. Harbeck, ed., *Coming Out of the Classroom Closet: Gay and Lesbian Students, Teachers, and Curricula*. New York: Haworth.

Watters, Alan. 1986. "Heterosexual Bias in Psychological Research on Lesbian and Male Homosexuality (1979–1983)." *Journal of Homosexuality* 13/1: 35–58.

Weeks, Jeffrey. 1991. "Pretended Family Relationships." In Jeffrey Weeks, *Against Nature*. London: Rivers Oram.

Weston, Kath. 1991. *Families We Choose: Lesbians, Gays and Kinship*. New York: Columbia University Press.

Williams, Walter L. 1992. "Benefits for Nonhomophobic Societies: An Anthropological Perspective." In Warren J. Blumenfield, ed., *Homophobia*. Boston: Beacon.

Willmott, Peter. 1987. *Friendship Networks and Social Support*. London: Policy Studies Institute.

▼

FAMILIES OF NATIVE PEOPLE, IMMIGRANTS, AND PEOPLE OF COLOUR

TANIA DAS GUPTA

LEARNING OBJECTIVES

In this chapter, you will learn that:

- the "family" form has not always been nuclear and heterosexual (Das Gupta, 1994; Latham and Pazdro, 1984; Chapter 4 in this text);
- women and men of colour and immigrants have not always had the right to live in a "family" context in Canada, a right that white Canadians take for granted (Thornhill, 1991; Brand, 1991). Therefore, roles played by men and women of colour have not been the stereotyped ones that white feminists often take for granted as a point of departure;
- when women of colour have been allowed to live in it, the "family" form has generally been oppressive to them, but it has also been a support and refuge in an otherwise hostile environment;
- immigrant women and women of colour have to go beyond gender to understand their situations in the world. This means that we have to take into account race and class oppressions as well as privileges (*Fireweed*, 1983; Vorst et al., 1991) and thus make alliances with the working class, and with men of colour, on these grounds;
- forms of resistance that have emanated from these varied realities and experiences have historically not been recognized as "feminist" because they don't adhere to a traditional mould. The mould itself needs to be re-examined because of its exclusionary parameters.

INTRODUCTION

This chapter presents an antiracist perspective on the "family" in Canada that departs from traditional discussion of the subject. Since it is often assumed that the "family" is of a standard form, variations are neither acknowledged nor discussed. Authors implicitly assume that the "family" unit is male-dom-inated, white, middle-class, nuclear, and heterosexual. This image does not allow for variations of class, **ethnicity**, or sexuality. Such a stereotype is rein-forced by ideological institutions and processes in society, most conspicuously by the mass media.

Therefore, traditional discussion of the "family" falls into an **essentialist** trap, reinforcing a **functionalist** notion of the "complementary" roles played by men and women. Conflicts and oppressions are not acknowledged, and, if they were, would be defined away as "deviance" (Parsons and Bales, 1955). Variations of "family" forms among people of colour, for example, extended families, single-parent families, and multiple-parent families, would also be seen as deviant and in need of being resocialized to conform to the dominant form.

This chapter looks at variations in families among Native people and people of colour in Canada and then analyzes how these variations, in most instances, have been socially organized according to the imperatives of a **capitalist** society and its associated interventionist state (Panitch, 1977). State policies in the area of immigration and racism have historically had a funda-mental effect on families and on communities of colour. We will see that peo-ple of colour have frequently been denied the right to have the "family" form of their choice and that this denial has been historically motivated by racism, an ideology that has been invoked explicitly or implicitly by the Canadian state. Also, we will see that the demand for "a family" has been one of the major organizing principles of **communities of colour** in Canada.

In this chapter, I put the word "family" in quotation marks to indicate that the word has sexist and racist connotations. Carol Yawney, an anthropol-ogist, has commented that we could use other words to refer to a **household**, such as "clan" or "band" (Personal communication). As a compromise, I use the plural "families" to indicate that there are many different forms of house-holds operating in different communities.

CRITICAL REVIEW AND THEORETICAL FRAMEWORK
▼

The most powerful critique of traditional theories and reports on the "family" came from feminist writers, activists, and theoreticians (de Beauvoir, 1952; Greer, 1970; Steinem, 1983), who pointed out that the roles played by women within their families were far from ideal and in fact reinforced a second-class role for women marked by oppression, boredom, and non-recognition. By ignoring the problems in families, particularly those arising from relationships between men and women, we were delivering not a complete picture of the institution, but a partial picture, one that represents a patriarchal vantage point.

By not looking at the experiences of women in families, we were perpetuating the invisibility of women's work as well as our silence in academic discourse. Feminist contribution to sociological theory has been, therefore, a focus on women's experience and making gender a framework for analysis (Smith, 1977).

A whole range of feminist literature on families has developed that looks at women's work in their homes (Dalla Costa and James, 1972; Fox, 1980; Luxton and Rosenberg, 1986) and its connection to work outside their homes (Armstrong and Armstrong, 1984; Connelly, 1978; Gannage, 1986). Among feminist writers, different approaches have been developed — namely, the liberal, radical, and socialist strains (Armstrong and Armstrong, 1984).

Socialist feminism most vociferously argues for the need to look at any social reality, including those of women, in the context of the larger political and economic relations that affect it. Historians such as Fox-Genovese (1982) argue that separating "official" (read: men's) and "other" (read: women's) history results in perpetuating, rather than challenging, the status quo. I would add that this argument is also accurate for white, Eurocentric history versus the history of people of colour. Socialist-feminist historians argue for the inclusion of political economy and class both in understanding gender and family and in engaging in a transformation process. They add that simply replacing "official" history with "women's" history maintains the ideological underpinnings of the former and the biological "otherness" of the latter, which forms a powerful ideology on which gender inequality is based.

Fox-Genovese writes of the "complexity of human motivation" that persuades members of oppressed communities to participate in and reproduce their own oppressions as well as that of others. This is the issue of **ideological hegemony**, which Antonio Gramsci pioneered (Wotherspoon, 1987). This also makes it imperative to look at ideological relations simultaneously with political and economic relations.

Cross-cultural variations in families have been pointed out by feminists such as Nett (1988, p. 83) and socialist-feminist anthropologists such as Reiter (1975); however, variations have been linked to different stages of economic development in societies. In other words, communities of colour have been studied anthropologically by white women but frequently in the context of looking at pre-capitalist societies. It is as if these communities of colour existed in the distant past and are now terminated. One is left to wonder what is happening in those societies today and how gender relations are being carried on within a global political economy. This omission of historical continuity perpetuates a **stereotype of** people of colour being stagnant and exotic, which fuels modern-day racist images of non-European societies.

When we look at the literature about racial and ethnic variations in families, we see a patriarchal bias. Issues of race and gender are conspicuously unexplored (Ishwaran, 1980). However, this strain of research did illustrate that families, as institutions, play a crucial role in reproducing ethnicity and also in facilitating the adaptation process for new immigrants and refugees. The problem with this literature is that it does not represent women's experiences in their families. Nor does it discuss gender and class relations. It assumes that the experiences of men and women within families are the same. It also does not relate families to the role of the state and the general political environment, although **multiculturalism** is often assumed as a benevolent given. Values, beliefs, and behaviours within families of immigrants and Native people are explored, often over generations, to study the effect of the **acculturation** process on the internal workings of families. The influence of the larger political economy on immigrants, Native people, and families of colour is a highly problematic one, and is closely tied to the racism and sexism that were the foundations of the project of nation building in which the state was and is actively involved.

Since the 1980s, there has been a growing literature documenting, from women's standpoints, the experiences of immigrant women and women of colour in families and communities in Canada (Brand, 1991; Brant, 1988; Das Gupta, 1986; *Fireweed*, 1983; Iacovetta, 1987; Latham and Pazdro, 1984; *Polyphony*, 1986). Much of this has been written by Native women, women of colour, and immigrant women. What was hidden in the household, and thus in history, is now slowly being uncovered, documented, and published.

Such writings on women's experiences not only fill a gap in "official" historical writings, but also provide a certain feminist perspective that has been a revitalizing force within the movements of women, organized labour, and people of colour (Leah, 1991). This perspective has been referred to in academic discourse as the "race, gender, class" perspective, that is, the intertwining of different yet simultaneous levels of oppression experienced by working-class women and women of colour (Vorst et al., 1991).

The demand for a "family" historically became an antiracist, feminist, and working-class agenda, given oppressive state policies. The state has maintained a capitalist mode of production as well as reproducing racist, sexist, and classist structures through its various policies, including immigration policies and such laws as the Indian Act. Through such policies, the state has regulated the "family" form of Native people, immigrants, and people of colour. It has rationalized doing so with various hegemonic ideologies, such as racism and gender. Hence, the "family" has become a terrain of struggle not just for men and women but also for communities of colour and immigrant communities vis-à-vis the state.

The questions this chapter will try to answer are: What have been the dominant structural characteristics of Native families, families of colour, and

immigrant families? How have these been outcomes of dominant state policies and practices? How have race, class, and gender ideologies mediated dominant policies and practices? And how have Native people, people of colour,
and immigrants resisted these policies and practices?

NATIVE PEOPLE
▼

GENOCIDE OF THE CULTURE, GENOCIDE OF THE FAMILY

It is erroneous to talk about Native families for two reasons. First, Native
peoples are composed of a number of distinct nations with different histories,
cultures, economic bases, languages, and dialects. So it is important to be specific when making sociological assertions. Second, the devastation of Native
families has been only one part of the Canadian government's genocidal policies. In their application to Native people, education, social services, economic development, and the justice system are euphemisms, as has been well
documented by both Native (York, 1989) and non-Native people (Johnston,
1983). The destruction of Native families has taken place in the context of
colonial domination, which has led to economic devastation, poverty, and
social disintegration.

When Europeans landed on this continent, they encountered well-devel-
oped, highly organized, and stable formations of Native societies, including
family formations. Families varied in lineage and locality, but they were
extended, and women and men related to each other with reciprocity and sharing (Bourgeault, 1991; Brant, 1988). Such family structures were supported
by an economic infrastructure that was itself based on reciprocity, sharing, and
production for subsistence of the community. The products of labour were
appropriated not by one class or group of people, but by the community or
band (Bourgeault, 1991; Van Kirk, 1980).

However, these arrangements were a hindrance to the European project
of colonization and capitalism. In order to subjugate and disempower Native
people, the mercantile colonizers embarked on a campaign to penetrate,
exploit, and distort Native families, and finally to destroy them altogether.

Bourgeault (1991) talks about the experience of the Dene-Chipewyan
people of the subarctic in the seventeenth century onwards, when the Hudson's
Bay Company and the North West Company established fur-trading posts.
The fur trade could not have been pursued without a suitable and sufficient
pool of labour. Native women were appropriated by selective "enslavement."
They were taught about mercantile trade and then used as conduits for
mobilizing their own band members to work as labourers for the trade post.

A male **comprador** class was thus created among the people, transforming Native egalitarian relations between men and women into hierarchical and dependent ones.

In the absence of white European women, white officials took "wives," often by force, initially from the Native community and later from the racially preferred Métis community (Bourgeault, 1991, p. 104; Canadian Association in Support of Native Peoples [CASNP], 1978, p. 34). These women were used to transport goods, prepare furs, make shoes, knit, stitch, and "keep house" for white men. Native men became the hunters and trappers for the companies, and also acted as middlemen in the fur trade. Women's labour was thus diverted from their own communities toward the maintenance of individual men and the colonial trading companies. Native men sometimes resorted to "several wives" in order to accomplish their middlemen roles. Bourgeault (1991) critiques the conclusion made by some that communal societies were polygamous by arguing that the existence of several wives was a creation of mercantile capitalism, imposed on egalitarian Native societies.

Initially, most Métis children were abandoned by their white fathers and grew up as Native people. Later, white fathers attempted to assimilate the children, particularly females, into European Christian culture with the assertion that Native culture was inferior.

As capitalism predominated and immigration from all over the world took hold, the labour of Native peoples, including the Métis, was not as crucial as it had been in the early years of capitalist development. Nor was Native peoples' labour as malleable as that of immigrants, since Natives retained the option of not assimilating into the predominant capitalist system. So the European colonialists, with the help of the Church, adopted a strategy of biological and cultural **assimilation** of Native peoples. At the centre of this approach lay an effort to destroy Native family formations, including by the destruction of Native children.

The net result of European colonization for the Nedut'en of British Columbia, for example, as no doubt for many other Native peoples in Canada, has been intergenerational alienation and breakdown of family life due to loss of traditional Native lands, culture, and systems.

Through conversion to European religions, sacred rituals and practices to ensure socialization of succeeding generations are no longer employed. Parents who were removed from their own families as children and sent to residential schools were not familiar with intimate familial relationships; when they raised their own children, they often used harsh, punitive methods that masked their good intentions. Children did not understand why their parents behaved as they did, and were sometimes resentful, further damaging familial relations (Fiske and Johnny, 1996).

Fiske and Johnny (1996) also relate the way that forced relocation of the Nedut'en for the purpose of providing labour for sawmills helped to dismantle their ancestral way of life. The new settlement was outside traditional lands, so older members of the group felt dislocated, while the youngsters were left to grow up in a village that gave no sense of continuity with the group's past. This has led to sadness and tensions in families, and a fear that the young generations have lost both respect for and understanding of time-honoured practices that made the Nedut'en family and community strong (Fiske and Johnny, 1996, p. 235).

Another negative impact on family life has been greater dependence on cash, supplanting the old system of co-operative communal production in which reciprocity and pooling of foods and other resources among extended kin was the norm. Family ties among various relatives were sustained in this way, particularly due to the obligations engendered by the performance of services that required payment in kind and reciprocity (Fiske and Johnny, 1996). Money does not have the same character; it does not create the same sense of responsibility for, and co-operation with, one's fellows.

Two institutions that have played very key roles in the destruction of Native children are the schools and the child-welfare agencies.

John's story (see Box 5.1) encapsulates the vicious cycle set up by the interplay of white institutions — the educational system, the "just-us" (justice) system, and the child-"welfare" system — as well as the predominant racist culture of everyday life, which have culminated in the devastation of Native individuals, families, communities, and nations.

Residential schools provide the most dramatic examples of what education did to Native children and to families. York (1989, p. 22) presents vivid documentation of the horror of missionary teachers and government officials threatening bodily harm or arrest to force Native parents to send their young children to residential schools. Residential schools were hostels where children were separated from their families, prevented from speaking their own languages and practising their own traditions, and made to practise a semi-militaristic lifestyle, including wearing uniforms and having their hair shaved off. They were brainwashed to believe in the "goodness" of the Bible and the "barbarism" of Native religions. All this happened with the aid of severe corporal punishment, and, frequently, these children were sexually abused. Generations of depression, alcoholism, suicide, and family breakdown are the legacy of such traumatic experiences and are described as the "residential school syndrome" by Native peoples themselves (York, 1989, p. 37).

The abuse at such schools seems to be only one part of a litany of abuse, including sexual abuse, that Native children experience at the hands of non-Native men in powerful positions. In some Native communities, up to 94 percent

BOX 5.1
▼
JOHN'S STORY

My mother is Mohawk, my father was Ojibway. My mother was single. At that time, the Children's Aid could scoop up children by declaring a parent unfit just for being single. My mother lied about my background by saying that I was French Canadian. If she had said that I was Native, I would have been scooped. This story was hidden from me until I was 11 years old.

Then, they [Children's Aid] farm them [children] out to white families. It does wonders to the mind. I have been mistaken as everything [Portuguese ...] other than Native. The children lose all links with their families. There is a brother serving a sentence now in Stoney Mountain. He was scooped and fostered by a single male who abused him physically and sexually. He [brother] drank and tried to commit suicide. Finally, he killed his father. Now, some reserve people are standing up to it [adoptions by non-Natives] and support- ing the mother and the child. In the 1920s, a law was passed that it was ille- gal for three or more Natives to gather together.

In the early 1970s, it was illegal to practise our culture — the pipe, the sweatlodge, burning sweetgrass. ... I am thankful to the elders who continued these practices, sometimes hidden in caves. Natives did not vote till the 1960s. Many Natives fought in the war. When they got back, they were treated not just as second-class citizens but as third-class citizens. A lawyer could go to jail for representing Natives.

I was the only Native in school [in the city]. Let's say I have a birthday party. I was not allowed to attend their birthday party. It messes you up. It plants the seed of hate. It creates anger. After a point, they [the white kids] weren't allowed [by white parents] to play with me. I remember rolling up into a tight ball on my porch just to be outside. My daughter has been called "half- breed." We have told her to fight back. She was called into the principal's office. Nothing happened to the child who started the whole thing. I told him that if you want me to discipline my child, and nothing happens to the other child, I'm not doing it.

I went to a training school, which is like a residential school. I was sent to the hole [solitary confinement] for standing up for some friends who were speaking in their [Native] language. I also experienced sexual abuse there.

If you're on the reserve, the secondary school is one or two hours away. You have to go in a car. The majority have to board there. You can imagine the racism in the town. Most drop out.

(continued)

(Box 5.1 continued)

I have been fifteen years in and out of institutions. I was lashing out against the racism and abuse. My mother married a European man. There was differentiation between their [white] children and me. Others have also had similar experiences. My mother tried to pass on traditional ways — I remember she gave me a pouch of tobacco every time she had a request. She was showing me respect.

Let me tell you about the "just-us" [justice] system. A Native man in Saskatchewan went in to sell his gun. He wanted to do it the right way. He went into a store instead of selling it privately. The owner said that he did not want to buy anything from an Indian. As he turned to leave the store, the owner shot some bullets near his legs. The Native man kept walking toward the door. Another bullet was shot near his hand. As he turned the doorknob, he was shot in the back. He lay near the door in his blood for five minutes before the ambulance was called. The killer got four years in jail, saying he didn't know if his gun was loaded or not and he is out on appeal.

When a Native person goes to court, [he or she] is asked if [she or he] is guilty. We have no concept of guilt. We have either "done something" or "not done something." Most of the Native inmates are in for petty crimes, and they haven't been able to pay the fines.

I came in touch with [Native] people in the last two years. With two other brothers who have done time, I have started the ... Circle with Youth. It is a healing process.

Source: Interview with author, 1992.

of the residents were sexually abused as children (York, 1989, p. 30). Most children attending residential school started young, and many stayed for years without holidays and without any contacts with their parents and their communities. Separating children from their families was one of the chief ways the institution could break all cultural links with Native education, culture, and language.

In the absence of good parental role models and the total absence of Native role models, residential schools produced generations of Native adults with minimal parenting skills, coupled with symptoms of residential-school syndrome. This frequently produced abuse within Native families (Locust, 1990). Diana Nason, a former program supervisor at Native Child and Family Services of Toronto, confirmed the persistence of this vicious cycle (interview with author, 1992).

Native children in residential schools retaliated by running away, dropping out, or conducting mass boycotts (York, 1989, p. 22), but many had to remain and endure the abuse. The movement for self-government in education gained strength in 1969, when residents of Saddle Lake Reserve, in north-eastern Alberta, demanded that some Native teachers be hired at the nearby residential school and later took control of the administration of the school after a sit-in that lasted a few weeks.

Now, Native bands operate schools on reserves, and some operate boards of education. This strategy has ended the abuse and the forced separation of Native children from their families and communities and is reversing the drop-out trends. Unfortunately, the federal government continues to cut back its commitment to fund Native education. There are still thousands of Native students who must attend provincial schools, where non-Native curricula, white teachers, and white officials dominate, and where they still face an alienated and colonial educational system that ignores the historical experience of Native peoples.

Just as the residential-school system was being phased out in the 1960s, the child-welfare system stepped into view in the form of Children's Aid Services, which removed Native children from their parents on the pretext that the parents were "inconsistent" or "abusive." This was a dominant phenomenon in most Native communities on- and off-reserve.

In 1979, a national report on adoption and welfare found that 20 percent of children in foster care were Native, while only 6 percent of the Canadian population were Native (Hudson and McKenzie, 1981, p. 63). In Manitoba, 60 percent of children in foster care were Native, while the Native population in the province was 12 percent of the total. In the 1970s, 80 percent of Native children in Kenora, Ontario, were in "care" (Native Child and Family Services of Toronto, 1991). This trend continued into the early 1980s (York, 1989, p. 206).[1] Most children were placed in non-Native homes, including homes outside Canada. In the 1990s, this trend is being reversed to a certain extent, with more Native empowerment and the growing movement in support of Native people adopting Native children (interview with Ken Richard, Executive Director, Native Child and Family Services of Toronto, 1998).

How did such high numbers of adoptions of Native children come about in cultures where "kids are considered as sacred gifts" and where "nobody owned the children, except the community" (Diana Nason, interview with author, 1992)? Hudson and McKenzie (1981) have answered this question by analyzing the non-Native child-welfare system as an agent of colonization of Native peoples. They have argued that this colonial relationship has three characteristics — namely, the lack of decision-making power in the Native community, the devaluation of Native parenting and child-welfare practices, and the nature of interaction between Native and non-Native societies that reproduces the subordination of the former and the domination of the latter.

The lack of decision-making power in the communities and families from which Native children have been removed is borne out by Native people's use of adjectives such as "scooped," "abducted," and "kidnapped" (Brant, 1988, p. 100). York (1989) describes several cases where government removed infants to hospitals for treatment and then placed them in foster homes near the hospital, where they remained, even though their parents had never been abusive to them.

Nason (interview with author, 1992) confirmed that, once a child's file is closed after adoption, it is difficult to get any information about her or his natural parents and family. In the case of **non-Status** and Métis children, it is even more difficult to trace family roots. Even today, there are about twenty Native foster homes in Metro Toronto. York (1989, p. 215) points out that the criteria used by child-welfare agencies to designate foster homes are class- and race-biased. For example, requirements for steady incomes and a separate bedroom for each adult family member automatically disqualify most Native homes, particularly on reserves. At present, out of fourteen Native child-welfare organizations in Ontario, only five are mandated to remove children "for protection" from abuse. Thus, the limitation of power of the Native community in this regard lends support to the colonization thesis advanced by Hudson and McKenzie (1981).

Native peoples are unique in Canada as being the only communities that have been defined by the government in a piece of legislation, the Indian Act, which was passed in 1876 (*Midnight Sun*, 1988, p. 78). The descendants of those who did not sign treaties or become registered are not defined as "Indian." Until 1960, a Native person had to renounce "Indian" status in order to vote, go to university, buy liquor, or live off-reserve. Before 1985, Native women who married non-Native men lost their status as "Indians" (as did their children) unless they subsequently married Native men. This meant that they could not reside on-reserve and they lost all inheritance rights. Moreover, they and their children could not go back to their families on-reserve in case of being widowed, separated, or divorced (CASNP, 1978, p. 4). This policy was challenged by Jeanette Corbiere-Lavell in 1973. Although she did not win her case, the campaign united large numbers of Native women and started a movement to reform the Indian Act.

The social workers and child-welfare workers are mainly middle-class non-Natives who undoubtedly bring their own biases in defining "abuse" and "dysfunctional families" (York, 1989; Johnston, 1983). Carol Locust (1990) discusses several examples of classifying traditional child-rearing practices as "abusive." The practice common to extended families of a child living with her or his grandparents, aunts, or uncles has often been interpreted as abuse. Diana Nason (interview with author, 1992) related a situation in which a Native couple used to leave their child with one set of grandparents on the weekends while they indulged in drinking. These parents were defined as "inconsistent parents" and their child was removed from them.

Children in Native cultures are treated as fully developed human beings deserving of full respect. Children are therefore not "forced" or "disciplined" into anything, a characteristic mentioned also by John (interview with author, anonymity requested, 1992). Older Native children have been known to take on significant household responsibilities, particularly around child care. These roles have sometimes been interpreted as "contributing to delinquency."

Similarly, Native parents who encourage their children to participate in traditional ceremonies, which may require them to be absent from school, have been blamed for not providing an environment conducive to educational success.

A "blaming the victim" mentality has always existed, as far as the Native community is concerned. Disproportionately high rates of post-neonatal deaths and a variety of illnesses are often used to justify classifying Native parents as "unfit," without explaining that these health problems occur predominantly as a result of poverty and discrimination.

In the face of such systematic genocidal policies, many in the Native communities have resorted to self-destructive behaviours such as alcoholism, sniffing gasoline, and suicide to escape the pain of daily survival (York, 1989; *Midnight Sun*, 1988, p. 78). This in turn has reinforced the predominant racist stereotypes that non-Native societies hold about Native people.

RESISTANCE TO GENOCIDE

After generations of colonial domination and the resulting politics of divide and rule, Native peoples have achieved a sense of unity for a common goal — self-government. As John said: "The Mohawk, Micmac, Ojibway, and others were united in the Oka crisis. In the West, the Blood, the Cree, and the Blackfoot Confederacy are talking together. ... They realize who the common enemy is" (interview with author, 1992). Groups such as Indian Rights for Indian Women and the Native Women's Association of Canada have taken up the struggle for women in these communities, including fighting discrimination contained in the Indian Act (CASNP, 1978).

With the presentation of the paper "Indian Control of Indian Education" by the National Indian Brotherhood in 1972, there emerged a movement for reclaiming Native indigenous values in education. Now, as a result of consistent Native lobbying, there is some recognition by non-Native people, particularly the government, that it is essential for Native peoples to educate their own children with their own curricula, teachers, and administration and, most important, with the involvement of their parents and local bands. However, the battle is far from over, for Native educators face a lack of funds from the federal government, which limits their objective. Most Native children still

attend provincial schools in which Native community participation is minimal. Therefore, their educational experience is still biased, foreign, and irrelevant, a situation that maintains their high drop-out rates.

York (1989, p. 26) describes one school where a boycott was organized
by four bands whose children attended the school. The Ojibway of Sabaskong
Bay created their own schools, hired their own teachers, and started schooling
their own children. In the end, the Indian Affairs department was forced to
fund the Native school.

Self-government in the area of social services and child welfare is also a
growing movement, with organizations such as Anishnawbe Health Toronto,
which provides culturally sensitive health care to Native people in Toronto,
and Native Child and Family Services (NCFS) of Toronto, which tackles child
welfare in the off-reserve population in Toronto. The NCFS has launched several innovative programs, based on Native values, to intervene in situations of
child abuse in Native families. For instance, they can remove a Native child to
a "Native support home" in the same city. They have also started a "customary care program" (NCFS, 1991), which is an adaptation of the principle of
the extended-family form so important in Native cultures. If parents are in
need of child-care support, they have the right to name an extended-family
member or trusted friend as an alternative caregiver. In the absence of such
options, NCFS can match parents with other Native families who have volunteered to extend such help. By means of these programs, NCFS is trying to
use Native values and traditions in promoting child welfare. An important
departure here from the non-Native system is the maintenance of ties between
children and their natural parents, keeping Native families together as well as
caring for children in their Native communities. NCFS will soon be mandated
to take children into protective custody (interview with Ken Richard, 1998).

IMMIGRANTS AND PEOPLE OF COLOUR
▼

THE CONSTRUCTION OF "SINGLE" AND "TEMPORARY" STATUS

As Iacovetta and colleagues (1998) demonstrate, "sojourners" to Canada have
been perhaps as common as settlers. Men from various Asian countries who
migrated to Canada in the nineteenth century have been generally referred to
as "sojourners," implying that they never intended to settle in Canada. The male
"sojourners" have been either single or married with families back home, living
in bachelor communities. These men came to Canada from rural villages to
work in railway- and road-building, in the lumber industry, and mining, to
name a few of their generally dangerous, unskilled, and low-paying jobs. They

engaged in this type of work arrangement in order to supplement their incomes in their countries of origin. They came alone and were "sojourners" not out of their own choice, but because women's entry into Canada and their employment here were restricted. On the other hand, women in specified numbers were recruited as domestics; they were single women or women who stated that they were single for official purposes. During the late nineteenth century and the early decades of the twentieth century, Canadian immigration policy favoured European settlers who would come to Canada's West to engage in agriculture. Thus, settlers were in the main white and comprised families, and "sojourners" were usually single, working-class, and non-white (Iacovetta et al., 1998).

Chinese Families

In the absence of appropriate and adequate European immigration in the late 1800s, and because of the near genocide of Native peoples, about 15 000 Chinese men were admitted into Canada to work on the railways, despite protests from B.C. politicians and people at large. However, once the railway was completed in 1885, the Chinese Immigration Act was passed to restrict the entrance of the Chinese by imposing a $50 head tax, which rose to $500 per head by 1903.

The wives of Chinese labourers usually stayed behind in China, not always because they wanted to, but often because they or their husbands could not afford the head taxes. Valerie Mah, a Toronto teacher and historian, called the Toronto Chinese community between 1878 and 1924 the "bachelor" society because of the absence of women (Dunphy, 1987). The head tax was a way of systemically excluding a group of people because of race, ethnicity, and sex.

The women who did come numbered under 100 in 1885, and either were the wives of merchants or were prostitutes (Van Dieren, 1984). The tiny middle class of traders and merchants in the Chinese community and their wives were not required to pay the head tax between 1911 and 1923. Furthermore, their economic status and ability to procure trade for Canada meant that, even when the period of exclusion was in effect from 1923 to 1947, during which no Chinese immigration was officially allowed, these men and women enjoyed special privileges. Given capitalism's constant search for investment, Canada has always encouraged entrepreneurial immigrants. However, it should be noted that there were very few women in this elite group of Chinese (Man, 1996, p. 273). The wives of immigrant businessmen became important as co-managers and unpaid workers, thus saving on labour expenses and also maintaining a passive labour pool.

The sexuality of people of colour is always a problem for a racist society. Single male Chinese workers posed a threat of **miscegenation** to white Canadians. Pon (1996) describes how Chinese masculinity was presented in the Toronto newspaper *Jack Canuck* in the early part of this century as being dangerous and feminine at the same time. Chinese men were thought to lust after white women, seeking to assuage their perilous hunger by luring these women behind the partitions of their laundries or restaurants into their private lairs, then seducing them with wine and opium so that they could have sexual relations with them. Many Canadians believed that white women were particularly susceptible to the cunning advances of these falsely smiling, docile-appearing Asian men, since white women were held to be naïve and weak. The very signs of oppression in Chinese men — the smiling subservience — were demonized by white writers for *Jack Canuck*. They warned their readers not to trust the apparent docility displayed by these Chinese men: the smiles were meant to lure innocents into their devious clutches, to the ultimate ruination of the innocents; the Chinese were mocking their white superiors with their smiles. When Chinese men attended Christian churches, seeking conversion, it was held that they were really seeking the company of unsuspecting white girls. Chinese men were even condemned for their audacity in erecting partitions in their small businesses to hide their private quarters from white scrutiny; they were accused in the pages of *Jack Canuck* of using their businesses as fronts for less legitimate pursuits, and readers were led to believe that Chinese men were carrying on all manner of dastardly deeds behind these barriers when the reality is that they were eating and sleeping there. Denied their families, Chinese men were evidently not to be allowed to have any privacy either. Relegated to the lower strata of Canadian society, largely as providers of services, Chinese men had to display their humility to white society in order to earn a living; as a result, they were even denied their masculinity, as their demeanour was not considered manly enough by white Canadians. Yet the sexuality of Chinese men was still believed to be dangerous, especially in the face of the weakness and gullibility of young white women. One solution to this dilemma was to import female Chinese prostitutes. However, the presence of prostitutes raised fears of a rise in the population of Chinese immigrants as well as the seduction of white boys (Van Dieren, 1984).

South Asian Families

As in the case of Chinese immigrants, immigrants from the Indian subcontinent, referred to as South Asians, were prevented from coming to Canada by systemic barriers. By an immigration stipulation of 1908, South Asians could land in Canada only by continuous journey. Yet the Canadian Pacific Railway, which operated the only continuous steamship passage on that route, was forbidden to sell any tickets. Moreover, under the Immigration Act of 1910, each Asian immigrant had to possess $200 to enter Canada. These two rules effectively prevented the entry of South Asians (Jamal, 1998).

Before World War II, male Punjabi labourers comprised most of the immigrants to Canada. They settled in rural areas of British Columbia but were denied basic rights extended to other citizens of Canada, such as the vote, the right to buy property, and to live wherever they chose (Dhruvarajan, 1996, p. 302).

South Asian women were banned from Canada, although, in 1910, the wives of two professional men entered (Doman, 1984). Immigration of South Asian women of all classes was decried by society at large, including white women's groups, for fear of encouraging the settlement of South Asians in Canada.

It was not until 1919 that South Asian women could enter Canada, and then only as wives. Repeated pressure from British colonial officials at the Imperial War Conferences, held between 1917 and 1919, had the ban removed. Yet few women and children emigrated to Canada because they were formally required to be registered as legitimate "wives and children" in India, and few procedures facilitated marriage registrations there until 1924. Between 1921 and 1923, only eleven women and nine children entered (Doman, 1984, p. 102). Older children could not emigrate to reunite with their parents, a rule that disregarded the fact that, unlike Canadian children, older children often lived with their parents up to the time of their marriage.

When women started coming in small numbers to join their husbands, they lived mainly in the home and occupied themselves with domestic work. Although the B.C. families were nuclear, their personal relations with women from other South Asian households continued the extended-family organizations they had been familiar with in India. Children growing up in this environment faced a dual culture (as do all immigrant children). They were expected to learn English and adapt to Canadian institutions, but they were also expected to retain many of their indigenous cultural values and traditions. For instance, youth, having grown up in Canada, were still expected to adhere to the arranged-marriage system, facilitated by relatives in India. Marriages would take place in India and then spouses would be brought back to settle in Canada. The practice continues today to a certain extent (Gogna, 1992).

Japanese Families

Before 1908, evidence suggests that the Japanese in Canada were mainly a community of single males and that some may have sought solace with prostitutes (Adachi, 1976; Kobayashi, 1978). Most lived with other men in company shacks and bunkhouses near their workplaces, just like their Chinese and South Asian counterparts.

In 1907, self-regulation of immigration from Japan was negotiated in the form of a gentlemen's agreement, according to which the Japanese government voluntarily restricted the number of emigrants to Canada. Canada resorted to this approach to maintain diplomatic relations with Japan, an ally of Britain at the time. The agreement covered the immigration of domestic and agricultural workers; wives, children, and parents were allowed to arrive freely until 1928. The agreement came on the heels of a race riot in British Columbia aimed at Chinese and Japanese immigrants.

Adachi describes the period after 1908 as the "family building phase" (1976, p. 87), when single men sought wives in several ways. Some visited Japan for arranged marriages; others sent for "picture brides" from a catalogue (Kobayashi, 1978, p. 4).

Traditionally, most Japanese marriages had been arranged. The parents selected a bride on the basis of such criteria as her ability to preserve family traditions, her domestic abilities, and her intelligence and accomplishments (Adachi, 1976, p. 88). A meeting of the prospective bride and groom would take place before the final approval of marriage.

For most Japanese men residing in Canada, the meeting before marriage was impossible. Thus, couples had to rely on photographs of each other, and eventually marriages were held by proxy. By all accounts, these marriages seemed fairly resilient, given the lack of parental interference, the inevitable possibility of disappointment upon meeting, and the women's encounters with the harsh living conditions in Canada.

Japanese women, like many women in other communities, were expected to be completely devoted to their husbands, children, and the home, although they laboured on farms as well as fulfilling their domestic obligations. Their labour played a crucial role in the success of Japanese farms, particularly in berry and small-fruit production (Adachi, 1976, p. 149). Perhaps the reason the Canadian government was open to the formation of families among the Japanese, but not among the South Asian and Chinese communities, was that unpaid family labour is an asset in small farming, as it allows the farmer to greatly minimize labour costs. This contrasts sharply to the conditions under which domestic workers have come into Canada. The latter have historically been encouraged to work in Canada as "single" women, away from their family members, including their young children. In their case, family members were seen as potential burdens on Canadian social services.

After 1928, however, in an effort to further limit the number of Japanese immigrants, women and children were included in the annual quota. This was a period of heightened racism against Asians in general, and the Japanese in particular. There was intense paranoia among white Canadians about being outnumbered and economically dominated by Japanese Canadians. By 1931, the number of picture brides coming into Canada had declined significantly.

Anti-Japanese feelings reached a zenith in the war years with the bombing of Pearl Harbor. In the name of national security, mass evacuations of

Japanese were begun in January 1942; all males between 18 and 45 had to be removed from the West Coast by April 1942. This resulted in the dismantling of families and the disruption of children's schooling. Most of the men were removed to work in road camps in other parts of Canada. Women and children were, initially, forced to reside in hastily converted public buildings, lacking complete privacy, before being moved to camps in the B.C. Interior, first to tents and then to shacks.

On June 24, 1942, the Canadian Security Commission decided to reunite married men in detention camps with their families, by transporting wives and children to the camps for the winter. As a result, the camps became extremely crowded and ill-equipped, and the movements of residents were closely monitored by security officials. Unmarried men in the camps were prevented from marrying lest they should try to stay with their wives. Even though the commission was supposed to provide the basic necessities of life, evacuees had to buy their own food with incomes between 22.5 and 40 cents an hour (Adachi, 1976, p. 259). The old and the infirm lived on provincial relief based on the number of family members. Japanese children were excluded from provincial schools, so that camp residents themselves had to build their own schools with their own finances and staff them with hastily trained Japanese teachers.

Familial authority and socialization processes were transformed in the semi-communal camp life (Maykovich, 1980, p. 68). The authority that Issei (first generation) parents had over their children was weakened, which then weakened parents' abilities to transfer their indigenous language and culture.

The disruption of families continued in the postwar years, when all Japanese Canadians were encouraged to go back to Japan or to work on sugar beet farms, extremely strenuous work. Many young, single members of the Nisei (the second generation) chose to move to Ontario and other Eastern provinces, away from their parents.

Adachi (1976) writes about the difficulty of gauging the psychological effects of internment on individuals, families, and the community. However, it is notable that the Nisei and the Sansei (third generation) are quite often assimilated into dominant Anglo-Canadian culture. The Sansei have about a 59 percent rate of intermarriage, compared with the 99 percent rate of **endogamy** of the Issei (Adachi, 1976, p. 362). Could this be a way of shielding themselves from the ravages of state racism that their Japanese parents and grandparents experienced?

Black Caribbean Families

If we look at the history of white European immigrant women, we find a pattern of large numbers coming to Canada as poor, single, young domestic workers (Barber, 1986; Conway, 1992; Lindstrom-Best, 1986). White women had a choice of settling in Canada or returning to their home countries. Between 1900 and 1930, about 170 000 British women came under this category. In 1929, 1288 out of 1618 Finnish women arrived as domestics. Immigration policies differed for domestics who were women of colour. If they came as temporary or contract domestic workers, they could not alter this status in Canada. If they did not fulfil their contractual agreements, they were forced to go back to their home countries.

Although there are some similarities between the conditions endured by Finnish domestics in the earlier decades of this century and women of colour who have more recently served as domestics, there are vast differences as well. In terms of similarities, Finnish domestics were required to live in the homes of their employers in sometimes dismal conditions; they were closely supervised by their employers, even on their days off; they were expected to subjugate their desire for family life to the needs of the families with whom they lived and, indeed, often lost any opportunity to form their own families. However, Finnish domestics enjoyed a number of advantages over their third-world counterparts. The Finnish community in Canada was primarily composed of domestics, so it organized around that phenomenon. Social events of all kinds were scheduled for Wednesday and Thursday afternoons, when most domestics had their free time. There were places in the community where the women could congregate and have coffee, talking over their troubles and obtaining information about other prospective employers. Even churches offered religious services to accommodate the schedules of the Finnish domestics. The support of such a community was empowering to these immigrant women, who were able to resist the oppression of their employers and change jobs to achieve some upward mobility (Lindstrom, 1998). They had options which third-world domestic workers most often do not.

Women of colour who have been brought to Canada as contracted domestic workers have been predominantly black Caribbean and Filipina women. These women have been, and still are, admitted for limited contractual periods. They remain in Canada only in the job and with the employer with whom the contract exists. The periods during which these women could, in fact, use the domestic scheme[2] to emigrate to Canada have been brief, so that few women have been able to take advantage of it. As a result of political lobbying by community organizations since 1981, domestic workers have been able to apply for immigration after two years of contracted work.

However, systemic barriers remain, since applicants have to fulfil certain conditions, such as maintaining stable employment, demonstrating financial-management skills, and demonstrating their involvement in the community. Just as in the case of Asian male immigrants in the early part of the twentieth century, it has been a policy of the government not to encourage the possibility of developing families among women of colour who came as domestic workers. Thus, their status as "single" and as "temporary" is deliberately organized by immigration policies.

Even when Chinese and Japanese women worked as domestic workers, they were restricted to working for Asian families. A law that restricted Chinese families from employing white domestic workers stood until 1929 (Dunphy, 1987). This could only reflect racism and the fear of miscegenation. The decision to admit certain groups of women as domestic workers while excluding others was perhaps guided not only by racial concerns and those arising from ethnocentrism. It is noticeable that the groups admitted under the domestic schemes have been, by and large, English-speaking and Christian, and more akin to Western, Anglo-Canadian culture. One can only suggest that these concerns were paramount, since many of these women would work as babysitters and nannies, and would therefore have a strong socializing influence on white children. Moreover, the role of black women as caregivers is a holdover from the history of slavery, of racism and sexism.

The first Caribbean domestic scheme admitted 100 women from Guadeloupe in 1910 and 1911 (Calliste, 1991). However, the scheme was ended because of information that these women were allegedly not completely "unattached," that is, that they had children. Many of these women were later deported on the grounds that they were allegedly "public charges." The real reason was, of course, that unemployment among white female domestic workers had gone up and women from the Caribbean were seen as competition. Also, part of the reason lay in the assumption that single mothers would become public dependants.

Black Caribbean female non-domestics and men who wanted to emigrate to Canada were systemically excluded by immigration regulations that admitted only farmers, farm labourers, domestics, wives, and minor children of residents in Canada, and British subjects from English-speaking countries (Calliste, 1991, p. 142). Besides, the Immigration Act of 1952 officially excluded "people on the basis of nationality, citizenship, ethnic origin … and their probable inability to become readily assimilated" (Calliste, 1991, p. 143).

The "singleness" of black domestic workers from the Caribbean was maintained in the second domestic scheme (1955–67), when a quota system was established for admitting as immigrants to Canada only unmarried women without children and not in common-law relationships. Proposed changes to immigration regulations in the early 1960s may have been what eventually prompted many of these women to apply to sponsor their close relatives, fiancés, and children. Not only was this very disappointing to Immigration officials (Calliste, 1991, p. 151), but they could not reconcile the fact that women breadwinners were sponsoring men as fiancés, a departure from traditional gender roles.

However, as other writers have pointed out, historically, black women have often been heads of households (Brand, 1988, 1991; Turritin, 1983; Yawney, 1983) — out-migration of male members to urban centres in the hope of increased income turned a significant proportion of families in Montserrat into female-headed ones (Turritin, 1983, p. 311). Brand (1988, p. 122) has argued that the depressed economic condition of black men generally has prevented them from participating in child and family maintenance. Therefore, black women have, out of necessity, been economically independent in supporting themselves and their children. Even though they earn some of the lowest incomes in Canada, their labour-force participation is one of the highest.

The determination of Immigration officials to maintain the singleness of black Caribbean women was dramatized in the case of the seven Jamaican mothers who applied to sponsor their children, previously unreported, in 1976. They were ordered to be deported for failing to report their children on their applications to come to Canada (Leah and Morgan, 1979). After an intensive struggle that involved community and labour groups, the seven women won their cases and were allowed to stay in Canada. At about the same time, there was another publicized case of a black Caribbean woman, a landed immigrant, who was ordered to be deported for being on welfare and receiving mothers' allowance because of lack of day care for her three preschool children. Her common-law husband had been deported earlier for the same reason (Leah and Morgan, 1979).

When black Caribbean workers applied to sponsor their fiancés and children in the early 1960s, the government responded by bringing in middle-class black Caribbean men who were university students, which in effect continued the lack of family reunification for these women (Calliste, 1991). An unequal sex ratio existed in the black Caribbean community until very recently.

Today, domestic workers come into Canada on temporary work permits, an arrangement begun in 1973. For two years, these workers remain as "unfree," after which they can apply for permanent residence. But, as mentioned before, this transition is marked by many barriers (Silvera, 1983, p. 18). In 1992, the Ministry of Employment and Immigration announced changes in the Foreign Domestic Movement program such that applicants now must have the equivalent of Grade 12 education, fluency in an official language, and either six months of training in caregiving or one year of work experience in this area (interview with Carol Salmon, counsellor, Intercede, 1998). Some of these criteria could effectively exclude women from the Philippines, India, and the Caribbean, where the required education is unavailable or inaccessible to working-class women.

IMMIGRANT DOMESTIC WORKERS AND WHITE FAMILIES

One of the issues that has rarely been discussed is the contribution of domestic workers in reproducing white Canadian-born families in Canada. By definition, they "mother" white Canadian-born children by cooking, cleaning, washing, dusting, and even fulfilling sexual services under coercion (Silvera, 1983, p. 61). While their own families, including those with very young children, are forced by immigration laws and employment conditions to remain far away from their mothers, these women nurture, feed, dress, and nurse their employers' children. They enable mainly upper-class and middle-class white women to escape their traditional gender roles to develop lucrative careers or to enjoy leisure time. By the same token, the government can save on crucial day-care services, which are urgently needed by working women with preschool children. In this process, domestic workers are prevented from ever establishing their own families and communities. There is almost an assumption that "they" don't "need" these families since they are assumed to be racially and socially incapable of nurturing and properly socializing their own children. This attitude has sometimes also been directed toward white, non–English-speaking European domestic workers, such as Finnish domestics (Lindstrom-Best, 1986, p. 20), although black domestic workers have been subjected to it most frequently.

Stasiulis and Bakan (1997; see also Bakan and Stasiulis, 1997) stress that foreign domestic workers in Canada are denied basic citizenship rights because of their entry status as temporary workers, not landed immigrants. Their citizenship in their countries of origin does not protect them from exploitation and oppression because of the vulnerable economic and political positions of these countries; many of them depend on the inflow of foreign currency from their citizens working abroad to service their debts and are extremely reluctant to take an international political stance that might endanger the ability of their nationals to find work in more prosperous countries. In Canada, because foreign domestic workers are classified as guest workers, they are excluded from most provincial labour legislation that might result in additional expense for Canadian employers, who usually belong to the upper classes of Canadian society. In addition, these temporary workers can be easily deported if their employers deem that they have not fulfilled the terms of their employment contract. Canada enjoys a reputation for being one of the best countries in which third-world women might find domestic work, so it attracts a large number of applicants. Many of these women hope that domestic work will be a stepping stone for permanent landed status for themselves, and the opportunity to sponsor their families. However, they are required by Canadian law to have a live-in arrangement with their employers for two out of the three years that they must be in Canada before they can apply for landed status.

The implications of the live-in requirement for foreign domestic workers are enormous. Stasiulis and Bakan (1997) indicate that research has shown the bargaining position of domestic workers to be significantly impaired when this requirement is in place. Their employers have much more control over them in such a case. The premises themselves are often oppressive, in the sense that domestics may find themselves living in basements without locks on their doors. Living in their employers' homes means that domestic workers are isolated from any sort of community that might provide them with solace and support; combined with the isolation of the job itself, the conditions under which these foreign workers must live for at least two years would be insupportable for most Canadians (Bakan and Stasiulis, 1996).

Familial ideology that promotes the mistaken notion that foreign domestic workers are one of the family is also a source of oppression. The division between the public sphere of work and the private sphere of family life is absent for domestic workers because their residence and their work are in the same location and involve the same individuals. There is an intimacy in the relations between domestic workers and their employers that is missing for other workers. This very intimacy can lead to exploitation because requests for more hours of work can be couched in terms of favours, and domestic workers may fear incurring the wrath of their employers, who could make their lives quite unbearable. Raises in pay may be circumvented by employers who bestow gifts upon their workers instead. The gifts and their giving, of course, remain within the power and control of the employers. Their receipt is not considered to be the right of the domestic workers. Finally, the fact that caring for children involves emotional investment makes domestic workers vulnerable to emotional and psychological exploitation. No matter how much love and devotion they feel for their charges, the children are not theirs and never will be. (See the various chapters in Bakan and Stasiulis, 1997, for more detailed information on the conditions foreign domestic workers in Canada are forced to endure.)

BLACKS IN CANADA
▼

SLAVERY

To understand the relations between black and white communities in Canada, one has to look back at the history of slavery in the Americas. It was in that context that racialized gender relations of working-class black women and white middle-class men and women crystallized (Brand, 1988). Within slavery, black women were used not only for the reproduction of Blacks, but also for the reproduction of children of white slave masters, including those born of brutal rapes.

Contrary to popular belief, slavery did exist in Canada, specifically in what became Quebec, Nova Scotia, Ontario, and New Brunswick, between 1629 and 1834 (Brand, 1988; Bolaria and Li, 1988; Chapter 1 in this text). **Black Loyalists** also came to Canada after the American Revolution, and as fugitives from slavery after 1800 via the **Underground Railroad**. There was no official prohibition of black immigration, although Blacks were frequently stopped at the border for alleged medical reasons (Thomas and Novogrodsky, 1983, p. 61).

In the absence of specific historical documentation on black communities, in particular on black women, in those times, one can speculate that their families resembled those in the United States and the Caribbean. Under slavery, the sexuality of black women and men, and the reproductive capacity of black women specifically, were owned and controlled by white slave masters. They determined whether women were to bear children, whose children they would bear, and whether they would marry. They also determined which of the male slaves should serve as "studs" for the purpose of increasing the slave population. Marriages, pregnancies, and families among Blacks were systematically prevented because pregnancy diminished the number of female "hands" on the plantation. Natural reproduction of slaves was not needed by whites at that time because importation of African slaves served the need for surplus labour (Brand, 1988; Dill, 1992, p. 220). It was only after 1807, when the slave trade was abolished, that women were expected to reproduce frequently, under coercion, in order to keep a stable enslaved labour supply.

Dill (1992) discusses the ambiguity that slave masters felt about black families. On the one hand, they recognized the family's role in the socialization of slave children. On the other hand, they recognized the potential for slave resistance to develop. It is clear from historical writings that slavery and racism prevented the development of traditional gender roles, with their associated traits of masculinity and femininity, from emerging in the black community. Black men were denied any stable role or participation in their families and in the destiny of their wives and children. Therefore, black men were denied the patriarchal role that white European and Canadian men performed in their families. As a result, black women were largely single mothers who worked equally with their male counterparts in slave labour. A traditional sexual division of labour within black families was not reinforced because black men and women achieved "equality" as unfree labour outside their families.

THE CONTEMPORARY SITUATION

Blacks in Canada have always occupied a subordinate position in economic, political, and ideological relations. This has had a distinct impact on black families (Calliste, 1996, p. 244). These two statements constitute the essential starting point of Calliste's essay on black families in Canada, particularly in Nova Scotia. She goes on to argue that racism has forced most Blacks to work in low-paying, unstable jobs, resulting in low socio-economic status, which then helps to break down family relationships. Sexism and class inequality combine with racism to create extremely limited employment opportunities for black women, many of whom have traditionally worked as domestics. Furthermore, immigration policy has historically discriminated against Blacks, preventing them to the greatest extent possible from establishing permanent residence, and making family formation in Canada difficult, while exploiting their labour power.

Racist attitudes toward black families in this country have resulted in these families having to make a number of adaptations. For instance, on the whole, black families in Canada are less likely to be formally married than Canadian families of all ethnic groups; Nova Scotian Blacks have the lowest rate of marriage of all. Calliste (1996, p. 252) states that this low marriage rate is due to high unemployment and low wages, and the pressure these put on marriages. Some other reasons cited for the low rate of marriage among Blacks is the shortage of black men due to immigration schemes that recruited black Caribbean women as domestics and nurses, and the greater tendency of black men to engage in interracial marriage. The high rate of single-parent, mother-headed families among Blacks is also due to a number of factors, some of which relate to socio-economic circumstances.

With regard to gender roles, Calliste (1996) suggests that there is a great deal of similarity between those played by Blacks and those played by whites. For example, a gendered division of labour exists wherein black women are expected to take the responsibility for domestic labour while black men do the outside tasks. When some women attempt to gain a more egalitarian sharing of domestic work, they may suffer from abuse, and their marriages may break down as husbands feel that their power is being threatened. In addition, there is a reluctance to deal openly with issues of family violence because the black community does not wish to reinforce racist stereotypes in the dominant society. Thus, many black women in these situations attempt to maintain racial solidarity with those who oppress them within their own families.

CHARACTERISTICS OF FAMILIES AMONG
"TEMPORARY" WORKING-CLASS CANADIANS
▼

Even though the Canadian government deliberately and systemically prevented the formation of families of colour before the 1950s, women, men, and children have organized themselves into households in order to create a sense of stability, of "family," and of community. These formations have often provided solace from the otherwise hostile environment permeated with racism and ethnocentrism.

Turritin (1983, p. 321) writes that the "sibling household" among black women from Montserrat was the predominant social arrangement in the postwar period; a woman and her sibling lived together. Friendship networks were also very significant in choice of residence. Silvera (1983, p. 31) writes about black Caribbean women referring to close friends as "church sisters." Unfortunately, even this was disrupted by government efforts to disperse domestics across the country (Calliste, 1991, p. 153). Women also created social clubs, centres, and recreational programs to facilitate social networks and support, friendship, and, later, self-advocacy organizations (Calliste, 1991, p. 152; Das Gupta, 1986, p. 17; Silvera, 1983, p. 125).

Brand (1988) speaks of the extended family in the black community, which is based on **matrilineage** and strong female support across generations, going beyond rules of paternity and "blood" relationships. Yawney (1983) discusses how lower-class family life in the Caribbean is marked by matrifocality, where women are heads of households and responsible for supporting their children. Relatives, neighbours, and friends take part in looking after children. In this network, elderly grandmothers, unemployed family members, family friends, and unattached individuals, particularly women, become key players in providing support to one another, particularly in child-rearing responsibilities.

Even in times of slavery, black people struggled to create families on their own terms. Research reveals that naming black children after their fathers and blood relatives was a way of maintaining family relations (Dill, 1992, p. 221). Preserving of African traditions in kinship ties was also significant. Constructing slave quarters using African building technologies and design reveals cultural resistance to racist oppression in Blacks' efforts to maintain family ties and privacy.

Chinese and South Asian men from the "bachelor" period continued their long-distance family lives by visits and sending money. Dill refers to this as the "split household family" (1992, p. 225). In Canada, Chinese men formed kinship associations based on surname, dialect, or territory (Johnson, 1983, p. 364). These were also social-support associations and facilitated the maintenance of links with their wives and children, and also enabled them to deal with the prejudices of the larger society. Perhaps this was an extension of the lineage, a social grouping that is significant in Chinese culture. Lineage involves a group of families descended from the same ancestor through the male line, living together in the same locality, owning common property, and worshipping common ancestors (Johnson, 1983, p. 361).

Among South Asian men, village and kin relations were used to establish "family"-like formations. During the long voyage to Canada, in restricted and crowded conditions, the men lived communally, cooking and eating together, and supporting each other. This pattern continued once they were in Canada. Four to twelve men would live together in a household, creating an extended "family"-like structure based on the Indian norm (Buchignani and Indra, 1985, p. 33; see also Dhruvarajan, 1996). They pooled their money for their necessities of life and shared household duties. It was apparently common for an unemployed member to do the cooking. In this set-up, the sick and the unemployed were well looked after. Living collectively also allowed these men to save money, despite the low wages that they earned. These early immigrants developed a reputation for being financially independent, a reputation that survived even the depression years. This pattern of collective and co-operative living continued even after some women and children started joining their husbands in Canada.

In these early years, the banning of wives and children, which prevented them from reuniting with their families, provoked the most intense anger and fuelled political organizing among British Columbia's South Asian community. The men realized that, without women, children, and families, their community would remain temporary, unstable, and stripped of social and political rights in Canada.

Evidence suggests that families among Japanese Canadians, once they started developing, were nuclear. Kobayashi (1978) writes that this resulted in the Nisei, the second generation, missing out on contacts with their grandparents, who traditionally would have played a significant role in the socialization of children. She questions the implications of that for these children and for future generations.

FAMILY BUILDING AMONG POSTWAR IMMIGRANTS
▼

Even though the government made an effort to encourage family reunification in the postwar era, many barriers were erected. Some of these were institutionalized and systemic, while others were a legacy of past antifamily and racist government policies. These barriers continue up to today, even though one of the cornerstones of the current immigration policy, as phrased in the Immigration Act of 1976, is "to facilitate the reunion in Canada of Canadian citizens and permanent residents with their close relatives from abroad" (Toronto Coalition for a Just Refugee and Immigration Policy, 1987).

When reunification took place, communities had to deal with the estrangement of couples (Dill, 1992) and with the fact that children born later than usual meant greater differences in age and in values between parents and children (Johnson, 1983).

Blacks

Similar problems have been mentioned with regard to black Caribbean women who sponsored their children to Canada in later years and who experienced tension in these relationships because they had been separated and had to deal with feelings of hurt, rejection, and indifference (Christiansen, Thornley-Brown, and Robinson, n.d., p. 76). These children faced new lives, separated from their siblings and caregivers, and had to develop, almost overnight, new relationships with their natural mothers, from whom they may have been separated for years. Some of these mothers may have married here, had other children, and established a "family" with which these newly arrived children had no familiarity (Calliste, 1996).

Chinese

With the repeal of the Chinese Immigration Act, Chinese immigration was restricted to wives and unmarried children under 18; this was later expanded to include sponsored relatives. However, these groups could not apply to come into Canada as independent immigrants until 1962 (Li and Bolaria, 1983, p. 93).

Since 1967, Chinese immigrants from Hong Kong have come to Canada in large numbers.[3] Many of these immigrants are middle class, highly educated, cosmopolitan, and able to speak English. In recent years more Chinese women than men have emigrated; some of them are independent immigrants, able to score high enough in the point system not to require sponsorship by a male family member. Yet, they have not been considered to have separate experiences from their male counterparts and so have disappeared into the statistics (Man, 1996).

In Man's (1996) study of 30 middle-class Chinese women from Hong Kong, the majority of them were family-class immigrants sponsored by their husbands. Despite the fact that most of them have post-secondary education or training of some kind and worked prior to immigration, they are classified by immigration law as dependants and, therefore, supposedly not bound for the labour market. Without Canadian experience and accreditation for their educational credentials, the women who had sought employment in Canada were either underemployed or unemployed.

The impact of immigration on the family lives of Man's (1996) subjects was varied. Some of the women found that their husbands' **un(der)employment** brought new intimacy and interdependence to their marriages. Others felt that their marriages were facing imminent breakdown because of the isolation they experienced as immigrants and because of the stress of unemployment. Some of the husbands were "astronauts"— men who spend up to half of the year in Hong Kong while their families remain in Toronto; their absences were due to their reluctance to give up their high-paying jobs in Hong Kong. One of the wives disliked the arrangement because of the burden of running her household by herself, while another enjoyed her newfound freedom and greater communication with her husband. In Canada, housework and child care were more solitary for these women because of the lack of extended family and relatives living in close proximity. Teenagers were less independent in Canada, so they felt resentful. Further, due to the higher cost of living in Canada and lower salaries, some women who had been able to hire domestic help in Hong Kong so that they could pursue their careers and other interests could no longer afford to do so. Now having a double day exhausted these women. Because managing the household is a source of pride for these Chinese women and is part of being a good wife, many are reluctant to ask their husbands to do their share of the work; it is a loss of face to do so. Thus, many of Man's subjects were too tired to do much more than work and manage the household duties, relinquishing thoughts of a social life such as the one they had had in Hong Kong. It would appear that these women immigrants' lives narrowed in focus upon moving to Canada.

South Asians

Unlike other landed immigrants, South Asians could not freely sponsor parents, grandparents, fiancés, or unmarried children (Das Gupta, 1986, p. 68). South Asian immigration was also restricted by yearly quotas. For instance, the quota for India was 150 in 1951 and 300 in 1957 (Buchignani and Indra, 1985). These were men by all accounts, since it was assumed that these immigrants could later sponsor their wives and their unmarried children under 21.

After the point system was introduced to immigration law in 1967 and race was no longer an explicit criterion for admission, South Asian immigrants who possessed professional and technical skills began to arrive in Canada from India. These immigrants usually entered in family units, and tended to live in metropolitan areas such as Toronto and Vancouver, although they often eschewed moving into ethnic enclaves.

First-generation South Asians bring with them certain cultural and religious beliefs and practices that are difficult to maintain in Canada, particularly once their children begin attending school and learning the beliefs and practices of the dominant culture in Canada. While adherence to traditions strongly influenced by patriarchy and familial orientations varies among Hindus of different educational, geographic, and class backgrounds, Dhruvarajan (1996) argues that there remains a cultural tendency to bestow superiority on the male head of the household, even though it might only be symbolic. In terms of their family lives, South Asian women shoulder most of the domestic responsibility and consider themselves to be housewives in spite of their work in the paid-labour market. They see their wages from their paid work as extra income to supplement that of their husbands. Immigration has caused a degradation of some of their skills because those skills are not required in the Canadian market; for example, one woman encountered by Jamal (1998, pp. 31–32) had expertise in a type of embroidery using gold and silver threads and sequins much in demand in her country of origin for the garment industry but apparently not widely sought in its Canadian counterpart. Hence, women like this one have been effectively pushed out of the labour market in this country, with commensurate hardship for themselves and their families.

SOCIAL CONSTRUCTION OF GENDER, RACE, AND CLASS IN POSTWAR FAMILIES OF COLOUR
▼

To facilitate family reunification, a category of immigrants was labelled as the "family class"; these would be given priority simply because they had "very close relatives" in Canada. Critics have pointed out that, in practice, the arbitrary definition of "family" and delays in the processing of these applications often keep families separated for long periods (Toronto Coalition for a Just Refugee and Immigration Policy, 1987). For instance, "family" does not include brothers and sisters over 19, or sons and daughters over 19. Fathers are not recognized as parents. A natural father has to legally adopt his child before he can sponsor her or him. An adoption process has to happen before the child's thirteenth year and can be fairly complicated. It has been said that overseas immigration officials tend to reject these applications. Similarly, de facto parents, such as aunts or grandparents, who may have brought children up in the absence of natural parents, are not recognized. Like natural fathers, they also have to legally adopt the children before sponsoring them over to Canada.

The formal definition of who would be considered "family" members illustrates the cultural and racial bias of the state. According to government definitions, several members of an extended family are not seen as "close" family members. Moreover, children who are young adults are assumed to be financially independent, living separately from their parents, and are thus not part of their parents' "family unit." There are also assumptions about the **neolocal**, which may not have relevance for **matrilocal** or **patrilocal** communities.

Even though family-class immigrants are said (according to immigration regulations) to be of first priority, in practice they are less of a priority than entrepreneurial immigrants (Cross Cultural Communication Centre, n.d.). In some countries, such as ones in the Caribbean, family-class applications fall in priority after student and work authorizations. Besides, the process of **family reunification** is often lengthy because of lack of resources in overseas immigration offices as well as bureaucratic obstacles. Normal processing time for family-class applications from the United States and Britain is between 71 and 116 days; those from India take 203 to 413 days, those from Guyana 518 days, those from Trinidad and Tobago, 462 days, and those from Zaire 637 days (Cross Cultural Communication Centre, n.d.).

The reasons for these delays in countries consisting mostly of people of colour are the lack of personnel and other resources to process the volume of applications. This practice of **systemic discrimination** allows "neutral" structures and practices to have an adverse effect on one group of people. For instance, there are 5 immigration offices in the United Kingdom, 10 in the United States, 4 in France, and 2 in Germany, while there is only 1 in India, serving 8 other jurisdictions; of 6 in Africa, 1 serves 23 other jurisdictions and 2 are in South Africa.

Processing of these applications from countries of colour takes an adversarial approach, in which it is difficult to reapply if an application is rejected, since the application loses its original priority. Moreover, a sponsor must have a certain level of income to be able to apply for "close family members" to join her or him. These discriminatory practices are similar to the Chinese head tax. The adversarial approach is revealed also in the case of conventional refugees who want to sponsor their close "family" members. A Minister's Permit is given to them only after a medical clearance and an interview of the applicants. There does not seem to be any consideration of applicants who may fear for their lives and who may want to leave their countries as soon as possible.

Thus, we can see that it is questionable whether family reunification is really a priority for the government, or if it is merely rhetorical. The 1986 Neilson Task Force Study Team report on citizenship, labour, and immigration recommended that the "assisted relatives" category should be virtually done away with by reducing the points acquired for having assistance from family members from ten to five (Canada, Task Force on Program Review, 1985). Currently, there is no longer an "assisted relatives" category.

Historically, it is noticeable that, when women have been allowed to enter Canada, they have been able to do so as wives and as dependants

(Estable and Meyer, 1989). Their dependent status is maintained by various institutional processes upon their arrival in Canada. The point system of immigration perpetuates systemic barriers for women and people of colour who want to immigrate as independent candidates since it emphasizes such things as education, skills, training, employability in "open occupations," and knowledge of English and/or French. Most women from the working classes and from racial minority groups would never qualify to immigrate on the basis of such criteria as they lack access to the required training. Thus, when women have come to Canada on their own, they have done so as "unfree" labour, as slaves, domestic workers, or seasonal farm labourers. Mostly, these have been black, Filipina, and Mexican women. Despite the recent demand for domestic workers, this occupation has not been added to the list of "open occupations" and thus does not earn any immigration points (Estable and Meyer, 1989, p. 39).

As soon as immigrants are defined as "family class," it is assumed that they are not good enough to work outside the home (hence the lack of insistence on earning points) and that their primary responsibility is with child care and housework. Another "family class" assumption is that women are not destined for the labour force. This in effect reproduces traditional gender ideology, even though the majority of immigrant women participate in the paid-labour force (in the most ill-paid and insecure sectors) at a greater rate than Canadian-born women.

However, women's dependence on men is reinforced by a variety of institutional processes. Until 1992, government-subsidized English/French as a Second Language (ESL/FSL) courses were not made accessible to those who have been sponsored. "Breadwinners" (read: men) were given first priority for admission to these courses. This policy affected women adversely, since more women than men lack the knowledge of an official language (Estable and Meyer, 1989, p. 20). This situation is exacerbated for older women.

Language classes are now available through programs known as Language Instruction for Newcomers to Canada (LINC) and Labour Market Language Training (LMLT). Unfortunately, these programs are not available for citizens. Since many people who do not speak English or French are citizens of Canada, they are ineligible for LINC classes. LMLT programs are available for citizens, but only for those whose occupations are deemed to be in demand locally. Training allowances are available only through Employment Insurance (previously known as Unemployment Insurance), but only to those who have worked a certain number of hours. Those who do not qualify for Employment Insurance will not get any allowance for learning English or French. This acts as a disincentive for learning English or French. Moreover, child-care provisions are inadequate, as only "childminding" is available, rather than quality

---

BOX 5.2
▼
THE PANDEY FAMILY

Mr. and Mrs. Pandey were in their later years when they immigrated to Canada to be with their sons who had immigrated before them and had established lives. They moved in with their eldest son and his family. Mr. Pandey, having retired from his job in India, took a job in his son's office in Winnipeg.

Problems developed between the two generations because of cultural differences. The son's wife was Canadian, not of Indian origin. The grandchildren do not speak any of the Indian languages so Mrs. Pandey, who could not speak any English at all when she first arrived, could not communicate with them or her daughter-in-law.

Source: Based on Vanaja Dhruvarajan, "Hindu Indo-Canadian Families," in Marion Lynn, ed., *Voices: Essays on Canadian Families* (Toronto: Nelson, 1996), pp. 305–307.

---

child care. The inaccessibility of ESL/FSL classes has long-term implications for immigrant families.

Moreover, women are not eligible for most subsidized social services unless they can prove that their sponsorship has broken down (Ng and Das Gupta, 1981). Often, Canada Employment Centres will invite the "heads of households" — that is, men — to their initial orientation sessions (Estable and Meyer, 1989, p. 47). It is assumed, perhaps falsely, that information will be automatically "passed on" to their sponsored relatives. Community organizations representing immigrant women agree that Employment Centre practices place women in a double bind. Women are denied access to training, upgrading, and ESL/FSL classes, but they cannot find waged work without enrolling in such courses. For job-training courses, a minimum level of English or French is necessary. So once again women are denied access if their spoken English is poor. In the absence of recognition of prior professional experience and qualifications, women are streamed into dead-end entry-level jobs (Estable and Meyer, 1989, p. 23; Jamal, 1998).

The dependence of immigrant women is dramatically perpetuated when they are in abusive relationships. When women are being sponsored as fiancées, the couple have to marry within 90 days and "prove" that the marriage is genuine by staying in it for a specified time (Lee, 1990). In such situations, women face a "choice" of breaking sponsorship and risking deportation or staying silently within an abusive marriage. If they decide to notify

Immigration authorities of their abuse, then they face the discretion of the official who judges the case on humanitarian grounds. Whether they remain in Canada may depend on their ability to speak English or French, their community contacts, their employability, and so on. However, given the abusive conditions in which they lived, it is unlikely that they will meet these criteria. Recently, as a result of pressure from immigrant women's advocacy groups, abused women who have been allowed to remain in Canada have become eligible for subsidized social services.

CONCLUSION
▼

The community histories presented here illustrate the politicization of the family vis-à-vis the Canadian state and dominant interest groups. Historical writings reveal that women, men, and children of colour have not always had the right to live in a "family" situation on their own terms. The descriptions of the conditions under which working-class Chinese, South Asian, and Japanese men and women in the early twentieth century, and, later on, black Caribbean women, lived and worked illustrate that they existed as "single" people in the Canadian context. Official immigration policy, as well as informal practices, ensured that this pattern was perpetuated. Families were, and continue to be, disrupted and actively prevented from forming, thus hampering the reproduction of the group and its community. Family disruption also ensures the temporariness of their residence in Canada. Moreover, it ensures the predominant whiteness of the population overall. The birth of the Métis was a result of coercive miscegenation practised by male colonists with Native women. Simultaneously, those women's indigenous family forms, which had been extended and egalitarian, disintegrated. Later on, the extended families and close relationships between Native parents and their children were broken down for the express purpose of terminating Native cultures, languages, religions, education, and economies. This was accomplished initially by missionary-led residential schools, and later by non-Native child-welfare agencies, both of which operated on the philosophy of superiority of white Christian culture and the natural inferiority of Native peoples.

At the same time, the Indian Act defined many members of the Native communities, particularly women married to non-Natives and their children, as non-Status, which, among other indignities, denied them the right to live on reserves with their families.

The experience of Blacks who came from the United States as slaves, Loyalists, and fugitives can be seen in the context of slavery in the Americas. Families of enslaved black people were completely controlled by white slave masters. Decisions regarding marriages, sexual relations, pregnancies, and cohabitation were made by white men. Like various Native nations, enslaved Blacks were also subjected to forced miscegenation, a form of violence toward women and a way to reproduce the slave population. In the absence of adequate research, I have speculated that this history must have had profound effects on their later migration to Canada and the establishment of their families here.

The Native nations, as well as immigrants of colour who were held captive as single and temporary workers, provided a pool of cheapened labour to fuel the development of colonial mercantile capitalism and, later, industrial capitalism. Native peoples provided labour for the fur trade, and Blacks and immigrants of colour were instrumental in land clearing, farming, lumbering, and the like. Later, all these communities were employed in factory, service, clerical, and domestic work.

The absence of immigrant families meant that the quantitative cost of reproduction was lower, since their families were not present in Canada. The spouses and family members of these immigrants, who lived outside Canada, subsidized them with their unpaid labour at home. This enabled Canadian employers to keep wages at a super-exploitative level and thus to reap high profits. However, qualitatively and psychologically, the absence of families meant increasing costs for these immigrant workers in the form of loneliness, alienation, and depression. For Native peoples, these effects reached an extreme level, with high incidences of self-destructive behaviour. The destruction of Native communities hardly presented itself as a problem to Canadian employers, since labour was plentiful through immigration. In fact, the presence of Native peoples and their rights as the original peoples of this land were seen by many as an impediment to the capitalist employment of land and natural resources.

Family members were generally allowed in for certain groups, such as Chinese merchants and the Japanese. Perhaps in these cases the value of families for stability and for reproduction was recognized by the government. The contribution of women and children as unpaid labourers in small businesses and on family farms (for which the Issei were gaining a reputation before their internment) was recognized also.

Legitimization functions of the state were accomplished by the genocide of Native families and the obstruction of family formation among immigrants. First, the state prevented the reproduction of these peoples, and thus the formation of their communities and nations, especially in the case of Native peoples. This removed any basis of power for them and was the formula for maintaining their vulnerability. That vulnerability was rationalized on overt and covert racism, thus fanning white racism, which was hegemonic in Canada at the time. By pursuing such policies, governments were catering to a racist public while maintaining the "cheapness" of people of colour and of Native people.

When family reunification was declared an official policy in the postwar period, traditional gender roles with their associated ideologies were reproduced through various institutional processes. Even if we are to accept these gender relations, family reunification has remained an uphill battle for many immigrants. Despite this history, Native people and people of colour have formed families in order to establish permanence, mutual support, and solidarity with each other. Same-sex, communal, and quasi-extended families have been formed as a bulwark against genocide and racism. These alternative families create a sense of support and solace from the harsh realities of life. The struggles for family reunification and for civil rights have been two of the most important organizing principles for immigrants and people of colour. For Native people, self-government in every aspect of their lives has been the fundamental demand for the restoration of their families and nations.

SUMMARY
▼

- State policies in the area of immigration and racism have historically had a fundamental effect on families and on communities of colour. People of colour have frequently been denied the right to have the "family" form of their choice and this denial has been historically motivated by racism. For many years, Canadian immigration policy ensured that working-class immigrants lived in Canada as "single" people, and families were actively prevented from forming within a number of immigrant groups.
- Through the Indian Act and various immigration policies, the state has maintained a capitalist mode of production as well as reproduced racist, sexist, and classist structures. Through such policies, the state has regulated the "family" form of Native people, immigrants, and people of colour.
- Native people, as well as immigrants of colour who were held captive as single and temporary workers, provided a pool of cheap labour to fuel the development of industrial capitalism in Canada.
- Despite this history, Native people and people of colour have formed families in order to establish permanence, mutual support, and solidarity with each other.
- The struggles for family reunification and for civil rights have been two of the most important organizing principles for immigrants and people of colour in Canada.
- For Native peoples, self-government has been fundamental for the restoration of families and nations.

NOTES
▼

I would like to acknowledge the assistance of Julianne Momirov and Maria Teresa Wilson in revising this chapter.

1. Statistics regarding the Native community are problematic, owing to the deeply varying definitions and perceptions of who a Native person is.
2. "Domestic Schemes" refers to special programs that the Canadian government has had to allow specified types and numbers of domestic workers to enter Canada.
3. This section is written by Julianne Momirov.

CRITICAL THINKING QUESTIONS
▼

1. How have the families of Native people, immigrants, and people of colour been different from the dominant "family" form in Canada?
2. How were these "differences" socially constructed?
3. How did racism and class considerations shape public policy around immigration and family matters?
4. How did sexism and class considerations shape public policy around immigration and family matters?
5. What is your own family history in Canada? How has that history been shaped by racism, sexism, and class realities?
6. Does immigration benefit immigrants? If so, describe how. If not, describe how it does not and why people would continue to seek immigration to Canada?

SUGGESTED READING
▼

Abigail B. Bakan and Daiva Stasiulis, eds. 1997. *Not One of the Family: Foreign Domestic Workers in Canada*. Toronto: University of Toronto Press.

This contemporary collection of articles reveals the contradictory and often conflictual circumstances under which foreign domestic workers labour in Canada.

Dionne Brand. 1991. *No Burden to Carry: Narratives of Black Working Women in Ontario, 1920s to 1950s*. Toronto: Women's Press.

A unique collection of accounts from Canadian black women who laboured in a variety of mostly working-class situations in Ontario during this century.

Bonnie Thornton Dill. 1992. "Our Mothers' Grief: Racial Ethnic Women and the Maintenance of Families." In Margaret L. Anderson and Patricia Hill Collins, eds., *Race, Class and Gender: An Anthology*. Belmont, CA: Wadsworth.

In a frankly revealing essay, Dill relates the challenges, and often grief, visible-minority women face when struggling to raise their children, maintain households, and create economic stability.

Franca Iacovetta with Paula Draper and Robert Ventresca, eds. 1998. *A Nation of Immigrants: Women, Workers, and Communities in Canadian History, 1840s–1960s.* Toronto: University of Toronto Press.

This collection of original essays chronicles the lives of immigrant women struggling to make a living in their new country.

Barbara K. Latham and Roberta J. Pazdro, eds. 1984. *Not Just Pin Money: Selected Essays on the History of Women's Work in British Columbia.* Victoria: Camosun College.

One of the first collections of accounts of the paid and unpaid labour of women from a variety of ethnic communities settled on the West Coast of Canada.

Jesse Vorst, Tania Das Gupta, Cy Gonick, Ronnie Leah, Alan Lennon, Alicja Muszynski, Roxana Ng, Ed Silva, Mercedes Steedman, Si Transkan, and Derek Wilkinson, eds. 1991. *Race, Class, Gender: Bonds and Barriers.* Toronto: Society for Socialist Studies, and Garamond.

This original collection of essays analyzes the impact race, class, and gender have on women's work and family lives.

Geoffrey York. 1989. *The Dispossessed: Life and Death in Native Canada.* Toronto: Lester and Orpen Dennys.

Travelling across Canada, York visits Native reserves varying in wealth from the very poor to the more economically stable, but all facing problems related to self-government, child-socialization, and adult-lifestyle issues.

REFERENCES
▼

Adachi, Ken. 1976. *The Enemy That Never Was.* Toronto: McClelland & Stewart.

Armstrong, Pat, and Hugh Armstrong. 1984. *The Double Ghetto: Canadian Women and Their Segregated Work.* Toronto: McClelland & Stewart.

Bakan, Abigail B., and Daiva Stasiulis. 1996. "Structural Adjustment, Citizenship, and Foreign Domestic Labour: The Canadian Case." In Isabella Bakker, ed., *Rethinking Restructuring: Gender and Change in Canada.* Toronto: University of Toronto Press.

———, eds. 1997. *Not One of the Family: Foreign Domestic Workers in Canada.* Toronto: University of Toronto Press.

Barber, Marilyn. 1986. "In Search of a Better Life: A Scottish Domestic in Rural Ontario." *Polyphony* 8 (1–2): 13–16.

Bolaria, B. Singh, and Peter S. Li. 1988. *Racial Oppression in Canada,* 2nd ed. Toronto: Garamond.

Bourgeault, Ron G. 1991. "Race, Class and Gender: Colonial Domination of Indian Women." In Jesse Vorst, Tania Das Gupta, Cy Gonick, Ronnie Leah, Alan Lennon, Alicja Muszynski, Roxana Ng, Ed Silva, Mercedes Steedman, Si Transkan, and Derek Wilkinson, eds., *Race, Class, Gender: Bonds and Barriers.* Toronto: Society for Socialist Studies, and Garamond.

Brand, Dionne. 1988. "A Conceptual Analysis of How Gender Roles Are Racially Constructed: Black Women." Unpublished MA thesis, University of Toronto.

———. 1991. *No Burden to Carry: Narratives of Black Working Women in Ontario, 1920s to 1950s*. Toronto: Women's Press.

Brant, Beth. 1988. "A Long Story." In Beth Brant, ed., *A Gathering of Spirit*. Toronto: Women's Press.

Buchignani, Norman L., and Doreen Indra. 1985. *Continuous Journey*. Toronto: McClelland & Stewart.

Calliste, Agnes. 1991. "Canada's Immigration Policy and Domestics from the Caribbean: The Second Domestic Scheme." In Jesse Vorst, Tania Das Gupta, Cy Gonick, Ronnie Leah, Alan Lennon, Alicja Muszynski, Roxana Ng, Ed Silva, Mercedes Steedman, Si Transkan, and Derek Wilkinson, eds., *Race, Class, Gender: Bonds and Barriers*. Toronto: Society for Socialist Studies, and Garamond.

———. 1996. "Black Families in Canada: Exploring the Interconnections of Race, Class, and Gender." In Marion Lynn, ed., *Voices: Essays on Canadian Families*. Toronto: Nelson Canada.

Canada. Task Force on Program Review. 1985. *Citizenship, Labour and Immigration: A Plethora of "People" Programs: A Study Team Report to the Task Force on Program Review*. Ottawa: The Task Force.

Canadian Association in Support of Native Peoples. 1978. *Bulletin* 18/4: 34–35.

Christiansen, Juliette M., Anne Thornley-Brown, and Jean A. Robinson. n.d. *West Indians in Toronto*. Toronto: Family Services Association of Metro Toronto.

Connelly, Patricia 1978. *Last Hired, First Fired: Women and the Canadian Work Force*. Toronto: Women's Press.

Conway, Shelagh. 1992. *The Faraway Hills Are Green: Voices of Irish Women in Canada*. Toronto: Women's Press.

Cross Cultural Communication Centre. n.d. "Processing of Family Class Applications." Unpublished paper. Toronto: Cross Cultural Communication Centre.

Dalla Costa, Maria Rosa, and Selma James. 1972. *Women's Subordination and the Subversion of the Community*. Bristol, England: Falling Wall Press.

Das Gupta, Tania. 1986. *Learning from Our History: Community Development by Immigrant Women in Canada, 1958–86: A Tool for Action*. Toronto: Cross Cultural Communication Centre.

———. 1994. "Political Economy of Gender, Race and Class: Looking at South Asian Immigrant Women in Canada." *Canadian Ethnic Studies* 26/1: 59–73.

de Beauvoir, Simone. 1952. *The Second Sex*. New York: Knopf.

Dhruvarajan, Vanaja. 1996. "Hindu Indo-Canadian Families." In Marion Lynn, ed., *Voices: Essays on Canadian Families*. Toronto: Nelson Canada.

Dill, Bonnie Thornton. 1992. "Our Mothers' Grief: Racial Ethnic Women and the Maintenance of Families." In Margaret L. Anderson and Patricia Hill Collins, eds., *Race, Class and Gender: An Anthology*. Belmont, CA: Wadsworth.

Doman, Mahinder. 1984. "A Note on Asian Indian Women in British Columbia 1900–1935." In Barbara K. Latham and Roberta J. Pazdro, eds., *Not Just Pin Money: Selected Essays on the History of Women's Work in British Columbia*. Victoria: Camosun College.

Dunphy, Cathy. 1987. "Canadian History of Chinese Women." *The Toronto Star*, July 14, p. G1.

Estable, Alma, and Mechtild Meyer. 1989. *A Discussion Paper on Settlement Needs of Immigrant Women in Ontario*. Ottawa: Immigrant Settlement and Adaptation Program.

Fireweed 16 (Spring 1983).

Fiske, Jo-Anne, and Rose Johnny. 1996. "The Nedut'en Family: Yesterday and Today." In Marion Lynn, ed., *Voices: Essays on Canadian Families*. Toronto: Nelson Canada.

Fox, Bonnie, ed. 1980. *Hidden in the Household: Women's Domestic Labour under Capitalism*. Toronto: Women's Press.

Fox-Genovese, Elisabeth. 1982. "Placing Women's History in History." *New Left Review* 133 (May/June): 5–28.

Gannage, Charlene. 1986. *Double Day, Double Bind: Women Garment Workers*. Toronto: Women's Press.

Gogna, Sarabjit. 1992. "Parents Will Find Right Man for Me." *The Toronto Star*, March 28, p. J1.

Greer, Germaine. 1970. *The Female Eunuch*. London: MacGibbon and Kee.

Hudson, Pete, and Brad McKenzie. 1981. "Child Welfare and Native People: The Extension of Colonialism." *The Social Worker* 49/2: 63–88.

Iacovetta, Franca. 1987. "Trying to Make Ends Meet: An Historical Look at Italian Immigrant Women, the State and Family Survival Strategies in Post-War Toronto." *Canadian Woman Studies* 8/2: 6–11.

Iacovetta, Franca, with Paula Draper and Robert Ventresca, eds. 1998. *A Nation of Immigrants: Women, Workers, and Communities in Canadian History, 1840s–1960s*. Toronto: University of Toronto Press.

Ishwaran, K., ed. 1980. *Canadian Families: Ethnic Variations*. Toronto: McGraw-Hill Ryerson.

Jamal, Amina. 1998. "Situating South Asian Immigrant Women in the Canadian/ Global Economy." *Canadian Woman Studies* 18/1: 26–33.

Johnson, Graham E. 1983. "Chinese Family and Community in Canada: Tradition and Change." In Jean Leonard Elliott, ed., *Two Nations, Many Cultures: Ethnic Groups in Canada*. Scarborough, ON: Prentice-Hall.

Johnston, Patrick. 1983. *Native Children and the Child Welfare System*. Toronto: Canadian Council on Social Development.

Kobayashi, Cassandra. 1978. "Sexual Slavery in Canada: Our Herstory." *The Asianadian* 1/3: 63–88.

Latham, Barbara K., and Roberta J. Pazdro, eds. 1984. *Not Just Pin Money: Selected Essays on the History of Women's Work in British Columbia*. Victoria: Camosun College.

Leah, Ronnie. 1991. "Linking the Struggles: Racism, Feminism and the Union Movement." In Jesse Vorst, Tania Das Gupta, Cy Gonick, Ronnie Leah, Alan Lennon, Alicja Muszynski, Roxana Ng, Ed Silva, Mercedes Steedman, Si Transkan, and Derek Wilkinson, eds., *Race, Class, Gender: Bonds and Barriers*. Toronto: Society for Socialist Studies, and Garamond.

Leah, Ronnie, and Gwen Morgan. 1979. "Immigrant Women Fight Back: The Case of the Seven Jamaican Women." *Resources for Feminist Research* 8/3: 23–24.

Lee, Betty. 1990. "Immigration and Immigrant Women." Paper presented at Symposium on Immigration, Settlement and Adaptation, May 28–29.

Li, Peter S., and B. Singh Bolaria. 1983. *Racial Minorities in Multicultural Canada*. Toronto: Garamond.

Lindstrom, Varpu. 1998. "I Won't Be a Slave! Finnish Domestics in Canada, 1911–1930." In Iacovetta et al., eds., *A Nation of Immigrants: Women, Workers, and Communities in Canadian History, 1840s–1960s*. Toronto: University of Toronto Press.

Lindstrom-Best, Varpu. 1986. "Going to Work in America: Finnish Maids, 1911–1930." *Polyphony* 8(1/2): 17–20.

Locust, Carol. 1990. "Discrimination against American Indian Families in Child Abuse Cases." *Indian Child Welfare Digest* (Feb./Mar.): 7–9.

Luxton, Meg, and Harriet Rosenberg. 1986. *Through the Kitchen Window: The Politics of Home and Family*. Toronto: Garamond.

Man, Guida. 1996. "The Experience of Middle-Class Women in Recent Hong Kong Chinese Immigrant Families in Canada." In Marion Lynn, ed., *Voices: Essays on Canadian Families*. Toronto: Nelson Canada.

Maykovich, Minako K. 1980. "Acculturation versus Familism in Three Generations of Japanese Canadians." In K. Ishwaran, ed., *Canadian Families: Ethnic Variations*. Toronto: McGraw-Hill Ryerson.

Midnight Sun. 1988. "Canada's Natural Resource." In Beth Brant, ed., *A Gathering of Spirit*. Toronto: Women's Press.

Native Child and Family Services of Toronto. 1991. *Annual General Report*. Toronto: Native Child and Family Services of Toronto.

Nett, Emily M. 1988. *Canadian Families: Past and Present*. Toronto: Butterworths.

Ng, Roxana, and Tania Das Gupta. 1981. "Nation Builders? The Captive Labour Force of Non-English Speaking Immigrant Women." *Canadian Woman Studies* 3/1: 83–85.

Panitch, Leo, ed. 1977. *The Canadian State: Political Economy and Political Power*. Toronto: University of Toronto Press.

Parsons, Talcott, and Robert F. Bales. 1955. *Family, Socialization and Interaction Process*. Glencoe: Free Press.

Polyphony 1986. 8(1/2).

Pon, Madge. 1996. "Like a Chinese Puzzle: The Construction of Chinese Masculinity in *Jack Canuck*." In Joy Parr and Mark Rosenfeld, eds., *Gender and History in Canada*. Toronto: Copp Clark.

Reiter, Rayna, ed. 1975. *Toward an Anthropology of Women*. New York: Monthly Review Press.

Silvera, Makeda. 1983. *Silenced*. Toronto: Williams-Wallace.

Smith, Dorothy E. 1977. "Some Implications of a Sociology for Women." In Nona Glazer and Helen Youngelson Waehrer, eds., *Woman in a Man-Made World*. Chicago: Rand McNally.

Stasiulis, Daiva, and Abigail B. Bakan. 1997. "Negotiating Citizenship: The Case of Foreign Domestic Workers in Canada." *Feminist Review* 57 (Autumn): 112–39.

Steinem, Gloria. 1983. *Outrageous Acts and Everyday Rebellions*. New York: Holt, Rinehart and Winston.

Thomas, Barb, and Charles Novogrodsky. 1983. *Combatting Racism in the Workplace: Readings Kit*. Toronto: Cross Cultural Communication Centre.

Thornhill, Esmeralda. 1991. "Focus on Black Women!" In Jesse Vorst, Tania Das Gupta, Cy Gonick, Ronnie Leah, Alan Lennon, Alicja Muszynski, Roxana Ng, Ed Silva, Mercedes Steedman, Si Transkan, and Derek Wilkinson, eds., *Race, Class, and Gender: Bonds and Barriers*. Toronto: Society for Socialist Studies, and Garamond.

Toronto Coalition for a Just Refugee and Immigration Policy. 1987. *Borders and Barriers. An Education Kit: Canada's Policy on Refugees/Family Reunification*. Toronto: Toronto Coalition for a Just Refugee and Immigration Policy.

Turritin, Jane Sawyer. 1983. "We Don't Look for Prejudice." In Jean Leonard Elliott, ed., *Two Nations, Many Cultures: Ethnic Groups in Canada*. Scarborough, ON: Prentice-Hall.

Van Dieren, Karen. 1984. "The Response of the WMS to the Immigration of Asian Women, 1888–1942." In Barbara K. Latham and Roberta J. Pazdro, eds., *Not Just Pin Money: Selected Essays on the History of Women's Work in British Columbia*. Victoria: Camosun College.

Van Kirk, Sylvia. 1980. *Many Tender Ties: Women in Fur Trade Society in Western Canada, 1670–1870*. Winnipeg: Watson and Dwyer.

Vorst, Jesse, Tania Das Gupta, Cy Gonick, Ronnie Leah, Alan Lennon, Alicja Muszynski, Roxana Ng, Ed Silva, Mercedes Steedman, Si Transkan, and Derek Wilkinson, eds. 1991. *Race, Class, Gender: Bonds and Barriers*. Toronto: Society for Socialist Studies, and Garamond.

Wotherspoon, Terry, ed. 1987. *The Political Economy of Canadian Schooling*. Toronto: Methuen.

Yawney, Carol. 1983. "To Grow a Daughter: Cultural Liberation and the Dynamics of Oppression in Jamaica." In Angela Miles and G. Finn, eds., *Feminism in Canada*. Montreal: Black Rose.

York, Geoffrey. 1989. *The Dispossessed: Life and Death in Native Canada*. Toronto: Lester and Orpen Dennys.

FAMILY POVERTY AND ECONOMIC STRUGGLES

LESLEY D. HARMAN

LEARNING OBJECTIVES

In this chapter, you will learn that:

- there are a number of myths about family life which need to be dispelled in order to understand family poverty in Canada;
- far from being carefree and blissful pockets of love and security, families, for many Canadians, are experienced as requiring a constant effort to keep the wolf from the door;
- Canada is a stratified society in which certain groups are less equal than others and tend to be more vulnerable to poverty; particularly disadvantaged are women, children, persons with disabilities, and aboriginal people;
- structural factors such as social reproduction and discrimination within a system of capitalism and patriarchy are the general causes of poverty in Canada today;
- economic hardship affects all social classes, including the middle class and the "working poor," primarily as a consequence of economic downturn;
- family poverty is deep and widespread in Canada today.

INTRODUCTION

The goal of this chapter is to discuss some of the sociological definitions, causes, and consequences of family poverty.[1] If you have ever heard someone say, "I can't afford to have children" or "I can't afford to work," you have witnessed an expression of the perpetual struggle that many people living in families today experience just to make ends meet. It is not unusual to hear people talk in economic terms about living in families, having children, and working. For those of you reading this book who have homes and children of your own, and all of the expenses that they may entail, this may not be news. For others of you who have had relatively few economic worries, it may come as quite a surprise that family poverty is a pressing concern today in Canadian society.

Perhaps the most enduring myth of family life is the belief that, once married with children, one will live happily ever after. But rarely discussed are the economic hardships, stresses, and pressures of family life. Far from being carefree and blissful pockets of love and security, families, for many Canadians, are experienced as requiring a constant effort to keep the wolf from the door. There are a number of myths about poverty, which we will seek to dispel in this chapter. The first such myth is that poor people are social "failures" who bring poverty on themselves. The second is that, if one works hard enough, one can be successful and avoid poverty. The third is that family poverty is not very extensive today in Canada. The fourth is that poverty is a new phenomenon in Canada.

In this chapter, it will be argued that Canada is a stratified society in which certain groups are less equal than others and tend to be more vulnerable to poverty. Structural factors such as **social reproduction** and discrimination are the general causes of poverty in Canada today. It will also be demonstrated that economic hardship affects all social classes, including the middle class and the "**working poor**," primarily as a consequence of economic downturn. Finally, it will be shown that family poverty is deep and widespread in Canada today. Particularly disadvantaged groups include women, children, persons with disabilities, and aboriginal people.

WHAT IS POVERTY?
▼

Canada is a very affluent society, and our standard of living is generally so much higher than that of those societies in which the majority of the earth's population live that it is sometimes hard to speak of poverty in absolute or objective terms and really be expressing anything meaningful. Indeed, defining poverty is difficult at the best of times.

RELATIVE AND ABSOLUTE POVERTY

One useful distinction is between *relative* and *absolute* poverty. By **relative poverty**, we mean that what is considered poor is relative to what the contemporary social standards are for "normal" and "wealthy." These standards change with economic fluctuations, technological developments, and changing definitions of the "good life." **Absolute poverty**, on the other hand, refers to a condition of mere physical survival. As Ross, Shillington, and Lochhead (1994, p. 4) point out, even the effort to determine absolute poverty is problematic, influenced as it is by contemporary societal norms, conditions, and services:

> The strictest application of this approach results in a standard of living sufficient only to keep the human body together ... whose components are food provided by a charitable group or food bank, shelter provided by a community hostel, second-hand clothing and access to basic remedial health care. The poverty line implied by such a budget would be very low; an annual income of $2,000 per person would probably cover it.

OBJECTIVE AND SUBJECTIVE POVERTY

Another useful distinction is between *objective* and *subjective* definitions of poverty. By **objective poverty,** is meant the prevailing definitions used by bodies whose purpose it is to collect, compile, and report data on poverty within the Canadian population, such as Statistics Canada and the Canadian Council on Social Development. In the most simple case, this involves setting an income level below which a family of four would be defined as living "in poverty." Roughly translated, this means that a family that spends more than 57 percent of its income on food, clothing, and shelter is considered to be poor (Lemprière, 1992, p. 18). In recent years, objective measures of poverty have become more sophisticated, taking into consideration such variables as the fact that the cost of living will vary between and within regions, and between types of family arrangement. So the definition of poverty is complex, even in objective terms, as illustrated by the Statistics Canada low-income cutoffs (see Table 6.1).

By **subjective poverty,** we refer to the way people feel about their standard of living. One may feel rich or poor entirely independently of Statistics Canada measures. For example, a full-time student living on a fixed allowance may run out of spending money early in the academic year and have to make do on $100. She might "feel" poor, even if her father is a millionaire and she stands to inherit a fortune. In this case, we would say that objectively she is rich (belonging to a wealthy family), but subjectively she feels poor. On the other hand, a homeless woman without a penny to her name might find a $100 bill in the park and feel like an heiress, if only for a day. In this case, we would say that objectively she is poor (because her annual income is virtually nothing), but subjectively she feels rich. The subjective definitions are important because we live in a society in which people tend to compare themselves with others; in which mass-media images of the "good life" are strong and compelling; in which children learn to demand consumer goods and feel inadequate, poor, and disadvantaged compared with other children if they do not have them. How we feel relative to others and relative to our perception of how

TABLE 6.1
▼
STATISTICS CANADA LOW-INCOME CUTOFFS, 1994

Size of Household	Population of Community of Residence				
	500 000+	100 000–499 999	30 000–99 999	Fewer than 30 000	Rural Areas
1 person	16 609	14 246	14 147	13 164	11 478
2 persons	20 762	17 806	17 685	16 455	14 348
3 persons	25 821	22 147	21 993	20 464	17 845
4 persons	31 256	26 809	26 623	24 773	21 600
5 persons	34 939	29 969	29 760	27 692	24 146
6 persons	38 622	33 128	32 897	30 610	26 692
7 or more	42 305	36 288	36 034	33 528	29 238

Source: Adapted from Statistics Canada, *Income Distributions by Size in Canada, 1992* (Catalogue no. 13-207-XTB). The authors have estimated the 1994 cutoffs by adjusting for estimated rates of inflation.

we should feel also weighs heavily in our enjoyment of life and our experience of "hardship."

Both objective and subjective measures of poverty seem to take as their standard middle-class values of the "good life," which render problematic much of the sociological discussion of poverty. If it is a middle-class value system that defines what it means to be poor, then it is also the same value system that evaluates those poor people and attempts to explain why they have "failed." Indeed, poverty is rarely thought of as a virtue, but rather as a failing. It would not be an exaggeration to say that, in our culture, poverty is regularly associated with evil, and those living in poverty are thought of as somehow less worthy than those who are not. Even our language reveals that one's "worth" or "value" is expressed in monetary rather than in other social terms. With these qualifications in mind, let us examine some of the figures on poverty in Canada today.

The data on objective family poverty are striking. One and a half million households now live in poverty in this country (Ross et al., 1994). Until the effects of the recession of the early 1990s began to be felt, it appeared as if family poverty was on the decline. By 1989, 13.6 percent of Canadians were living in poverty, a marked decrease from 16.8 percent in 1984 (Ross, 1992, p. 60). However, as Table 6.2 indicates, by 1991 the rate increased to 15.9 percent, with 13 (21.1) percent of Canadian families living in poverty (Ross et al., 1994).[2] Particularly striking are the figures of 60 percent for lone-parent

TABLE 6.2
▼
POVERTY RATES AND TOTAL NUMBERS IN POVERTY, 1973, 1981, 1986, 1991: STATISTICS CANADA AND CANADIAN COUNCIL ON SOCIAL DEVELOPMENT DEFINITIONS

	1973		1981		1986		1991	
	Number ('000s)	Rate (%)	Number ('000s)	Rate (%)	Number ('000s)	Rate (%)	Number ('000s)	Rate (%)
FAMILIES								
Statistics								
Canada	701	13.4	721	11.3	801	11.8	949	13.0
CCSD	906	17.4	1 307	20.5	1 444	21.2	1 543	21.1
UNATTACHED INDIVIDUALS								
Statistics								
Canada	767	40.2	940	37.5	1 004	34.5	1 259	36.6
CCSD	756	39.7	991	39.5	1 103	37.9	1 280	37.1
TOTAL HOUSEHOLDS								
Statistics								
Canada	1 468	20.6	1 661	18.7	1 805	18.6	2 209	20.6
65 years								
and over	506	41.0	533	33.7	433	24.2	522	25.0
under 65								
years	962	16.3	1 129	15.4	1 372	17.3	1 687	19.5
CCSD	1 664	23.3	2 297	25.9	2 547	26.2	2 822	26.3
65 years								
and over	582	48.3	1 495	20.5	1 782	22.5	2 043	23.6
under 65								
years	1 082	18.2	803	34.9	765	30.0	779	27.6
TOTAL PERSONS								
Statistics								
Canada	3 269	16.2	3 339	14.0	3 597	14.4	4 230	15.9

Source: David P. Ross, E. Richard Shillington, and Clarence Lochhead, *The Canadian Fact Book on Poverty, 1994* (Ottawa: Canadian Council on Social Development, 1994). Statistics Canada data based on Survey of Consumer Finances microdata tapes.

families headed by females and 38 percent for young families headed by individuals 24 years or younger. In Ontario, the rate of family poverty is now 31.8 percent, doubtless a reflection of the enormous hardship produced by the recent economic recession. The only promising sign from the data is the substantial drop in poverty — 25 percent — among the elderly.

THE WORKING POOR AND THE NEAR POOR
▼

Often rendered invisible is a category called the "working poor." These are families in which the main earner worked 49 weeks during the year or more, but who remained poor. In 1991, 28.6 percent of all non-elderly poor households fell into this category, and 60 percent of these families had dependent children (Ross et al., 1994, pp. 76–79). In addition, the "**near poor**" are those "whose standard of living closely resembles that of the poor and is much different from that of typical (or middle-income) households" (Ross and Shillington, 1990, p. 64). This category is important to include because the low-income cutoffs tend to be arbitrary and it is misguided to believe that those who fall immediately above these lines are not experiencing economic hardship. Ross and Shillington found in examining the incomes of households sitting at 110 percent of the poverty line (in other words, earning an income 10 percent higher than the poverty line), that the additional family income amounted to only the equivalent of a daily bus or metro fare for each member of the household. They concluded that this was "not enough to permit a change in the way households live. For all practical purposes, households in this income range are just as poor as households that are classed as poor under the Statistics Canada definition of poverty" (1990, p. 65). Accordingly, 12 percent of female lone-parent households, 15 per cent of elderly couples, 15 percent of no-income households, 8 percent of single-income households, and 4 percent of dual-income households would be classified as living near poverty (1990, pp. 68–70).

Because the objective measures of poverty are arbitrary and subject to revision at any time, it is important to consider those Canadians who live close to poverty and to realize that they are exempt only from the measure and the label "poor," not from the experience of economic difficulty. Indeed, so much of the effect of poverty stems from the subjective experiences of those undergoing it that the objective measures give us only a very partial picture at best. Nevertheless, what the figures do tell us is that there is deep and extensive family poverty in Canadian society today and that the situation seems to be getting worse, not better.

THE HISTORY OF POVERTY IN CANADA
▼

For many born in the post–baby boom generations, it would seem that the recent economic recession in Canada has brought about new and dreadful poverty for the first time. A glance at the pages of history, however, tells us that poverty has been a constant feature of life in Canada.

RECENT QUINTILES

One graphic indication of the consistency in income distribution in Canada is the Statistics Canada breakdown of national income into **quintiles**. The population is divided into fifths on the basis of wealth, and the percentage of total national income shared by that fifth is indicated. In Table 6.3, it is striking to note that, consistently between 1951 and 1987, the bottom fifth of the population has shared approximately 4 percent of the total national income, while the top fifth has shared between 42 and 43 percent. Beyond the quintile figures, Ryan notes, the figures for wealth indicate even greater inequality than income. In 1980, 18.8 percent of the national wealth was owned by the top 1 percent of the population, while 57.1 percent of the national wealth was owned by the top 10 percent (Ryan, 1990, p. 49). The conclusions to be drawn from these figures are fairly straightforward. Social inequality is a real, enduring, and consistent feature of life in Canadian society. The figures defy the myths that poverty is a new phenomenon and that the situation of the poor is dramatically improved by social spending.

THE GREAT DEPRESSION

During this century, Canada experienced a catastrophic blow to its economy, which became known as "the Great Depression." Lasting from 1929 to 1939,

---

TABLE 6.3
▼
DISTRIBUTION OF TOTAL NATIONAL INCOME IN CANADA*

	Bottom fifth	Second fifth	Middle fifth	Fourth fifth	Top fifth
1951	4.4%	11.2	18.3	23.3	42.8
1975	4.0	10.6	17.6	25.1	42.6
1979	4.2	10.6	17.6	25.3	42.3
1984	4.5	10.3	17.1	25.0	43.0
1987	4.7	10.4	16.9	24.8	43.2

*Statistics Canada figures for families and unattached individuals. Figures given are before taxes, but include results of government transfer payments, such as family allowance, Employment Insurance benefits, Canada and Quebec Pension Plans, Old Age Security, and Guaranteed Income Supplements.

Source: Michael T. Ryan, *Solidarity: Christian Social Teaching and Canadian Society*, 2nd ed. (London, ON: Guided Study Programs in the Catholic Faith, 1990), p. 49. Reprinted with the permission of the Guided Study Program in the Catholic Faith.

the period has been referred to as Canada's "ten lost years" (Broadfoot, 1973). Following the collapse of the New York Stock Exchange in 1929, Canada's fledgling economy crumbled. Broadfoot summarizes the events:

> Canada's markets began to collapse. The U.S., to protect its own, erected high tariff walls, shutting out Canadian goods. The prairie wheat economy tottered as the $1.60 a bushel price of 1929 skidded to 38 cents in $2\frac{1}{2}$ years. By that time, even the weather had turned against us: the drought was destroying the West, and Canada like the rest of the world was deep into the worst depression in history.
>
> As the West and wheat went, so did the rest of Canada. Farmers stopped buying. Eastern factories closed, or laid off hundreds. Construction virtually stopped. Banks no longer lent money; instead, they called in loans. Less and less money was put into circulation and fewer and fewer goods were produced and more and more factories were shut down and the rolls of the poor grew longer and longer and the gloom and despair deepened.
>
> Depression is a downward spiral and there was nothing to halt it. At times, the spiral was slowed, but it was never halted. When the upturn began around 1937 or 1938, it was a long, long struggle. (p. vii)

Broadfoot's book is a collection of interviews with people who survived the Great Depression. Their stories reveal the difficulties of the age, which seem almost unimaginable today. For millions of Canadians, life became a matter of sheer survival. They were living in "absolute" poverty. In 1932, it was estimated that an Ontario family of five would need $6 to $7 a week to eat nutritiously (Grayson and Bliss, 1971, p. xiv). Many were required to survive on $10 or less per month (Broadfoot, 1973). Government relief was received by about 20 percent of the population in the worst year of the Depression (Grayson and Bliss, 1971, p. x). But as Grayson and Bliss point out, "These figures ignore the tens of thousands who were too proud to fall back on 'charity' and the millions whose standards of living fell but not quite far enough to force them onto relief" (p. x). One account puts the unemployment and social-assistance situation into perspective:[3]

> Lethbridge in '32, and I'm sure, quite sure of that date, had about 20 percent unemployed. That doesn't mean what it does today. It meant 20 percent of the men *who had worked* were on the dole. Men on the bricks. It *didn't* mean wives who might have wanted to work, or had once worked because, you see, not many women worked. Waitressing, five and ten, a few banks, secretaries. ... And it didn't mean young people who had come out of high school or school and couldn't get a job. There were no jobs for them, and they were not listed as employables.
>
> ... The 20 percent of 1932 was only the men, the heads of families. It meant one father of a family in five had no work and so his wife

and their five kids were on the relief too. Total all that up and it makes a terrible high total.

Another way. One family in five was out of work. Two families were not on relief but so deep in debt and so far into poverty that they would have taken relief if they could have. The fourth family was just getting by, and the fifth family, the merchants, the lawyers, all the professional men, the grain people and the retired people living in town, they were doing very well. Very well indeed. (p. 68)

Few were spared. However, as the following story of a young immigrant shows, the wealthy seemed to profit from the misfortunes of others:

There was this fellow, Steve Metarski. He'd come over from Poland, the Ukraine, over there, as a kid of 14 or so and worked building railroad and became a subcontractor, and when he married my cousin he was about 45. He was what you would call The Solid Citizen. ... His first wife had died and he had this lovely house in a good part of Hamilton. ...

About 1930 ... construction just went crash and Steve lost his business in six months. Apparently it was just plain murder. Assets didn't cover debts at the bankruptcy auction so they — and who *they* are, I just don't know — but they took his house and he got his lawyer to work something out so he'd still have possession and ownership as long as he made the payments. Monthly. But man, he'd bought the house in, say, the mid-twenties, and he had a big chunk of a house left to pay, and it was a hell of a house, and interest was about 8 or 9 percent. We think 9 percent high today? Think what it was then. I'm in the business and I would say it would be crushing.

... Here was Steve, no business, no job, no cash buried in the backyard and with some screwy deal between the bank and his creditors and where was his out? There was none.

Sally said he never made more than two payments, and had to sell furniture to do that. Then the house was swiped out from under him and sold at about a quarter of actual worth to some guy in Burlington. The guy moved in with his wife and kids and let Steve and Sally live in the basement, and Sally was the maid and Steve did work around the yard, stoked the furnace and was the guy's chauffeur. A chauffeur, for Christ sakes!

Look at it this way. Say, on July 1, 1930, Steve still had a business and a fine house and a nice wife. By January 1, 1931, six months later, he's zilch. Living in the basement in his own house and his wife is the maid upstairs, and the cook. (pp. 8–9)

In another story, a survivor recounts how, during the Depression, poverty was considered a crime:

I never so much as stole a dime, a loaf of bread, a gallon of gas, but in those days I was treated like a criminal. By the twist in some men's minds,

men in high places, it became a criminal act just to be poor, and this per-
colated down through the whole structure until it reached the town cop
or the railway bull and if you were without a job, on the roads, wandering, you automatically became a criminal. It was the temper of the times.

I was, you could say, a wanderer. One of the unfortunates. A victim of the economic system? Perhaps. Certainly, most certainly a casu-
alty in the battle between ignorant men who were running this country.
There are two places in Ontario, in the fair city of Toronto and down at
the even fairer city of London, where ancient records will show that I am
a criminal. A criminal in that I violated the Criminal Code of Canada
and thereby gained a criminal record for begging. Jail.

If you were poor but had a house and sent your kids to Sunday
school, if you had no money and nothing for food, then you were unfortunate and people looked after you. If you left home, like I did, so my
brothers and sisters would have more food and more room to sleep, then
you became a criminal. You did not have to commit a criminal act. Mr.
[R.B.] Bennett saw to that. You just had to be you, without money.
Throw the guy in jail. Get him out of town. Lay the stick to his back-
side. Hustle him along. There's no more soup and bread and there won't
be tomorrow so you guys get the hell out of here, see? How many times
have I heard these things. (pp. 19–20)

One survivor speaks of finding the family's papers after the death of
her father in 1968. The receipts told the tale of how her father had paid for
the land:

You know what that old man had done? He had been paying off that land
at two dollars a month, five dollars, sometimes ten, sometimes the receipt
would read that instead of money, Connor, the owner, had taken a steer
as payment. The things made me just break down and cry. Every month,
he never missed a month, Dad made some sort of payment. Just the
interest sometimes; and a big deal for him was a bottle of whisky at
Christmas and sometimes a package of Picobac for his pipe.

He scraped and scraped and scraped and scraped some more and
he kept us, Mother, me, my cousin from Calgary who was an orphan, he
kept us on that farm. In those days a man would hang on to his land as
if it was life itself. I guess it was. Those old and faded receipts. Two dollars, four. His life's blood. (p. 63)

Another survivor questions the official government statement that no
one in Canada was starving, with the following tale:

R.B. Bennett said nobody in Canada was dying of starvation and if he
meant like Biafra, kids with big bloated bellies, no, not that kind of starvation. But I know one family which lost three children from hunger.
Lack of food, malnutrition, then diarrhea which they couldn't fight

because they were so weak — and that to me is dying of starvation. They were my sister's kids. ... (pp. 91–92)

It was a dreadful period in Canadian history, but not so long ago. At its worst, the Depression saw whole families lose their homes, their life savings, and all of their belongings. Many went hungry. The government set up "relief camps," where it is estimated that more than 200 000 single homeless men were "interned" between 1933 and 1936, ostensibly to offset a revolution, and paid 20 cents a day (Grayson and Bliss, 1971, p. xv). The memories are bitter, but many wonder, "Could it happen again?"

THE "NEW" POVERTY

With the economic hardships brought about by the recession of the early 1990s, politicians, planners, scholars, and citizens are wondering if we have entered a period of "new" poverty. While most tip-toe around the word "depression," perhaps for fear of causing things to get even worse, there would seem to be a growing resignation among the population that the current economic slump will be with us for some time. For Dean and Taylor-Gooby (1992), looking at Britain, this "new" poverty has been brought about primarily by the rise in unemployment. With long-term unemployment has come a general increase in the welfare rolls and the growth of the segment of society dependent on government support (see Figure 6.1). Accompanying unemployment as a factor in the new poverty has been the dramatic increase in lone-parent households, primarily headed by women. The general vulnerability to poverty of women who are not supported by men is known as the "**feminization of poverty**." Together, unemployment and the feminization of poverty are the forces at work in the "new" poverty.

CAUSES OF FAMILY POVERTY
▼

Why do some families become poor? Sociologists have debated this question for decades. In the short space allowed, we can only highlight some of the issues.

THE "CULTURE OF POVERTY" ARGUMENT

For many Canadians who have grown up in poverty, the likelihood of having a better life in their adulthood is remote. Some sociologists have attributed this to what they call the "**culture of poverty**" (Lewis, 1966). By this they mean that poor families tend to develop fatalistic values and attitudes about their lot in life, devaluing education, career aspirations, and the usual middle-class def-

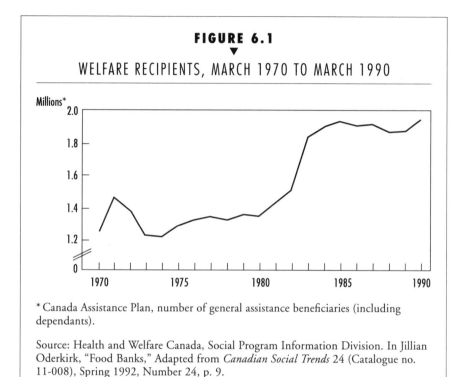

FIGURE 6.1
▼
WELFARE RECIPIENTS, MARCH 1970 TO MARCH 1990

*Canada Assistance Plan, number of general assistance beneficiaries (including dependants).

Source: Health and Welfare Canada, Social Program Information Division. In Jillian Oderkirk, "Food Banks," Adapted from *Canadian Social Trends* 24 (Catalogue no. 11-008), Spring 1992, Number 24, p. 9.

initions of success. They develop a sense of hopelessness of ever getting out of their situation and live with a type of survival mentality. This, in turn, becomes a self-fulfilling prophecy in which failure is inevitable and poverty is seen to cause more poverty. This orientation is contrasted sharply with that of families who share a more middle-class orientation to success, career advancement, and an ever-brighter future.

Since families are the context for the most lasting socialization, these attitudes and values developed in early childhood prove to be important in the subsequent orientation of the child. Within the culture of poverty, it is argued, parents look forward impatiently to their children being able to contribute to the family's income. Prolonged school attendance will take away from the more immediate gratification offered by dropping out and getting a job. For the child as well, the prospect of having spending money to buy a car or stereo equipment, things that cash-strapped parents cannot afford, may draw them away from school work and career aspirations.

Thus, the value placed on higher education by middle-class families is not always shared by the poor. Not only is university or college education costly, but it is often derided as not being "real work." As Willis (1981) found in his study of working-class youths in Britain, the prevalent attitude was that schooling is a waste of time because poor children will probably fail anyway, so what's the use of trying? In contrast, the middle-class orientation toward education is one that seeks more and better education for children, in recognition of the fact that occupations and incomes in Canadian society tend to be positively correlated with the amount of education attained. In turn, the likelihood that a high-school drop-out will get a well-paying job is very slim indeed (Canadian Council on Social Development, 1991). In addition to a lack of encouragement, poor children often have school problems because of poor diet and health care, and limited time and space at home to study. Because of all of these factors, children from poor families simply do not have the resources to compete successfully and tend to do more poorly in school than children from wealthy families. This is often taken, by families, schools, and governments alike, as evidence that they shouldn't be there in the first place.

THE "SOCIAL REPRODUCTION" ARGUMENT

The "culture of poverty" concept has been roundly criticized (Leacock, 1971). Most significantly, it has been indicted for being invented by middle-class social scientists who tend to divide the world into "us" and "them." As we have shown, they assumed that the reason for poverty and its perpetuation is that poor people share values and attitudes that render them incapable of competing in the dominant culture defined by middle-class standards of success. It follows that, to eliminate poverty, one should begin by changing the values and attitudes of the poor to make them coincide with those of the dominant culture.

It is precisely this solution to poverty that is problematic, because it ignores the structural basis of poverty — that wealth in Canadian society is concentrated in the hands of a few elite groups. Lone-parent families, the aged, the unemployed, aboriginal people, and persons with disabilities cannot single-handedly, by altering their attitudes and values, change this rigid and enduring economic structure, or their place in it. To assume that they can takes all responsibility for poverty away from the rich and the state and allows for "**blaming the victim**" (Ryan, 1971). Critics of the culture of poverty approach admit that the values and attitudes of the poor differ from those of successful middle-class people, but they see these as the result of poverty, not its cause. Focussing exclusively on changing their attitudes is thus blaming them for their problems.

Blaming the victim is as popular a pastime when discussing poverty today as it was more than 25 years ago, when Ryan (1971) brought the term into the sociological vocabulary. He was accusing social scientists who used the "culture of poverty" concept of merely engaging in a more sophisticated version of victim-blaming than that frequently engaged in by the general public. Often we tend to dismiss the troubles of others as a consequence of their own failings, rather than looking for larger structural reasons for social injustice.

Such victim-blaming is rooted in the belief that success and achievement in North American society are attributable to the hard work and ability of the individual. This is equivalent to thinking of our society as a **meritocracy** — that all have an equal chance of success and those at the top are those with the most merit. Attitudes such as "the poor are poor because they deserve it," or "people on welfare are lazy bums who don't want to work," or "anyone can make it if they really want to" reflect an unrealistic view of the current economic system and hold poor people responsible for their own misfortune. As Dean and Taylor-Gooby (1992) point out, attitudes toward the poor basically contain a dual concern with "delinquency" and "dependency." They argue that both are the source of general fear, for, to quote Elliot Liebow, "the one threatens the property, peace and good order of society at large; the other drains its purse" (1967, p. 6).

Meritocracy as a principle that explains poverty is contrasted with the "social reproduction" approach. Critics of the culture of poverty concept, such as Leacock (1971) and Ryan (1971), argue that we have to look at the structural reasons for why the rich get richer and the poor get poorer in capitalist society. Why is it that the distribution of income between classes has been so remarkably intransigent over the past 40 years, as seen in Table 6.3 on page 194? We must recognize that there are important class differences in our society, and members of the well-to-do classes enjoy opportunities and privileges simply because of their class positions.

One useful tool for this is the concept of "**cultural capital**," or the cultural and financial resources that support a middle-class lifestyle. According to the social-reproduction point of view, success in capitalist society is more likely if one has cultural capital (Lipset, 1972). Cultural capital includes everything, from the financial backing to attend university and have all of the resources to educate one into the middle-class values and culture system, to "connections" in the business world that ease a child's entry into the job market, to more subtle indications like language. Bernstein (1973) argued that middle-class children learn "elaborated" codes that provide an entry into the middle-class world, while children without cultural capital tend to learn "restricted" codes that do not provide access to upward mobility. Thus, the concept of cultural capital helps us to understand the barriers that children from disadvantaged groups may experience, through no fault of their own, because their families have not had the means to provide them with the tools necessary to compete in a middle-class world. There is, then, a tendency for the social reproduction of class membership. Middle-class families not only have the means to provide their children with higher education, but also the orientation that encourages this. The tendency for families with cultural capital is to pass this on to their children (Bourdieu and Passeron, 1977).

CAUSES OF MIDDLE-CLASS POVERTY

Economic struggles can affect families from any class, and this has been increasingly apparent during the recent recession. Children from poor backgrounds regularly encounter a **glass ceiling**, confirming what they already know: you can't get out of the class you were born into. For middle-class families, however, it may come as a shock to realize that the future may hold the real possibility of economic hardship. **Vertical intergenerational mobility** refers to the tendency of children to be upwardly or downwardly mobile relative to their parents' status. Although it is the goal of many middle-class parents to give their children what they did not have, including childhood experiences as well as opportunities for advancement when they are adults, the likelihood of achieving upward mobility is becoming increasingly rare. There are not many ways that the child of a doctor and a lawyer can surpass her parents. Thus, we often encounter a net *downward* intergenerational mobility in the higher-income groups, producing relative poverty for these children (Porter, 1979).

For most Canadian home-owners, the single-family dwelling is the most substantial investment they will make during their lives. And while there are those wealthy citizens who do not need to work to earn a living, who live in homes that are debt-free, 89 percent of Canadians are work-dependent, which means that they must work in the paid labour force or have another source of regular income in order to cover their cost of living (Rinehart, 1987). Mortgage payments or rent payments must be made every month. Children must be fed and clothed, and their many needs somehow provided for. Other expenses related to living up to the middle-class lifestyle, including one or more cars, holidays, and a variety of consumer goods, may be affordable only through bank loans or credit card debts, which will have to be reduced through regular payments. A middle-class family may find that a variety of unexpected changes in their situation will make them experience economic hardship. Even though they have steady jobs, a sudden dramatic increase in interest rates may send a family's mortgage payments sky-high. Unexpected repairs on a house or car may entail major financial outlays. Economic downturn may result in fewer hours, fewer sales, or fewer contracts for workers, thus reducing their net income. When the connection with the paid workforce is severed, through unemployment, illness, or death of a worker, the household unit may find itself quickly imperilled, on the brink of financial disaster. Disability or lengthy illness of a breadwinner may mean little or no income, and possible job loss. The birth of a child may mean a reduction in the net family income while one parent stays at home with the baby or continues to work while paying for child care. Clearly, in our current economic times, many families cannot count on a predictable source of income and a predictable set of expenses. This may help to explain why one outcome of the recession has been a severe self-imposed restriction on consumer spending.

Because it is getting more and more expensive to live up to the standards set by and for middle-class society, and because fewer and fewer jobs have long-term security attached to them, more and more families find it necessary to have two incomes in order to make ends meet. Indeed, the dual-income family is now the norm. By 1987, a full 70 percent of married Canadian women under 65 were employed, with 36 percent employed full-time all year and 34 percent employed less than full-time all year (National Council of Welfare, 1990, p. 21). By 1991, two-thirds of mothers with children at home were in the paid labour force. However, "regardless of age, mothers working full-time … earn less than women without children at home" (Logan and Belliveau, 1995, p. 28).

One of the greatest stresses on family life is the financial strain introduced by a new baby. Joy at the arrival of this tiny new life may be tempered by the prospect of having another mouth to feed. Particularly when there have been no previous children and no hand-me-downs, there is an initial outlay of a lot of money for furniture and clothing. The weekly grocery bill may soar when the costs of formula, baby food, and diapers are added on. A parent who stays home has lost a substantial part of her income during the initial period of maternity leave, followed by a total absence of income once the maternity-leave period is up. Many families find themselves financially strapped, and women in particular experience a great deal of conflict over whether to return to work. The dilemma is often shaped by the availability of affordable child care, the income of the parent, and the flexibility of the occupation. To return to work after the birth of a baby means that the family will most likely have to employ a caregiver to look after the child, unless there are relatives who would do it for free (rare in this day and age).

Although the cost of child care varies regionally and with the type of service provided, it is reasonably safe to assume that an earner would have to be making a considerable amount more than the minimum wage to justify paying for child care. In addition, a worker requires an appropriate wardrobe and transportation, and often must pay more money for meals than she would spend at home. After taxes, it is not unusual to hear a woman say, "I can't afford to work." What this means is that it would end up costing her more to work and hire someone to look after her child than to stay at home and forfeit her income. While it may be the case that men can't afford to work in some situations, the current wage structure is gender-biased in such a way that, by 1995, women made only 73 percent of the salaries that men did (*Canadian Social Trends*, 1997). Women who are on a career track may delay childbearing for several years, being aware of the costs to their career, as well as to their financial situation, of having a child. Thus, it is not unusual to hear a woman say, "I can't afford to have children."

So, clearly, economic struggles for families are produced by and produce conflicts around work and home. These struggles are seen to be primarily women's problems, as women have been the caregivers in our society — not only for children, but also for the elderly. In fact, much of the care of the old and the sick is done within the voluntary sector, through the unpaid domestic labour of full-time homemakers (Hooyman and Ryan, 1987). And just as it is taken for granted that women will care for children without pay or recognition, so it is taken for granted that the old and the sick will be taken care of. For the full-time homemaker to return to work may present "elder-care" as well as child-care dilemmas. Care of the elderly is expensive and, as aging is often associated with poverty in our society, may not be affordable without significant strain on the household budget. Unlike the day-care solution, however, care of the elderly often involves a relatively permanent assignment to an institution. Similar to the guilt experienced by parents who place their children in day-care centres, the guilt experienced in placing one's parents in a "home" suggests just how strong the social pressures are to take care of them within family settings.

The 1990s have brought us into the uneasy realization that the entire definition of work is being questioned, hurried along by the dramatic rise in unemployment across all occupations and all social classes. As Burman (1988) has noted, unemployment can deal an enormous blow to one's self-esteem, as well as placing a family in economic difficulty. In cases of long-term unemployment of a sole breadwinner, families may experience considerable stress. Low self-esteem, diminished hope for future employment, substance abuse, strained family relationships, and social stigma within the community can all be consequences of long-term unemployment. As well, lengthy financial dependency on the state may mean net downward mobility for family members, having long-term consequences for the life chances of children. As more and more Canadians experience unemployment first-hand, it is imperative that as a society we begin to lift the social stigma placed on individuals and families when the economy does not favour them, and begin to look at larger structural reasons for their individual hardship. The days in which it was safe and smug to blame the victim are fading fast as we begin to realize that few are truly secure in their jobs.

BOX 6.1
▼
POOR FAMILIES LOSING MARKET SHARE

A study released in March 1997 by the Canadian Council on Social Development (CCSD) called *Left Poor by the Market: A Look at Family Poverty and Earnings* shows that poor families fare worse in the labour market than they did 10 years ago. Study authors Grant Schellenberg, CCSD research associate, and David Ross, CCSD executive director, compared labour-market conditions in 1984 and 1994, two similar points in the business cycle. They found that families living below the poverty line experienced a decline in wages and that fewer of them were actively seeking employment.

Hardest hit were families headed by young adults (under age 35) and lone parents. Poor families headed by adults between the ages of 54 and 65 years also lost ground over the decade, as rates of unemployment for that age group climbed. The authors found that the most severe drop in average earnings of poor families occurred in Ontario, and that families in New Brunswick experienced the most improvement in their situation.

"Clearly, the lack of jobs, and a decrease in minimum wages over the decade have hurt Canada's lowest income earners hardest," says Schellenberg.

"We undertook this study because governments today are reducing public spending on social programs, with the expectation that poor families will be able to increase their self-reliance through their own earnings from the marketplace. Unfortunately, this report suggests that the marketplace is in an even weaker position than it was a decade ago to provide all families with earnings that would take them above the poverty line," says Ross.

"More than half a million Canadian families relied on public income supports to keep them above the poverty line in 1994. Without those government transfers, the number of poor Canadian families would have jumped by 56 percent that year. And the average depth of poverty would have gone up by 70 percent, or $5700 per poor family," says Schellenberg.

Source: Adapted from Canadian Council on Social Development, *Communique*, released March 18, 1997. Reprinted with permission of the Canadian Council on Social Development.

DISADVANTAGED GROUPS
▼

In Canadian society today, certain groups of people are systematically disadvantaged. Of particular interest are women, children, persons with disabilities, and aboriginal people. When people belong to more than one of these

categories, for example, Aboriginal children or disabled women, their susceptibility to poverty tends to increase.

WOMEN

It has been argued so far in this chapter that the myths of family life have concealed widespread family poverty and economic struggles in Canadian society.
What has become increasingly evident is that women's economic dependency
within patriarchal society has made poverty very likely for them if they live
alone. Lone-parent families headed by females are the most likely families to
be poor (Ross and Shillington, 1990, p. 41). This is symptomatic of a larger
trend known as "the feminization of poverty."

The term "feminization of poverty" means that, without the support of
a man, a woman is likely to be poor. This problem is widespread in Canadian
society. According to the National Council of Welfare (1990, p. 15), 84 percent of all women will spend at least part of their adult lives without husbands,
having to support themselves and their children. Today, 75 percent of never-
married female single parents, 52 percent of previously married female single
parents, 44 percent of unattached women over 65, and 33 percent of unattached women under 65 are living in poverty in Canada (National Council of
Welfare, 1990, p. 3). At every stage of their lives, women are more prone to
poverty than men, and more likely to be trapped, and eventually die, in a life
of poverty (Harman, 1992).

The Working Poor

Changes in women's work both in and out of the home have paralleled changes
in the nature of the household as an economic unit. The interdependency
between the private and the public realms necessitates that most families
engage in both social and biological reproduction in the private realm and productive labour (earning an income) in the public realm, as demonstrated in
Figure 6.2.

The gendered division of labour has ensured that women occupy the private realm and men occupy the public realm. Women's work has been restricted
to the "double ghetto" of unpaid domestic labour in the home and poorly paid,
low-status pink-collar jobs in the paid labour force (Armstrong and Armstrong,
1978). Men's work, on the other hand, has been compartmentalized into the
highly paid, high-status white-collar sector and the traditionally physical blue-
collar sectors. Both arenas of "men's work" have been seen to reflect men's
greater suitability for the hard, cold, aggressive, competitive marketplace that
is the public realm, while both arenas of "women's work" have been seen to
reflect women's greater suitability for the soft, emotional, passive, and nurtur-

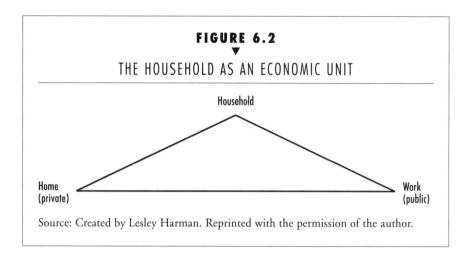

FIGURE 6.2
▼
THE HOUSEHOLD AS AN ECONOMIC UNIT

Household

Home
(private)

Work
(public)

Source: Created by Lesley Harman. Reprinted with the permission of the author.

ant roles of wife, mother, and overall caregiver. Although in recent years more and more women are being employed in non-traditional occupations, a substantial majority of women continue to be employed in the traditional pink-collar sectors (clerical, teaching, nursing, social work, and domestic activities). In 1988, 76 percent of women in the paid labour force worked in these traditional female jobs (National Council of Welfare, 1990, p. 21). And while it is also true that more and more men are doing unpaid domestic labour in the home, women continue to do the bulk of the housework. When they also work in the paid labour force, they are often forced to work a "double day" — to do a full day's work outside of the home during the day, followed by the equivalent amount of time doing the domestic labour required to keep the household operating (Luxton, Rosenberg, and Arat-Koc, 1990).

Significant shifts in the paid labour force in recent years, particularly the dramatic rise in unemployment during the current recession, are important in understanding family poverty. Women's participation in the paid labour force has steadily increased, from 28 percent of all workers in 1961 to 44 percent in 1988 (National Council of Welfare, 1990, p. 20). By 1989, 58 percent of Canadian women were in the paid labour force (Parliament, 1990, p. 18).

According to Pat Armstrong (1984), while women have progressively been moving into the workforce, it is a fallacy to assume that they have been "taking jobs away from men." Rather, there are several forces at work. First, because of economic downturn, many previously single-income families have experienced economic difficulties, and women have been "pushed" out of the home into the labour force. They have also been "pulled" out by the opening up of low-paying, typically pink-collar jobs as the state has expanded dramatically since the last war, to the point of being the largest employer in Canada.

Technological changes such as the computer revolution, through which desktop computers have become standard office fare and data processing has become an industry in its own right, have opened up vast opportunities for work in a traditionally female-dominated field, at the same time dramatically changing the skills and job requirements associated with clerical work. For example, "filing" — manually sorting and storing paper documents, once occupying armies of poorly educated and poorly paid women — has taken on a totally new meaning over the past twenty years. Now the mountains of paper have been reduced to electromagnetic fields stored on computer memory, and the physical act of filing to the pushing of a button. Computer innovations have also been responsible for job losses in some blue-collar areas, typically the arena of "men's work." The worker composition of the automobile industry, for example, has been significantly altered by the introduction of robots to perform work that men once did. Unemployment in blue-collar areas has also served to push women into the workforce, in some cases to become the sole breadwinner in families.

The reasons for women's increased labour-force participation are rooted in the larger structural relations of patriarchal, capitalist society. The triangulation between home, work, and household (see Figure 6.2) means that women are often caught between realms when they strive to "have it all." It is difficult for women to thrive financially without being dependent on a male breadwinner. As the biological reproducers of the species, women have been socially cast into roles that place priority on motherhood. When women work for an income they tend to be discriminated against, as it is assumed that their paid labour is less significant than that of men. Women's paid labour can become a poverty trap, with a catch-22: many women cannot make enough money in the paid labour force to pay someone else to look after their children, therefore ensuring that they will stay home, thus disadvantaging themselves when they do seek re-entry into the labour force. Financial independence becomes increasingly difficult. If women live without men, either by choice or by necessity, they are often forced to become dependent on the state through Family Benefits payments.

Lone Parents

In 1991, lone-parent families made up 13 percent of all Canadian families (Oderkirk and Lochhead, 1992, p. 27). This figure is not much different from that in 1941, when just over 12 percent of all Canadian families were lone-parent families (1992, p. 27). The major demographic differences, however, are that in 1941 death of a spouse was the most frequent cause of lone-parenting, whereas today lone-parent families tend to be more the result of separation, divorce, and widowhood (79 percent), or never-married women raising their children alone (16 percent) (1992, p. 28).

Throughout the life cycle, living in a potentially pregnant body means that reproduction will significantly affect women's material existence. Teenage pregnancy frequently leads to early and long-term poverty. Along with high rates of separation, divorce, and widowhood, these life events result in 82 percent of lone-parent families being headed by women (1992, p. 27).

A study of gender differences in lone-parent families reveals that, as with other disadvantaged groups, lone parents are doubly disadvantaged when they are women. In general, female lone parents tend to be younger, less well educated, and more likely to live in poverty than male lone parents. In 1991, lone mothers with dependent children constituted 30 percent of all poor families, compared with 24 percent in 1981, indicating that female-headed lone-parent families are making up an increasing proportion of Canada's poor (Ross et al., 1994, p. 63). In 1993, 76 percent of these families with children under 7 were poor, while 81 percent of never-married mothers were raising their children in poverty (Ross, Scott, and Kelly, 1996, p. 3). The rates of poverty and major sources of income, broken down by sex, are provided in Figure 6.3, and the 1993 rates among Canadian families in Figure 6.4.

As we will see in Chapter 8, the prospects for getting out of a life of poverty are often bleak for female lone parents, who often become dependent on the state and face systemic blocks to their opportunities to "get off the system." Early pregnancy, whether in a marriage or not, virtually excludes the possibility of women getting enough education and training to develop a career that might eventually lead to economic independence. And as women age, their job prospects are not always very favourable. In old age, women usually outlive their male partners and may find themselves impoverished, living on a fixed income and all alone. Increasingly, we are witnessing the ultimate tragedy of the feminization of poverty in the growing visibility of homeless women.

CHILDREN

In 1989, it was brought to the attention of the Canadian public that more than one million Canadian children under the age of 16 are growing up in poverty (Barter, 1992, p. 11). The House of Commons passed a motion stating a goal of eliminating poverty among children by the year 2000 (Kitchen et al., 1991). The 1990s were to be the decade in which child poverty was redressed in this country. However, child poverty is on the rise. By 1994, one in five Canadian children was living in poverty (Ross et al., 1996, p. 1).

Children are particularly vulnerable to poverty. Living in families means that they are dependent, economically as well as emotionally, on the family

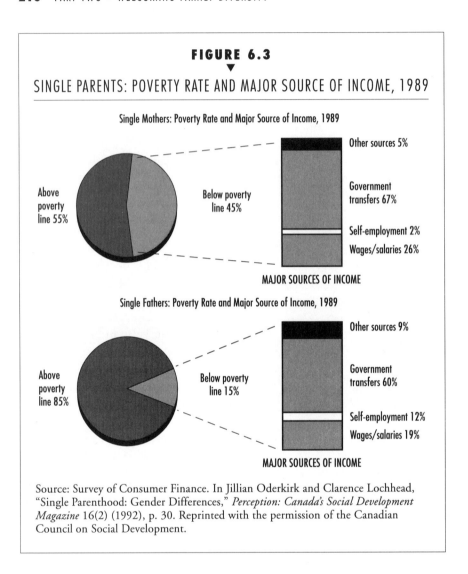

FIGURE 6.3
▼
SINGLE PARENTS: POVERTY RATE AND MAJOR SOURCE OF INCOME, 1989

Single Mothers: Poverty Rate and Major Source of Income, 1989

Above poverty line 55%

Below poverty line 45%

Other sources 5%

Government transfers 67%

Self-employment 2%

Wages/salaries 26%

MAJOR SOURCES OF INCOME

Single Fathers: Poverty Rate and Major Source of Income, 1989

Above poverty line 85%

Below poverty line 15%

Other sources 9%

Government transfers 60%

Self-employment 12%

Wages/salaries 19%

MAJOR SOURCES OF INCOME

Source: Survey of Consumer Finance. In Jillian Oderkirk and Clarence Lochhead, "Single Parenthood: Gender Differences," *Perception: Canada's Social Development Magazine* 16(2) (1992), p. 30. Reprinted with the permission of the Canadian Council on Social Development.

unit. If the family is poor, so are the children. And as the lessons of the Great Depression should tell us, the "lost years" spent in childhood poverty have long-term consequences for the life chances of children.

Poverty can affect the life chances of a child even before she is born. Kitchen and colleagues (1991) report that low-income expectant mothers tend to have poorer diets, probably a result of inadequate nutritional education and insufficient funds to purchase adequate or healthier food. Poor maternal diet "increases the likelihood of prenatal and neonatal mortality or prematurity" (1991, p. 5). Indeed, the figures on infant mortality show a significant class

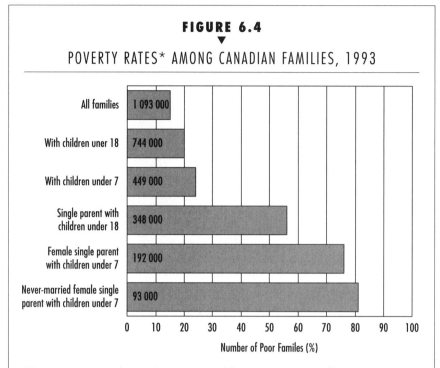

FIGURE 6.4

▼

POVERTY RATES* AMONG CANADIAN FAMILIES, 1993

All families — 1 093 000

With children uner 18 — 744 000

With children under 7 — 449 000

Single parent with children under 18 — 348 000

Female single parent with children under 7 — 192 000

Never-married female single parent with children under 7 — 93 000

Number of Poor Families (%)

* Poverty is measured using Statistics Canada's Low-Income Cutoffs (LICOs), 1986 base (for the years 1981 to 1991).

Source: Prepared by the Canadian Council of Social Development, using Statistics Canada's Survey of Consumer Finances microdata tape.

difference. In 1986, the rate of infant mortality was 10 per 1000 for the lowest-income quintile, while it was 5 per 1000 for the highest-income quintile (Canadian Institute of Child Health, 1989, p. 98).

For the children who do survive birth, a life of poverty means that they will very likely not have adequate nutrition to develop to their full physical and mental potential. It is also a fairly strong predictor of stress, and even violence in the home. As we have already seen, poor children do not have the cultural capital or the opportunities to strive for middle-class goals, and will likely have their opportunities for getting out of the class they were born into severely curtailed. Children living in poverty have twice the likelihood of developing chronic illness, physical disability, or emotional difficulties; poor academic attainment; dropping out of high school; living in unsafe housing; and smoking. The social reproduction of poverty is most striking when it is shown that, in 1990, 18 percent of poor female teenagers became pregnant, compared with 4 percent of teenagers from higher-income homes (Ross et al., 1996).

PERSONS WITH DISABILITIES

"Disability" is defined by the World Health Organization as "any restriction or lack (resulting from an impairment) of ability to perform an activity in the manner or within the range considered normal for a human being" (Statistics Canada, 1989, p. xxi). The definition contains the essence of the experience of being in a disabled body: that the world of work, family, and life in general is the privileged sphere of non-disabled people, the "normals." It was not so long ago that individuals who did not strictly conform to the category of "normal" were considered freaks, unentitled to work in the public sphere, or to have love, happiness, and family in the private sphere (Goffman, 1963). This has meant systematic blocks to opportunities for advancement, in formal education and in the workplace, and almost certain poverty and dependency for the disabled.

There has been increasing awareness in recent years that persons with disabilities are routinely discriminated against in the job market, and they now constitute one of the recognized "target groups" of visible minorities in efforts to promote diversity in the workplace. Nevertheless, years of disadvantage at the hands of a discriminatory labour market have left disabled persons as a group more vulnerable to poverty.

Adults with disabilities tend to have lower incomes than non-disabled Canadians. In 1986, 40 percent of Canadians with disabilities aged 15 to 64 were employed, while 70 percent of non-disabled adults were employed (Nessner, 1990, p. 5). But these figures should be interpreted carefully, as 51 percent of adults with disabilities defined themselves as not in the workforce, and hence not "unemployed." Many persons with disabilities who are not in the workforce depend on various forms of state support, such as disability pensions, to get by. Such incomes tend to be low and geared at providing a subsistence level of survival. Consequently, adults with disabilities tend overall to have significantly lower incomes than other Canadians. In 1985, the median income for adult men with disabilities was $13 000, while it was $20 900 for non-disabled males (Nessner, 1990, p. 5).

When gender and disability are combined, we find that women with disabilities are doubly disadvantaged. If non-disabled women are more prone to poverty than men, and systematically make less money in the labour market, then one might expect that women with disabilities would be even more vulnerable to poverty. Statistics seem to bear this out. According to Barile (1992, p. 32), 66.1 percent of women with disabilities working in regulated industries earned less than $20 000, while only 14.6 percent of men with disabilities did. At the other end of the wage scale, 2.7 percent of women with disabilities made over $40 000, while the figure climbed to 20.6 percent for males with disabilities.

ABORIGINAL PEOPLE

To be an aboriginal person in Canada today is to face a strong likelihood of poverty, disease, and a short lifespan. As we saw in Chapter 5, aboriginal people have faced a history of hatred and discrimination in Canadian society at the hands of a violent and imperialistic state. The injustices done to this group are only beginning to be appreciated; however, the scars are deeply felt in a community in which an aboriginal person will die, on average, ten years sooner than other Canadians, and in which an aboriginal person is three times more likely to end up in jail than in a high-school graduating class (Comeau and Santin, 1990, p. 2).

Demographics indicate that, as a group, aboriginal people have been structurally maintained in a situation of poverty. According to Frideres (1998), the average aboriginal income is 70 percent of a non-aboriginal income; unemployment ranges between 17 percent among off-reserve aboriginal people to 57 percent among those on-reserve, compared with the national average of 10 to 11 percent; and the high-school completion rate is two-thirds the national rate. The dependency ratio — the proportion of the population not in the workforce (the young and the old) relative to the population in the workforce — is twice as high among aboriginal people as in the general population.

As a rule, aboriginal culture has not shared the dominant middle-class values, so higher education — with the value placed on competition — and paid employment — with the value placed on consumerism — have not typically been viewed with the same importance. Coupled with **systemic discrimination** and racism at the hands of schools and employers, aboriginal people have occupied a distinct and certainly disadvantaged social position within Canada.

CONSEQUENCES OF POVERTY
▼

POOR-QUALITY FOOD AND HEALTH

While we may debate the definitions and causes of poverty, for poor Canadians it has very real and bleak consequences. Poverty means having little money to get through the month and buy even life's necessities: shelter, food, and clothing. Poor families may find that they have to buy the cheapest food in order to get through the month, and go hungry when that has run out. You may have noticed that, for much food there is a negative correlation between its price and its nutritional value. Additives and high fat content are common in low-priced foods. If consumed in large quantities, such foods may be cancer-causing. Certainly the links between fat and chronic disease such as cancer and heart problems have now been established, as has the link between such chronic disease and poverty (Antonovsky, 1967; Hay, 1988). Lack of education may keep the poor unaware of how their own life expectancy may be diminished by their poor diet. Clothing, particularly winter clothes to protect against the harsh Canadian climate, are expensive and may be simply unaffordable, increasing the likelihood of illness.

The increased use of food banks, emergency shelters, and other charitable organizations providing life's necessities gives us a clue as to how desperate many Canadians now are. The number of food banks in Canada has mushroomed from one, in Edmonton, in 1981, to 292 by October 1991. Food-bank use is most common in Ontario, where 28 of every 1000 people are recipients of monthly aid. As Figure 6.5 indicates, more than 40 percent of the recipients in Canada are children, and families with children received two-thirds of the food relief in 1990. Most of the people who make use of food banks are on welfare (Oderkirk, 1992, p. 7).

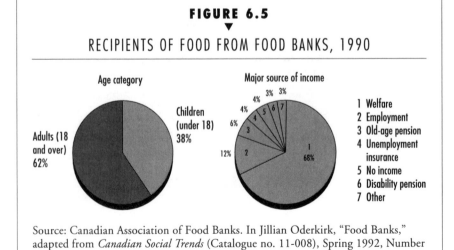

FIGURE 6.5
▼
RECIPIENTS OF FOOD FROM FOOD BANKS, 1990

Age category

Adults (18 and over) 62%

Children (under 18) 38%

Major source of income

3% 3%
4%
4%
6%
12%
68%

1 Welfare
2 Employment
3 Old-age pension
4 Unemployment insurance
5 No income
6 Disability pension
7 Other

Source: Canadian Association of Food Banks. In Jillian Oderkirk, "Food Banks," adapted from *Canadian Social Trends* (Catalogue no. 11-008), Spring 1992, Number 24, p. 8.

As an indication that poverty does not just strike the uneducated members of society, Toronto's Daily Bread Food Bank records show that the education level of food-bank recipients is going up. In 1991, 9 percent had graduated from college or university (compared with 4 percent in 1987), 9 percent had some college or university (4 percent in 1987), and 22 percent had graduated from high school (5 percent in 1987) (Oderkirk, 1992, p. 12). In total, 40 percent of those who used this food bank had a high-school diploma or more.

WELFARE

Welfare may be the last resort for those who are able to work but whose Employment Insurance benefits have run out, or for those who are unable to work because of illness, physical disability, or having to raise preschool children. Welfare payments across Canada fall miserably below the low-income cutoffs, keeping recipients destitute and often in such misery that they become unable to extricate themselves from this state. In 1990, there were 1.93 million welfare recipients in Canada, with families constituting the majority, at 63 percent (Oderkirk, 1992, p. 11).

HOMELESSNESS

Thousands of Canadian men, women, and children face homelessness today. Although economic struggles can be experienced by members of all social classes, the experience of being homeless is perhaps the closest one can come to the absolute poverty that Ross and Shillington describe (1990, p. 236). For here, the fragile connections between public and private realms have been severed. There is no private realm, there is no household, and there is no steady work.[4]

Homelessness is a general category for those who have no fixed address. It is telling to focus on the language we use, and to realize that within the label "homeless" is contained a world of meaning. "Homelessness" denotes deficiency; there is something very important missing, and that is "home." As we have seen above, the connections between home, household, work, and family are so strong in our society that they form a web that contains us within the class system. When the web is broken, the swift and steady descent to homelessness takes one out of the class system altogether, to the nether regions of the "underclass."

No one knows how many homeless people there are, and this is primarily because the homeless are not part of the larger system of control through which the state monitors the lives and activities of its citizens. Although efforts have been made to count and keep track of the homeless, the problem is that they are not locatable according to the same criteria as are the "homeful." Those who are connected in the web of relations between home and work are locatable through an array of codes and numbers. A fixed address locates one, as does a telephone number. Paid employment locates one, as does a social insurance number, bank account, credit card, driver's licence, and health insurance number. The myriad ways in which the homeful are accountable also enable the state to exercise control over them.

Not so for the homeless, whose descent to the underclass puts them so "low" as to be outside and below the entire system of membership of our society, disentitling them from even the most basic of rights and privileges, such as enumeration for voting. Indeed, it is not unusual to hear the homeless referred to as "less than human," belonging "in the gutter." Such talk reveals the bitter truth that what is really valued in our society, that which is seen to give us our humanity, is "homefulness" and property ownership. In this sense, not much has changed in attitudes toward the homeless since the Great Depression.

The experience of homelessness is to lose claim to the private realm altogether. As much as we idealize the home as the place where one can "be oneself," the realization that simple, taken-for-granted daily routines such as bathing and sleeping cannot be performed in private suggests the bleak reality of homelessness. Imagine for a moment what you would do if you did not have a place to go to sleep, eat, rest, keep your things, and have some privacy. Perhaps you have found yourself in a strange city with no money and nowhere to go. Chances are, however, that help was just at the other end of the phone: the bank, your parents or friends, some source of support to tie you into the world of the homeful. For the homeless, there are no such ties. Soup kitchens, food banks, emergency shelters, and handouts provide the necessities of life. Public washrooms, public transportation, public libraries, and all-night doughnut shops become "home," and the daily routines of life are practised there for all the world to see.

When I was interviewing women for my study on homeless women (Harman, 1989), one woman told me that "the city is a great place ... if you have money." Her experience of the abject poverty of homelessness was to see another side to the city, the underside, with its filth, violence, hunger, cold, and despair. Living on the street means being basically exposed to the elements — the winter cold, the rain, and the blazing heat of summer. Inadequate food, shelter, and clothing increase susceptibility to disease. Women in particular are targets of violence: rape, theft, and the day-to-day degradation of being treated as less than human. Fear of violence may make women reluctant to fall asleep at night, wandering about in search of a quiet, safe place.

The visibly homeless are only a part of the picture, however. In fact, there are many different stages and shapes that homelessness may take. Women's economic dependency means that they are more vulnerable to becoming homeless. Watson and Austerberry (1986) distinguish between **concealed homelessness** and **potential homelessness** as two categories that are applicable to women. By "concealed homelessness," they mean the condition of living temporarily with friends or family. While appearing to be homeful, the individual may in fact be relying on the goodwill of others for a roof over her head. By "potential homelessness," they mean those, particularly women, who could be homeless at any time or will be soon. Here we see that by virtue of their dependency on male breadwinners whose paid labour provides a roof over their heads, these women are not yet homeless. However, if they leave the situation, or the male breadwinner becomes unable to work for any reason, the interconnections between home and work cannot be maintained, and the entire family, or just the women and children, might quickly become homeless.

Homelessness might be temporary, as in the case of an abused woman who leaves her husband and takes her children to stay at a shelter until she gets on her feet. Although many such women do not have adequate job skills or support in the community to survive economically, some are able to become self-supporting. Sadly, many of the women in this situation find themselves chronically dependent on emergency shelters. For many such clients, the "hostel becomes a home" (Harman, 1989). Here, a substitute for the shelter of the homeful is provided. Food, clothing, and structured domestic activities such as cooking and cleaning serve to reproduce the domestic roles familiar to many once-homeful women. In this way, women's dependency on the male breadwinner is replaced by dependency on providers of social services. Unfortunately, the alternatives to this kind of life are limited, as there is not sufficient affordable housing or community support to give these women the kind of opportunities required for them to be independent. Those who avoid the hostel route, for example, teenage runaways, may find themselves doomed to a life on the street, working as prostitutes, addicted to drugs, and involved in petty crime.

CONCLUSION
▼

Family poverty and economic struggles affect men, women, and children in Canada today who are all struggling to make ends meet and maintain some kind of a lifestyle in the face of economic uncertainty. We have seen that the definitions and meanings of poverty are problematic, influenced as they are by middle-class values of the "good life." We have distinguished between relative and absolute poverty and objective and subjective definitions of poverty. We have seen that there is disagreement as to the causes of poverty, with some sociologists tending to blame the victim in identifying a culture of poverty and others recognizing that poverty is an inevitable outcome for some within a stratified system in which the rich tend to get richer. Certain groups, such as women, children, persons with disabilities, and aboriginal people, are more susceptible to poverty than those who occupy positions of privilege.

The consequences of poverty mean that life is a constant struggle. Long-term unemployment can be stressful on family relations as well as affecting the opportunities available to children. The contemporary living arrangements of most Canadians necessitate some kind of balance between the public and the private realms; losing that balance may mean severe economic struggle. For 1.9 million Canadians, living on welfare has meant relying on the safety net of the state to meagerly support them. The homeless live the closest to absolute poverty in Canadian society today, with many homeless or potentially homeless women being concealed through the charity of friends, community, or the state.

Our discussion of family poverty began with a list of four poverty myths: that poor people are social "failures" who bring poverty on themselves; that if one works hard enough, one can be successful and avoid poverty; that family poverty is not very extensive today in Canada; and that poverty is a new phenomenon in Canada. In contrast to these myths, we have learned that poverty is most often a consequence of factors beyond an individual's control; that poverty strikes even those who are well educated, from affluent families, and working full-time; that family poverty is a deep and widespread reality for millions of Canadians; and that social inequality has been a persistent fact of life in Canada during this century, with the most devastating experience being that of the Great Depression.

It would be wrong to offer false hope in times of economic uncertainty. Nevertheless, one can hope that, by revealing the poverty myths through a sociological perspective on poverty, we might all gain a more realistic understanding of the problem. The task of the future would seem to be to avoid blaming the victim and to begin examining how we can work collectively to improve the life chances of all Canadians.

SUMMARY
▼

- There are different meanings and definitions of poverty, including relative versus absolute poverty, and objective versus subjective poverty.
- People living near poverty, such as the working poor and the near poor, experience economic hardship.
- Unemployment and the feminization of poverty are the forces at work in the "new poverty."
- The "culture of poverty" argument tends to blame the victim.

- The "social reproduction" argument finds that social classes tend to reproduce themselves intergenerationally.
- The most economically disadvantaged groups in Canada today are women, children, persons with disabilities, and aboriginal people.
- Consequences of poverty include poor-quality food and health, welfare dependency, and homelessness.

NOTES
▼

1. The author gratefully acknowledges the valuable insights offered by Bernard Hammond during the preparation of this chapter. This chapter is dedicated to my children — Matthew, Daniel, and Beth.
2. Of the objective measures of poverty, the Statistics Canada figures tend to be the more conservative, with the Canadian Council on Social Development (CCSD) determining higher low-income cutoffs, and therefore higher rates of poverty. As with all attempts to use statistical calculations to measure the social world, the "operationalization of variables" determines what one finds. For the purposes of this chapter, the Statistics Canada figures are listed, with CCSD figures following in parentheses.
3. Extracts from Grayson and Bliss (1971) are reprinted with permission by the University of Toronto Press.
4. An understudied population among the homeless are the working poor, who have paid employment but still cannot find affordable housing and are forced onto the street or into charitable shelters. This discussion focusses on those who are without steady paid employment.

CRITICAL THINKING QUESTIONS
▼

1. Reflect on times when you might have experienced "subjective" poverty and compare those experiences with a state of "objective" poverty. What does living in poverty mean to you? How difficult is it to define poverty?
2. Compare and contrast the "culture of poverty" argument with the "social reproduction" argument. Why do you think it is so easy and so popular to blame the victim?
3. Why do you think it has been so easy to blame unemployment on women, when the facts point to economic, technological, and policy reasons for this state of affairs?
4. Identify some ways to minimize child poverty in Canada.
5. Empty your wallet and examine the variety of codes and numbers that are in some way identified with your name. Imagine your life without these connections,

and you will have made the first step in imagining what it might be like to be homeless.

6. Play "The Poverty Game" in your class. This board game was created by a group of single mothers in British Columbia. The game enables participants to experience vicariously many of the challenges of trying to get through the month on a fixed income while raising children.

SUGGESTED READING
▼

Sheila Baxter. 1988. *No Way to Live: Poor Women Speak Out.* Vancouver: New Star.
Poor women talk about their lives in poverty.

Barry Broadfoot. 1973. *Ten Lost Years 1929–1939: Memories of Canadians Who Survived the Depression.* Toronto: Doubleday.
First-hand accounts of life in Canada during the Great Depression.

Lesley D. Harman. 1989. *When a Hostel Becomes a Home: Experiences of Women.* Toronto: Garamond.
A participant observation study of homeless women in Toronto in the mid-1980s.

Lesley D. Harman. 1992. "The Feminization of Poverty: An Old Problem with a New Name." *Canadian Woman Studies* (Summer): 6–9.
An overview of the ways in which women are more likely than men to live in poverty at all stages of their lives.

Brigitte Kitchen, Andrew Mitchell, Peter Blutterbuck, and Marvyn Novick. 1991. *Unequal Futures: The Legacies of Child Poverty in Canada.* Toronto: Child Poverty Action Group and Social Planning Council of Metropolitan Toronto.
A discussion of the causes and consequences of child poverty in Canada today.

REFERENCES
▼

Antonovsky, Anton. 1967. "Social Class, Life Expectancy, and Overall Mortality." *Millbank Memorial Fund Quarterly* 45: 31–73.

Armstrong, Pat. 1984. *Labour Pains: Women's Work in Crisis.* Toronto: Women's Press.

Armstrong, Pat, and Hugh Armstrong. 1978. *The Double Ghetto: Canadian Women and Their Segregated Work.* Toronto: McClelland & Stewart.

Barile, Maria. 1992. "Disabled Women: An Exploited Underclass." *Canadian Woman Studies* 12/4: 32–33.

Barter, Kenneth A. 1992. "The Social Work Profession and Public Welfare." *Perception: Canada's Social Development Magazine* 16(2/3): 11–14.

Bernstein, Basil. 1973. *Class, Codes and Control,* vol. 1. London: Routledge and Kegan Paul.

Bourdieu, Pierre, and Jean-Claude Passeron. 1977. *Reproduction in Education, Society and Culture*. Beverly Hills, CA: Sage.

Broadfoot, Barry. 1973. *Ten Lost Years, 1929–1939: Memories of Canadians Who Survived the Depression*. Toronto: Doubleday.

Burman, Patrick. 1988. *Killing Time, Losing Ground: Experiences of Unemployment*. Toronto: Thompson Educational.

Canadian Council on Social Development. 1991. "Tackling Canada's High Drop-Out Rate." *Social Development Overview* 1 (Fall): 7–8.

Canadian Institute of Child Health. 1989. *The Health of Canada's Children: A CICH Profile*. Ottawa: Canadian Institute of Child Health.

Canadian Social Trends. 1997. "Social Indicators." *Canadian Social Trends* 47 (Winter): 31.

Comeau, Pauline, and Aldo Santin. 1990. *The First Canadians: A Profile of Canada's Native People Today*. Toronto: James Lorimer.

Dean, Hartley, and Peter Taylor-Gooby. 1992. *Dependency Culture: The Explosion of a Myth*. New York: Harvester Wheatsheaf.

Frideres, James S. 1998. *Aboriginal Peoples in Canada: Contemporary Conflicts*, 5th ed. Scarborough, ON: Prentice-Hall.

Goffman, Erving. 1963. *Stigma: Notes on the Management of Spoiled Identity*. New York: Simon and Schuster.

Grayson, L.M., and Michael Bliss. 1971. *The Wretched of Canada: Letters to R.B. Bennett, 1930–1935*. Toronto: University of Toronto Press.

Harman, Lesley D. 1989. *When a Hostel Becomes a Home: Experiences of Women*. Toronto: Garamond.

———. 1992. "The Feminization of Poverty: An Old Problem with a New Name." *Canadian Woman Studies* (Summer): 6–9.

Hay, David A. 1988. "Mortality and Health Status Trends in Canada." In B. Singh Bolaria and Harley D. Dickinson, eds., *Sociology of Health Care in Canada*. Toronto: Harcourt Brace Jovanovich.

Hooyman, Nancy R., and Rosemary Ryan. 1987. "Women as Caregivers of the Elderly: Catch-22 Dilemmas." In Josefina Figueria-McDonough and Rosemary Sarri, eds., *The Trapped Woman: Catch-22 in Deviance and Control*. Beverly Hills, CA: Sage.

Kitchen, Brigitte, Andrew Mitchell, Peter Blutterbuck, and Marvyn Novick. 1991. *Unequal Futures: The Legacies of Child Poverty in Canada*. Toronto: Child Poverty Action Group and the Social Planning Council of Metropolitan Toronto.

Leacock, Eleanor Burke, ed. 1971. *The Culture of Poverty: A Critique*. New York: Simon and Schuster.

Lemprière, Tony. 1992. "A New Look at Poverty." *Perception: Canada's Social Development Magazine* 16(2/3): 18–21.

Lewis, Oscar. 1966. "The Culture of Poverty." *Scientific American* 215/16: 19–25.

Liebow, Elliot. 1967. *Tally's Corner: A Study of Negro Streetcorner Men*. London: Routledge and Kegan Paul.

Lipset, Seymour M. 1972. "Social Mobility and Equal Opportunity." *The Public Interest* 29: 90–108.

Logan, Ron, and Jo-Anne Belliveau. 1995. "Working Mothers." *Canadian Social Trends* 36 (Spring): 24–28.

Luxton, Meg, Harriet Rosenberg, and Sedef Arat-Koc. 1990. *Through the Kitchen Window: The Politics of Home and Family*, 2nd ed. Toronto: Garamond.

National Council of Welfare. 1990. *Women and Poverty Revisited*. Ottawa. Ministry of Supply and Services.

Nessner, Katherine. 1990. "Profile of Canadians with Disabilities." *Canadian Social Trends* 18 (Autumn): 2–5.

Oderkirk, Jillian. 1992. "Food Banks." *Canadian Social Trends* 24 (Spring): 6–14.

Oderkirk, Jillian, and Clarence Lochhead. 1992. "Single Parenthood: Gender Differences." *Perception: Canada's Social Development Magazine* 16(2/3): 27–32.

Parliament, Jo-Anne B. 1990. "Labour Force Trends: Two Decades in Review." *Canadian Social Trends* (Autumn): 16–19.

Porter, John. 1979. *The Measure of Canadian Society: Education, Equality, and Opportunity*. Toronto: Gage.

Rinehart, James. 1987. *The Tyranny of Work*. Toronto: Harcourt Brace Jovanovich.

Ross, David. 1992. "Current and Proposed Measures of Poverty, 1992." *Perception: Canada's Social Development Magazine* 15(4)/16(1): 60–63.

Ross, David P., Katherine Scott, and Mark Kelly. 1996. *Child Poverty: What Are the Consequences?* Ottawa: Canadian Council on Social Development.

Ross, David P., and Richard Shillington. 1990. *The Canadian Fact Book on Poverty, 1989*. Ottawa: Canadian Council on Social Development.

Ross, David P., E. Richard Shillington, and Clarence Lochhead. 1994. *The Canadian Fact Book on Poverty, 1994*. Ottawa: Canadian Council on Social Development.

Ryan, Michael T. 1990. *Solidarity: Christian Social Teaching and Canadian Society*, 2nd ed. London, ON: Guided Study Programs in the Catholic Faith.

Ryan, William. 1971. *Blaming the Victim*. New York: Pantheon.

Statistics Canada. 1989. *Health and Activity Limitation Survey: Subprovincial Data for Ontario*. Ottawa: Statistics Canada.

Watson, Sophie, and Helen Austerberry. 1986. *Housing and Homelessness: A Feminist Perspective*. London: Routledge and Kegan Paul.

Willis, Paul E. 1981. *Learning to Labor: How Working-Class Kids Get Working-Class Jobs*. New York: Columbia University Press.

PART THREE

▼

CONFRONTING CHANGE

▼

"POLITICIZING THE PERSONAL": FEMINISM, LAW, AND PUBLIC POLICY

DOROTHY E. CHUNN

LEARNING OBJECTIVES

In this chapter, you will learn that:

- historically, feminists in Canada and elsewhere have placed great emphasis on the role of sociolegal reforms in achieving equality for women;
- despite many changes over the years, family law and policy always have privileged the **nuclear family** form;
- sociolegal reforms related to families always have differential impacts on women that are linked to class, race, ethnicity, (dis)ability, and sexual orientation;
- sociolegal reform is a necessary but not sufficient basis for achieving equality for all women.

INTRODUCTION

Increasingly, many scholars, activists, and policy-makers have embraced the revisionist view that societal institutions are social constructs created within the constraints of particular structures at particular times (Foucault, 1980; Garland, 1985; Weeks, 1986). Thus, state, law, and family are not always and everywhere the same in a specific society or in societies with similar histories. In Canada, for example, it is possible to identify three major periods of social transformation since 1840: the development of industrial capitalism and a laissez-faire state, corporate capitalism and a welfare state, and transnational capitalism and a neo-liberal form of state (Brodie, 1995; Chunn, 1992; Evans and Wekerle, 1997; Moscovitch and Albert, 1987; Panitch, 1977; Ursel, 1992).

These changes in forms of capitalist organization and social relations were accompanied by analogous transformations in the forms of **patriarchal** relations, albeit all of them were linked to the nuclear, or bourgeois, family model premised on heterosexual marriage, the sexual division of labour, and the "**public/private** split" (Barrett and McIntosh, 1982; O'Donovan, 1985; Zaretsky, 1976). It is this model of "the **family**" that has been, and continues to be, dominant in Canadian law and social policy related to the so-called private sphere (Boyd, 1997; Brodie, 1996; Eichler, 1997; Luxton, 1997; Pulkingham and Ternowetsky, 1996).

Revisionist analyses of sociological reform in capitalist societies, both historical and contemporary, also reveal that reform is an inherently contradictory phenomenon (Chunn, 1992; Donzelot, 1980; Foucault, 1977, 1980; Garland, 1985). Such reforms always are the product of political struggle and negotiation. Hence, they invariably generate positive as well as negative effects, which, in turn, are mediated by gender, race, class, sexual orientation, age, and (dis)ability. On the one hand, then, law and public policy help maintain the status quo of structured inequalities by buttressing particular forms of social and family organization. At the same time, law and public policy are not merely unitary instruments of oppression wielded by white, bourgeois, heterosexual men (Boyd, 1997; Brophy and Smart, 1985; Gavigan, 1993, 1998; Smart, 1984, 1986).

Since the late nineteenth century, feminists and the organized women's movements in Canada have played a prominent role in campaigning for legal and policy reforms and thus in the transformations outlined above (Adamson, Briskin, and McPhail, 1988; Bacchi, 1983; Black, 1988; Kealey, 1979; Latham and Pazdro, 1984; Rooke and Schnell, 1987; Ross, 1995; Strong-Boag, 1976).[1] Like their counterparts in other Western market societies (Brophy and Smart, 1985; Zaretsky, 1982), they were instrumental both in constructing the foundations of the welfare state and in the reordering of that state since the 1960s.[2] Moreover, female teachers, social workers, and health-care workers have played a crucial part in staffing welfare bureaucracies. Thus, women helped create and run the welfare state as well as constituting a large number of its clients, and therefore cannot be viewed simply as passive victims of a "male" state (Andrew, 1984; Bacchi, 1983; Baines, Evans, and Neysmith, 1991; Burt, 1988; Dale and Foster, 1986; Gordon, 1988, 1990; McCormack, 1991; Wilson, 1977; Zaretsky, 1982).

This chapter examines the historical and contemporary role of women, especially feminists, in constructing the Canadian welfare state through their successful advocacy of legislation and policies governing the "private" sphere of the family. The discussion centres on four topics: (1) major feminist theoretical perspectives on family, law, and the state that historically have guided reform demands; (2) selected reforms in the areas of **family law** and public policy that were inspired and/or supported by first-wave and second-wave feminists in Canada;[3] (3) the differential and contradictory impact of those reforms on women; and (4) concluding comments on future directions and strategies for feminists concerned with law and social policy.

FEMINIST THEORETICAL PERSPECTIVES ON STATE, LAW, AND FAMILY
▼

The history of **feminism** is really the history of diversity (Bacchi, 1991). Consequently, while feminists begin with the assumption that the majority of women in most societies occupy a subordinate position vis-à-vis men and that feminists must concentrate on altering the dynamics of power to achieve true equality for women, they often diverge in their explanations of why and how women are subordinated, and on the best means of bringing about change. Thus, all feminist perspectives on law and social policy operate with particular conceptions of the state, law, and family that, in turn, shape the legislation and policies promoted by adherents of the various theories.

The following discussion outlines the major theoretical perspectives on state, law, and family that have guided Canadian feminists and the implications of each for legislative and policy reforms to improve women's position in both the public and the private spheres.

In Canada, social or maternal feminism was the dominant perspective associated with the first wave (Bacchi, 1983; Latham and Pazdro, 1984; Roberts, 1979; Strong-Boag, 1976). The second wave was initially associated with liberal feminism (Adamson et al., 1988; Black, 1988), but radical and **socialist feminism** began to exert an important influence on campaigns around law and social policy during the 1970s (Adamson et al., 1988; Barrett and Hamilton, 1986; Boyd and Sheehy, 1986). More recently, theoretical critiques by aboriginal women, women of colour, and lesbians have stimulated a rethinking of the ways in which feminists conceptualize state, law, and family (Andrew and Rodgers, 1997; Bannerji, 1993; Herman, 1994; Monture-Angus, 1995; Razack, 1998; Wendell, 1996).

Although first-wave feminism in Canada followed a somewhat different developmental trajectory than it did elsewhere,[4] the catalyst for the emergence of an organized women's movement was the same as in other Western market societies — the legal invisibility of women, particularly married women, during the nineteenth century. Governed by laws based on the unity doctrine,[5] a wife was viewed as mere extension of her husband and had the "status ... of an infant or institutionalized incompetent" (Kieran, 1986, p. 41; see also Backhouse, 1991, ch. 6). Indeed, great effort was expanded to force the First Nations to conform to this patriarchal, authoritarian marriage law (Backhouse, 1991, ch. 1). Single women had more rights than their married sisters, but the rise of organized feminism was clearly linked to a desire to end the legal subordination of all women — more specifically, of white, middle-class women.

Because first-wave feminists were activists rather than academics, they did not articulate explicit formal theories. However, their theoretical perspectives on state, law, and family can be abstracted from writings and speeches of prominent feminist leaders. What we discover is that maternal or social feminists were hardly revolutionaries seeking to transform the status quo. Indeed, they initially accepted the nineteenth-century liberal conception of the state as a neutral arbiter of the common good. Only after some experience with the laissez-faire state did maternal feminists begin to articulate what might be characterized as a liberal reformist view, that, to safeguard the common good, the state might have to intervene on behalf of the disadvantaged (e.g., women) and help them to improve their position vis-à-vis more powerful individuals and groups (e.g., men). As Nellie McClung put it, "More and more the idea is growing upon us that certain services are best rendered by the state, and not left to depend on the caprice, inclination, or inability of the individual" (1976, p. 322; see also Bacchi, 1983).

FIRST-WAVE FEMINISTS AND REFORMS

For maternal feminists, law was a pivotal means of addressing women's devalued status relative to men. It was a positive instrument of social engineering and reform that could assist and empower women through legislation and policies that recognized their special needs and distinct qualities. Thus, maternal feminists strongly embraced the idea that women are different from men; not inherently inferior, but rather possessed of unique characteristics by virtue of their ability to mother and perform other domestic tasks (McClung, 1976). At the same time, they assumed that women could, and should, work with men to obtain legislation and policies that would enhance the status of wives and mothers in "their proper sphere" (McClung, 1976).

The maternal-feminist assumptions that nurturing and caregiving are "feminist" qualities, and providing and protecting are "masculine" traits, reflected an uncritical belief in the normality of the bourgeois family model and acceptance of the idea that the family is one based on a heterosexual marriage relationship in which each member of the nuclear unit has a specific role. The sexual division of labour leaves husband and wife in charge of separate but equal spheres of activity. He is predisposed to enter the public arena and to act as provider/protector, while she is similarly inclined to manage the private realm of the family as caregiver/housekeeper. Children exist in a "natural" state of dependency on parents and must not be allowed to act like adults; they must go to school, eschew paid employment, and be supervised in their leisure activities (Chunn, 1990; Foucault, 1980; Mandell, 1988).

SECOND-WAVE FEMINISTS AND REFORMS

Ultimately, the failure of both maternal and liberal first-wave feminists to challenge assumptions about the sexual division of labour and the public/private split was rectified by their second-wave successors. When liberal feminism re-emerged in the 1960s, however, adherents operated with conceptions of state, law, and family that differed little from those of their nineteenth-century precursors. They, too, viewed the state as a mediator or neutral arbiter, primarily in the public sphere. Thus it was assumed that once women obtain the same access to and opportunity to compete in the public sphere as men, the state will not treat their interests any differently from those of men. Like their historical counterparts, then, liberal feminists of the 1960s believed that discrimination against women could be removed through the implementation of reforms on an ad hoc, piecemeal basis and without any fundamental restructuring of societal institutions (Adamson et al., 1988; Andrew and Rodgers, 1997; Boyd and Sheehy, 1986).

Similarly, second-wave liberal feminists continued to emphasize law as the route to women's equality, and the guarantor of it once achieved. During the 1960s, however, liberal feminists no longer had to concentrate all their energies on the fight to attain legal personhood and political rights. As a result, they were able to shift their attention to the development of legal strategies for eliminating sex discrimination and implementing equality, not only in the areas of education and employment, but also more generally in all societal institutions, including the family. Moreover, by conceptualizing women and men in terms of sameness rather than difference, liberal feminists assumed that women could work co-operatively with men in pursuit of equality and that, indeed, such alliances were crucial to achieve it (Boyd and Sheehy, 1986; Williams, 1990).

Again, in contrast to their historical precursors, 1960s liberal feminists made a direct link between liberation and economic independence. The solution to "the problem with no name" (Friedan, 1963) was paid employment for married women. Thus, although liberal feminists did not develop an overt critique of the family, they implicitly challenged the sexual division of labour by arguing for the movement of married women *en masse* into the public realm. The stage was set for the "grass roots" radical and social feminists of the 1970s, who mounted an explicit critique of the bourgeois family model that was encapsulated in the slogan "**the personal is political**." Although both groups came out of the "new left" Marxist-influenced political movements of the time, they formulated very different analyses of women's subordination (Adamson et al., 1988; Barrett, 1988; Black, 1988; Boyd and Sheehy, 1986).

Like maternal feminists, radical feminists operate on the assumption of difference between men and women. Unlike maternal feminists, however, radicals argue that there are two gender classes, with diametrically opposed and irreconcilable interests. They point to patriarchy — men's dominance over women — as a transhistorical phenomenon that is predicated on male control over women's sexuality and reproduction. Therefore, gender oppression is primary; all other oppressions — class, racial — are secondary to or flow from it (Barrett, 1988; Black, 1988; Boyd and Sheehy, 1986).

Given these assumptions, radical feminists have very little faith in either the state or the law within existing structures, viewing them as simply "male protection rackets" (MacKinnon, 1987, p. 31). In short, the state and law are literally man-made, reflect men's interests, and cannot be viewed as amenable to any sort of social-engineering or piecemeal reform. Therefore, the liberal emphasis on law reform is misplaced in the radical-feminist view and women should stop looking to the male-dominated state to help them. If women want to be free, they will have to liberate themselves through consciousness-raising and the creation of alternative structures (MacKinnon, 1987).

For radical feminists of the second wave, the nuclear family is a major site of women's oppression. In "politicizing the personal," they have emphasized the need for women to avoid the enslavement that is the result of "**compulsory heterosexuality**" as exemplified by heterosexual marriage (Rich, 1980). Women must separate from men — politically and/or physically — if they wish to regain control over their sexuality and reproductive decisions.

While radical feminists exploded the ideology of "separate spheres" with a critique of "compulsory heterosexuality" and marriage, socialist feminists were launching a different project that led them in the same direction — namely, the reformulation of orthodox Marxist theory, which is gender-blind and, except for Engels's work (1964), offers virtually no analysis of the "private" sphere.[6] In contrast to radical feminists, socialist feminists reject a transhistorical conception of patriarchy, that is, the idea that women's oppression is everywhere and always the same. Indeed, they begin with the assumption that these relations assume different forms as changes in social organization occur. Thus, it is necessary to be historically and culturally specific in the analysis of women's subordination (Barrett, 1988; Burstyn and Smith, 1985).

Socialist feminists went on to link the women's secondary status in capitalist societies to the undervalued work that they perform inside and outside the family. Most women straddle, and are subordinate in, both the public and private spheres because their work is unpaid domestic labour and/or underpaid clerical and service employment. Thus, any analysis of women's inequality must focus on the family, or more specifically, on how women are psychologically, economically, and physically subordinated through heterosexual marriage (Barrett and McIntosh, 1982; Luxton, Rosenberg, and Arat-Koc, 1990).

Given their concerns, socialist feminists conceptualize the state and law very differently from how liberal and radical feminists do. While the state is neither a neutral arbiter of individual rights nor a weapon of men, it is central in reproducing women's subordination through law and social policy. At the same time, socialist feminists insist that we have to distinguish between different forms of state and law over time. In our liberal democratic society, for example, while law can be a direct instrument of gender oppression, the ideological influence of law is much more important in maintaining women's subordination. That is to say, law (as well as social policy) incorporates certain assumptions about men and women and the relations between them that are accepted uncritically by most of the people who make, administer, or are subject to it (Barrett and McIntosh, 1982; Gavigan, 1988, 1993).

Although various ideologies affect law and social policy, socialist feminists consider **familial ideology** to be crucial to the perpetuation of women's subordination in Canada and other liberal democracies (Barrett and McIntosh, 1982; Gavigan, 1988, 1993). After all, a minority of people in these societies actually live in the ideal type of nuclear-family unit where the wife/mother is a full-time homeworker and the husband/father is the sole breadwinner. Yet polls and research reveal that young women continue to believe that they will marry for life and be full-time homemakers, at least when their children are young (Luxton et al., 1990). Similarly, many of the people who draft and implement legislation and social policies act in accordance with these assumptions about marriage and the "normal" family. Thus, law may not be a direct instrument of male power, but it helps reproduce women's inequality nonetheless.

Moreover, law must be viewed not just as an ideological mechanism that helps perpetuate unequal gender relations, but also as one that reproduces class inequalities. Thus, gender and class relations are intertwined, with neither necessarily assuming primacy in explaining women's subordination. Therefore, working-class women may share common interests with, say, both working-class men and middle-class women.

Unlike their radical counterparts, then, socialist feminists view law as a means of working toward equality for women. Law is not an "absolute good" in the liberal-feminist sense, but women themselves, or women and men together, can sometimes obtain sociolegal reforms that further their collective struggles against class and gender inequities in capitalist liberal democracies like Canada. For example, socialist feminists assume that a reform such as a national day-care program might be most directly beneficial to working-class and/or single mothers who are in the labour force. Yet it would also help some middle-class women and men who have custody of children. Over the long term, then, legal and social policy reforms can raise political consciousness and contribute to a transformation of the status quo (Adamson et al., 1988; Boyd and Sheehy, 1986).

Recently, the three dominant theoretical perspectives associated with second-wave feminism have been subject to extensive critique because they speak primarily to the experiences of white, able-bodied, and/or heterosexual women. Feminists of colour and aboriginal women have documented the absence of an analysis of race and ethnicity in these theoretical frameworks (Bannerji, 1993; Herbert, 1989; Kirkness, 1988; Monture, 1989; Monture-Angus, 1995; Ng, 1988; Razack, 1992, 1998; Williams, 1990). Lesbian feminists have noted a similar theoretical silence on the issue of sexual orientation (Herman, 1990, 1994; Robson, 1992, 1994). Likewise, the failure of feminist theory to address women with disabilities has been underscored (Mosoff, 1997; Wendell, 1996). As a result, many feminists are rethinking their theoretical positions and attempting to respond to the critiques in their current work on law, family, and social policy (Boyd, 1997; Gavigan, 1993, 1998; Mossman and MacLean, 1997).

We turn now to an examination of how Canadian feminists have "politicized the personal," both historically and in the contemporary context, through the advocacy of legal and policy reforms related to social reproduction.[7]

FEMINIST REFORMERS AND SOCIAL REPRODUCTION: HISTORICAL SHIFTS IN FAMILY LAW AND PUBLIC POLICY
▼

In retrospect, it is clear that first- and second-wave feminists exercised an important influence on law and social policy in Canada. The first wave helped to promote reforms that collectively shaped the welfare-state structures that regulated the "private" sphere of the family, or reproduction. The second wave played a major role in bringing about reforms that have reordered those structures since the 1960s. During both periods, feminists worked under the umbrella of national women's organizations and, often, in concert with men. The National Council of Women of Canada, formed in 1893, brought feminist and non-feminist women together in a common goal to protect and uphold the family (Strong-Boag, 1976). Almost eighty years later, the National Action Committee on the Status of Women was established in 1972 to represent women's interests and concerns and to press for the implementation of the numerous recommendations of the 1970 Royal Commission on the Status of Women (Black, 1988). Since the 1960s, status-of-women councils — federal and provincial — have also exerted a strong influence on law and social policy related to the family.

UPGRADING WOMEN'S STATUS IN THE FAMILY

Historically, both England and Canada have created a two-tiered system of family law: one related primarily to the propertied classes, and one focussed primarily on the underclasses of society (Chunn, 1992; Mossman and MacLean, 1986, 1997). What is less well known is how first-wave feminists helped to reshape this dual system in the emergent welfare state. Although first-wave maternal feminists did not challenge the sexual division of labour, they did "politicize the personal" because of a desire to upgrade women's status in their "proper sphere" of the family. From the 1880s onward, the maternal feminist focus on making the "separate but equal" doctrine a reality led to the promotion of numerous laws and policies aimed at regulating both biological (McLaren and McLaren, 1998; McLaren, 1990) and social reproduction (Strong-Boag, 1976; Ursel, 1986).

Maternal feminists were particularly concerned to reinforce women in their motherhood role and to keep mother-led families together in the midst of the "social disorganization" generated by the rapid industrialization and urbanization of Canada between 1880 and 1940 (Ursel, 1986; see also Strong-Boag, 1976). As well as promoting educational initiatives aimed at preparing women for marriage and a domestic "career" (Strong-Boag, 1976, 1988), they joined in campaigns for the implementation of legislation and policies that gave mothers and wives some rights when a marriage failed. On the one hand, maternal feminists fought for reforms in divorce, custody, and property law, which benefited mainly middle- and upper-class women who could afford legal counsel. On the other hand, they promoted child- and family-welfare laws related to guardianship, maintenance, and support, which primarily assisted women in marginal families (Chunn, 1992; Snell, 1991).

If we look at custody and guardianship, we find that, although nineteenth-century law was not static, the courts consistently upheld the absolute right of fathers to legal control of their children under English common law (Backhouse, 1991, ch. 7; Kieran, 1986). However, by the beginning of the twentieth century, urban reformers, including feminists, had obtained legislation in a number of provinces that accorded some recognition to the importance of women's motherhood role. For example, in 1897 British Columbia laid the foundations of the "tender years" doctrine by authorizing judges to award custody of children under the age of 7 to non-adulterous mothers who were deemed "fit" parents (Backhouse, 1991, p. 204). The principle, reiterated as late as 1955 in *Weeks* v. *Weeks*, that "all other things being equal, a young child should be with its natural mother" came to dominate custody and guardianship decisions in the twentieth century.

Married women also gained new rights to property in the nineteenth century. Under the unity doctrine, a wife was legally obliged to hand over to her husband everything she had — land, furniture, money, including wages, and even the clothes on her back. However, three successive reform "waves" culminated with the implementation of separate property regimes in some provinces by 1900 (Backhouse, 1992). In Ontario, for instance, a series of legal reforms dating from 1859 ultimately were consolidated and expanded with the enactment of the Married Women's Property Act in 1884, which gave husbands and wives control over their own property, whether it was acquired before or during the marriage (Kieran, 1986; Morton, 1988). Other provinces followed suit. Subsequently, when a marriage failed, each partner kept what was his or hers.

With regard to financial support, feminists and other reformers obtained provincial legislation during the late nineteenth and early twentieth centuries that imposed a legal obligation on husbands and fathers to support their wives and children upon marital breakdown or their children in cases of unmarried parenthood. Previously, men could abandon their dependants and leave them destitute while retaining legal control over wives and/or children (Kieran, 1986, p. 49). However, rapid industrialization and urbanization from the 1880s onward brought disproportionate numbers of women and children to the growing cities and left increasing numbers of mother-led families living in destitution when male breadwinners did not join them. This "**feminization of poverty**" was one reason behind the enactment of desertion statutes, which allowed nonadulterous wives and mothers to obtain maintenance orders from the courts that compelled the male deserter to pay support or face sanctions, including a jail term. Ontario enacted the first Deserted Wives' Maintenance Act, in 1888, and other provinces followed (Chunn, 1992).

In cases when a deserter could not be located and when the male protector/breadwinner was absent from the family because of death or mental or physical incapacity, the state assumed the financial role of husband and father through the payment of mothers' pensions or allowances. "A broad spectrum of articulate, middle-class Canadians" (Strong-Boag, 1979, p. 25) had promoted such an income-support policy since the turn of the century without success. But the increase in mother-led families during World War I generated a strong perception that "the family" was in crisis and provided the catalyst for implementing this reform to help "deserving" women fulfil their "natural" homemaker role; that is, to enable mothers to engage in part-time rather than full-time employment outside the home or to earn without leaving the home. Thus, the recipients of pensions or allowances were considered state employees and were expected to supplement their government salaries with other earnings (Strong-Boag, 1979, p. 27; Kitchen, 1987; Little, 1994).

From a contemporary vantage point, it is obvious that first-wave, or maternal, feminists were major players in formulating and implementing legislation and public policies governing the private sphere of reproduction in the emergent Canadian welfare state. Together with other reformers, they created a system of family and welfare law that remained intact until the 1960s and 1970s, when another generation of feminist reformers came of age.

SOLVING THE "PROBLEM WITH NO NAME"

Second-wave feminism developed in the general context of the civil rights movements that characterized Canada and other liberal democracies during the 1960s. Women, the poor, racial and ethnic minorities, and gay men and lesbians began to enter the political arena in an effort to temper, if not eradicate, discrimination based on gender, race, class, and sexual orientation; that is, to implement the principle of formal legal equality in every social institution.

In Canada, feminist agitation ultimately helped persuade the federal government to establish the Royal Commission on the Status of Women, whose 1970 report set the second-wave reform agenda for the next two decades. The commissioners placed great faith in law as a vehicle of social change and adopted the same pragmatic focus as their first-wave sisters (Andrew and Rodgers, 1997; see also Brodie, Gavigan, and Jenson, 1992). However, their emphasis on rights and formal legal equality contributed, first, to a complete overhaul of the family law and social policy that maternal feminists had worked so hard to achieve and, second, more generally to a restructuring of the Canadian welfare state.

Whereas maternal feminists had "politicized the personal" to enhance the position of women within the family, their second-wave successors were determined to create the conditions whereby there would be flexibility and interchangeability of roles for men and women in both the public and the private spheres. Since 1968, then, Canada's family law system has been reordered extensively along liberal egalitarian lines. The federal divorce law and provincial legislation governing marriage and separation are no longer sex-specific or predicated on "fault." Rather, they are gender-neutral and based on the principle of **formal equality** between spouses — with no rights to property, custody, and maintenance, and no familial roles based on sex (Eichler, 1997).

Custody

Family law is now based on the assumptions that women are no more predisposed than men to assume child-care responsibilities and that fathers and mothers are equally capable of parenting. For example, the introduction to the 1979 B.C. Family Relations Act stated that the law was designed to acknowledge "the changing roles of spouses" and to "place parents on more equal footing in custody and access disputes." Therefore, when a marriage ends, children should be placed with the parent who can best serve their interests. Thus, the "tender years" doctrine that worked in favour of women who were deemed "fit" mothers has been displaced by the gender-neutral "best interests of the child" principle (Boyd, 1989a, 1989b).

The notion of equal parenting also underlies the parental-leave program implemented through an amendment of the Unemployment Insurance Act (now the Employment Insurance Act) in 1990. In addition to the fifteen weeks of maternity benefit that employed pregnant women may claim under the act, either parent can take ten weeks of paid leave following the birth or adoption of a child. The rationale for parental leave is the reduction of work–family conflict and the potential for changing the gendered division of labour both at home and in the workplace (Evans and Pupo, 1993; Iyer, 1997).

Marital Property

Both federal and provincial family laws now stipulate that the division of marital property will be governed by the principle of equalization incorporated in a deferred-community-property regime. That is to say, as a general rule, separate property rights exist so long as the marriage is intact, but if the relationship dissolves, all marital property is shared equally between the spouses (Steel, 1985). Moreover, the concept of property has been greatly expanded to cover "virtually anything of which one could conceive" (Morton, 1988, p. 260). For example, the 1986 Ontario Family Law Act includes not only the usual things such as land, but also deferred-profit-sharing plans, pensions, and interests in estates or trusts (Morton, 1988).

Spousal and Child Support

Canadian family law now is based on the principles of spousal self-sufficiency and equal parental responsibility for child support, and it applies to legal and common-law marriages and, in British Columbia, to same-sex relationships of at least two years' duration. Gone are the sex-specific clauses that characterized the divorce, desertion, and other family-related legislation promoted by first-wave feminists, obliging men to maintain their dependants and requiring women to be non-adulterous to qualify for support. Today, the courts assume that, in most cases of marital breakdown, each spouse can attain economic independence and contribute financially to the upkeep of their children. Therefore, spousal-support orders usually are short-term with the sole purpose of allowing the dependent partner to become self-supporting (Mossman and MacLean, 1997).

However, the increasing number of people, and primarily women and children, who become state dependants following a marital breakdown also has generated court decisions and public policies aimed at ensuring the provision of adequate spousal and/or child support by non-state sources. Since the early 1980s, several Supreme Court of Canada judgements (e.g. *Moge* v. *Moge*) have allowed contributions to a marriage that impact on the ability of a spouse to attain self-sufficiency and independence upon separation and divorce to be factored into judicial decisions about spousal support. Similarly, the federal **child-support guidelines** implemented in 1997 attempt to link child-support awards to both the costs of raising children and the income of the payor.

Enforcement of support orders has been addressed as well. When the historical pattern of default on support orders continued after new family-relations laws were implemented during the 1970s and 1980s, several provinces, including Manitoba, Ontario, and British Columbia, established maintenance-enforcement programs to reduce the astronomical rate of non-compliance. The programs essentially are state-ordered collections on behalf of the persons who are not receiving the support ordered by the courts. For example, an individual who consistently fails to pay maintenance without good reason may have his or her wages garnisheed.

Notwithstanding the reforms outlined above, family-welfare law still is premised on sex-specific assumptions about morality and the family unit. The "man in the house" rule, now the "spouse in the house" rule, remains in the social-assistance legislation of every province (Gavigan, 1993, 1998; Mossman and MacLean, 1997). Although apparently gender-neutral, the spousal rule almost always is applied to women who live with men rather than the reverse (Carruthers, 1995; Martin, 1992).

THE CONTRADICTORY AND DIFFERENTIAL EFFECTS OF FAMILY LAW AND SOCIAL POLICY
▼

Even a cursory examination of the effects of the family-law and social-policy reforms promoted by first- and second-wave feminists reveals the contradictory and differential results of such reform. Every innovation generated both intended and unintended outcomes. If we begin with an analysis of the reforms advocated by maternal feminists, we can see that they had a number of positive consequences in practice. First, the legal recognition of the work performed by women in their role as mothers and, to a lesser degree, wives was a concrete acknowledgement that the "private" sphere of reproduction was important and should be taken into account when a marriage ended. Clearly, the "tender years" doctrine assisted many women in their attempts to gain custody or guardianship of their children. Similarly, desertion legislation and enforcement mechanisms, such as family courts, gave women without means legal assistance in obtaining support for themselves and their children. The early family courts in Ontario collected substantial sums on behalf of women and children, as did the superintendent of child welfare, who dealt with unmarried mothers' cases (Chunn, 1992).

Second, such reforms as mothers' pensions represented some recognition of social or state responsibility at the provincial level to directly oversee the well-being of disadvantaged individuals and if necessary to contribute materially to their subsistence rather than simply leaving the burden to families and charities in the "private" sector or to local governments. During the interwar years, increasing numbers of women received "state salaries for mothers," and the provinces moved toward the assumption of sole responsibility for aid to mother-led families. In British Columbia, for example, the number of mothers or foster mothers receiving allowances rose from 636 in 1919–20 to 1751 in 1938–39, and the amount expended by the province increased from $612 645 in 1927–28 to $790 101 in 1938–39 (Strong-Boag, 1979, pp. 26, 28–30).

Third, although statistics are lacking, it seems probable that feminist-supported legislation and policies to shore up the nuclear family left poor, white women and children without male breadwinners at least marginally better off in the urban, industrial context than they might have been otherwise. Similarly, the liberalization of federal divorce law in the 1920s meant that middle- and upper-class women could now obtain a divorce on the same grounds as their husbands, while the implementation of separate property regimes saved some women from the destitution that previously befell many wives who were divorced or deserted by their spouses (Backhouse, 1992; Kieran, 1986, ch. 7; Snell, 1991).

NEGATIVE EFFECTS OF FIRST-WAVE REFORMS

With hindsight, the negative consequences of family-related legislation and policies supported by maternal feminists are readily apparent. First, these sociolegal reforms entrenched the ideology of separate spheres and thus helped to perpetuate the structured dependency of women within marriage. In short, first-wave feminists sanctified the bourgeois-family model and the sexual division of labour. Thus, married women acquired more power within the family not so much in their own right as women, but because of their role in social reproduction, particularly as mothers (Brophy and Smart, 1985, ch. 1; Chunn, 1992). The failure of maternal feminists to attack the economic dependency

---

BOX 7.1
▼
MURDOCH V. MURDOCH

The Murdochs were Alberta ranchers who separated in 1968 after 25 years of marriage, during which time Irene Murdoch had worked alongside her husband to the extent that he did not have to hire a hand. However, when she sued for half-interest in their property, cattle, and other assets, the Alberta courts and, ultimately, the Supreme Court of Canada decided that Mrs. Murdoch was entitled to alimony but had no claim on the value of the property because she had not made "a direct financial contribution" to the ranch; the work she had carried out for 25 years was "the work done by any ranch wife." In short, Mr. Murdoch held the title to the property, and Irene Murdoch "was expected to hoe, mow, dehorn, brand (and cook, clean, and bear and raise children)" with no hope of a share of it when the marriage ended (Kieran, 1986, p. 142; see also Morton, 1988).

---

of women within marriage was ultimately underlined by cases like *Murdoch* v. *Murdoch* (see Box 7.1), which revealed a basic weakness of the separate-property regime.

Second, the family-related reforms promoted by maternal feminists were all premised on, and therefore reinforced, the sexual double standard. Whether women applied for custody, maintenance, or mothers' allowances, they were routinely scrutinized for moral fitness. "Uncondoned adultery" by a wife and mother automatically barred her from obtaining maintenance for herself upon marital breakdown and led to the rescinding of existing support orders if the husband could prove to the court that she had engaged in immoral conduct. Similarly, a woman who received public assistance because her male breadwinner had absconded or who drew a mothers' pension was subject to the discriminatory "man in the house" rule. If she resided with a man, authorities assumed that he must be supporting her and she became ineligible for state benefits. The same rule did not apply to men. Indeed, some women have been charged with fraud for collecting public assistance at the same time that they shared living quarters with a man, and a few were actually jailed (Porter and Gullen, 1984).[8] Thus, only the morally "deserving" received state assistance; the "undeserving" were punished through loss of their children, denial of financial assistance, and even criminal prosecution.

Third, for the most part, maternal feminists supported legislation and policies that emphasized the responsibility of individual men for maintaining their dependants — wives, children, parents. Thus, they sought and achieved the use of state power to enforce the "privatization of the costs of social reproduction" (Fudge, 1989), that is, to maintain women in their "natural" role as caregivers and housekeepers when the male breadwinner was no longer part of the family unit. Moreover, although state agencies such as family courts collected and distributed considerable sums of money to women and children, the majority of men defaulted on or were chronically in arrears with their support payments (Chunn, 1992). Even when the state assumed some direct financial responsibility for social reproduction, as exemplified by the implementation of mothers' pensions, the emphasis remained on individual family units and case-by-case assessment of eligibility.

Finally, the differential effect of the legislation and policies supported by first-wave feminists must be underscored. White middle-class, heterosexual women, and to a lesser extent their counterparts in the "respectable" working classes, did benefit from family-law reforms related to custody, property, and support. However, white women in the ranks of the working and dependent poor, particularly single mothers, had to trade off the assistance they received from the paternalistic state against increased surveillance and scrutiny of their family life (Chunn, 1992; Little, 1994). And lesbian women, women of colour, and aboriginal women were invisible in the statutes and public policies outlined above. Indeed, Asian Canadian and South Asian Canadian women (and men) and First Nations women (and men) did not even have voting rights until the 1940s and 1950s, respectively (Kirkness, 1988; Williams, 1990). Moreover, most aboriginal women living on-reserve did not live in nuclear-family units and were governed entirely by the federal Indian Act. Thus, provincial legislation and policies related to marriage, matrimonial property, maintenance, and other family matters were irrelevant to their lives (Turpel, 1991). Similarly, First Nations women have been embroiled more often in guardianship battles with the state than with the fathers of their children (Monture, 1989).[9]

POSITIVE EFFECTS OF SECOND-WAVE REFORMS

Notwithstanding the overhaul of family law and social policy since the 1960s, the effects of sociolegal reforms achieved, in part, by second-wave feminists have been just as contradictory as those of their first-wave precursors. On the positive side, the implementation of formal legal equality in family law ended the blatant sexual discrimination and enforced dependency that characterized the old desertion statutes and the mothers' allowances legislation. Women were no longer held accountable to a sexual double standard in the form of adultery clauses under the new family relations acts.

Parental leave also reinforces the feminist critique of the sexual division of labour. By facilitating the assumption of child-care responsibilities by fathers, the policy helps to undercut the widespread assumption that women are naturally predisposed toward, and better at, nurturing than men. Moreover, the policy has the potential to improve women's position in the paid workforce because they can remain attached to the labour force on "leave" while they stay home to care for a child, rather than "leaving" the ranks of the employed altogether (Evans and Pupo, 1993; Iyer, 1997).

A second positive result of second-wave family law reform has been the increased recognition of women's financial contribution to marriage through the implementation of deferred-community-property regimes for the division of family assets upon marital breakdown. Redefining assets to include social benefits (such as pensions) and intangible assets (such as university degrees) has improved the lot of women who, like Irene Murdoch (see Box 7.1), had never been part of the paid workforce when divorce ended a long-time marriage and of women who left the labour force and/or worked part-time to accommodate child-care responsibilities (Keet, 1990; Steel, 1985).

Third, legal and social-policy reforms advocated by second-wave feminists have recognized, to some degree, that there are different types of cohabitation, that many common-law and same-sex relationships are similar in nature to formal heterosexual marriages. Thus, the maintenance sections of the provincial family relations acts now apply to heterosexual, common-law unions and, in British Columbia, to same-sex relationships. Moreover, the 1997 Ontario Court of Appeal decision in the case of *M.* v. *H.* upheld the claim of M. for spousal support from H., her financially better off former partner. M. had argued that the Ontario Family Law Act discriminated on the basis of sexual orientation because it did not apply to same-sex partners, one of whom was dependent upon the other when the relationship ended. If the Supreme Court of Canada upholds the OCA decision in *M.* v. *H.*, the door will be open to define same-sex unions as common-law unions in all family-law provisions governing support.[10]

While family law on the division of property still applies only to married couples, heterosexual and, in British Columbia, same-sex, common-law couples now are able to rely on constructive-trust doctrine when dividing property at the end of a relationship. In 1992, for example, the B.C. Supreme Court found that Michael Forrest and William Price "lived in a lengthy, sexually faithful relationship for thirteen years" and shared "a committed, caring, and loving relationship, tantamount in all respects to a traditional heterosexual marriage." Therefore, Forrest, who assumed the homemaker role, was entitled to a share of Price's assets (*Vancouver Sun*, 1992, p. B1). This judgement has obvious implications for future cases involving same-sex couples who dissolve a long-term relationship (Duclos, 1991; Gavigan, 1995).

FAMILY LAW AND WOMEN'S INEQUALITY

Although few feminists regret the repeal of legislation and social policies rooted in paternalism, they have been confronted with some negative and unintended consequences of the gender-neutral family law and policy they struggled so hard to achieve (Andrew and Rodgers, 1997; Busby, Fainstein, and Penner, 1990; Fineman, 1991). Clearly, the implementation of formal legal equality in family law and social welfare has not only failed to end women's structured dependency, but has also intensified it in some instances upon marital breakdown. So we have to ask how it is that family law, which is premised on the principle of liberal egalitarianism, continues to help reproduce and sustain women's inequality. After all, gender-neutrality means that there are no rights to custody, maintenance, and property based on sex.

The short answer is that strict adherence to the principle of formal equality in the absence of **substantive equality** leads to inequality; treating unalikes in the same way simply perpetuates differences. However, we also need to examine the role of ideologies in reproducing women's subordination, that is, the assumptions and beliefs about family and equality that influence how judges interpret and administer gender-neutral legislation. In short, the rules can change, but the people who apply them do not automatically adjust their thinking (Gavigan, 1988).

An examination of custody and access outcomes since the implementation of gender-neutral law suggests that the overall effect of the reform has been to increase the power of fathers to lay claim to their children (Bourque, 1994; Boyd, 1989b). Since the 1970s, the percentage of cases where mothers retain sole custody of children after a separation or divorce by agreement with the fathers has dropped and, in contested cases, men have a good chance of "winning" (Bertoia and Drakich, 1993; Boyd, 1989b, p. 845). Moreover, from the late 1980s onward, judicial decisions in cases involving disputes over access of non-custodial fathers to their children have favoured fathers over mothers (Bourque, 1994; Boyd, 1997a; Taylor, Barnsley, and Goldsmith, 1996). Clearly, the new "politics of custody" places feminists in a quandary. They have long advocated equal parenting, but formal legal equality seems to mean that fathers gain at the expense of mothers. This trend reflects the combined influence of ideologies related to family, motherhood, fatherhood, and equality on judicial interpretation of such malleable concepts as "the best interests of the child" (Boyd, 1989a, 1989b; Drakich, 1989).

Notwithstanding the reform of custody law, some judges have continued to interpret "the best interests of the child" principle in terms of the old "tender years" doctrine, which empowered mothers so long as the woman in question adhered to the norms of the "good" mother — white, middle-class, heterosexual, and married. A review of the outcomes in contested cases involving young children since the implementation of gender-neutral law reveals that, regardless of her parenting abilities, a lesbian mother almost always loses custody to the father unless she hides her sexual orientation and appears to fit the norm (Arnup, 1989). One of the clearest judicial statements about the need for mothers to be, or appear to be, heterosexual was the judgement handed down by a B.C. Supreme Court justice in the 1987 case of *Elliott* v. *Elliott* (Sage, 1987). Mr. Elliott obtained custody of his 7-year-old daughter, who was then residing with her mother, because Ms. Elliott had established a live-in relationship with a lesbian partner. In awarding custody to the father, Mr. Justice MacKinnon was very explicit about his reasoning: "Whatever one might accept or privately practise, I cannot conclude that indulging in homosexuality is something for the edification of young children" (Sage, 1987, pp. 1, 8).

In some cases, the "best interests of the child" principle is equated with the availability of a stay-at-home mother or mother figure. Regardless of sexual orientation, then, a mother who engages in full-time or part-time employment to support her children may well lose custody to a husband who has a new homemaker-wife, a housekeeper, or some other surrogate mother to look after the children (Boyd, 1989a, 1989b, 1997a). At the same time, a woman can be a full-time mother and still lose custody of her children if she is forced to rely on welfare and thus lives at or below the poverty line. More often than not in such cases, the father is economically secure and the court will award custody to him because he can provide a better standard of living for the children. Thus, the "best interests of the child" are equated with material comfort (Boyd, 1989a, 1989b).

Judges also seem to be swayed by the ideology of fatherhood and the demands of **fathers' rights** groups in assessing "the best interests of the child" (Drakich, 1989). In Canada and elsewhere, they are handing down judgements about custody and access that are based on assumptions that children must have a father in their lives and that contemporary men are equally involved in parenting their children. Such decisions not only privilege the nuclear-family form, but also ignore the facts that some fathers are bad role models and that most fathers do not contribute equally to the care of their children prior to divorce (Bourque, 1994; Boyd, 1998; Taylor et al., 1996). Moreover, studies of fathers' rights show that they want neither sole responsibility for children nor an equal division of child care and responsibility. They want equal status as legal parents, which really is a demand "to continue the practice of inequality in postdivorce parenting but now with a legal sanction" (Bertoia and Drakich, 1993, p. 612).

Proposals for mandatory **joint custody** of children also reflect ideologies of fatherhood.[11] While Canadian law contains no presumption in favour of joint custody, the federal Divorce Act, 1985 and some provincial statutes allow joint custody as an option. Moreover, the "friendly parent" provision in the Divorce Act, which directs courts to operate on the principle that children should have as much contact with each parent as is in their "best interests," sometimes forces women to accept a joint-custody arrangement with a spouse who has been physically or sexually abusive. If she resists, the mother may lose custody altogether because she is perceived as being unco-operative and/or as putting her own interests before those of the children (Bourque, 1994; Rosnes, 1997). Such was the decision in *LiSanti* v. *LiSanti*, a case where the wife went to a women's shelter with her children to escape the alleged abuse of her husband. The court awarded Mr. LiSanti interim custody of the children on the grounds that Mrs. LiSanti's "abrupt departure" was "a complete denial of the husband's custodial rights" and that "the best interests of the children, were they ever first considered by her, would have militated against such a result" (Boyd, 1989b, p. 848).

Clearly, then, judicial determinations of custody based on notions of equal parenting and justified by what is best for the children often work to the disadvantage of mothers. An examination of the results of gender-neutral law governing spousal and child support reveals the same general pattern: women lose and men gain overall when the courts adhere strictly to the principle of formal legal equality. The liberal feminists who strongly critiqued the old paternalistic divorce and desertion statutes and pressed hard for family-law reform to implement formal legal equality did not anticipate such an outcome. They believed that "the problem with no name" (Friedan, 1963) would recede and ultimately disappear once women entered the paid labour force in large numbers and achieved economic independence from men.

MARITAL BREAKDOWN AND ECONOMIC INEQUALITIES

The liberal-feminist failure to adequately theorize women's work at home as well as in the labour force was realized only over time. Simply moving married women into paid employment did not produce liberation because most often they found themselves trying to cope with a double day: eight hours of low-paid service and clerical work in the "pink ghetto" and more hours of unpaid domestic work to service their families (Evans, 1991; Morton, 1988, 1993). The significance of the devalued nature of women's work in both the public and the private spheres was painfully revealed as the divorce rate in Canada began spiraling upward after the 1968 divorce-law reform introduced some "**no-fault**" grounds for divorce.[12]

Under the principle of formal legal equality enshrined in provincial family relations acts since the 1970s and in the 1985 Divorce Act, the courts have assumed that women are as capable of achieving self-sufficiency as men, despite the evidence that in most cases they are substantially less able to be self-supporting (Morton, 1988; Mossman and MacLean, 1986, 1997). In 1994, Canadian women with full-time, full-year paid employment still made only 70 percent of the earnings of their male counterparts, and among all earners that year women made 62 percent as much as men (Luxton and Reiter, 1997, p. 204; see also Evans, 1991).

When marriages break down, women are much more likely than men to be plunged into poverty, and with marriages ending at an unprecedented rate, the "feminization of poverty" has increased. Moreover, although women have always been more vulnerable to poverty than men, now middle- and upper-class women are joining the ranks of the poor after separation or divorce (Evans, 1991). Why has this occurred? Partly because the courts have consistently failed to consider, first, the value of women's unpaid contributions to family or social reproduction and, second, the significant negative effect on their opportunities and advancement in paid work of leaving the labour force for years at a time to take care of children (Bailey, 1989, p. 628; Keet, 1990; Morton, 1988, 1993). In short, when the courts make determinations about spousal and child support and property, they do not take into account the substantive inequality in the economic situations of men and women upon marital breakdown. They tend to interpret self-sufficiency not in terms of previous standards of living, but in terms of earning any sort of living at all (Bailey, 1989; Keet, 1990; Morton, 1988, 1993).

Nonetheless, the courts have adopted contradictory positions on the issue of who is responsible for an ex-spouse when she or he does not attain self-sufficiency. A "trilogy" of cases (*Caron* v. *Caron, Pelech* v. *Pelech, Richardson* v. *Richardson*) decided by the Supreme Court of Canada (SCC) in 1987 established what became known as the "causal connection test": if a spouse who applies for maintenance or an increase in existing maintenance demonstrates "that he or she has suffered a radical change in circumstances flowing from an economic pattern of dependency engendered by the marriage," the court may "exercise its relieving power." In the 1987 "trilogy," the point at issue was whether mutual agreements between ex-spouses that set potential limits on the maintenance obligations of one to the other were valid. The main argument put to the SCC was that, after signing a separation agreement that set limits on her ex-husband's financial responsibilities, each of the three ex-wives found that her financial position changed for the worse and only further support from her former spouse would enable her to get off social assistance. However, the SCC found no relationship between the changed economic situation of the three women and their previous marital relationships. Therefore, the state, and not their ex-husbands, was deemed to be responsible for their maintenance (Bailey, 1989).

In contrast, the 1992 Supreme Court of Canada decision in *Moge* v. *Moge* supported the claim of the ex-wife that her former husband who had not lived with her for many years should continue to pay spousal support. The SCC was swayed by the argument that women's unpaid contributions to a marriage, such as domestic labour and child care, typically were undervalued in spousal-support awards, and this undervaluing is linked to the feminization of poverty as divorce and separation increase. Thus, "the responsibility for women's poverty should rest wherever possible with a man with whom they have had a recognized relationship" (Boyd, 1996, pp. 176–77).

Whether they uphold state or individual responsibility for maintenance, the courts seem to be telling women that they should be married, that the solution to their situation is to find another male breadwinner who will enable them to play their proper role as primary caregiver and supplementary wage-earner. In other words, a position of structured dependency on men is what they should aspire to. Thus, although judges are not directly instructing women to marry, their adherence to assumptions about the "normal" wife/ mother living in a nuclear family seems to be guiding their decision making, with dire consequences for separated and divorced women.

Overall, family-law reforms implemented since the 1960s have continued the historical emphasis on the "privatization of the costs of reproduction," albeit now women have been factored into the equation (Fudge, 1989). The question is: How do we ensure that individual men or individual women assume responsibility for themselves and for their dependent children? This focus in law and social policy has two major effects.

First, it generates poverty, primarily for women and children. For example, the maintenance-enforcement programs implemented in some provinces have reduced the default rate on support payments and the federal child-support guidelines have established minimum levels of support, but neither policy can eliminate or even substantially ameliorate poverty since both spousal- and child-support awards generally are so low (Eichler, 1991; Pulkingham, 1994). Similarly, the new property laws do not guarantee a fifty-fifty split of all assets between spouses. In some provinces, property owned by one spouse for strictly business purposes is excluded; legal marriage contracts can override an equal division of assets; and upon application from one of the spouses, the courts have discretion to order an unequal division of property if judges determine that it would not be just or fair to enforce the equalization principle (Keet, 1990; Morton, 1988).

Second, emphasizing individual responsibility for the "personal" preempts the creation of new social programs. For example, the use of tax exemptions and/or credits for child-care expenses incurred by parents reinforces the idea that social reproduction is a personal rather than a public issue. Moreover, the financial rewards for the work entailed in caring for children are so low that it remains overwhelmingly "women's work" because men have no "incentive for giving up the status and rewards associated with male models of paid labour" (Ferguson, 1991, p. 94). Such individualized approaches to caring simply perpetuate the sexual division of labour (Teghtsoonian, 1997).

Finally, we need to examine the differential effect of the legislative and policy reforms promoted by second-wave feminists. In retrospect, the lack of focus on class, race, and sexual orientation in many feminist campaigns for sociolegal change is very obvious. Again, white, bourgeois, heterosexual women, and to a lesser extent their counterparts in the more affluent sectors of the working class, have gained the most from the reordering of family law since the 1960s. Thus, many couples have no property to split when their relationships dissolves. Or, if common property exists, it is most often a house with a mortgage, so there is nothing to divide except mutual debt. Similarly, as low as they are, child- and spousal-support obligations imposed on the working poor may mean that two families are impoverished rather than one. Moreover, the legal recognition of different forms of family such as common-law relationships seems to be directly correlated with the extent to which they resemble traditional heterosexual marriages and is often aimed more at keeping people off welfare than at any democratization or abandonment of familial ideology.

The same disparities are generated by child-care policies. During the 1980s, only slightly more than 50 percent of pregnant women in paid employment claimed maternity benefits under Unemployment Insurance, probably because the benefit was so low that only women and/or couples with a good income could afford to do so. The situation is even worse under the Employment Insurance Act because the benefit remains low (about 55 percent of average insurable earnings); eligibility now is based on hours, not on weeks, worked; and the maximum weekly payment has been reduced (Iyer, 1997, p. 187). Since the benefit for parental leave is the same, the outcome will likely be that a preponderance of middle- and upper-class heterosexual women take advantage of the program (Evans, 1991, pp. 196–97). Tax credits and exemptions for child care are also most helpful to more affluent professional women and couples who can afford to hire domestic workers or to support a stay-at-home mother (Macklin, 1992).

Obviously, none of these programs is particularly relevant to single low-income parents, most of whom are women and/or members of racial and ethnic minorities. Moreover, the growing reliance of affluent families on poor women of colour to provide child care has created conflicts among feminists about the exploitation of some women by other, more privileged women (Arat-Koc, 1990; Macklin, 1992; Ng, 1988).

Thus, feminist support for individualized solutions to the problem of housework, motherwork, and wifework has helped some women. But it has also depoliticized the issue and made it less likely that in the near future the state will implement comprehensive social programs that would benefit the majority of Canadian families. At the same time, it is painfully apparent that aboriginal women, immigrant women, and women of colour face difficulties that were simply not part of the picture of women painted by the 1970 Royal Commission on the Status of Women (Abner, Mossman, and Pickett, 1991; Arat-Koc, 1990; Williams, 1990).[13]

CONCLUSION
▼

The mixed and often negative effects of feminist-inspired legislation and social policies have helped to fuel a backlash against feminism in the form of a pro-family movement exemplified by REAL Women of Canada and fathers' rights groups (Bertoia and Drakich, 1993). Women are exhorted to "Blow Feminism, Girls, Find Mr. Right" (*Vancouver Sun*, 1991, p. A5). A perhaps more significant development, however, is that "ideological debate" among feminists themselves about women's position in families, along with the concomitant disillusionment of many feminists with the process of sociolegal reform, has diluted, and even erased, feminist impact on contemporary law and policy (Peters, 1997; Smart, 1986, 1989).

Nonetheless, many feminists continue to see law and the state as critical sites of struggle (Adamson et al., 1988; Gavigan, 1993; Razack, 1991). In the current climate of conservatism, feminists cannot simply abandon the legal and policy arenas to the proponents of "family values" (Peters, 1997, p. 49). However, it also is clear that sociolegal reforms per se cannot end women's inequality. Thus, feminists must think carefully about the unintended as well as the intended consequences of the family-related reforms they advocate, and strategize about how they can reinject feminist perspectives on family law and policy into the political and public cultures (Boyd, 1997; Luxton, 1997).

SUMMARY
▼

- Historically, feminist movements in Canada and elsewhere have been dominated by theoretical perspectives that place primary emphasis on using law to achieve equality for women with men. First-wave, maternal feminism promoted sociolegal reforms that would guarantee women's "separate but equal" status in the family, while second-wave, liberal feminism advocated family-related legislation and policies based on gender-neutrality.

- Neither maternal nor liberal feminists explicitly challenged the idea that the "normal" family is a nuclear unit based on a heterosexual, marriage relationship, a sexual division of labour, and the public/private split. Consequently, family-related sociolegal reforms consistently have privileged the nuclear-family model regardless of whether they were promoted by feminists or by non-feminists.

- Nonetheless, feminist-inspired reforms related to families clearly have "politicized the personal" and contributed to greater equality for some women vis-à-vis men over time. Historically, maternal feminists helped make women legally visible in their roles as mothers and wives through the implementation of legislation and policies giving them rights to custody, financial support and property. Contemporary liberal feminists helped to entrench formal legal equality for women with men in the family through the implementation of gender-neutral legislation and policies governing custody, maintenance, and property.

- However, the negative and differential impact of family-related reforms reveals the weaknesses of both maternal and liberal feminism and demonstrates that feminists cannot litigate their way to equality. Through their belief in "separate but equal spheres," first-wave, maternal feminists achieved reforms that entrenched women's dependency on marriage and a male breadwinner. Likewise, second-wave, liberal feminists secured reforms that asserted women's formal equality with men, but ignored the substantive inequality with men that most women experience. Moreover, neither maternal nor liberal feminists factored differences among women into their reform proposals. Thus, the main beneficiaries of family-related reforms historically have been the most privileged women in society (i.e., white, middle-class, and respectable working-class women).

- Despite the contradictory and differential effects of sociolegal reforms, feminists can use law in conjunction with initiatives in other arenas, such as the media and politics, to work toward the achievement of full equality for all women in Canada. Above all, feminists must promote legislation and policies that recognize the differences as well as the commonalities among women and between women and men that treat unalikes differently in order to move beyond simple formal equality toward substantive equality. They need to think about both employment and pay equity; about extended, single-parent, and same-sex families as well as heterosexual, nuclear ones; and about the complex ways in which race, class, sexual orientation, and (dis)ablity intersect with gender to reproduce structured inequalities. In short, feminists have to focus on moving the women at the bottom up to effect any fundamental change in society.

NOTES
▼

1. This chapter focusses primarily on feminist reform activities in Anglo-Canada, where provincial family law is derived from English precedents.
2. In this chapter, the welfare state is conceptualized as a set of services and ideas that operates at two levels: the "male stream," where aid (e.g., Employment Insurance) is a right or entitlement; and the "female stream," where assistance (e.g., mothers' allowance) is charity meted out to the "deserving" (Gordon, 1988; see also Wilson, 1977).
3. The terms "first-wave" and "second-wave" feminism denote the organized feminist movements that emerged in Canada and elsewhere during the late nineteenth and early twentieth centuries and during the 1960s, respectively.
4. In the United States and England, for example, liberal feminism predated maternal feminism and exercised a strong influence on feminist activism from the 1850s onward, whereas, in Canada, the two perspectives emerged almost simultaneously during the late nineteenth century. Moreover, first-wave feminism had a less-distinct presence in Canada than elsewhere because feminist activists tended to be subsumed within the larger social, moral, and urban reform movements that emerged in Anglo-Canada from the 1880s to the 1920s and in the aftermath of those movements between the wars (Bacchi, 1983, 1991; Roberts, 1979).
5. The most succinct statement of the unity doctrine is attributed to Sir William Blackstone, the English legal commentator: "In law husband and wife are one person, and the husband is that person" (Kieran, 1986, p. 41).
6. Radical and socialist second-wave feminists critiqued the three major assumptions underlying the bourgeois family model: first, that the nuclear family is the natural, inevitable, and highest family form; second, that there is a sexual division of labour; and third, that there is a public/private distinction.
7. There are two interrelated forms of reproduction: biological reproduction of the species is linked to the physical processes of conception, pregnancy, and birthing; social reproduction of the species is linked to the "motherwork," "wifework," and "housework" that women perform to maintain the physical and emotional health of individual family members, and hence of the society as a whole (Luxton et al., 1990, pp. 58–61). For reasons of space, this discussion focusses on law and social policy related to social reproduction.

8. In a 1982 Ontario case, for example, a 50-year-old woman received a three-month jail term for a $19 373 welfare fraud even though her lover did not provide financial support for her or her children and he also had another woman friend. The judge said the courts must punish women who "are prepared to allow themselves to be used in that fashion" (Porter and Gullen, 1984, p. 215).

9. Historically, the First Nations were shockingly overrepresented among children in care and adopted children (Monture, 1989, p. 2). More recently, First Nations have asserted control over child welfare, but current privatization policies in Canada may erode this control through underfunding (Kline, 1997).

10. While this book was in press, the Supreme Court upheld the decision of the Ontario Court of Appeal in *M*. v. *H*.

11. Indeed, both legislators and the judiciary have demonstrated some support for proposals to implement mandatory joint custody as a way of acknowledging the presumed increase in men's involvement in parenting. Joint custody sounds appealingly egalitarian. Yet in U.S. jurisdictions where it has been implemented, fathers are benefiting at the expense of mothers because women often remain the primary caregiver (physical custody), but men have equal say in decision making about the children (legal custody) and thereby continue to exercise control over their ex-wives. Men can also obtain reduced child support because they are supposedly caring for the children half of the time.

12. Although the Canadian divorce rate fell in the late 1980s, it remains significantly higher than prior to the 1968 law reform: in 1951, one in every 24 marriages ended in divorce; in 1990, one couple divorced for every 2.4 who married (Mossman and MacLean, 1997, p. 119).

13. The commissioners did not even address the situation of aboriginal women who lost their Indian status if they married non-Indian men. They had to leave their reserves, could neither inherit nor hold property on the reserve, and were denied recognition as Indians, as were their children (Kirkness, 1988; Turpel, 1991).

CRITICAL THINKING QUESTIONS
▼

1. Compare and assess the policy implications of the various feminist perspectives on state, law, and family.

2. Discuss the similarities and differences between first-wave, maternal feminists and second-wave, liberal feminists with respect to their views on family, law, and social policy.

3. Compare and evaluate the relative strengths and weaknesses of radical and socialist feminist approaches to "politicizing the personal."

4. Outline and assess the argument that feminist movements in Canada and other Western countries have reflected the experience of and improved the position of a select group of women in those societies.

5. Explain the "two-tiered system" of family law in Canada and discuss the feasibility of creating one system of family law that will reflect the reality of, and apply equally to, very different types of family.

6. Given the contradictory effects of family-related legislation and social policies, discuss the pros and cons of using law as a feminist strategy to achieve women's equality.

SUGGESTED READING
▼

Carol Baines, Patricia Evans, and Sheila Neysmith, eds. 1998. *Women's Caring: Feminist Perspectives on Social Welfare*, 2nd ed. Toronto: Oxford University Press.
> The essays in this collection reveal how much of the caring work in our society is done by women. Within the home, this work often is hidden in the roles of mothers, daughters, and wives; outside the home, caring work frequently is undervalued as women do volunteer work or low-paid jobs.

Abigail B. Bakan and Daiva Stasiulis, eds. 1997. *Not One of the Family: Foreign Domestic Workers in Canada*. Toronto: University of Toronto Press.
> This book documents the institutionalized unequal treatment of immigrant domestic workers in Canada. Since the 1940s, the number of women recruited from third-world countries to work in Canadian homes has increased markedly, while the rights of citizenship for such workers have declined.

Dorothy Chunn and Dany Lacombe, eds. In press. *Law as a Gendering Practice*. Toronto: Oxford University Press.
> The essays in this collection illustrate the complex and contradictory workings of legal discourse in the construction of "woman." They show how legal struggles over meanings about gender are reproduced, legitimized, and, perhaps, refashioned.

Martha A. Fineman and Isabel Karpin, eds. 1995. *Mothers in Law: Feminist Theory and the Legal Regulation of Motherhood*. New York: Columbia University Press.
> In this book, feminist theorists examine the legal issues surrounding motherhood. They show how law defines the ideal and the deviant mother, often without reference to the actual practices of motherhood.

Margaret Hillyard Little. 1998. *No Car, No Radio, No Liquor Permit: The Moral Regulation of Single Mothers in Ontario, 1920–1997*. Toronto: Oxford University Press.
> This book outlines how state financial assistance to single mothers in Canada historically has been contingent upon their adherence to "proper" moral standards. Single mothers deemed to be immoral have experienced the denial or loss of benefits.

Dorothy Roberts. 1997. *Killing the Black Body: Race, Reproduction, and the Meaning of Liberty*. New York: Pantheon Books.
> This book analyzes and illustrates the impact of racism on legislation and policies related to biological and social reproduction in the United States.

REFERENCES
▼

Abner, Erika, Mary Jane Mossman, and Elizabeth Pickett. 1991. "'No More Than Simple Justice': Assessing the Royal Commission Report on Women, Poverty and the Family." *Ottawa Law Review* 22/3: 573–606.

Adamson, Nancy, Linda Briskin, and Margaret McPhail. 1988. *Feminist Organizing for Change: The Contemporary Women's Movement in Canada.* Toronto: Oxford University Press.

Andrew, Caroline. 1984. "Women and the Welfare State." *Canadian Journal of Political Science* 17 (December): 667–81.

Andrew, Caroline, and Sandra Rodgers. 1997. *Women and the Canadian State.* Montreal: McGill-Queen's University Press.

Arat-Koc, Sedef. 1990. "Importing Housewives: Non-Citizen Domestic Workers and the Crisis of the Domestic Sphere in Canada." In M. Luxton, H. Rosenberg, and S. Arat-Koc, eds., *Through the Kitchen Window: The Politics of Home and Family,* 2nd ed. Toronto: Garamond.

Arnup, Katherine. 1989. "'Mothers Just Like Others': Lesbians, Divorce and Child Custody in Canada." *Canadian Journal of Women and the Law* 3: 18–32.

Bacchi, Carol Lee. 1983. *Liberation Deferred? The Ideas of the English-Canadian Suffragists, 1877–1918.* Toronto: University of Toronto Press.

———. 1991. *Same Difference: Feminism and Sexual Difference.* Sydney: Allen and Unwin.

Backhouse, Constance. 1991. *Petticoats and Prejudice: Women and the Law in Nineteenth-Century Canada.* Toronto: The Osgoode Society.

———. 1992. "Married Women's Property Law in Nineteenth-Century Canada." In Bettina Bradbury, ed., *Canadian Family History: Selected Readings.* Toronto: Copp Clark Pitman.

Bailey, Martha J. 1989. "*Pelech, Caron,* and *Richardson.*" *Canadian Journal of Women and the Law* 3/2: 615–33.

Baines, Carol, Patricia Evans, and Sheila Neysmith, eds. 1991. *Women's Caring: Feminist Perspectives on Social Welfare.* Toronto: McClelland & Stewart.

Bannerji, Himani, ed. 1993. *Returning the Gaze: Essays on Racism, Feminism and Politics.* Toronto: Sister Vision Press.

Barrett, Michele. 1988. *Women's Oppression Today: The Marxist Feminist Encounter.* Revised edition. London: New Left Books.

Barrett, Michele, and Roberta Hamilton, eds. 1986. *The Politics of Diversity.* London: Verso.

Barrett, Michele, and Mary McIntosh. 1982. *The Anti-Social Family.* London: Verso.

Bertoia, Carl, and Janice Drakich. 1993. "The Fathers' Rights Movement: Contradictions in Rhetoric and Practice." *Journal of Family Issues* 14/4: 592–615.

Black, Naomi. 1988. "The Canadian Women's Movement: The Second Wave." In S. Burt, L. Code, and L. Dorney, eds., *Changing Patterns: Women in Canada.* Toronto: McClelland & Stewart.

Bourque, Dawn. 1994. "'Reconstructing' the Patriarchal Nuclear Family: Recent Developments in Child Custody and Access in Canada." *Canadian Journal of Law and Society* 10/1: 1–24.

Boyd, Susan B. 1989a. "Child Custody, Ideologies and Employment." *Canadian Journal of Women and the Law* 3/1: 111–33.

———. 1989b. "Child Custody Law and the Invisibility of Women's Work." *Queen's Quarterly* 96/4: 831–58.

———. 1996. "Can Law Challenge the Public/Private Divide? Women, Work, and Family." *Windsor Yearbook of Access to Justice* 15: 161–85.

———. 1997a. "Looking Beyond Tyabji: Employed Mothers, Lifestyles, and Child Custody Law." In S.B. Boyd, ed., *Challenging the Public/Private Divide.* Toronto: University of Toronto Press.

———. 1998. "Lesbian (and Gay) Custody Claims: What Difference Does Difference Make?" *Canadian Journal of Family Law* 15/1: 131–52.

Boyd, Susan B, ed. 1997b. *Challenging the Public/Private Divide: Feminism, Law, and Public Policy.* Toronto: University of Toronto Press.

Boyd, Susan B., and Elizabeth A. Sheehy. 1986. "Feminist Perspectives on Law." *Canadian Journal of Women and the Law* 2/1: 1–51.

Brodie, Janine. 1995. *Politics on the Margins: Restructuring and the Canadian Women's Movement.* Halifax: Fernwood.

Brodie, Janine, ed. 1996. *Women and Canadian Public Policy.* Toronto: Harcourt Brace & Company, Canada.

Brodie, Janine, Shelley A.M. Gavigan, and Jane Jenson. 1992. *The Politics of Abortion.* Toronto: Oxford University Press.

Brophy, Julia, and Carol Smart. 1985. *Women-in-Law.* London: Routledge and Kegan Paul.

Burstyn, Varda, and Dorothy E. Smith. 1985. *Women, Class, Family and the State.* Toronto: Garamond.

Burt, Sandra. 1988. "Legislators, Women, and Public Policy." In S. Burt, L. Code, and L. Dorney, eds., *Changing Patterns: Women in Canada.* Toronto: McClelland & Stewart.

Busby, Karen, Lisa Fainstein, and Holly Penner, eds. 1990. *Equality Issues in Family Law.* Winnipeg: Legal Research Institute of the University of Manitoba.

Carruthers, Errlee. 1995. "Prosecuting Women for Welfare Fraud in Ontario: Implications for Equality." *Journal of Law and Social Policy* 11: 241–62.

Chunn, Dorothy E. 1990. "Boys Will Be Men, Girls Will Be Mothers: The Regulation of Childhood in Vancouver and Toronto." *Sociological Studies in Childhood Development* 3: 87–110.

———. 1992. *From Punishment to Doing Good: Family Courts and Socialized Justice in Ontario, 1880–1940.* Toronto: University of Toronto Press.

Dale, Jennifer, and Peggy Foster. 1986. *Feminists and State Welfare.* London: Routledge and Kegan Paul.

Donzelot, Jacques. 1980. *The Policing of Families.* New York: Pantheon.

Drakich, Janice. 1989. "In Search of the Better Parent: The Social Construction of Ideologies of Fatherhood." *Canadian Journal of Women and the Law* 3/1: 63–87.

Duclos, Nitya. 1991. "Some Complicating Thoughts on Same-Sex Marriage." *Law and Sexuality* 1: 31–62.

Eichler, Margrit. 1991. "The Limits of Family Law Reform, or the Privatization of Female and Child Poverty." *Canadian Family Law Quarterly* 7: 59–83.

———. 1997. *Family Shifts: Families, Policies, and Gender Equality.* Toronto: Oxford University Press.

Engels, Friedrich. 1964. *The Origin of the Family, Private Property and the State.* New York: International Publishers.

Evans, Patricia M. 1991. "The Sexual Division of Poverty: The Consequences of Gendered Caring." In C. Baines, P.M. Evans, and S. Neysmith, eds., *Women's Caring: Feminist Perspectives on Social Welfare.* Toronto: McClelland & Stewart.

Evans, Patricia, and Norene Pupo. 1993. "Parental Leave: Assessing Women's Interests." *Canadian Journal of Women and the Law* 6/2: 402–18.

Evans, Patricia M., and Gerda R. Wekerle, eds. 1997. *Women and the Canadian Welfare State: Challenges and Change.* Toronto: University of Toronto Press.

Ferguson, Evelyn. 1991. "The Child-Care Crisis: Realities of Women's Caring." In C. Baines, P.M. Evans, and S. Neysmith, eds., *Women's Caring: Feminist Perspectives on Social Welfare.* Toronto: McClelland & Stewart.

Fineman, Martha. 1991. *The Illusion of Equality: The Rhetoric and Reality of Divorce Reform.* Chicago: University of Chicago Press.

Foucault, Michel. 1977. *Discipline and Punish.* New York: Pantheon.

———. 1980. *The History of Sexuality,* vol. 1. New York: Vintage.

Friedan, Betty. 1963. *The Feminine Mystique.* New York: Dell.

Fudge, Judy. 1989. "The Privatization of the Costs of Reproduction." *Canadian Journal of Women and the Law* 1: 246–55.

Garland, David. 1985. *Punishment and Welfare.* Brookfield, VT: Gower.

Gavigan, Shelley A.M. 1988. "Law, Gender and Ideology." In Anne F. Bayefsky, ed., *Legal Theory Meets Legal Practice.* Edmonton: Academic Printers and Publishing.

———. 1993. "Paradise Lost, Paradox Revisited: The Implications of Familial Ideology for Feminist, Lesbian, and Gay Engagement to Law." *Osgoode Hall Law Journal* 31/3: 589–624.

———. 1995. "A Parent(ly) Knot: Can Heather Have Two Mommies?" In Didi Herman and Carl Stychin, eds., *Legal Inversions: Lesbians, Gay Men and the Politics of Law.* Philadelphia: Temple University Press.

———. 1998. "Legal Forms, Family Forms, Gender Norms: What Is a Spouse?" Unpublished paper. North York, ON: Osgoode Hall Law School, York University.

Gordon, Linda. 1988. "What Does Welfare Regulate?" *Social Research* 55/4: 609–29.

———, ed. 1990. *Women, the State and Welfare.* Madison: University of Wisconsin Press.

Herbert, Jacinth. 1989. "'Otherness' and the Black Woman." *Canadian Journal of Women and the Law* 3/1: 269–79.

Herman, Didi. 1990. "Are We Family? Lesbian Rights and Women's Liberation." *Osgoode Hall Law Journal* 28: 789–815.

———. 1994. *Rights of Passage: Struggles for Lesbian and Gay Legal Equality.* Toronto: University of Toronto Press.

Iyer, Nitya. 1997. "Some Mothers Are Better Than Others: A Re-examination of Maternity Benefits." In S.B. Boyd, ed., *Challenging the Public/Private Divide.* Toronto: University of Toronto Press.

Kealey, Linda, ed. 1979. *A Not Unreasonable Claim: Women and Reform in Canada 1880s.* Toronto: Women's Press.

Keet, Jean. 1990. "The Law Reform Process, Matrimonial Property, and Farm Women: A Case Study of Saskatchewan, 1980–1986." *Canadian Journal of Women and the Law* 4(1): 166–89.

Kieran, Sheila. 1986. *The Family Matters: Two Centuries of Family Law and Life in Ontario.* Toronto: Key Porter.

Kirkness, Verna. 1988. "Emerging Native Women." *Canadian Journal of Women and the Law* 2/2: 408–15.

Kitchen, Brigitte. 1987. "The Introduction of Family Allowances in Canada." In Allan Moscovitch and Jim Albert, eds., *The "Benevolent" State: The Growth of Welfare in Canada.* Toronto: Garamond.

Kline, Marlee. 1997. "Blue Meanies in Alberta: Tory Tactics and the Privatization of Child Welfare." In S.B. Boyd, ed., *Challenging the Public/Private Divide.* Toronto: University of Toronto Press.

Latham, Barbara K., and Roberta J. Pazdro, eds. 1984. *In Her Own Right: Selected Essays on Women's History in B.C.* Victoria: Camosun College.

Little, Margaret. 1994. "Manhunts and Bingo Blabs: The Moral Regulation of Ontario's Single Mothers." *Canadian Journal of Sociology* 19/2: 233–47.

Luxton, Meg, ed. 1997. *Feminism and Families: Critical Policies and Changing Practices.* Halifax: Fernwood.

Luxton, Meg, and Ester Reiter. 1997. "Double, Double, Toil and Trouble ... Women's Experience of Work and Family in Canada, 1980–1995." In P.M. Evans and G.R. Wekerle, eds., *Women and the Canadian Welfare State.* Toronto: University of Toronto Press.

Luxton, Meg, Harriet Rosenberg, and Sedef Arat-Koc, eds. 1990. *Through the Kitchen Window: The Politics of Home and Family,* 2nd ed. Toronto: Garamond.

MacKinnon, Catherine. 1987. *Feminism Unmodified: Discourses on Life and Law.* Cambridge, MA: Harvard University Press.

Macklin, Audrey. 1992. "*Symes* v. *M.N.R.*: Where Sex Meets Class." *Canadian Journal of Women and the Law* 5/2: 498–517.

Mandell, Nancy. 1988. "The Child Question: Links Between Women and Children in the Family." In Nancy Mandell and Ann Duffy, eds., *Reconstructing the Canadian Family: Feminist Perspectives.* Toronto: Butterworths.

Martin, Dianne L. 1992. "Passing the Buck: Prosecution of Welfare Fraud; Preservation of Stereotypes." *Windsor Yearbook of Access to Justice* 12: 52–97.

McClung, Nellie. 1976. "What Will They Do with It?" In Ramsay Cook and Wendy Mitchinson, eds., *The Proper Sphere*. Toronto: University of Toronto Press.

McCormack, Thelma. 1991. *Politics and the Hidden Injuries of Gender: Feminism and the Making of the Welfare State*. CRIAW Papers no. 28. Ottawa: Canadian Research Institute for the Advancement of Women.

McLaren, Angus. 1990. *Our Own Master Race: Eugenics in Canada, 1885–1945*. Toronto: McClelland & Stewart.

McLaren, Angus, and Arlene Tigar McLaren. 1998. *The Bedroom and the State: The Changing Practices and Politics of Contraception and Abortion in Canada, 1880–1980*, 2nd ed. Toronto: McClelland & Stewart.

Monture, Patricia A. 1989. "A Vicious Circle: Child Welfare and the First Nations." *Canadian Journal of Women and the Law* 3/1: 1–17.

Monture-Angus, Patricia. 1995. *Thunder in My Soul: A Mohawk Woman Speaks*. Halifax: Fernwood.

Morton, Mary E. 1988. "Dividing the Wealth, Sharing the Poverty: The (Re)formation of 'Family' in Law in Ontario." *Canadian Review of Sociology and Anthropology* 25/2: 254–75.

———. 1993. "The Cost of Sharing, the Price of Caring: Problems in the Determination of 'Equity' in Family Maintenance and Support." In J. Brockman and D.E. Chunn, eds., *Investigating Gender Bias in Law: Socio-Legal Perspectives*. Toronto: Thompson Educational.

Moscovitch, Allan, and Jim Albert, eds. 1987. *The "Benevolent" State: The Growth of Welfare in Canada*. Toronto: Garamond.

Mosoff, Judith. 1997. "'A Jury Dressed in Medical White and Judicial Black': Mothers with Mental Health Histories in Child Welfare and Custody." In S.B. Boyd, ed., *Challenging the Public/Private Divide*. Toronto: University of Toronto Press.

Mossman, Mary Jane, and Morag MacLean. 1986. "Family Law and Social Welfare: Toward a New Equality." *Canadian Journal of Family Law* 5: 79–110.

———. 1997. "Family Law and Social Assistance Programs: Rethinking Equality." In P.M. Evans and G.R. Wekerle, eds., *Women and the Canadian Welfare State*. Toronto: University of Toronto Press.

Ng, Roxana. 1988. "Immigrant Women and Institutionalized Racism." In S. Burt, L. Code, and L. Dorney, eds., *Changing Patterns: Women in Canada*. Toronto: McClelland & Stewart.

O'Donovan, Katherine. 1985. *Sexual Divisions in Law*. London: Weidenfeld and Nicholson.

Panitch, Leo, ed. 1977. *The Canadian State: Political Economy and Political Power*. Toronto: University of Toronto Press.

Peters, Suzanne. 1997. "Feminist Strategies for Policy and Research: the Economic and Social Dynamics of Families." In M. Luxton, ed., *Feminism and Families*. Halifax: Fernwood.

Porter, Marion, and Joan Gullen. 1984. "Sexism in Policy Relating to Welfare Fraud." In J.M. Vickers, ed., *Taking Sex into Account*. Ottawa: Carleton University Press.

Pulkingham, Jane, 1994. "Private Troubles, Private Solutions: Poverty among Divorced Women and the Politics of Support Enforcement and Child Custody Determination." *Canadian Journal of Law and Society* 9/2: 73–97.

Pulkingham, Jane, and Gordon Ternowetsky, eds. 1996. *Child and Family Policies: Struggles, Strategies and Options*. Halifax: Fernwood.

Razack, Sherene. 1991. *Canadian Feminism and the Law: The Women's Legal Education and Action Fund and the Pursuit of Equality*. Toronto: Second Story.

———. 1992. "Using Law for Social Change: Historical Perspectives." *Queen's Law Journal* 17/1: 31–53.

———. 1998. *Looking White People in the Eye: Gender, Race, and Culture in Courtrooms and Classrooms*. Toronto: University of Toronto Press.

Rich, Adrienne. 1980. "Compulsory Heterosexual and Lesbian Existence." *Signs: Journal of Women in Culture and Society* 5/4: 631–60.

Roberts, Wayne. 1979. "'Rocking the Cradle for the World': The New Woman and Maternal Feminism, Toronto, 1877–1914." In L. Kealey, ed., *A Not Unreasonable Claim*. Toronto: Women's Press.

Robson, Ruthann. 1992. *Lesbian (Out)Law: Survival under the Rule of Law*. Ithaca, NY: Firebrand Books.

———. 1994. "Resisting the Family: Repositioning Lesbians in Legal Theory." *Signs: Journal of Women in Culture and Society* 19/4: 975–96.

Rooke, Patricia T., and Rudy L. Schnell. 1987. *No Bleeding Heart: Charlotte Whitton. A Feminist on the Right*. Vancouver: University of British Columbia Press.

Rosnes, Melanie. 1997. "The Invisibility of Male Violence in Canadian Child Custody and Access Decision-Making." *Canadian Journal of Family Law* 14/1: 31–60.

Ross, Becki L. 1995. *The House That Jill Built: A Lesbian Nation in Formation*. Toronto: University of Toronto Press.

Sage, Barbara. 1987. "B.C. Lesbian Mother Denied Custody of Daughter." *The Lawyers' Weekly* 6/38: 1, 8.

Smart, Carol. 1984. *The Ties That Bind*. London: Routledge and Kegan Paul.

———. 1986. "Feminism and Law: Some Problems of Analysis and Strategy." *International Journal of the Sociology of Law* 14: 109–23.

———. 1989. *Feminism and the Power of Law*. London: Routledge.

Snell, James G. 1991. *In the Shadow of the Law: Divorce in Canada, 1900–1939*. Toronto: University of Toronto Press.

Steel, Freda M. 1985. "The Ideal Marital Property Regime — What Would It Be?" In Elizabeth Sloss, ed., *Family Law in Canada: New Directions*. Ottawa: Advisory Council on the Status of Women.

Strong-Boag, Veronica. 1976. *The Parliament of Women: The National Council of Women of Canada, 1893–1920*. Ottawa: Museum of Man.

———. 1979. "'Wages for Housework': Mothers' Allowances and the Beginnings of Social Security in Canada." *Journal of Canadian Studies* 14/1: 24–34.

———. 1988. *The New Day Recalled: Lives of Girls and Women in English Canada, 1891–1939*. Toronto: Copp Clark Pitman.

Taylor, Georgina, Jan Barnsley, and Penny Goldsmith. 1996. *Women and Children Last: Custody Disputes and the Family Justice System.* Vancouver: Vancouver Custody and Access Support and Advocacy Association.

Teghtsoonian, Katherine. 1997. "Who Pays for Caring for Children? Public Policy and the Devaluation of Women's Work." In S.B. Boyd, ed., *Challenging the Public/Private Divide.* Toronto: University of Toronto Press.

Turpel, Mary Ellen. 1991. "Home/Land." *Canadian Journal of Family Law* 10/1: 17–40.

Ursel, Jane. 1986. "The State and the Maintenance of Patriarchy: A Case Study of Family, Labour and Welfare Legislation in Canada." In J. Dickinson and B. Russell, eds., *Family, Economy, and State: The Social Reproduction Process under Capitalism.* Toronto: Garamond.

———. 1992. *Private Lives, Public Policy: 100 Years of State Intervention in the Family.* Toronto: Women's Press.

Vancouver Sun. 1991. "Blow Feminism, Girls, Find Mr. Right." (Nicole Parton). Nov. 9, p. A5.

———. 1992. "Gay Man Wins Property Settlement." (Larry Still). Nov. 5, p. B1.

Weeks, Jeffrey. 1986. *Sexuality.* London: Tavistock.

Wendell, Susan. 1996. *Rejected Body: Feminist Philosophical Reflections on Disability.* New York: Routledge.

Williams, Toni. 1990. "Re-forming 'Women's' Truth: A Critique of the Report of the Royal Commission on the Status of Women in Canada." *Ottawa Law Review* 22/3: 725–59.

Wilson, Elizabeth. 1977. *Women and the Welfare State.* London: Tavistock.

Zaretsky, Eli. 1976. *Capitalism, the Family and Personal Life.* New York: Harper and Row.

———. 1982. "The Place of the Family in the Origins of the Welfare State." In Barrie Thorne and Marilyn Yalom, eds., *Rethinking the Family.* New York: Longman.

CASES CITED
▼

Caron v. *Caron* (1987) 7 RFL (3d) 274 (SCC)

Elliott v. *Elliott*, unreported case

LiSanti v. *LiSanti* (1990), 24 RFL (3d) 178

M. v. *H.* (1997), 25 RFL (4th) 116 (Ont. CA)

Moge v. *Moge* (1992) 3 SCR 813

Murdoch v. *Murdoch* (1973) 41 DLR (3d) 367 (SCC)

Pelech v. *Pelech* (1987) 7 RFL (3d) 225 (SCC)

Richardson v. *Richardson* (1987) (3d) 304 (SCC)

Weeks v. *Weeks* (1955), 3 DLR 704 (BCCA)

▼

DIVORCE: OPTIONS AVAILABLE, CONSTRAINTS FORCED, PATHWAYS TAKEN

CAROLYNE A. GORLICK

LEARNING OBJECTIVES

In this chapter, you will learn that:

- female single-parent families outnumber male single-parent families by more than four to one, and it is possible that 45 percent of Canadian children will experience separation/divorce before the age of 18;
- (mis)perceptions are apparent in divorce discussions;
- controversy exists as to the long-term impacts of divorce on children;
- low-income women are witnessing a redefining of mothering through employability programs;
- frequently missing from the divorce literature are the voices of divorced women and children in defining, framing, and guiding their experiences.

INTRODUCTION

Divorce is likely to be viewed as an ending rather than a beginning. Clearly it is an end to some relationships; it weakens some and strengthens others. Divorce may also initiate an interactive process of individual and social realignments, strains, hopes, and expectations combined with perceptions of available options, institutional and individual constraints, and paths chosen. Divorce is also a process in which gender inequities persist and are sustained. In this context, it is useful to recognize everyday interactions and their effects on the lives of family members, relatives, and friends. In that light, the life experiences of divorced women guide the discussion in this chapter.

The first section of the chapter addresses conclusions drawn from the divorce literature and their influence on policy assumptions and reform activities. The second section offers an illustration of the options perceived, the constraints forced, and some of the pathways taken by a particular group of low-income female single parents who found themselves characterized as "welfare moms."

Out of every ten Canadian marriages, at least four are expected to end in divorce (Statistics Canada, 1997a). Between 1970 and 1986, the divorce rate increased, from 18.6 to 43.1 percent. In 1987, the divorce rate peaked at 50 percent of all marriages. Since then, the rate has been decreasing. Nevertheless, by 1996, there were 1 138 000 single-parent families in Canada, with female single-parent families out numbering male single-parent families by more than four to one. Of all single-parent families, one-third have been divorced, and one-fifth were separated. One in every five children lives in a single-parent family (Statistics Canada, 1997a). It is possible that 45 percent of Canadian children will experience separation/divorce before the age of 18 years (Statistics Canada, 1997a).

Discussions of divorce-rate trends include the impact of legal divorce reforms such as family-law changes, expanded judicial services, and shortened waiting periods. Other explanations focus on women's financial independence, through increased participation in the labour force, as a factor in women's decision to divorce. Yet other explanations emphasize supportive societal attitudes regarding divorce. Still others view the increase in divorce as a disruption of traditional family values and as comparable to an epidemic or disease. Reflecting a neo-conservative and deviance perspective, Frum (1996) argues that

> Canada faces no social problem more important than the strengthening of the family — reducing the number of births outside marriage and cutting the rate of divorce. To achieve that aim, we must revitalize the institution of marriage. How? By ensuring that laws and customs favour marriage over all other ways of life.

Whether one is offering explanations for divorce-rate trends or attitudes, it is also useful to address conclusions drawn from the divorce literature and their influence on policy assumptions and reform activities.

(MIS)PERCEPTIONS OF DIVORCE
▼

Perceptions of divorce have been framed and challenged by individual, familial, and societal experiences and reinforced through the media and professional and research information. Divorce has been categorized and described in numerous academic/professional writings (several journals focus specifically on divorce) and self-help/how-to-survive-divorce books, which have proliferated as the number of individuals experiencing divorce has increased. Much of the social-psychological information may be grouped under two general approaches: divorce viewed as initiating negative and pathological responses, and divorce as a positive self-realization experience (Arendell, 1986).

IS DIVORCE A PATHOLOGICAL RESPONSE OR A POSITIVE SELF-REALIZATION EXPERIENCE?

How people adjust to divorce has received significant theoretical and speculative attention. Some theories promote a **deviance model of divorce** characterized by stages of denial, mourning, anger, and readjustment; by a significant, continuous loss of self-esteem for women (Weiss, 1975); and as creating long-term negative consequences for children and a period of "diminished parenting" (Wallerstein and Kelly, 1980). This traditional monolithic model pathologizes divorce by describing the divorcing family as deviant and emphasizing the problems emerging from this deviance (Eichler, 1993). Elements of this approach have been found in professional responses (some therapeutic and casework activities) that emphasize divorce as a crisis as opposed to a lengthy, continuous process of adjustment (Strauss, 1988).

The reverse of the deviancy model is the view of marital separation as an opportunity for personal growth. Divorce is seen as challenging individuals to increase or reinforce their adaptive abilities by interacting with and responding to the challenges and crises that are integral to divorce (Weitzman, 1985; Strauss, 1988). Several possibilities exist, such as enlarging, not decreasing, supportive family ties with remarriage: children may have more than two parents and a greater number of relatives. An expansion of friendship ties and opportunities is also viewed as a possibility. Divorce may also be understood as a mass resistance of women against oppressive familial and social structures. It may certainly have a liberating outcome for women, men, and children leaving a hostile family environment.

In any case, it is misleading to emphasize either greater personal-growth opportunities or negative and pathologizing divorce outcomes, for each places the onus for adaptability or change on the individual. For the individual responding to changes in the aftermath of divorce, however, it is less a question of ability than one of opportunity, with women frequently having fewer economic, legal, and labour-market opportunities than men (Eichler, 1993, 1997). Furthermore, to picture divorce as primarily either positive or negative is to overlook the complexity of the process itself and the differing concerns and capacities of individual family members. For example, when women leave a physically and/or emotionally abusive relationship, the initial relief at separation and the degree of predictability in the aftermath of departure has the possibility of translating into enhanced self-worth. This exists along with the personal stress, fear, and worry about money, housing, and legal outcomes that accompany the departure.

Missing from both of these assumptions is the significance of race and ethnicity for divorcing families. It is undoubtedly more difficult for recent female immigrants to initiate and obtain a divorce. Why is this, and what solutions should be forthcoming? Are some racial or ethnic groups more supportive of divorce than others? If so, what forms of support exist? And what are the policy and advocacy implications of these differences? Also, how might a woman who is disabled define and respond to the divorce process? The questions are numerous; the answers in the research literature are few.

In spite of the contradictions and omissions in these two general assumptions, they underlie much of the divorce literature. The following discussion of some myths and realities surrounding divorce emphasizes the pervasiveness of these assumptions.

IS DIVORCE A COMMONALITY OF NEGATIVE EXPERIENCES?

Divorce in this "commonality of experiences" context is a life-cycle transition experienced negatively by all involved individuals (former spouses, children, grandparents, friends, and other family members) (Ahrons and Rogers, 1987). The social and psychological impact is difficult for everyone, with no individual or group suffering more or adapting better than another. Timing of individual and familial adaptation is also significant. Two to three years is frequently perceived as the crucial period of "adaptability" for most members of divorced families.

Recognizing the diversity of individual experiences and understandings, hopes and expectations, and strains and stresses throws into question arguments for commonality in adaptation and timing. Furthermore, to view divorce as another life transition masks the different short- and long-term outcomes experienced by gender (husband versus wife, son versus daughter). For example, missing from the commonality of experiences discussion is the economic vulnerability of women (and their children) and the direct link with their post-divorce experiences. In sum, overemphasizing the commonality of experiences ignores the differing divorce realities and the diversity of experiences of family members. Stating that the experiences of divorcing family members are entirely negative offers a picture of the family as coming to an end, with few constructive or positive initiatives forthcoming.

ARE POST-DIVORCE PROBLEMS TRANSITIONAL BECAUSE THE PARENT IS LIKELY TO REMARRY?

As noted, the deviancy model of divorce presents this family type as short-term, aberrant, and "no longer intact." Frequent comparisons are drawn between "intact" families — the preferred, normative, and "necessary family structure" — and "not intact" families. The divorced family presumably becomes "intact" again if divorced spouses remarry and form another nuclear family, sometimes referred to as blended, step-, reconstituted, or bi-nuclear. The **blended family** contains spouses who may have been divorced, widowed, or never married, and with or without children. Within this family unit are various configurations of stepparents and step-/adopted siblings, as well as step-grandparents/aunts/uncles/cousins.

Most children living in step-families are in a blended form of the couples' biological children and the wife's child(ren) from a previous marriage. Nine percent of children under 12 years of age are members of a step-family, with approximately 50 percent being stepchildren and 50 percent born or adopted into the step-family (Statistics Canada, 1997a). The most frequent step-relationship was that of stepfather–stepdaughter, with stepfathers outnumbering stepmothers five to one. In spite of the fact that stepmother–stepdaughter was the least frequent relationship, the "wicked stepmother" myth, emerging from folk tales and children's stories such as "Cinderella" and "Snow White," persists. Cheal (Human Resources Development Canada, 1996) discovered that National Longitudinal Survey of Children and Youth (NLSCY) data did not support the traditional stepmother myth. Stepmothers were not harsher or more inconsistent in their interactions with their stepchildren than were biological/adopted mothers with their biological/adopted children. It appears that the majority of children in step-families have moderate to good relationships with their parents, which is remarkable, given the various permutations of interactions and complexities that might emerge as family members negotiate their roles and positions. Ferri and Smith (1998), in acknowledging the stresses and strains experienced by step-families, argue for greater support of these families, such as recognition of particular circumstances, the myriad and complex relationship structures and processes, and the formidable time and financial-resource challenges. Ferri and Smith (1998) maintain that

> the challenge facing those in step families is particularly great, not only because of the complex new relationships involved, but also because, for biological parents at least, and for many step-parents too, the failure of earlier relationships may have left a vulnerable legacy in terms of material hardship and emotional insecurity.

The literature on step-families, although growing, tends to use a comparative (that is, blended versus nuclear family) approach, or contains descriptions of emerging personality and familial traits, or presents hurdles overcome in spousal or parental relationships. In short, the measuring stick remains the nuclear family and the degree to which the blended family is able to approximate it.

Although nuclear families numerically predominate, the possibility increasingly exists for a child or an adult to move in and out of a variety of family structures over time. Remarriage is increasing with one in five persons married in the early 1990s having been previously married. More than a quarter of individuals in common-law relationships are divorced. Common-law families increased the fastest of any other family structure between 1991 and 1996. One couple in seven were living common-law by 1996 (Statistics Canada, 1997a).

In response to the perception that single-parenting is transitional, there are two considerations. First, the labour-force participation of females (and, for some, greater financial independence) may lead to a postponement of remarriage or influence a decision not to remarry. Second, it is not entirely clear that remarriage will resolve any or most post-divorce problems. Indeed, remarriage may lead to another divorce.

DOES DIVORCE HAVE A LONG-TERM NEGATIVE IMPACT ON CHILDREN?

The assumption here is that, although divorcing spouses ultimately tend to adapt to marital separation, children are more likely to experience emotional and physical trauma for a long time (Wolchik and Karoly, 1988; Wallerstein and Kelly, 1979; Pett, 1982). The "missing" father and the "emotionally overwrought" mother are to blame, and there are long-term negative consequences of divorce and growing up in an "aberrant" single-parent family. Numerous factors have been discussed as indicators of long-term negative impacts on children. One example is the age of the child. A 1998 Statistics Canada study of 23 000 children under the age of 11 years noted that 20 percent of children ages 10–11 saw their parents separate before they were 5 years old. This was an increase from 12 percent of a similar group in 1973, and 6.5 percent in 1962. Subsequently the number of young children witnessing divorce has tripled over the past two decades.

What are the experiences of children dealing with divorce? A recent study, which tracked 2000 families over 20 years, discovered that children of high-conflict divorces fared better than children of apparent low-conflict divorces where marital hostility was not overt (Amato and Booth, 1997). Divorce in the latter family situation was more of a surprise and jarring for children who experienced a diminished sense of trust leading to psychological distress in later years. Others argue that child-adjustment factors relate to income, level of couple animosity, and custodial parents' childrearing skills (Ambert, 1989). Still others contend that children of divorce are sick more than children in two-parent families. Statistics Canada (1992) found that 56 percent of children of single-parent families have at least one health problem, compared with 49 percent of children from two-parent families.[1] The implication is that children in two-parent families have safe and comfortable environments, and those in single-parent families do not. A recent study concluded that the majority of children in single-mother families did not have more emotional and behavioural problems and academic and social difficulties than children from two-parent families, although it did argue that risk factors and rates were greater for children of single-parent families (Lipman, Offord, and Dooley, 1996).

What is much less clear is whether these health or behavioural conditions are a direct result of divorce or a drop in the standard of living, or some combination that might ensue from divorce. Also, what is defined as long-term versus short-term negative effects and how might these be delineated or measured over time? Studies also reveal that comparable negative impacts are observed in both discordant two-parent families and high-conflict divorces.

Certainly, there are several intervening and controlling factors beyond the implied assumption that, by divorcing, parents will make their children sick. Nevertheless, those kinds of links are made and compounded. For example, it is sometimes said that, if a parent works, she is likely to cause harm to her children. An employed mother seeking custody may frequently discover that working fathers are lauded as dedicated, responsible parents for providing child support, while working mothers are not necessarily viewed in a favourable manner.

Controversy over whether divorce has long-term negative impacts on children seems to have altered public opinion. More specifically, there appears to be an attitude shift regarding divorce and its effect on children among certain age groups. Statistics Canada (1997b) noted that 44.5 percent of 15- to 29-year-olds said they would remain in a bad marriage for their children, compared with 39.5 percent of 30- to 49-year-olds. Of those over the age of 50, 52 percent consistently reported they would remain in bad marriages for the children's sake. Overall, 40 percent of adult Canadians would stay in an unhappy relationship for their children, with 60 percent of males choosing to remain, compared with 33 percent of females. It is difficult to predict the extent to which these changing attitudes will have an impact on marital separation in the future. Those most willing to stay in a relationship for the children's sake, such as the 15- to 29-year-old group compared with the 30- to 49-year-old group, may not have married and are predicting their possible behaviour.

What are the long-term implications for children of parents staying together, or remarrying, compared with divorcing? Perhaps what makes this a difficult period for some children and not others is not the divorce itself, but myriad influences from family relationships, income decline, and residential changes combined with the child's age and sex. Perhaps analysis in the divorce literature should stress "mother presence" rather than "father absence" to draw a clearer picture of the ambiguities surrounding these questions. Perhaps a greater emphasis on context and interaction of factors should be pursued. Perhaps also worth revisiting is whether only cross-sectional data provide sufficient answers to time-based questions. And perhaps a greater effort in listening to divorce experiences interpreted by children is a direction worthy of pursuit.

DO DIVORCED FATHERS OFFER SUFFICIENT AND CONSISTENT ALIMONY AND CHILD SUPPORT?

The argument here is that divorced, non-custodial fathers have been sufficient and consistent in their alimony and child-support payments. In fact, downward financial and social mobility have been the experience of most women and children after divorce, and this decline is directly linked to inadequate, erratic, and missing financial support. Public recognition of the numbers of female single-parent families relying on social assistance has led to accusations against a group referred to as "**dead-beat dads.**" Some, however, believe that dead-beat dads are a myth. The co-chairperson of the joint Commons–Senate committee examining access to children of divorce by grandparents and non-custodial parents contends: "the idea of deadbeat dads, I find objectionable … that is a myth created by the feminist agenda. There are just as many deadbeat mothers as there are deadbeat fathers" (*London Free Press*, 1998). This is an interesting observation, given the significantly higher numbers of custodial mothers compared with custodial fathers.

A recent national study indicated that 47 percent of court-ordered support payments are made on time, and 33 percent are at least six months late, while out-of-court settlements have led to 75 percent making regular payments (Statistics Canada, 1997b). Provinces have implemented a variety of punitive measures responding to support orders in default. Before the implementation of the Family Support Plan in Ontario, 85 percent of family-support orders were in default. With the introduction of the mandatory deduction order under the Family Support Plan, the number of defaults has been decreasing. Nevertheless, in spite of court orders, 80 000 Ontario parents are not receiving child support, with a total $1.2 billion in arrears. The details of why this trend is occurring are not clear. There is some speculation that at least one segment of those parents in arrears over child support are members of the working poor whose incomes may be based on seasonal or part-time employment.

Several measures have been put in place to collect owed child support. Recently, Ontario has increased efforts by suspending driver's licences, and in some cases jail sentences have been imposed. In 1997–98, 1145 warnings of Ontario driver's licence suspensions have been sent, and 288 defaulters have had their licences suspended. Other possible methods of solving the arrears problem include seizing lottery winnings over $1000 (although one wonders how many child-support orders this would affect), withdrawing half the money held by delinquent parents in joint bank accounts, and allowing courts to collect money from a third party found hiding defaulting parents' assets. With a possible $10 000 fine to both the non-custodial parent and his or her employer, a clear responsibility is placed on the parent who has been issued an alimony/child-support order and the employer to ensure that the order agreement is fulfilled. In 1993, the Ontario government extended the garnishee of wages to five years from one year to minimize the need for yearly renewals. As well, up to half of Employment Insurance benefits may be garnisheed for support payments. Another child-support search option is the Debtguard Internet site, which uses framed stamp-sized photos in a mock "Most Wanted" poster, including details of occupations and whereabouts.

In addition to irregular or non-existent and unpredictable child-support payments, the custodial parent may also run into barriers with the agency in charge of assisting the child-support payment process. Ontario's now centralized Family Responsibility Office has come under criticism from custodial parents, women's support groups, opposition MPPs, and the province's ombudsman. Much of the criticism rests with the "inequitable and inadequate" delivery system that leave some families without income support that has been garnisheed from the non-custodial parent's wages.

Legal reforms such as "no-fault" divorce have failed to ameliorate the financial crisis experienced by divorced women and their children. In fact, the post-separation income discrepancy between former spouses has continued. Three years after marital separation, the incomes of women and children had dropped by at least 30 percent; while, on average, men's incomes were more than double those of their former wives (Economic Council of Canada, 1992; National Forum on Family Security, 1993). Furthermore, Pask (1993, p. 187) argues that, "if men were to uniformly pay one-third, instead of less than one-fifth, of their gross income as support, the percentage of women and children in poverty would be reduced from 58 percent to 26 percent."

There are many conceptual and methodological difficulties in measuring the economic impact of divorce. Some of the studies are based on differing research designs (cross-sectional or longitudinal) and varying income measures (drop in income, drop in expected income, negative-income events, or additional "need" measures). Also the politics of poverty-line definition influence discussions of depth of poverty for female single-parent families. Questions worth pursuing include: Do younger divorced women experience a greater drop in standard of living than older divorced women? Do upper-income divorced women experience the same relative decline as lower-income divorced women? And what influence do socio-economic status and age have on men's economic experiences after divorce? Do race, ethnicity, or disability influence a woman's income drop? Or are predetermined factors at work? As Morgan (1991) contends, the economic gains and losses experienced by women in the aftermath of divorce have been predetermined by forces existing prior to the marriage's ending.

Regardless of the omissions and inconsistencies in the literature on economic decline in the aftermath of divorce, the family wage becomes the husband's wage as the measuring stick in alimony/child-support decisions. Even before divorce, however, the family wage does not always reflect an equitable sharing of household resources. This inequity in some families may be compounded by husbands who use a disproportionate amount of household resources (Wilson, 1977).

In sum, although there is no clear consensus on the extent of economic decline (or how to measure it), a drop in standard of living does occur for the custodial mother. This drop depends on the non-custodial father's pattern of financial support, and legal processes that enhance or detract from that support.

DO CUSTODIAL MOTHERS CHOOSE TO WORK OR PARENT FULL-TIME?

An Organisation for Economic Co-operation and Development publication (1993), *Breadwinners or Child Rearers: The Dilemma for Lone Mothers*, offers an international comparison of the influences on the labour-force participation of female single parents compared with married mothers. Although a comprehensive and detailed discussion of the issue is presented, the prevailing assumption is that there is an element of choice for female single parents between paid employment and full-time parenting. Accompanying this perceived choice, however, are the negative stereotypes of divorced mothers in the labour force. As MacLean (1991, p. 36) comments, "Working women have been characterized after divorce as independent, self-sufficient women and non-working women as alimony drones, attempting to live off their ex-husbands or as welfare scroungers living off the taxpayer."

The latter stereotype is reinforced by changes in social-welfare policy directed at those single mothers dependent on social welfare. Welfare to Work programs across the country have targeted two groups: youth and female single parents receiving social assistance (Gorlick and Brethour, 1998). Within this context, employability is **redefining mothering**. The definition of mothering is up for grabs as each province appears to redefine mothering for program convenience. The definition of "full-time" mothering is based on the age of the child. Subsequently, in British Columbia, a single mother on social assistance is expected to enter a welfare to work program when her child reaches the age of 7 years. In Quebec, Manitoba, Alberta, the significant child ages are 2 years, 6 years, and 6 months, respectively. In the past, the age markers for employability had been in some provinces 18 to 19 years. This downward shift in the child's age has been accompanied by a gender-neutrality trend toward single-mother employment (Evans, 1997). In short, a single mother's entitlements are predicated upon her role as worker as opposed to mother (Duncan and Edwards 1997).

In sum, a custodial mother is frequently placed in a no-win position in which she attempts to balance parental and work responsibilities with economic pressures. There may appear to be a choice between parenting and employment; the reality is, there is no such choice.

ARE MOTHERS WHO DO NOT SEEK OR ARE NOT GRANTED CUSTODY IMMORAL AND UNFIT PARENTS?

The mother is most often the custodial parent. However, two countervailing trends are emerging. An increasing number of fathers are requesting custody of their children, and there is a greater awareness of mothers who are not seeking or who are not granted custody. In the United States, fathers seeking custody are successful 40 to 70 percent of the time, and the number of father-led single-parent families there has doubled since 1980 (*Newsweek*, 1993). As Quinn (*Newsweek*, 1993, p. 64) comments:

> Depending on the judge, a father's chances are best if he earns substantially more than the mother; if he takes a new wife who will stay home with the kids (mothers are apparently fungible); if he handled part or most of the parenting; if the children are older; if the mother has a paying job; or if she violates a norm, by taking a lover or admitting she is gay.

Predominantly ignored in the divorce literature are the experiences of non-custodial mothers. Edwards's (1989) study is an exception; it identifies the variety of choices made by, and the perceptions of, non-custodial mothers, including the following: "I still feel most people do not understand children not living with their mothers. There is an automatic stigma. What must be wrong with her? She must not be a very loving or dedicated person or mother. She must be a drunk or prostitute or something evil" (p. 30).

Some of the non-custodial mothers in the Edwards study lost custody battles, some chose to be the non-custodial parent, some regained custody; some developed positive relationships with their children, others did not. Many are living in new family configurations; some are living alone. Their accounts show a diversity of reasons, and myriad responses. Clearly, though, blaming the mother prevails when women are non-custodial, while the single custodial father is portrayed in the media as long-suffering, thoughtful, and responsive to his children's needs. It must be remembered that, in spite of the array of television shows featuring single custodial fathers, this group is a statistical minority, as are non-custodial mothers.

ARE REFORMED DIVORCE LAWS REMOVING THE GENDER BIASES IN DIVORCE?

Until 1968, divorces in Canada were granted if one of the spouses had committed adultery, if desertion or imprisonment had taken place, or if spouses had lived apart for three years. A relative liberalization of divorce laws after 1968 led to increased divorce rates. In 1985, the "**no-fault**" **divorce** law was passed, and in the ten weeks immediately after its passage the number of divorce cases in Canada tripled, to 49 000. The new law reduced the waiting period to apply for a divorce to one year, and granted an uncontested divorce after a three-year separation.

One of the outcomes of the legal reforms has been a "**get self-sufficient quick**" orientation primarily directed to those women who have interrupted their employment for marriage and/or child care. This approach assumes that in most current marriages both spouses have careers, and that wives generally have kept working full-time or intermittently throughout the marriage. This orientation, reinforced by judicial indifference to gender wage inequities, influences decisions regarding retraining periods for the dependent spouse. Frequently, the time frames for education or retraining are unrealistic, given the duration of academic or professional training, demands of single parenting, and lack of opportunity to engage full-time in these educational and retraining programs.

A 1992 decision has the potential for altering one aspect of this "get self-sufficient quick" orientation. A Hamilton, Ontario, family court ordered that a divorced wife receive compensation for career loss. This initiative was based on the assumption that, if damages can be calculated for personal-injury accidents, then it should be possible to calculate loss of income that results from marital commitments. Although innovative, this approach will have more benefit for women who have left higher-income, professional careers than for women from lower-income, secretarial/clerical positions. Furthermore, even if the divorced woman is eligible, she does not receive compensation if her former husband cannot afford it.

A 1992 Supreme Court decision will also alter the "get self-sufficient quick" approach in divorce settlements. In delivering the decision on the *Moge* case, in which the husband argued that his wife had time to become self-sufficient, Justice Claire L'Heureux-Dubé found that the financial consequences of the end of a marriage extend beyond the simple loss of future earning power or losses directly related to the care of children. They will often encompass loss of seniority, missed promotions and lack of access to fringe benefits such as pension plans and insurance....

This decision was based on the assumption that support payments should function as a vehicle for an equal sharing of the economic consequences of marriage and divorce. In some instances, support payments may continue for an indefinite period. Frequently, however, there is not sufficient income for long-term substantial support. In the *Moge* case, for example, the former wife's monthly support is $150. A more recent case before the Supreme Court raises the question of support standards for short-term marriages (see Box 8.1). Thus, the extent to which this decision will balance the financial inequities that emerge in most families is questionable.

In a legal context, it is not useful to examine women's approach to economic support after divorce primarily in terms of whether or not they seek employment. As MacLean (1991, p. 43) suggests,

we have to stop thinking of the woman's role as head of household after divorce as not financially dependent or independent, working or not working, and begin to perceive it as negotiating an income package from a variety of sources, public and private, collective and individual. The divorced woman then would have to contend with only the cost of being a woman, rather than the cost of divorce as well.

As of May 1997, Federal Divorce Act changes focussed on the child-support award process. More specifically, child support is now calculated using the income of the non-custodial parent based on average awards in each province. Also Federal Income Tax Act changes mean that child support will not be tax deductible for non-custodial parents, and custodial parents will not have to pay income tax on the money they receive. Critics of these changes contend that they take away the discretionary powers of the courts regarding child support and provide for an annual review of the orders that maybe very stressful for some women, particularly those who have been abused. Furthermore, these changes may increase the possibility of litigation; lead to more parents lobbying for joint or sole custody rather than pay child-support costs; and may result in a significant federal tax grab, given that non-custodial parents usually have a higher income than custodial parents. Have these reforms eased gender inequities? Is there greater economic security for children? It is premature to offer a clear and precise response to the impact of these child-support changes. Recently, another joint Senate–Commons review of child custody and access has emerged as a result of the acrimonious parliamentary debate over Bill

---

BOX 8.1
▼
TOP COURT WEIGHS THE PRICE OF MARRIAGE

"When you say 'I do' does it really mean that — legally, forever?" asks lawyer Carol Hickman, who is defending Frank Bracklow in his fight against a challenge from his disabled ex-wife for long-term monthly support. The court is being asked to rule on whether a sick or disabled spouse is entitled to indefinite financial support based on need if the disability is not a result of the collapse of the marriage.

Sharon Bracklow, who suffers from a mood disorder, an obsessive-compulsive disorder, and an immune-system disorder, is unlikely to work again. She lives in subsidized housing and receives disability benefits of $787 a month since a court allowed her ex-husband to stop sending her monthly cheques of $400 three years ago.

Sharon Bracklow's lawyers argue that she cannot survive financially on her own, so the burden should fall on family members rather than on the welfare system. "One is simply not allowed to abandon a spouse to destitution at the end of a marriage if one has financial resources which might assist in relieving the other's financial circumstances," her lawyers say in a submission to the court. Spouses should expect that they are potentially assuming financial responsibility for their spouses in the event of economic hardship, including job loss, her lawyers argue.

Frank Bracklow's lawyers counter that he has already paid his fair share and a ruling in his ex-wife's favour would reduce marriage to "the purchase of a lifetime policy of disability insurance."

The courts have long established support standards for long-term marriages, but this case could set a benchmark for support obligations arising from shorter marriages (such as Bracklow's) when one of the partners is disabled or unable to work.

Source: Adapted from "Top Court Weighs Price of Marriage," *The Toronto Star*, November 6, 1998, pp. A1 and A33. Reprinted by permission of *The Canadian Press*.

C-41, in turn offering some controversial recommendations (see Box 8.2). However, other elements of the divorce process continue to raise questions as to who fares better.

Divorce mediation, intended to minimize the hurdles of the process, has not been entirely successful. Mediation assumes an equal bargaining power, and has led some women to forgo the legal protection of the adversarial system.

BOX 8.2
▼
REPORT OF THE JOINT SENATE–COMMONS COMMITTEE ON CHILD CUSTODY AND ACCESS, DECEMBER 1998

Formed as a compromise to the acrimonious debate regarding Bill C-41, which established mandatory child-support guidelines, the joint Senate–Commons Committee on Child Custody and Access itself became a controversial forum, complete with warring factions, charges of bias, and political interference. The primary premise throughout the report is that both parents, whatever their differences, are capable, responsible, and acting in good faith. Some of the recommendations that have been proposed include:

The terms "custody" and "access" should be replaced by "shared parenting":
The implication of this change is that separating parents should develop co-parenting plans and share information on their childrens' health, education, and social lives.

False accusations of spousal abuse should be reviewed:
The government should review the Criminal Code to assess if it punishes a parent who falsely accuses a spouse of abuse in the context of a child-custody dispute.

The importance of grandparents:
Careful consideration by the courts should be given to the importance of grandparents and other family members in the lives of children in child-custody and -access decisions.

The voices of children in child-custody and -access disputes:
The courts should ensure that children have a voice in family disputes, possibly through legal representation.

Recommendations from this committee regarding changes to the 30-year-old Divorce Act must be passed by the House of Commons and the Senate before becoming law.

Sources: Editorial, *The Globe and Mail*, December 11, 1998, p. A26; Editorial, *The Canadian Press*, November 22, 1998, p. A1.

And, whether voluntary or ordered by the court, mediation may reinforce psychological and economic inequalities between spouses (Strauss, 1988).

Similarly, joint custody was intended to equitably divide the financial and emotional burdens of child custody. Consistent and sufficient support payments, it was thought, would accompany this arrangement as a result of the father's greater involvement in his children's lives, in turn reducing con-

BOX 8.3

▼

WOMAN ABUSE MUST BE PART OF CUSTODY AND ACCESS CONSIDERATIONS

Legislation should be drafted to better protect battered women and their children. Many abused women and their children face extreme dangers at the time of separation and divorce. As part of the abusers' pattern of control and domination, victims have usually been threatened that if they dare leave, they, their children, or their families will be seriously hurt or killed. Abused women are at most risk of being killed by an abusive partner after separation. In Canada, intimate femicides account for between 61 and 78 percent of all killings of women where an offender is identified. Abused women report they have been terrorized by their abusive partner's threats to abduct their children. In 1990, there were 432 reports of parental child abduction where charges were laid. Half of all abductions occur during a court ordered visitation.

The Canadian family law systems do not adequately deal with custody and access disputes. Canadian custody and access statutes (with the exception of Newfoundland and Labrador) make no specific reference to violence as a factor to consider in determining custody and access arrangements. Continuing to award custody and access to abusive men jeopardizes the safety of, and sometimes the lives of, women and children. Furthermore, it does not support those men for whom joint custody or access arrangements would be in the best interests and needs of their children.

Source: Megan Walker and Bina Osthoff, London Battered Women's Advocacy Centre, "Woman Abuse Must Be Part of Custody and Access Considerations," *The London Free Press*, October 19, 1998.

flicts over money and parenting responsibilities. The expectation of a friendly and co-operative relationship either at the time of divorce or soon thereafter is not a reality for most divorcing spouses, and subsequently joint custody is infrequently an option. Furthermore, family violence appears to escalate at the time of marital separation. Family law, however, has not responded to this reality for some families in terms of custody and access considerations.

In conclusion, 86 percent of children from separated/divorced families live with their mothers, and 7 percent live with their fathers. Seven percent live in joint custody or with other relatives, or are cared for by social agencies. A startling 42 percent of children rarely or never see their fathers again after their parents separate (Statistics Canada, 1997b).

THE AFTERMATH OF DIVORCE:
SINGLE MOTHERS ON WELFARE
▼

Between 1991 and 1996, the number of female-single-parent families increased faster (by 20 percent) than the number of male-single-parent families (Statistics Canada, 1997b). This increase in and high incidence of poverty among female-single-parent families continues to exacerbate the lack of resources available, threatening the life chances of this family group (Canadian Council on Social Development, 1996). Recent social policy and program changes have reaffirmed the individual-responsibility model, which assumes that the low-income single mothers are in that position as a result of individual choice and should be able to alter it as a result of individual action. This section outlines findings from a panel study of single mothers on social assistance, offering a picture over time of the experiences of low-income single mothers, including some of the options, constraints, and paths they have confronted and addressed. Although the findings are based on the activities of individuals, the need for social responsibility when developing social policy to assist this family group is implicit.

The study "Economic Stress, Social Support, and Female Single Parents," conducted by Carolyne Gorlick, consisted of four sets of interviews between 1986 and 1997 with the original sample of 150 single mothers receiving welfare.[2] Close to 51 percent of the single mothers (who had at least one child under 16 living at home) in the first interviews were separated, 31.3 percent divorced, 4 percent widowed, and 14 percent never-married. At the time of the first interviews, in 1986, 60 percent had separated in the past three years; more than half had separated during the preceding year. Approximately two years later, in 1988, 85 percent of the original sample were reinterviewed. Interviews with 150 single mothers not on social assistance and employed have been completed. The third round of interviews, with 80 percent of the original sample, was completed in 1993. Interviews with the children of the original group occurred in 1994. A fourth round of interviews has been recently completed.

"**Single mother on welfare**" is a phrase that evokes different images for different people. For some, the notions of dignity, struggle, and injustice are invoked. For others, hopelessness, immorality, and incompetence are suggested. It is important to understand who single mothers on social assistance are, and how they are responding to changes in their individual and family lives. Three themes emerged from the panel study: the social diversity that exists among single mothers, the prevalence of change in their lives, and the nature of the constraints they face that affect their choice of path.

State welfare policies directed at low-income or "sole-support" parents are complex and contradictory. From the deterrence principle inherent in low social-assistance rates, to the inter- and intra-regional inequities in the delivery of welfare, to the monitoring of recipients, the governing principles of legislation and their contradictory effects on women are apparent. Most legislation is influenced by a body of poverty literature that emphasizes the distorting, debilitating, and pathological effects of poverty on an individual's social and psychological experiences. These assumed links are incomplete and potentially misleading (Gorlick and Pomfret, 1993).

This pathological perspective (with elements comparable to the deviancy model of divorce) sees the poor as predictably, yet helplessly, yielding to overwhelming external constraints, unable to do anything to change their situation and their responses to it. When active, their response to poverty is often characterized as delinquent, deviant, or criminal, and judged ineffective and destructive for society, others, and themselves. Missing from most of this discussion is an image of the low-income single mother as a competent actor or agent for social change. Also missing is the acknowledgement that a single mother may refuse to surrender passively to her environment, or that even "bad" environments frequently contain enabling, as well as constraining, elements.

What emerges from this panel study of low-income single mothers is a portrait that stresses their persistent willingness and ability to deal with their circumstances in a positive, active, and determined manner. This does not minimize the difficulties, barriers, and problems confronting them and their children, nor does it suggest a "do-nothing" social-policy response to these families. Rather, the "voices" of women interviewed reveal their competencies, their resiliency, and their determination. It is these voices that are glaringly absent from discussions of divorce and the economic vulnerability of women and their children. And it is these voices from which models of social responsibility should be drawn.

SOCIAL DIVERSITY AMONG SINGLE MOTHERS
▼

Popular opinion and policy statements gloss over the diversities among single mothers, focussing instead on their presumed similarities. Low-income mothers in particular are often viewed in this manner. Many myths persist. For one, mothers on welfare are often viewed as young, never married, and with a number of children. Young single parents are not in the majority, as only 3 percent (under age 20) are receiving welfare (National Council of Welfare, 1998). Data from the panel study also challenge these stereotypes: the average age of

single mothers is 32 (the range is 19 to 56), and they have one or two children living at home (the range is 1 to 6). These figures are comparable to
national data trends (National Council of Welfare, 1998). Clearly, the reason
for applying for social assistance as a single parent coincides with child-bear-
ing years for women as welfare requests drop after age 40 (National Council
of Welfare, 1998). This trend may also be the result of social-assistance eligibility based on the age of the child and presence in the family home.

Another myth holds that single mothers continue having more children
in order to remain on social assistance. As the average number of children per
family suggests, this is not the case. One single mother from the study noted:
"It is mind-boggling to think that there are people that think that being on
welfare is so terrific that we would want to have more children to stay on."

For most single mothers, time on social assistance is short, not lengthy, as
the myth suggests. National data indicated that those with a disability, followed
by single parents, were most represented in the 25+ month category, which was
the longest welfare time measure used. National databases have not provided
an accessible tracing of "time on welfare." Studies that have focussed on the
duration of social assistance indicate that, for single mothers, the length of time
tends to be less than three years (Ontario Social Assistance Review Committee,
1988; Duncan, 1984). Preliminary findings by Gorlick of the final set of interviews indicate that one-third of single mothers were still on social assistance over
the ten-year period. This finding may have been the result of a recessionary
period that, despite being followed by a period of economic growth, has not
enhanced female employment opportunities. Another consideration is that
missing from the sample may be those who have accessed employment or education or have remarried and have moved on and are no longer accessible. These
missing respondents might have an impact on the proportion remaining on
social-assistance. Also a portion of this social-assistance group had a child under
13 years of age and/or were engaged in educational upgrading.

It is perceived that single mothers on welfare have low levels of education. Many of the single mothers in the panel study are fairly well educated.
At the study's outset, more than half had some post-secondary education, with
a quarter of them being graduates of either community college or university.
On the other hand, at least a quarter of the single mothers did not graduate
from secondary school. Many were upgrading their education during the ten-
year period. In the final interview round, 41 percent had earned a college
diploma or university degree, 17 percent had some post-secondary education,
25 percent had graduated from secondary school, and 11 percent had not
graduated from high school.

Throughout the ten years, single mothers consistently indicated that
they hoped to be off social assistance in one year or five years. Frequently the

longer time frame was related to educational and training periods. In the final round of interviews, although 23.5 percent were not engaged in exiting social assistance, 38.3 percent were employed full-time, and 11 percent part-time, 10 percent were looking for work, 5 percent were enrolled in an educational program, and 9 percent were combining looking for work, enrolled in an educational program, and working part-time or full-time.

Finally, it is inappropriate to assume that single mothers on welfare are all alike, or that they have similar values and attitudes, common parenting styles, or comparable hopes and expectations. Yet this assumption prevails; for example, punitive changes to student-assistance programs are based on the assumption that most single mothers on welfare are unlikely to pay their student-loan debts (Gorlick, 1992). Also time on social assistance varies, with some single mothers having the resources and opportunities to exit welfare earlier than others. This is also true for other social-assistance family groups, yet there is less tendency to attach a common label to them. This picture of single mothers on welfare is further limited because it dismisses or ignores the significance of time and change in their lives.

THE PREVALENCE OF CHANGE IN THE LIVES OF SINGLE MOTHERS

Clearly, for this group of single mothers and their children, financial uncertainty accompanies the emotional upheaval of marital separation. Sixty-six percent of women in the panel study said they sought spousal support soon after separation. Of those, 60 percent received the support. For many, though, the payments became erratic and unpredictable, and insufficient to sustain a family, in turn assuring their reliance on social assistance. For the majority of single mothers, their former husband's earnings had been the primary contribution to family income before separation, even though 76 percent of the single mothers had been employed. The majority were employed full-time, with 66 percent of them in the service and clerical sectors. Immediately after separation, 54 percent were employed, primarily part-time in the service and clerical settings. It has been well documented that low income levels and inadequate health-care benefits in these work settings cannot sustain a family's income needs (Duffy and Pupo, 1992). This inadequate income combined with child-care difficulties has led many single mothers to apply for social assistance.

From the initial interviews, information was collected concerning the reasons for separation and its effects. The primary reason cited for separation was mental and/or physical abuse. Sixty-six percent indicated that separation was their idea; for 13 percent, the idea came from their former husbands; and, for 21 percent, separation was a mutual decision. Eighty-four percent said the separation was final. Whatever the reason for marital separation, the beginning of the process set this family on a journey of profound and far-reaching downward mobility. The perceived speed and intensity of changes in the lives of these women and children are structural as well as personal or individual.

Monthly Income Decline

About 75 percent of the single mothers experienced a drop in their monthly income as a result of marital separation. In some instances, the drop was quite dramatic: between $1667 and $3333 each month. Between the first and second interview, 62 percent noted that their monthly income had risen slightly through increases in employment or social assistance; 11 percent reported a decrease. Some of the single mothers experienced a decrease when they obtained full-time employment. In spite of this income decrease and the loss of certain benefits provided by welfare, they were determined to leave social-assistance programs. The inadequacy of social assistance and the growing demand for food banks are continuous reminders of the severity of this situation. Mother–child relationships are altered, with each sometimes trying to protect the other. As one child noted, "I don't feel poor. My mum puts me ahead of herself so I can get what I need" (Cheryl, 15 years old, in Gorlick, 1995, p. 292). Studies have shown that low-income mothers experience material deprivation for their children and may suffer nutritionally (Gorlick, 1995).

Residential Changes

Eighty-six percent of the single mothers changed residences after they were separated. Also, 45 percent changed residences between the first and second interviews. Reasons given for moving include wanting a better residence, leaving a high-crime area, avoiding problems with superintendents, being evicted, wanting to be closer to school or work, and needing a different size of accommodation. Single mothers suggested that these residential changes were particularly difficult for their children, who found themselves frequently adapting to different schools and new friends. Contrary to expectations, the majority of the single-parent families were not in public housing, but rather in the private rental market. National data support this, with 77 percent of single-parent families on welfare renting, 11 percent in subsidized housing, 6 percent own their own home, and 6 percent other or unknown (National Council of Welfare, 1998). Compared with other family types on social assistance nationally (couples with or without children, unattached persons), single-parent families were more likely to rent. Spector and Klodawsky (1993, p. 249), examining the housing patterns and needs of single-parent families, observe:

Threats to security of [housing] tenure due to economic eviction are less the case where public assistance through rent geared to income programs are available. Here, rental or housing charge payments remain a constant proportion of income, as long as income remains below an upper threshold. Publicly funded housing, however, is geared towards providing relatively short-term relief for the poorest of families. There may be a requirement to increase rent and eventually to vacate once a single parent increases her income through employment and/or through the earnings of teenage children.

Although the majority of single mothers were not living in co-operative housing, it appeared to be the most favoured. Those living in co-operative housing indicated that it was a satisfactory and a continuous alternative.

Changes in Marital Status, Family Composition, and Health

Twenty-two percent of the single mothers changed their marital status between the first and second interviews, usually because of divorce finalization, although a small number remarried. During this period, in 18 percent of the families, at least one child left home, to live either with the father or alone. Family composition continued to change over the ten-year period, although very few remarried, and fewer still had more children.

Change also has an impact on single mothers' perceived health. Mothers felt that their health worsened with discontinuing social assistance, residential changes, and obtaining full-time employment. As one mother explained, "I am going off Family Benefits soon, because I have a job. But I am scared — really scared — that I may be taking too much of a chance for myself and the kids, because I'm not sure what the future will hold" (Cathy, Interview 3, in Gorlick, 1995, p. 294).

Changing Network of Friends and Relatives

In the aftermath of separation, single mothers enter a social world consisting primarily of female friends and their children (Gorlick and Pomfret, 1993). Friends, children, and relatives do not promote marital reconciliation; the majority agree with the separation or do not voice an opinion. Single mothers perceive that most of their social support came from other females: female rather than male friends, their mothers rather than fathers, and female rather than male relatives. The one exception is that single mothers feel their sons provide as much close and esteem support as their daughters do. Between interviews, increased social support was the trend, although for some there was a decrease, and others felt the levels of support remained constant. Most of the single mothers did not interact with former spouses, although some maintained a relationship with their in-laws. Invariably, relationships altered, in both positive and negative ways. One single mother commented:

> "It was hard enough when my former husband would show up at Christmas with expensive gifts for the kids, when he didn't take much notice of them the rest of the year. I got used to that. But when my [married] sister would insist that her kids open up their more expensive gifts while my kids looked on, well, that hurt." (Gorlick, 1995, p. 290)

In sum, the importance of female friends and their own children in the lives of single mothers is consistent and strong. Furthermore, single mothers in this study are very satisfied with the social support they continue to receive.

Changes Perceived by Children

Children identified residential, school, friendship, and family changes (Gorlick, 1995). Ninety percent of children said they have moved residence (50 percent of whom moved four to seven times); 79 percent changed schools (27 percent more than four times); and 65 percent said their friends changed. Some children (21 percent) remembered frequent changes in child-care arrangements. For many children, interaction with fathers had been infrequent and periodic, although 63 percent of the children had some contact with fathers. Seventy-three percent were 4 years of age or younger when their parents separated, with 10 percent born to never-married mothers. Throughout these constant changes, the children viewed their mother as the most important and consistent adult in their lives.

THE NATURE OF STRAINS CONFRONTING SINGLE MOTHERS, AND PATHS CHOSEN
▼

One of the prominent strains for single mothers is lack of money, which, for the women in the panel study, is accompanied by the stigma of welfare. A variety of negative attitudes are perceived by low-income single mothers and are reinforced by particular policies and programs. The Ontario Family Benefits Act, for example, functioned to devalue single mothers by offering social assistance to the mother for the child. The implication is that welfare is reduced as each child leaves home, leaving the possibility of a middle-aged mother without financial support after having engaged for several years in domestic and parental care. By that time, the single mother may be too old to find employment and too young to collect pension benefits.

Another strain comes from the experience of single-parenting. Strains exist both for those single mothers on social assistance and for those who are employed. While 80 percent of single mothers on social assistance indicate a greater companionship with their children after separating, they also recognize conflict in these relationships (Gorlick and Pomfret, 1993). For both employed and unemployed single mothers, the prevalence of conflict is the same with daughters and sons. But significant gender differences emerge in the type of conflict. Most mothers report that their primary conflict with daughters occurs around their daughters' assertion of independence. With sons, mothers tend to cite their anger with separation, hyperactive behaviour, personality conflict, and stubbornness, and say that the male children were "going through a stage."

Gender differences also appear in the ways mothers prefer to deal with the conflict. With both sons and daughters, mothers prefer to deal with the conflict through communication (slightly more so with daughters). Providing a good parenting role is the second most preferred method for dealing with conflict with daughters. With sons, the second most preferred method is to do nothing.

Overall, children act simultaneously as constraints and enablers in their mothers' lives. It should not be forgotten, however, that a lack of financial resources combined with a child's request for, say, sports equipment or money for school trips or clothing, frequently augments the strains of single parenting.

To what extent do these changes and strains result in emotional or psychological distress for single mothers? It has been suggested that single mothers on social assistance have a low regard for themselves, a low self-esteem. True, some do. However, 80 to 90 percent of single mothers see themselves at positive to very positive self-esteem levels. Differences in self-esteem scores between employed single mothers and those on social assistance are modest. In general, single mothers on welfare maintain a view of themselves that is at least as favourable as that of their employed counterparts (Gorlick and Pomfret, 1993).

Single mothers on social assistance routinely seek out and engage in numerous activities with the hope of ending their dependence on welfare. Both the variety of paths taken and the persistence with which they are pursued, sometimes under the most trying circumstances, are impressive. They seek various kinds of employment, and additional education or training to increase their employability. Technically, this group would have been better off economically if they had remained on social assistance. Yet they chose to leave the welfare rolls.

Single mothers, whether on social assistance or not, have high educational aspirations for their daughters and sons. About 80 percent of both groups want their children to have some type of post-secondary education. They also have high aspirations for themselves. Single mothers convey that they are not letting the circumstances of their lives — the number of children they have, whether they have preschool children, length of time they are on social assistance, their age or educational level — have an overwhelming negative impact. Age, for example, was not a factor in parental participation in educational upgrading or training. Thus, it is never too late or too early to support single mothers opting to engage in these programs. Most of us think that the more children the single mother has, the less likely she is to enroll in a training program or post-secondary studies, or to undertake full- or part-time employment. Contrary to expectations, however, parents with more children are slightly more likely than those with fewer children to undertake educational upgrading, such as completing secondary school.

Time on social assistance, time to initiate and engage an exit strategy, time to enter/re-enter the labour market are all aspects of low-income familial time. The manner in which individuals define time influences responses to perceived choices. For some, the embarrassment of a lengthy welfare dependency emerged with the aging of their child/ren, and for others it came at the end of educational upgrading and the frustrating search for a job. There is a negative correlation between time on social assistance and self-esteem, hopes for the future, and anticipation of future income. The longer single mothers were on social assistance, the more likely they were to believe their futures would remain the same or get worse. Self-esteem showed little measurable drop until after six years on social assistance (Gorlick, 1995).

There appears to have been a perceived period of grace, after which decline in mothers' self-esteem was apparent. Being on social assistance while your children were young appeared more socially acceptable. As children aged, mothers perceive that they are recategorized from full-time caregiver to labour-market entrants, and pressures to successfully obtain full-time paid employment become significant. In sum, single mothers did not want to remain on social assistance for long periods of time; there were, however, differing perceptions of labour-market-entry timing, defined by changing child-care needs, aspirations, health status, and familial readiness, as well as employment preparedness. Nevertheless, training and educational programs are bridges to nowhere without significant labour-market changes. As one single mother put it, "Retraining was unrealistic because there are no jobs. I bought into the dream that was not based on reality and now I owe $5400 and all I have is a boost to my ego" (Elaine, Interview 3, in Gorlick, 1995, p. 293).

CONCLUSION
▼

The preceding discussion has articulated some of the myths and realities surrounding divorce. Frequently, divorce is viewed as an ending, rather than as a starting point for realignments and changes within and outside the family. Frequently, divorce is seen as a negative experience or a positive and constructive outcome, rather than as a contradictory process involving elements of both. Too often divorced families are presented as "on hold," waiting to form another nuclear family. The complexity and contradictory nature of the divorce process should forewarn us of the misleading direction of an either/or analysis, the indifference to time and process in the research literature, and the sometimes simplistic assumptions about divorce found in policy articulation and development.

While change is a predominant feature of the lives of separated single mothers, the extent to which they and their children are subjected to it varies considerably. For some, income increases. For others, it decreases. For still others, it remains the same. And a similar pattern repeats itself for place of residence, marital status, and other social and personal indicators. These changes, in turn, may reinforce or modify the strains these women confront. It is misleading and unfair to characterize female single parents as a dispirited group who have given up on themselves and their children, expecting society to take care of them. Despite the uncertainty, the unpredictability, and the strains and stresses in their lives, these women are actively resisting any temptation to simply hand over responsibility for living their lives to others. While no doubt constrained and affected by the circumstances of their lives, they are not passive, and are exerting their ability to act upon the conditions of their lives, rather than merely responding to them.

From the panel study, it is clear that single mothers are agents, not subjects, and that their responses should not be viewed only through the therapeutic and policy lens as those of clients or recipients. Constraint-oriented social-policy and structural inequities premised on deterrence — as in the case of low welfare payments and misleading assumptions about the nature of single mothers — should be replaced by approaches facilitating, fostering, and supporting choices single mothers have already made.

SUMMARY
▼

- Divorce initiates an interactive process of individual and social realignments, strains, hopes, and expectations combined with perceptions of available options, institutional and individual constraints, and paths chosen. Divorce is also a process in which gender inequities persist and are sustained.

• It is misleading to emphasize either greater personal-growth opportunities or negative and pathologizing divorce outcomes, for each places the onus for adaptability or change solely on the individual.

• Comparisons are drawn between "intact" families — the preferred, normative, and "necessary family structure" — and "not intact" families. The divorced family presumably becomes "intact" again if divorced spouses remarry and form another nuclear family, sometimes referred to as blended, step-, reconstituted, or bi-nuclear.

• What makes this a difficult period for some children and not others is not the divorce itself, but myriad influences from family relationships, income decline, and residential changes combined with the child's age and sex.

• "Single mother on welfare" is a phrase that evokes different images for different people. For some, the notions of dignity, struggle, and injustice are invoked. For others, hopelessness, immorality, and incompetence are suggested. It is important to understand who single mothers on social assistance are and how they are responding to changes in their individual and family lives.

NOTES
▼

1. These data were initially released by Statistics Canada as 56 percent of single-parent families having children with a least one health problem, and 9 percent of two-parent families in the same circumstance (December 1992). This information was repeated in many newspapers across Canada. It was a couple of days before Statistics Canada noticed that, in fact, the appropriate statistic was not 9 percent, but 49 percent. Significant here is that this statistical bias went unchallenged. Perhaps one may speculate that this error supports common negative perceptions of single-parent families.

2. This discussion is based on the panel study "Economic Stress, Social Support and Female Single Parents." Funding for the panel study of low-income female single parents and their children has been provided by Human Resource Development Canada, the Social Sciences and Humanities Research Council of Canada, and the Thérèse F.-Casgrain Fellowship on Women and Social Policy. Findings are included to generalize where possible to the larger provincial or national single-parent populations and offer additional insights from a smaller sample.

CRITICAL THINKING QUESTIONS
▼

1. Discuss policy related to the family from the perspective of individual versus social responsibility models.

2. Discuss the commonalities and diversities that might exist between a female social worker and a single mother on social assistance. You may want to consider the public–private division affecting the female life experience; the significance of caring as individuals, in the family, the community, and society; and women relating to other women.

3. Identify a social policy that affects divorced families. In what manner does this policy offer support to, or create barriers for, single-parent families?

4. Undertake a content analysis of several academic journals focussing on divorce. What theoretical approaches emerge? What themes of divorce as a social problem are present? What feminist interpretations? Are there, for example, illustrations of the significance of "mother presence" as well as "father absence" in the divorce literature?

5. Female single parents and their children experience downward social mobility and economic stress in the aftermath of marital separation. Identify and discuss the key policy and structural changes that might alleviate these negative experiences.

SUGGESTED READING
▼

Christa Freiler and Judy Cerny. 1998. *Benefiting Canada's Children: Perspectives on Gender and Social Responsibility.* Ottawa: Status of Women Canada.
   A challenge to Canada's disgraceful response to child poverty, through the articulation and promotion of innovative child-benefit policies.

Margrit Eichler. 1997. *Family Shifts: Families, Policies and Gender Equality.* Toronto: Oxford University Press.
   A significant discussion of the "individual responsibility" versus "social responsibility" models inherent in perceptions of the family and influential in the policy context.

Susan McDaniel. 1998. "Families, Feminism, and the State: Canada in the 1990s and Beyond." In Les Samuelson and Wayne Antony, eds., *Power and Resistance: Critical Thinking about Canadian Social Issues.* Halifax: Fernwood.
   An interesting overview of family policy in Canada; trends, context, comparative understandings from a feminist perspective.

Simon Duncan and Rosalind Edwards. 1997. *Single Mothers in an International Context: Mothers or Workers?* London: UCL Press.
   This book challenges the debate that stereotypes single mothers as either a threat or a passive victim, by focussing on the interplay between single motherhood, state policies, labour market structures, and neighbourhood/community supports and constraints.

REFERENCES
▼

Ahrons, C.R., and R. Rogers. 1987. *Divorced Families; A Multi-Disciplinary Developmental View.* New York: W.W. Norton.

Amato, Paul, and Alan Booth 1997. *A Generation at Risk: Growing Up in an Era of Family Upheaval.* Cambridge, MA: Harvard University Press.

Ambert, A. 1989. *A Study of Relationships.* Greenwich, CT: JAI Press.

Arendell, T. 1986. *Mothers and Divorce: Legal, Economic and Social Dilemmas.* Los Angeles: University of California Press.

Canadian Council on Social Development. 1996. *The Progress of Canada's Children.* Ottawa: Canadian Council on Social Development.

Duffy, A., and N. Pupo. 1992. *Part-Time Paradox: Connecting Gender, Work and Family.* Toronto: McClelland & Stewart.

Duncan, Greg. 1984. *Years of Poverty, Years of Plenty: The Changing Economic Fortunes of American Workers and Families.* Ann Arbor, MI: Survey Research Center, Institute for Social Research, University of Michigan.

Duncan, Simon, and Rosalind Edwards. 1997. *Single Mothers in an International Context: Mothers or Workers?* London: UCL Press.

Economic Council of Canada. 1992. *The New Face of Poverty: Income Security Needs of Canadian Families.* Ottawa: Supply and Services.

Edwards, Harriet. 1989. *How Could You? Mothers Without Custody of Their Children.* Freedom, CA: Crossing Press.

Eichler, Margrit. 1993. "Lone-Parent Families: An Unstable Category in Search of Stable Policies." In B. Galaway and J. Hudson, eds., *Single-Parent Families in Canada.* Toronto: Thompson Educational.

———. 1997. *Family Shifts: Families, Policies and Gender Equality.* Toronto: Oxford University Press.

Evans, Patricia. 1997. "Divided Citizenship? Gender, Income Security, and the Welfare State." In Patricia Evans and Gerda Wekerle, eds., *Women and the Canadian Welfare State: Challenges and Change.* Toronto: University of Toronto Press.

Ferri, Elsa, and Kate Smith. 1998. *Step-parenting in the 1990's.* Family and Parenthood: Policy and Practice series. London: Family Policy Studies Centre.

Frum, D. 1996. "The Sexual Revolution's Next Goal." *Reader's Digest* (May), p. 37.

Gorlick, Carolyne. 1992. "The Female Single Parent Student." *Canadian Woman Studies* 12/4.

———. 1995. "Listening to Low Income Children and Single Mothers: Policy Implications Related to Child Welfare." In Joe Hudson and Burt Galaway, eds., *Child Welfare in Canada.* Toronto: Thompson Educational.

Gorlick, Carolyne, and Guy Brethour. 1998. *National Welfare to Work Programs: From New Mandates to Exiting Bureaucracies to Individual and Program Accountability.* Ottawa: Canadian Council on Social Development.

Gorlick, Carolyne, and A. Pomfret. 1993. "Hope and Circumstance: Single Mothers Exiting Social Assistance." In B. Galaway and J. Hudson, eds., *Single-Parent Families in Canada.* Toronto: Thompson Educational.

Human Resources Development Canada. 1996. *Growing Up in Canada.* National Longitudinal Survey of Children and Youth, no. 1. Ottawa: Statistics Canada and Human Resources Development Canada.

Lipman, E., David Offord, and Martin Dooley. 1996. "What Do We Know about Children from Single Mother Families?" In Human Resources Development Canada, *Growing Up in Canada*. National Longitudinal Survey of Children and Youth, no. 1. Ottawa: Statistics Canada and Human Resources Development Canada.

London Free Press. 1998. "Deadbeat Dad a 'Myth,' MP Says." March 9, p. 1.

MacLean, Mavis. 1991. "Surviving Divorce: Women's Resources after Separation." In Jo Campling, ed., *Women in Society: A Feminist List*. London: Macmillan.

Morgan, D. 1991. *The Family: Politics and Social Theory*. London: Routledge and Kegan Paul.

National Council of Welfare. 1998. *Profiles of Welfare: Myths and Realities*. Ottawa: Minister of Supply and Services.

National Forum on Family Security. 1993. *Family Security in Insecure Times*. Ottawa: Canadian Council on Social Development.

Newsweek. 1993. "Jane Bryant Quinn." January 25, p. 64.

Ontario Social Assistance Review Committee. 1988. *Transitions*. Toronto: Ministry of Community and Social Services.

Organisation for Economic Co-operation and Development. 1993. *Breadwinners or Child Rearers: The Dilemma for Lone Mothers*. Labour Market and Social Policy Occasional Papers, no. 12. Paris: Organisation for Economic Co-operation and Development.

Pask, E. Diane. 1993. "Family Law and Policy in Canada: Economic Implications for Single Custodial Mothers and Their Children." In B. Galaway and J. Hudson, eds., *Single-Parent Families in Canada*. Toronto: Thompson Educational.

Pett, M.G. 1982. "Correlates of Children's Adjustment Following Divorce." *Journal of Divorce* 5/5: 25–33.

Spector, A., and F. Klodawsky. 1993. "The Housing Needs of Single-Parent Families in Canada: A Dilemma for the 1990s." In B. Galaway and J. Hudson, eds., *Single-Parent Families in Canada*. Toronto: Thompson Educational.

Statistics Canada. 1992. *Marriage and Conjugal Relationships in Canada*. Ottawa: Minister of Supply and Services.

———. 1997a. *1996 Census: Marital Status, Common-Law Unions and Families*. (October 14). http://www.statcan.ca.

———. 1997b. "Canadian Children in the 1990s." *Canadian Social Trends* (Spring).

Strauss, M.B. 1988. "Divorced Mothers." In B. Birns and D. Hay, eds., *The Different Faces of Motherhood*. New York: Plenum Press.

Wallerstein, J., and J. Kelly. 1979. "Children and Divorce: A Review." *Social Work* (November): 468–75.

———. 1980. *Surviving the Break-Up*. New York: Basic Books.

Weiss, R.S. 1975. *Marital Separation*. New York: Basic Books.

Weitzman, L. 1985. *The Divorce Revolution*. New York: Free Press.

Wilson, E. 1977. *Women and the Welfare State*. London: Tavistock.

Wolchik, S., and P. Karoly, eds. 1988. *Children of Divorce: Empirical Perspectives on Adjustment*. New York: Gardner Press.

9

▼

FAMILY VIOLENCE: ISSUES AND ADVANCES AT THE END OF THE TWENTIETH CENTURY

ANN DUFFY AND JULIANNE MOMIROV

LEARNING OBJECTIVES

In this chapter, you will learn that:

- in the last three decades, family violence has emerged as a central theme in the sociology of the Canadian family;
- recent research advances have provided an increasingly accurate and disturbing portrait of the frequency and costs of family violence in Canada;
- our societal responsiveness to family violence is undermined by our ideological commitment to a Disneyesque notion of the family and our historical acceptance of family violence as normative;
- sociological and feminist analyses are generating an increasingly sophisticated understanding of family violence and its societal roots;
- current attention is focussed on the "diversities" of women's experience of family violence;
- social-policy responses to family violence, despite advances, are still plagued by inadequacies.

INTRODUCTION

Family-violence issues have become part of the lexicon of popular culture. Canadians would be hard-pressed to find a daily newspaper that didn't contain some coverage of wife abuse, child abuse, elder abuse, or any of the other manifestations of violence and conflict in intimate relations. TV movies and talk shows have broached every aspect of family violence, from incest and femicide, to sibling violence and child murder. Academic research has grown exponentially in this area, and numerous publications are now devoted to specific topics under the general rubric of violence among family members. Numerous policy initiatives have been launched, often at great public expense, both to explore the dimensions of family violence and to hew out some solutions to the violence. Only the most isolated members of our society have been untouched by the deluge of information on what was once an unspoken concern and invisible issue.

Here, we set forth a general outline of the current state of knowledge on family violence. Tremendous work has been accomplished in naming and defining the nature of family violence. Drawing in particular on historical examinations of family violence, the social definitions of family violence, and the power relations that underlay these definitions, have been increasingly exposed. Where once a man beating his wife[1] or parents smacking their child was almost a normative part of patriarchal social existence, these actions are now much more likely to be identified as unacceptable and abusive. Further, the parameters for understanding abuse have been extended well beyond simple physical violence to include emotional, psychological, and other forms of abuse. As the conceptualization of family violence and its constituent parts have been clarified, examinations of the dimensions of violence, including frequency and patterns, have dramatically improved. Today, we have a much greater appreciation of how routine and widespread violence among family members is. Not surprisingly, this refined image has been accompanied by increasingly complex and sophisticated theoretical explanations of the causes,

---

BOX 9.1
▼
CHILDHOOD AMIDST THE VIOLENCE

A little girl stands in a darkened doorway, staring wide-eyed with fear at the scene before her. Her beloved father is beating her mother with his fists. Her mother is trying to fend him off, at the same time attempting to protect her head. She is screaming and crying hysterically. Her husband is swearing at her, accusing her of unspeakable things, each accusation seeming to make him angrier and angrier, making him hit her harder and harder. His face is like a mask of fury and hatred. The little girl cowers against the door frame, tears filling her eyes. She watches her mother fall down upon the floor, her body going limp. Blood is trickling from her mouth. Her father kicks his wife again and again, until he seems to spend his energy and his anger. Then he slams out of the house. The little girl stares with horror at her mother, thinking she must be dead. Cautiously, she goes over to have a closer look at her, afraid of what she might find, her mind racing. What should she do? What if her mother is really dead? Would her father come back? How could she help her mother?

consequences, and patterns of abuse. On the cutting edge of these empirical and theoretical developments is a growing body of knowledge devoted to the diversities — racial/ethnic; sexual orientation; age; social class; dis/ability — which have previously been glazed over in discussions of family violence.

These various advances, however significant, must be balanced with an acknowledgement that much remains to be explored and much remains to be done. In particular, our increasingly precise vision of the violence has not translated into effective solutions. Policy initiatives remain fragmented and, too often, ineffective. More important, many of the ideologies that underlie family violence are alive and healthy. Indeed, to some degree the expansion of research and policy interest in family violence has promoted a pathological and individualistic perception of the problem. Perpetrators are seen as defective or criminal, and the solutions are embedded in psychiatry or criminal justice. A broader framework that is based in the societal foundation to family life and intimate relations, and that works from the premise of supporting "good" families and positive relationships rather than eradicating violent family members, has yet to be articulated.

A PROFILE OF FAMILY VIOLENCE IN CANADA IN THE 1990s
▼

Not surprisingly, it is enormously difficult to accurately capture the rates and patterns of domestic violence. On an individual level, victims frequently are embarrassed by their victimization, and intimidated by their victimizers, while perpetrators fear prosecution. On an institutional level, these problems are further compounded by the lack of agreement on basic definitions of key concepts such as "abuse" and "violence." As a result, traditional techniques of social research, such as questionnaires and personal interviews, have met with relatively little success. It is only in the 1990s that significant strides have been made in creating reliable databases that detail the rates and patterns of family violence (Statistics Canada, 1998).

Of particular significance was the 1993 Canadian Violence Against Women Survey (CVAWS). This internationally acclaimed study surveyed a nationally representative sample of Canadian women about their experiences with violence, especially violence at the hands of intimates. Anonymity was assured by computer-generated telephone sampling, and interviewers were provided with specialized training to elicit sensitive information. The result is a landmark research document that reveals a disturbing picture of pervasive and persistent violence against women.

Almost one in three women has experienced violence from an intimate partner. The CVAWS found that 29 percent of women who had ever married or lived in a common-law relationship revealed at least one episode of violence by a husband or live-in partner (Johnson, 1996, p. 136). CVAWS data also reveal that assaults on wives occur with alarming frequency. Two-thirds (63 percent) of women reporting violence indicated that it had occurred more than once, and one-third (32 percent) revealed more than ten episodes (Johnson, 1996, p. 138). This research also underscores the seriousness of the violence involved. In almost half (44 percent) of all violent relationships, a weapon was used at some point.

BOX 9.2
▼
THE COMPLEXITIES OF WOMAN ABUSE

Woman abuse may entail any varied combination of the following:

1. Physical Violence
   - kicking, shoving, punching, biting, beating, slapping
   - with or without weapons
   - forced confinement

2. Sexual Abuse
   - forced intercourse
   - intercourse with unwanted violence
   - forced sexual acts, e.g., forced viewing of pornography

3. Economic Abuse
   - preventing employment, e.g., disabling her car
   - forced ending of employment
   - forced economic dependency (demanding control over all wages)
   - withholding family monies or information about family finances

4. Social Abuse
   - restricting or ending contact with friends or relatives, e.g., limiting access to transportation
   - monitoring phone calls
   - creating geographic isolation, e.g., moving to remote location

5. Emotional Abuse
   - name-calling
   - use of threats and intimidation, e.g., threatening to commit suicide or to take custody of children
   - ignoring
   - inflicting damage on property or on family pets
   - establishing a climate of terror and unpredictability

Not surprisingly, in one-third (34 percent) of the cases, the women stated that they feared their lives were in danger (Johnson, 1996, p. 140).

Recent research initiatives such as the CVAWS put the lie to any efforts to minimize or explain away the violence presently taking place in Canadian families. Further, current research efforts are also clarifying the complexity of relationship violence. *Changing the Landscape: Ending Violence — Achieving Equality*, the 1993 Report of the Canadian Panel on Violence Against Women, for example, went beyond physical violence to include the sexual, psychological, financial, and spiritual dimensions that violence may assume (Canadian Panel on Violence Against Women, 1993, p. 22). While much remains to be learned about many aspects of intimate violence, a considerable research record has been established, for example, on the use of sexual violence in marriage (Johnson, 1996; Russell, 1982).

In short, researchers have made tremendous strides toward providing an increasingly accurate, if alarming, portrait of violence against women in intimate relationships. These achievements have not been mirrored in other elements of family violence. Put simply, for example, there "are simply no national estimates of the prevalence of child abuse in Canada" (Statistics Canada, 1998, p. 21). Despite the fact that provincial legislation seeks to ensure that all professionals (and, in some locales, all citizens) are legally required to report any suspected instances of child abuse, national data on either reported or substantiated cases of child abuse are not available. This is largely the result of both the private nature of the offence and the lack of consensus on operational definitions of child abuse. As a result our understanding of the national dimensions and patterns of abuse are in some respects still in their infancy.

However, on the plus side, Canadian researchers have been at the international forefront in research on sexual violence against children (Badgley, 1984). Further, the current gaps in the research record are being steadily filled in. The *Ontario Incidence Study of Reported Child Abuse and Neglect* is the first province-wide report on the annual incidence of child maltreatment (Trocme et al., 1994). These statistics suggest that annually (1993) 1 child in 50 in Ontario was involved in a reported case of child abuse, and the majority of substantiated cases of abuse involved neglect (36 percent) or physical abuse (34 percent). Similarly, a recent study undertaken by McMaster University and the Clarke Institute of Psychiatry surveyed a random sample of almost 10 000 Ontario residents concerning their recall of child maltreatment (Gadd, 1997, pp. A1, A6). These researchers found that one in three boys and one in five girls, according to adult recall, suffered some form of physical abuse as children. These studies confirm the impression that many children in our society are routinely subject to violence in the course of their family lives. Many of the unanswered questions about the dimensions and seriousness of this social problem will be answered when the Child Maltreatment Division of Health Canada fulfils its recent commitment to create a national incidence study of child abuse and neglect (Statistics Canada, 1998, p. 21n).[2]

Understandably, the research record on the least-well-known and most recently identified manifestations of family violence — such as elder abuse, sibling abuse, and teen abuse — are least well developed. Among these, elder abuse has captured the greatest attention and is furthest along the road to social recognition and policy responses. Drawing upon U.S. research and regionally defined samples, most researchers today suggest that between 2 and 4 percent of Canadian seniors are the victims of elder abuse, and that female seniors are more likely to be abused (Podnieks et al., 1990; see McDonald and Wigdor, 1995). Other forms of family violence are relatively unexplored and still must rely heavily on anecdotal evidence.

DETAILING THE COSTS OF FAMILY VIOLENCE
▼

Despite the current gaps in our knowledge of family violence, the existing research record clearly documents an extensive and onerous social problem. Drawing upon that limited understanding, analysts have been able to tally some of the direct costs of family violence. For example, it is estimated that sexual assault and physical abuse of women and girls (including wife abuse, marital rape, incest, and child abuse) costs Canada $4.2 billion a year in medical expenses, workdays lost, and so on (Priest, 1996, p. A1). The Centre for Research on Violence Against Women calculates that battered women who are unable to work lose $7 million a year in wages, and that the welfare system spends $1.8 million a year to support women who flee abusive relationships (Gurr et al., 1996, p. 6). Such analyses, of course, omit the indirect costs of jobs and careers that are abandoned, ambitions that are destroyed, and self-esteem that is undermined.

The human costs are incalculable. Analysts point to depression, feelings of helplessness, and generalized anxiety, as well as the ill health, injuries, and even death, which may be the physical outcomes of intimate violence (Giles-Sims, n.d.; Danica, 1988). Those who grow up in a violent family or living as an adult in an abusive relationship may, for example, have a difficult time establishing and maintaining friendships, confiding in relatives, trusting intimate partners, relating to children, and functioning effectively at work. In short, it is possible to speculate that the lives of those who experience family violence are impoverished on every level — emotional, physical, economic, social. As for the immediate social effects of abuse, harm to other family members, marital dissolution and diminished quality of life for the family as a whole may all ensue. Of course, the larger community will not escape unscathed. Economic productivity and educational attainment are likely to be adversely affected. Elevated use of medical, hospital, counselling, police, judicial, and penal services places an increased strain on community and social services. The list goes on. All these outcomes contribute, in turn, to an overall social instability and degeneration.[3]

THE IDEOLOGY OF THE PEACEFUL FAMILY
▼

Despite all we have learned about family violence and its devastating consequences, our understanding continues be mired down by our blind faith in the ideology of the peaceful family. Although there is ample evidence to indicate that men have long been, and still are, violent toward the women of their families, that mothers and fathers throughout recorded history have treated their children cruelly, that brothers and sisters have for generations abused one another, and that adult children have misused their aged parents, there still exists in our society a powerful ideology that romanticizes the family as a site of love, devotion, and understanding — the "haven in a heartless world" (Lasch, 1977). It is here, we are told, we will experience our most intimate and fulfilling relationships. When we are confronted with irrevocable proof that someone is suffering brutal treatment at the hands of a family member, the ideology explains away the perpetrator as a "sick" or deviant individual and the family as "dysfunctional." Faced with instances of family violence, we do not tend to question our fundamental beliefs about the family or the kind of society in which such families are found. We would rather cling to our "Disneyesque" idealizations about the family, so appealing at a visceral level, than confront the more complex and less reassuring realities of family life. Such tenacity is as true for members of the media, who tend to present cases of family violence in an individualized and sensationalized fashion, as it is for the average Canadian. Even the victims of family violence often continue to embrace this ideology, as evidenced by the fact that women who have been battered by a previous spouse often enter into another marital relationship, and children who have been abused grow up to create families of their own.

The tenacity of "the rhetoric of harmony" may account for the enduring nature of the family as an institution, as well as most people's reluctance to acknowledge that violence within the family is far from an aberration (Miller, 1990). Sociologist Leslie Miller argues that the rhetoric promotes beliefs about family relations and implicitly delineates what kinds of behaviours are possible or not possible. It goes without saying that the rhetoric invalidates violent relations among intimates. When violence *does* characterize family relations or an abusive episode occurs, family members are quick to redefine the action itself or to revoke family membership when family members do not behave properly within the parameters of the ideology. In other words, if a brother mistreats his sister, parents will redefine his abusive behaviour as "roughhousing" or perhaps make a statement such as "Boys will be boys." Or, if a man becomes violent with his wife, she may say that she "didn't recognize" him, that he was not the same man she married. Often the transformative agents — notably, alcohol and other drugs — are used to explain away the irreconcilable actions. In these instances, the behaviour and the person are redefined so that the rhetoric of family harmony may remain unchallenged, rather than questioning the social context that would contribute to the behaviour or the person's assumption that she or he could engage in such behaviour. The rhetoric of family harmony thus serves as a social smokescreen.

Further, and perhaps more important, the rhetoric of harmony in the family exists in tandem with the rhetoric of danger on the street (Miller, 1990). In other words, a corresponding ideology about strangers and the public sphere supports and helps to constitute the rhetoric of the family by allowing violence to characterize those relations. As repeatedly evidenced by surveys of public opinion, many Canadians consider it entirely reasonable to expect contacts with strangers to be violent and to fear strangers (Johnson, 1990). In contrast, those same people would consider it entirely *inappropriate* to experience family relations as violent and to fear family members. As a result when violence *does* occur between intimates, there is a knee-jerk reaction to explain it in a way that deflects the cause away from the idealized family relations themselves.

Noted Canadian feminist Meg Luxton has also written about what she refers to as "**familialism**," or the glorification of an idealized nuclear family, consisting of a "socially and legally recognized heterosexual couple" (1988, p. 238) with children who all share a warm, loving, and stable relationship. Because this type of family is the ideal model, any deviation from this norm is often stigmatized as inferior or pathological. Family members are likely to feel shamed that they are unable to live up to the ideal. The feeling of shame, in turn, is likely to both contribute to violence among family members and keep victims of violence silent, forcing them to tolerate the abuse.

The decision to tolerate abuse may be bolstered by related societal ideologies such as the notion that single-parent, mother-headed families are inferior child-rearing arrangements and the belief that "children of divorce" are generally maladjusted and prone to behavioural and emotional problems (see Amato, 1991, 1993). In addition, many abuse victims must face the reality that most single mothers and their children do suffer financial deprivation and high levels of stress (exacerbated by current trends by neo-conservative governments to drastically reduce social spending) (National Council of Welfare, 1998). In this economic and ideological context, it is not hard to understand why women, children, and seniors would strive to remain within the more traditional configuration of the family and maintain the ideal.

HISTORICAL ROOTS OF FAMILY VIOLENCE
▼

Despite the powerful and persistent ideology of the peaceful family, historical and cross-cultural evidence clearly documents that violence among intimates is deeply embedded in our historical traditions and cuts across both time and national boundaries. In 2500 B.C., a man could engrave his wife's name on a brick and use it to beat her for the heinous crime of talking back to him (DeKeseredy and MacLeod, 1997, pp. 7–9). Scolding, nagging, or talking back were grounds for being burnt at the stake in the Middle Ages, along with adultery. Pregnant women did not escape such a fate. In her work on the history of women in Western Europe from 1500 to 1800, Olwen Hufton (1995, pp. 266–91) recounts stories of women taking abusive husbands to court but effectively being on trial themselves. Although husbands were not free to treat their wives as abusively as they pleased without risking court action, they were considered to be legally superior to their wives. Neighbours approved of a husband's violence against his wife if she violated her gender role. Indeed, complainant wives risked chastisement by the court if they were judged to have overstepped the strict confines of their gender role. In fact, a woman had to be flawless to have any plausibility as a complainant in court against her abusive husband. Of course, this degree of perfection was rarely attainable, particularly since their flaws were largely *due to* the abuse they had suffered. In other words, if they had been raped, beaten, abused, or impregnated, they were deemed to be defective, a judgement that negatively influenced their credibility, despite the fact that they were in court seeking redress from the man who had rendered them so.

The treatment of Canadian women had a long-standing precedent not only in Canada, but in the countries of origin of most Canadians. Rape was literally a class affair in Western Europe between 1500 and 1800. Hufton (1995, pp. 269–70) argues that the life circumstances of working-class girls made it far less likely they would be believed if they complained of having been raped by a man. Because these young women lived their lives within the public sphere much more so than did their higher-class counterparts, having to sleep in kitchen corners or go out into the streets to run errands, they would be much more accessible prey to delivery men and soldiers whiling away idle hours. If there was any sort of acquaintance between the young woman and her assailant, regardless of how brief or superficial, the court would consider that she had encouraged him to make sexual overtures to her. Thus, working-class girls were more likely to be the victims of rape and less likely to report their victimization. Furthermore, if pregnancy resulted from the assault, the courts would decree that rape had not occurred at all, since it was believed at that time that a woman's pleasure was necessary for her to conceive; since a pregnant woman would have enjoyed the sexual experience, a rape could not have taken place. Only in the case of a lower-class man raping a woman of a higher social class, or raping a child, would the assailant be convicted. In such a case, there was little or no question that rape had ensued (Hufton, 1995, pp. 269–70). Thus, sexual assault was determined by class.

The abuse of children had similarly gone on for centuries under the guise of "parental discipline." Many of us are familiar with the admonition that sparing the rod will "spoil the child." Such treatment of children is likely the result of the historical notion that children, like women, belonged to men. Being the head of the household and family, the man was expected to be in control of those over whom he ruled. Therefore, he had every right to use any amount of force he deemed necessary to ensure obedience. Furthermore, as the undisputed authority over the family, the patriarch was expected to do what was, in his opinion, best for its well-being. That well-being, at times, may have had to be achieved at the expense of particular members, such as its youngest ones. Thus, in ancient times, infants may have been killed or allowed to die if there were already too many mouths to feed or if the babies themselves had some sort of defect. Alternatively, children may have been sold if the family were in dire need. From about the eighteenth century onward, Western religious beliefs have frequently admonished parents to break the will of children to attain complete obedience and control over them (Duffy and Momirov, 1997, p. 55). Other expressions of family violence, such as elder abuse and sibling abuse, were similarly embedded in the historical traditions of Canadian society. Sibling abuse, for example, was dismissed as "sibling rivalry" until quite recently, considered to be normal behaviour among brothers and sisters unless it went to extremes. Violent and abusive behaviour of many different sorts between siblings is well known in Western society. Judaeo-Christian literature recounts stories about one brother killing the other, another brother tricking his brother out of an inheritance, and several brothers selling their father's favourite son (and their brother) into slavery, meanwhile advising their father that his favourite had been killed. The history of royal houses in Western Europe is riven with the same types of stories of thoroughly nasty behaviour. The sheer length of time and breadth of geographical space in which such abusive behaviour among family members has occurred has probably contributed to its tacit acceptance by so many. History and geographical prevalence have helped to normalize family violence to such a degree that ironically it has become virtually unnoticeable. In other words, it "hides in plain sight."

Given these deep historical roots, it is not surprising to find ample evidence of the "normalization" of violence and abuse in the history of Canadian families. In the 1800s, in Canada, a woman seeking divorce after repeated beatings by her husband was often chastised for not having left after the first beating; yet women who *did* leave their marriages after only a couple of beatings were chastised for not being patient enough with their husbands. Judgements frequently implied that the women themselves were at fault when they appeared in court as complainants against their abusive husbands. Because women were supposed to conform to their husbands' standards, if a husband were violent, it was considered to be a wife's responsibility to change him. Courts in Canada were even less sympathetic to the plight of women who suffered male violence in common-law relations, usually due to the fact that these women were deviating from domestic ideals (Prentice et al., 1988, p. 148).

The history of violence against women in Canada is neatly summarized by Constance Backhouse (1991, pp. 167–72) in a story about Esther Hawley Ham, who, in approximately 1814, after having given birth to a child, had to return to her parents' home to recuperate from illness. Her husband presented himself at the Hawley home, making threats, demanding that his wife return home with him and shaking a whip at her. Despite her parents' concern, Esther had little choice but to follow her husband's wishes. Her parents subsequently discovered that their daughter had been physically and emotionally abused by her husband virtually throughout their marriage. Upon learning this, the Hawleys went to their daughter's home and rescued her. From that time on, Esther resided with her parents, although she did make several attempts to reconcile with her husband, who treated her in an abusive fashion each time. Eventually Esther's father sued her husband in court in an attempt to force him to contribute to Esther's support.

Backhouse (1991) posits that such civil action was the recourse for more well-to-do women who could not, for whatever reason, obtain a divorce from their abusive husbands but did not wish to remain in the marriage.[4] Usually it was a male relative who brought the suit on behalf of these women. The drawback to this action was that a wife had to be "fully justified" in her desire not to live with her husband (1991, p. 171). Unfortunately for Esther Hawley Ham, the judge hearing her case chose not to believe her evidence — or rather chose not to believe its severity. He considered that Esther's husband had used only a "moderate" amount of chastisement when he had used a whip to beat her. He was critical of Esther's parents' intervention in the entire matter. The claim for alimony was denied (1991, pp. 174–75).

In Backhouse's (1991, pp. 175–76) estimation, this particular court decision provided the basis for the denial of protection from abuse for women in Canada for the next 100 years. Women could be brutalized by men, but the courts refused to do anything to help them. In fact, judges expressed their abhorrence at having to hear of such things, which they considered improper for the public sphere. They would do their utmost to put the blame for the abuse on the women victims. Clearly, the victimization of women was not restricted to the private domain.

English common law and its principle of "marital unity" were at the heart of such inhumane treatment by the judicial system. Marriage by law made husband and wife one person — that was, of course, the husband. A woman, as a result, could not sue her husband, regardless of what he did to her, for it would be tantamount to suing herself. Or, more to the point, it would be as if *he* were suing *himself*. It must have seemed a ridiculous notion to nineteenth-century Canadians that a man could be so harsh to "himself" as to warrant being sued in court. Furthermore, wives could not be sexually assaulted within marriage because it was believed that, having married, they have given irrevocable consent to sexual intercourse at all times for the rest of their married lives. Any potential objections to such a legal position were silenced after the Canadian Parliament hurriedly passed legislation stating that a Canadian man could not be convicted of raping his wife (Backhouse, 1991, pp. 177–78).[5]

Nineteenth-century women did not meekly accept this blatant sexism; numerous personal and public efforts were made to demand more egalitarian marriage relations. As the laws began to slowly improve for women, many judges worked very hard to thwart any changes, countering whatever gains women had made. Women refused to be daunted. One of the women's groups fighting for justice for women, particularly when it came to family violence, was the Woman's Christian Temperance Union, whose call for the abolition of alcohol was based on the often intimate connection between alcohol consumption by men and the abuse of women and children. Their efforts and those of other early social reformers who sought to protect the welfare of children remind us that while the history of family violence is long and dreary, it is also highlighted by persistent individual and social acts of conscience and courage.

FAMILY VIOLENCE IN CROSS-CULTURAL PERSPECTIVE
▼

Viewed from an international perspective, it appears that violence against women in intimate relations is virtually commonplace at this point in history (Neft and Levine, 1997). Furthermore, it appears to be a growing, rather than diminishing, problem, despite the claim by some post-feminists that equality for women has been achieved. Yet it is largely tolerated or ignored by most societies in which police and judicial officers turn a blind eye, considering relations between a husband and wife to still be a "private" matter. This tolerance by society and its enforcers means that women are generally reluctant to report their victimization. They know that little is likely to be done to stop the abuse, and they know that they will be made to suffer doubly as the victims of the abuse and the victims of the system's tolerance and tacit endorsement. Shame and humiliation are frequently all women end up with when they report their victimization.

Further, when viewed transnationally, violence against women is not simply a matter of men abusing them; in fact, the violence is frequently of a more systemic nature. For example, among a sample of more than 600 families in southern Asia, it was found that 51 percent of these families had killed a newborn female infant (Neft and Levine, 1997, p. 152). In some countries, like Bangladesh, Brazil, Kenya, and Thailand, more than 50 percent of women homicide victims have been murdered by a current or former partner. While some North Americans may console themselves by thinking that these countries are vastly more patriarchal and less enlightened than Canada and the United States, their complacency is ill-placed. In Canada women are nine times more likely to be killed by their spouses than by a stranger, and in the United States the figure for female homicide victims murdered by a current or former spouse is 42 percent (Wilson and Daly, 1994).

Women of all ages experience violence throughout the world. Family violence accounts for most of the injuries suffered by women in most countries (Neft and Levine, 1997). Many are sexually abused as children and teenagers. This is true in highly industrialized "first world" countries, like Canada, the United States, New Zealand and Norway, as well as those of the third world. Some reports indicate that the figure may be as high as one-third. In many parts of Asia, hundreds of thousands of young women are pressed into prostitution either by outright coercion or by trickery (Neft and Levine, 1997).

In some countries, abusive husbands are punished only if the abuse has been deemed to be "excessive." In such cases, it is usually the severity of the wife's injuries that determines the "excess." For instance, in Nigeria a man is not allowed to "correct" his wife in such a way that results in her having a hospital stay of more than 21 days (Neft and Levine, 1997). Dowry deaths have increased in India despite an amendment to the penal code by the government stating that the husband or his family would be held responsible if a bride died an unnatural death within the first seven years of marriage. Dowry deaths typically occur when a husband or his family is not satisfied with the amount of money, gifts, or other valuables a bride has brought as dowry to the marriage.

They may harass her, kill her, or drive her to suicide. Since the courts require concrete evidence of cruelty or harassment, many cases are not brought to justice (Neft and Levine, 1997, p. 155).

Significantly, a Pakistani writer reminds us that the configuration of domestic violence against women should not be premised solely on the Western model. In some countries, it is not strictly men who perpetrate family violence; in fact, other women are often perpetrators as they work to preserve complex familial power relations (Seager, 1997, p. 107). That women participate in the abuse and oppression of other women demonstrates how truly insidious **patriarchy** is. Within its hierarchical system of power relations, women become divided from one another and, in effect, end up abusing themselves because of their own alienation and humiliating subjugation to notions of male supremacy.

UNDERSTANDING FAMILY VIOLENCE
▼

MAINSTREAM SOCIOLOGY

Efforts to understand and resolve family violence have taken myriad forms. Not surprisingly, considerable attention has focussed on individual victims and perpetrators, and explanations have often been couched in psychiatric or psychological terms. Men who batter women, for example, have been described as suffering from poor impulse control, addiction, depression, and low self-esteem. These personal pathologies are then traced back to the abuser's family of origin, with its "angry and ambivalent mother" and "shaming and rejecting father" (Dutton, 1995). Similarly, the behaviour of child abusers has been explained in terms of various psychological aspects such as self-centredness or simply as an expression of mental illness (Tower, 1996). While these kinds of explanations offer a seemingly common-sense approach to the violence and clearly imply specific solutions (notably, counselling and psychotherapy), they fail to explain a variety of anomalies. Why do two women growing up in the same family display profoundly different parenting styles? Why does family violence follow general social patterns, for example, of gender and poverty?

As a result of these kinds of concerns, some analysts have opted for a more interactive framework. Abuse is located not simply within the abuser and his or her personal characteristics, but in the idiosyncratic nature of the relationship between the abuser and the abused. Concretely, this perspective calls attention to specific aspects of the abusive relationship. For example, in explaining the etiology of child abuse, these analysts focus on relationship elements such as unwanted and unhealthy pregnancy, difficult labour, physical illness or disability in the child or parent (Tower, 1996). From this perspective, abuse may be triggered by specific aspects of the relationship. In the absence of these triggers, the same individual may not display abusive behaviour. The net result of this interactive approach is a line of analysis that is more broadly framed and flexible; but, it is still unresponsive to the larger societal factors — cultural beliefs and values, institutional elements — which may be crucial in setting the stage for abusive, dysfunctional families or, conversely, for supportive, non-violent families. It is precisely these kinds of issues that have stimulated an outpouring of sociological and feminist theorizing on family violence and have generated some of the most innovative and challenging perceptions.

Mainstream sociologists have drawn, in part, on the prevailing frameworks in their discipline. Socialization literature, for example, was helpful in explaining the "**intergenerational transmission**" of violence. Viewed from this "**social learning** perspective," growing up in an abusive family socializes children to become victimizers or victims (Tower, 1996). Violence is normalized and rationalized in the family of origin and, as a result, violent patterns of interaction are more likely to be played out in the family of procreation. These violent family scripts are not randomly distributed through the general population, but are complexly influenced by social class, ethnicity, and, in particular, gender. For example, growing up in a traditionally patriarchal community will likely increase the possibility of intimate violence between male and female and child and adult. This socialization approach is, then, helpful in suggesting explanations for the interconnections between intimate violence and, for example, gender and social-class roles.

Socialization similarly sets the stage for the growing literature on "male support theories." Put simply, this perspective examines the ways in which social ties (friendships) with abusive peers may be associated with higher rates of woman abuse. In other words, when a man's friends encourage him to use physical force to dominate his wife or girlfriend, he is more likely to engage in this behaviour. Needless to say, many other factors may enter into this equation. Membership in all-male organizations such as fraternities and the use of alcohol may, for example, intensify the relationship between male support for abuse and actual violent behaviour. Currently theories are being developed and tested to reflect this complexity (DeKeseredy and MacLeod, 1997).

Sociologists have also sought to develop more macro-level theories that seek to incorporate the role of major institutions into their analysis of family violence. James Garbarino's "**ecological model**" of child abuse (1977), for example, examines the situational impact of two macro elements — ideological support for the use of physical force against children and the adequacy of social-support systems in families. In a dramatic effort to grasp the implications of the "bigger picture," his theory drew attention to the prevailing beliefs and values in the culture along with societal responses to family issues such as family and children's services, day care, and housing. From this and other early work, sociologists have developed a variety of macro-level theories. Among the most notable of these is "**exchange/social control theory**."

Exchange theory works from the premise that individuals seek rewards and avoid punishment or costs. From this perspective, family members engage in violence "because they can." In other words, violence is used in the family when its rewards outweigh its costs. However, this cost/reward calculation does not simply depend on personal factors such as who is bigger and stronger. Clearly, this perspective allows for inclusion of other variables, such as who is employed and, therefore, has greater financial assets; who receives more education; and who is likely to be supported by agencies of social control (police, social welfare officers). If the use of violence is likely to be punished by the police and/or stigmatized by the community; if the victim is in a position to inflict financial, social, or religious penalties on the abuser; and if there are other effective means of action at the disposal of the abuser, violence is less likely to be employed. Conversely, if the violence is likely to be kept secret, if the punishment is non-existent or light or if there are rewards for being violent, then the likelihood of a violent outcome is increased (Gelles and Cornell, 1990). This, and other efforts at sociological theorizing, suggest that sociology continues to move toward an increasingly sophisticated and complex analysis of family violence.

FEMINIST INITIATIVES

Sociological efforts to develop an understanding of family violence have received a tremendous impetus from the evolution of feminist theorizing. Indeed, in many instances, it is difficult to separate feminist and sociological advances on the topic. Certainly the emergence of family violence as an issue owes an enormous debt to the modern women's movement.

Feminists of the second wave, coming of intellectual age in the late 1960s and early 1970s in both the United States and Canada, began to problematize gender and power relations between men and women. They promoted public recognition that women were second-class citizens and they questioned the underlying assumptions of social and cultural structures. By meeting together and sharing their personal experiences, these women realized that male violence was quite common — not the rare pathology traditional belief had promoted (Thorne-Finch, 1992, p. 121). They protested this violence against women (and their children), taking the blame from the shoulders of the victims and firmly placing it upon the male perpetrators. In practical terms, by the 1970s they laid the foundation for the shelter movement, and by the 1980s had established wife abuse in Canadian public consciousness. Most important, feminists demonstrated that, in contrast to popular notions about the rarity of family violence and its relation to "sick" individuals, violence within families was common in its various forms (Loseke, 1989, p. 191).

In part in response to the popularization of feminism, the American mass media began in the mid-1970s to focus their attention on the matter of wife beating. Lurid stories of extreme physical and emotional abuse, going far beyond the realm of what most people could tolerate, began to circulate. It was pointed out that this abuse had serious consequences not just for its female victims, but also for children who witnessed it and, perhaps most important, for future generations. The stories also illuminated that those involved in family violence were not necessarily poor, uneducated, mentally ill, alcoholic, or "different" in any way from those in non-abusive family situations. Female victims' behaviour did not differ from that of non-abused women. They were battered simply because they were women, the batterers were men, and the social context was patriarchal. The accounts of experts were not drastically different from media accounts (Loseke, 1989, 191–97).[6]

While modern feminists were tremendously important in publicizing woman abuse, feminist analysis has had a dramatic, if uneven, impact on theorizing family-violence issues. In particular, feminists have underlined the role of patriarchal culture in legitimating and perpetuating male violence against both women and children. Intimate violence was both rejected as either pathology or innate human trait and conceptualized as a manifestation of particular social arrangements and specific patterns of gender socialization. This, in turn, has generated an enormous outpouring of research and analyses on "masculinities" (Messerschmidt, 1993; Miedzian, 1991).

Further, feminist analyses have drawn attention to the political dimension of family violence. Power and control have been presented as central aspects of abuse — abusers abuse because they have the power (gender, political, economic, social, religious) and because abuse ensures their continued direct and indirect control over their victims (DeKeseredy and MacLeod, 1997, p. 42). Rather than reflecting individual pathologies or personal strategies, family violence is understood to be rooted in the fundamentals of social structure and gender relations.

These and other feminist initiatives have provided a tremendous impulse to theorizing on family violence, and the outcome continues to reverberate through the field (Duffy and Momirov, 1997). The interplay with mainstream sociological thought is, however, far from tranquil. In some instances, a kind of polarity has emerged in which feminist analysis is viewed as irreconcilable with sociological approaches and research. For example, some soci-ologists have tended to downplay the gendered nature of woman abuse with the use of gender-neutral terms such as "spouse abuse" and "partner violence." The implication is that wife abuse is a reciprocal matter between husbands and wives, dissociated from the social inequality between men and women. This analysis is, in turn, supported by research suggesting that men and women engage in roughly equal numbers of "acts" of violence. While these and other conflicts between mainstream sociology and feminism are important to be aware of, they do not signal a great divide between the two perspectives on family violence.

Most mainstream sociologists do not reject the fundamentals of feminist analysis. For example, they are usually quick to acknowledge that woman-ini-tiated violence in "partner violence" is typically less severe and less likely to result in injury than is male violence. Further, mainstream texts routinely acknowledge the feminist perspective and include it in any "debates" on the topic. Finally, in recent issues of one of the most prestigious mainstream U.S. journals, the *Journal of Marriage and the Family*, a growing number of explic-itly feminist articles are being included (Johnson, 1995; Gilgun, 1995). While there may not have been a feminist paradigm shift in sociological theorizing, clearly feminist thought has had and continues to have a profound impact on our understandings of family violence (Thompson and Walker, 1995).

The impact of feminist analysis seems to be particularly important in Canadian research. Most Canadian analysts, whether they subscribe to large-scale surveys or one-on-one interviews and whether they emphasize gender antagonisms or not, adopt some version of a feminist perspective. Indeed, the polarization between feminist and sociological analysis appears to be a more American phenomenon. Although a significant anti-feminist backlash has been popularized in the Canadian media, within Canadian academic work on family violence, disputes appear to be situated more between varieties of fem-inist thought than between feminist and non-feminist analysis (DeKeseredy and MacLeod, 1997).

In both Canada and the United States, feminist theorizing is likely to continue to play a central role. In particular, recent feminist interest in and inclusion of "diversities" in their work is likely to set the stage for an increas-ingly synergistic relationship between mainstream sociology and feminism.

As feminists examine the ways in which race, ethnicity, (dis)ability, social class, sexual orientation, age, geographic isolation, and so on, affect women's experiences, they will be drawing upon and adding to well-established socio-logical traditions. The net result may be an opportunity to further integrate feminist and traditional approaches to family violence (Anderson, 1997).

INTEGRATING "DIVERSITIES" INTO
FAMILY-VIOLENCE ANALYSIS
▼

Clearly, at the cutting edge of current work on family violence is the inclusion of diversities. Previous analyses tended to treat the experience of family violence, such as wife abuse, as a generic occurrence and ignored the impact of social class, race, ethnicity, sexual orientation, and so forth. For example, other aspects of an abused woman's life — her professional status, her ethnic background, her age — were all represented as subordinate to her status as victim. Conversely, the experiences of abused women who were outside the assumed norm were ignored. However, just as modern feminism has increasingly acknowledged the need to recognize and locate the concerns and issues of specific groups of women — lesbians, black women, older women, Native women — so, too, has feminist analysis of family violence targeted diversities.

While it isn't possible in a brief review to do justice to the body of literature generated by this initiative, a quick sampling reveals the impact on family-violence analysis. In Canada, for example, considerable effort has been directed toward understanding Native women's experience of abuse — both as children and as adults. Violence against Native women is not simply another expression of violence against women. It is violence framed by centuries of oppression and conditioned by ongoing racial antagonisms. Concretely, this means the violence may be rooted in communities besieged by unemployment, poverty, and addiction; it may be conditioned by a history of abusive schools and unsympathetic social services, by the routine derogation of Native culture and traditions, and by exclusion from mainstream realities. While patriarchy may be the critical ingredient, it is filtered through the important prisms of racism, colonialism, and classism. Native women explain the connections:

> People tell us our ancestors were very strong and I believe that. Everybody knew their roles, everybody had a place before white people came. When they did come, that's when all the dysfunction started. They took our land and Indians were mistreated. Everything was taken away from them and the whole family was disrupted. (Baxter et al., 1995, pp. 283–84)

As these remarks are echoed by indigenous people around the globe — Maoris in New Zealand, Australian Aborigines and so on — it is clear that family violence cannot be fully understood outside of its historical and cultural context (Smallwood, 1996; Cutts, 1996).

The implications of this understanding are not simply "theoretical." Clearly, the experiences of Native women (as well as immigrant and refugee women) point to the importance of going beyond a simple gender-based analysis. While Native (immigrant or refugee) men may be the perpetrators of the violence, they are also the victims of racism, economic marginalization, and social powerlessness. Finally, the traditional solutions — shelters and the criminal justice system — are clearly less appropriate when fleeing to a shelter means "leaving their communities and the support, familiarity, and cultural traditions that these communities represent" and when jailing the abuser merely adds to the aboriginal prison population and "does nothing to help him deal with his own feelings of inadequacy and alienation" (DeKeseredy and MacLeod, 1997, p. 19). In short, the experiences of Native, immigrant, and refugee women clearly raise a number of key theoretical and practical issues.

Explorations of violence between women in same-sex couples have had equally potent implications for family-violence analysis. Until the 1990s, relatively little had been published about violence in lesbian couples. However, it was clear that partner abuse in lesbian relationships was an important, unexplored aspect of women's experience of violence (Renzetti, 1992). Clearly, same-sex violence underscores the importance of factors beyond gender-based inequalities: "I had a lot of issues about violence against women and subscribed completely to a gender analysis of the issue. I guess I heard about lesbian battering back in 1991. I was stunned — the dynamics were so complex and difficult to sort out" (Murray and Welch, 1995, p. 109). While it was important for lesbians to be simply heard on the issue of intimate violence, ending the silence has had momentous implications for feminist analysis. On the one hand, it pushes feminists to focus on the power and control perspective rather than the interplay of genders; on the other hand, it emphasizes the important conditioning effect of the larger social context: "I think lesbian battering is very similar to battering in heterosexual relationships because it has similar characteristics ... physical, emotional and sexual coercion, or violence, are used to gain and maintain power and control" (Murray and Welch, 1995, pp. 110–11). However, the experience is located in a homophobic social context, where police, social-service agencies, and even friends, may be not only unsympathetic, but openly antagonistic to hearing charges of lesbian violence. Victims may be loath to act not only because they fear the victimizer or mistrust the social-support system, but also because they fear stigmatization as a lesbian, because they don't want to contribute to homophobia, and because they expect their accounts to be trivialized and minimized. Clearly, lesbian battering reveals a complex interplay between misogyny, **homophobia** and **sexism**. It also evokes the role of other factors, such as racism and ableism (Murray and Welch, 1995). Currently, feminist analysis is struggling to come to terms with this complex interconnection of forces.

THE STRUGGLE FOR SOLUTIONS[7]
▼

Although tremendous forward strides have been made in uncovering and understanding family violence, we are still very much handicapped by an incomplete grasp of the issue. However, whatever the limitations of our facts and insights, the plight of numerous victims has necessitated social intervention, particularly with regard to child, woman, and elder abuse. In the late twentieth century, we are expending considerable societal resources to respond to family violence. These efforts continue to be plagued by missteps and a perceptible lack of commitment. While much has been done, a great deal more remains to do, redo, and undo.

Most Canadians are aware of the social-service agencies, children's aid organizations, shelters, and hot lines that today respond to family-violence emergencies. They realize that the criminal justice system — police, courts, jails, and prisons — are often called upon to deal with the more serious cases of family violence. Most will have also received some information about societal efforts to improve and expand our responses to woman, child, or elder abuse. However, many Canadians are not cognizant of the many ways in which current solutions are riddled with shortcomings and hamstrung by inadequate funding. Even a quick overview of the present situation reveals not only that much has been achieved, but also that much needs to be done both to protect gains and to push for more effective measures.

CHILD ABUSE

Although child abuse has the longest history as an identified form of family violence, societal responses are riddled with problems. Children's Aid Societies, for example, routinely lack the finances to provide the level of investigation and supervision to ensure that children are adequately protected in their homes. Despite public inquiries and societal outrage, reports continue to surface of children and young teenagers being "abused, neglected and killed under the protection of government-funded agencies." Even when children (including very young children) are removed from abusive homes, they are likely to be "bounced from one foster home or group home to another as often as every few months." Although promised, computer systems that would ensure that all children are properly "tracked" and do not fall through administrative cracks are still not available (Donovan and Welsh, 1998, p. A3). Agencies point to underfunding, inadequate training, weak child-protection laws, too few staff, and onerous caseloads, while provincial governments often point to the need for fiscal restraint and tax cuts.[8]

The death of Kassandra Shepherd exemplifies the problems. While under the supervision of the Peel Children's Aid Society, the 3-year-old was killed by a blow to her head by her stepmother. The case worker for Kassandra was responsible for 36 other cases at the time. The subsequent inquiry made 73 recommendations, in particular urging more funding, smaller caseloads, and more workers. The Peel Children's Aid Society was able to implement 31 of these recommendations, reducing the caseload to 14 to 1, but "lack of funds ... keeps it from acting on the others." To fully implement the proposed changes, the agency would need to spend "at least $160 [million] to $180 million more" (Gillespie, 1998, p. B3).

While governments have been loath to provide funding, there has been some legislative movement. The Ontario government, for example, is proposing massive changes to its child-welfare laws. Among the key ingredients in this

---

BOX 9.3
▼
THE VALUE OF A CHILD'S LIFE

In July 1998, a 30-year-old father was jailed for 21 months for child abuse. He was convicted of failing to provide the necessities of life to his 5-year-old daughter. The girl, who was not expected to ever recover from her emotional and physical abuse, had been starved and was "so painfully thin" that her skin hung in folds; she was not yet toilet trained, and her vocabulary was limited to fewer than five words. Her mother, who is intellectually at the level of a child of 6 to 8 years of age, has previously had five other children. Children's Aid removed three of these children, and the fathers have custody of the other two.

Despite the fact that child-care workers from the Children's Aid Society and other organizations had visited the family 48 times over the course of 33 months, the child was not apprehended. Only when the father brought his daughter to the hospital to visit her mother (who had just delivered another baby) did her severe malnourishment and profound anemia result in removal from the home and criminal charges.

When conferring his sentence on the father, the judge lashed out at the system: "It is admittedly difficult to measure the comparative weights of competing evils but I confess to having great difficulty understanding what value system Parliament had in mind when it decided that two years imprisonment was a fitting maximum punishment for a parent who, by neglecting to provide the necessities of life to his or her child, actually endangers that child's life" (Crook, 1998, pp. B1, B8).

legislation is the addition of "neglect" to the law and according neglectful behaviour the same significance as physical abuse; the dramatic shortening of the length of time young children and infants remain "in care" before seeking a permanent adoptive home and increased scrutiny of parents' history of violence (wife abuse, child abuse, or criminal activity). These proposals are particularly important because they appear to tip the balance away from parental rights and toward enhanced children's rights (Welsh and Donovan, 1998, p. A6).

This struggle to determine the limits of parental rights is also being waged in the national debate over the "spanking law." Under Section 43 of the Canadian **Criminal Code** (based on an 1892 law), parents are legally allowed to physically discipline their children, provided the force is "reasonable." Children's rights advocates are challenging this "licence" to spank as abusive and outdated. Just as we no longer accept a man's "right" to discipline his wife, we should not tolerate the use of force and violence against children. Currently, a children's rights group is planning a constitutional challenge of Section 43 (Black, 1998, p. A5).

Clearly, child abuse is becoming a more broadly framed issue, and its evolution has very general societal implications. Nowhere is this more evident than in contemporary discussions of child poverty. If parents are abusive when they are neglectful and fail to provide adequately for their children, what is to be said about a society (or government) that does not ensure all of its children have adequate food, shelter, and clothing, and some rough equality of opportunity. In some sense, the federal government acknowledged this responsibility when it set a deadline of the year 2000 for the elimination of child poverty. At present, about one in five Canadian children is living in poverty, according to the National Council of Welfare, and that figure appears to be increasing (Eggertson, 1998, p. A7). Across Canada, social-service cuts and increased use of food banks speak to the growing plight of the poor. In Ontario, for example, 57 percent of welfare mothers surveyed reported some hunger — adults and children missing meals and cutting portions in the previous 30 days — and 22 percent reported severe hunger (Monserbraaten, 1998a, p. B1). Viewed from this perspective, child neglect appears to be both increasing and firmly attached to government priorities.

WOMAN ABUSE

The struggle to formulate solutions to woman abuse has been equally uneven. In the last two decades, there have been enormous improvements in the availability of shelters, increased services for battered women, the provision of counselling for the children of abused women and for male batterers, and educational initiatives, including television advertising. Efforts have been

---

BOX 9.4
▼
PATTERNED TRAGEDY: THE STEPS FROM
ABUSE TO FEMICIDE TO INQUIRY

Between 1977 and 1996 in Canada, 1525 wives were killed by their husbands (Statistics Canada, 1998, p. 28).

Step 1: A woman is in a relationship characterized by escalating violence and threats.

Step 2: The woman reaches out for help — perhaps fleeing to a shelter and seeking assistance from the criminal justice system.

Step 3: The response from the criminal justice system is ambiguous and/or ineffective; that is,

a) the assailant is mistakenly released on bail without the knowledge of the victim, or
b) the violent assailant is granted access to his children, or
c) poor communications between police forces results in critical errors, such as not knowing that he previously acquired a gun permit or that he has previously been charged with violent offences.

Step 4: The woman tells several people, including the police, that the man is going to kill her. Often, she takes specific steps, such as making out her will.

Step 5: The woman is killed.

Step 6: There is an inquiry (formal, informal, and/or media-generated) to examine what went wrong, and attention often focusses on why the woman didn't leave earlier, and so on.

Source: Based on media reports throughout the 1980s and 1990s; see, for example, the 1998 inquiry into the murder in Ontario of Arlene May.

---

launched to ensure that all women, regardless of age, disability, language, race, or ethnicity, have access to both shelters and services. In addition, there have been important changes in the responsiveness of the criminal justice system. Notably, for example, criminal-harassment legislation has been enacted so that women who are being harassed — followed, spied on, and so on — by their intimate partner have good legal recourse.[9]

While these and other steps have improved the lot of many abused women, the progress has been decidedly uneven. Once again, funding cutbacks are a central concern. For example, shelter workers in Ontario (whose budgets were cut in 1995–96 and in 1996–97) complain that funding reductions have meant abused women are allowed shorter stays at the shelter and must wait up to three to six months for counselling services. At the same time, help lines are missing more calls than they receive because of insufficient funding and resulting staff shortages. Also, funding for special programs for women from racially and culturally diverse communities, language interpretation services, services for the disabled, and legal aid have all been cut. The criminal justice system continues to be plagued by inadequate training for police, crown attorneys, and judges. Crown attorneys are burdened with onerous caseloads and lack the time to respond to and track domestic abuse cases. The president of the Ontario Crown Attorneys Association reported, for example, that prosecutors are hamstrung by lack of funding, resources and personnel. A survey of trial crowns found that almost 75 percent of them had less than five minutes to read and prepare each case before going to bail court (Infantry, 1998, p. A6; Darroch, 1998a, p. B4; Darroch, 1998b, p. B4).

As with child abuse, many of these flaws and inadequacies in the system come to the fore when a murder inquiry reveals a pattern of systemic failures. For example, in Ontario, in 1996, Arlene May was killed by her lover, Randy Iles. A subsequent inquiry revealed the assailant had a history of abusive relationships. When he murdered May, he was on bail for the fourth time for stalking, assaulting, and threatening to kill her. The criminal justice system allowed Iles's release despite the fact he had repeatedly threatened to murder May and despite the fact he had flouted a bail order to keep away from her. Finally, a court clerk's error allowed him to keep a firearms-acquisition permit, which allowed him to buy the murder weapon. Predictably, the inquest jury came back with recommendations calling for stiffer sentences for abusers, mandatory counselling, improved communication between the police and crown attorney's office, and greater police leeway to confiscate firearms and permits from those charged with domestic violence (*Toronto Star*, 1998a).

In short, the problem of woman abuse is far from a final solution. Despite important advances, the proliferation of useful recommendations, and repeated calls for "zero tolerance," the violence persists. Particularly in the current period of political conservatism and economic restraint, it is not clear whether there is the societal will to maintain our progress, let alone make further advances.

ELDER ABUSE

Since it is one of the most recently excavated forms of family violence, it is not surprising to find that solutions to elder abuse are limited. Drawing upon experiences associated with woman and child abuse, there have been efforts to provide educational resources and to familiarize the general public with the issue. In some instances, elder abuse is woman abuse "grown old," and senior women are using the shelters and counselling services available to all battered women. However, not surprisingly, much remains to be done.

A number of proposals are currently being promoted. Elizabeth Podnieks, of Ryerson Polytechnic University, calls for a national network so that information, policies, and educational materials can be more effectively shared. There is also a need for a clear criminal justice response to elder abuse. At present, according to Podnieks, Canada has prosecuted at most two cases of elder abuse. In contrast, San Diego, California, has successfully prosecuted more than 150 cases of physical and financial elder abuse. The difference lies in the presence of specific Criminal Code laws that deal with elder abuse. Now, Canadian prosecutors must rely on general theft and battery laws that ignore the specific dynamics of dependency and trust characterizing many elder abuse cases (Carey, 1998b; Carey, 1998a, p. A4).

The Ontario Older Women's Network is calling for training for women's shelter staff so that they can deal more effectively with the special health and social needs of older women; expansion of the safe shelter concept so that older women have access to subsidized housing for seniors; a 24-hour multilingual emergency phone line; and strengthening other services, including peer counselling, support groups, home services, and community day programs (Henderson, 1998, p. L3; Monsebraaten, 1998b, p. A9).

While the simple proliferation of proposals speaks to the vitality of social activists involved with elder abuse, it is clear that much remains to be accomplished. In the context of funding cutbacks and multiplying demands, the question of adequate resourcing will remain central for the foreseeable future. It remains to be seen whether our responses to elder abuse will keep pace with the demographic pressure from a rapidly aging population.

CONCLUSION
▼

The preceding brief overview of family violence in Canada reveals myriad complex issues that demand a societal response. Clearly our understanding of family violence, particularly certain aspects, is in its early stages. In every direction — research, analysis, policy — much remains to be done. However, it is important not to be overwhelmed by the sheer volume of human suffering, the tortuous complexity of the issues, or the glacial pace of social change. Researchers, analysts, and, especially, grass-roots advocates have made enormous strides. Many questions have been raised about behaviours that, for centuries, were taken for granted as normal and inevitable. Lively public debates have been instigated. People are more aware of their conduct in the family and its impact on loved ones. Many parents are reconsidering the wisdom of spanking their children or allowing their children to engage in "sibling rivalry." Such progress should not be ignored or deprecated. It is profoundly important for those who are victimized by family violence directly and for the rest of the Canadian population who may not even be aware that they are being victimized indirectly.

More and more people are cognizant of the fact that the problem of violence within the family cannot be ignored or normalized any longer. Despite its spotty record, the media have made attempts to report cases and cover inquiries. They have been instrumental in bringing this matter to the attention of the general public. Now, there are centres devoted to research on family violence, and governments are making efforts to address the problem on the level of both research and services. University courses and books now routinely discuss the phenomenon of violence in their presentations of family life so that young adults can understand the prevalence and parameters of the problem.

In short, family violence has acquired a significant place on the public agenda — an achievement in itself.

SUMMARY
▼

- Since the late 1960s, family violence has emerged has a central issue in the sociology of the Canadian family.
- As a result of this recognition, an increasingly accurate statistical database on forms of family violence is emerging.
- Despite these advances, societal understanding of family violence is hindered by the ideological blinders of "familialism."
- Confronting family violence entails coming to terms with our collective history, in which many expressions of violence were considered socially acceptable, even desirable.
- Our historical commitment to violent families is clearly reflected in many family practices around the globe.
- Mainstream sociology and feminist analysis have contributed enormously to the development of an in-depth understanding of family violence and its cultural roots.
- Success in articulating solutions (policies) for family violence has been more difficult to achieve, and in the current political and economic context, policy initiatives are particularly hard to launch.

• The achievements of the last three decades, particularly in dragging family violence into the public domain, have been momentous and bode well for future progress on the issue.

NOTES
▼

1. The media frequently refer to violence against women in intimate relations as "wife abuse." However, women in the shelter movement and scholars working in the field typically use the term "woman abuse," since it is both more encompassing and more political (see Dekeseredy and MacLeod, 1997, p. 20). For the purposes of this chapter, the term "woman abuse" is used.

2. Research in the United States suggests that violence against children is an immense social issue. The U.S. National Committee to Prevent Child Abuse indicated that, in 1993, there were almost 3 million reports of child abuse and 1 million confirmed cases. In this year, an estimated 1300 children, almost all under 5 years of age, died of child abuse (Edmonds, 1994, p. 8A).

3. There are a number of good sources of information on the World Wide Web relating to various aspects of family violence. For example, Alksnis and Taylor (n.d.), Edleson (1997a), and Maxwell (1994) discuss the impact on children of witnessing family violence. Edleson (1997b) also delineates the overlap between woman battering and child maltreatment in an attempt to provide a more integrated approach to the field.

4. Until 1968, divorces were extremely difficult and time-consuming to obtain in Canada. See Chapter 8.

5. This aspect of the "rape law" was not changed until 1983, with the introduction of the new sexual-assault law, under which it was possible for a man to be charged with sexually assaulting (raping) his wife.

6. For a comprehensive and enlightening discussion of the role of mass media in socially constructing the varied forms of family violence, see the theoretical treatment by Spector and Kitsuse (1987) and Best's collection of essays employing this theory (1989).

7. For a fuller discussion of the struggle to provide solutions to family violence, see Duffy and Momirov, 1997.

8. National polls indicate that Canadians consider children a public-spending priority and are willing to pay higher taxes in order to ensure children's well-being. A recent poll found that 61 percent believe Canada spends "too little" on children, and 74 percent would support a tax increase if the monies were directed to children's welfare (Monserbraaten, 1998c, p. A3).

9. Manitoba, for example, recently (May 1998) introduced the "toughest measures in the country to protect victims of domestic violence and stalking" (*Toronto Star*, 1998c). Victims will be able to obtain a "protection order" over the phone at any time in order to keep away a stalker or abusive partner. Similarly, British

Columbia (April 1998) has earmarked $610 000 for violence-prevention pro-
grams (*Toronto Star*, 1998b).

CRITICAL THINKING QUESTIONS
▼

1. Consider in what ways the status of women in society — economic, political,
   religious, educational, social — has an impact on women's experience of family
   violence and renders it significantly different from men's. Are there important
   parallels to the relationships between children and adults?

2. Frequently, social policy must balance the needs and rights of parents against the
   needs and rights of children. Discuss whose rights should be considered key in
   a variety of scenarios — parents' rights to physically reprimand children versus
   children's rights to physically resist their parents; children's rights to "divorce"
   their parents; and so on.

3. Analysts have become increasingly aware of the impact of "diversities" on the
   experience of family violence. Consider the ways in which social class and race
   affect women and children's experience of abuse. Outline specific ways in which
   social policy might respond to these differences in experience.

4. If you were asked to design a year 2000 community project around the issue of
   family violence, what one direct or indirect issue (teen abuse, poverty, and so on)
   would you target, and why?

5. With the increasing proportion of elderly, and especially older elderly in the population, abuse of the elderly is likely to become increasingly prominent as a family-violence issue. Identify some concrete steps that might be taken at both the
   societal and the community level to help reduce the abuse of our seniors.

SUGGESTED READING
▼

Elly Danica. 1988. *Don't: A Woman's Word.* Toronto: McClelland & Stewart.
   A riveting and disturbing first-hand account of one woman's experience with
   childhood abuse.

Walter DeKeseredy and Linda MacLeod. 1997. *Woman Abuse: A Sociological Story.*
Toronto: Harcourt Brace & Company.
   An invaluable combination of sociological theory, current research, and personal
   experiences relating to women's experience of violence.

Holly Johnson. 1996. *Dangerous Domains: Violence Against Women in Canada.*
Toronto: Nelson Canada.
   A detailed analysis of woman abuse, drawing in particular on the data generated
   by Statistics Canada's Canadian Violence Against Women Survey.

Ann Duffy and Julianne Momirov. 1997. *Family Violence: A Canadian Introduction.* Toronto: James Lorimer.

The first Canadian text to provide an overview of Canadians' experience with and understanding of woman, child, elder, and other family abuse.

Leslie Timmins, ed. 1995. *Listening to the Thunder: Advocates Talk about the Battered Women's Movement.* Vancouver: Women's Research Centre.

The voices of 22 grass-roots activists discussing their experiences and strategies.

REFERENCES
▼

Alksnis, Christine, and Jo-Anne Taylor. n.d. "The Impact of Experiencing and Witnessing Family Violence during Childhood: Child and Adult Behavioural Outcomes." http://www.csc-scc.gc.ca/crd/famviol/fv04e/fv04e.htm.

Amato, Paul R. 1991. "The 'Child of Divorce' as a Person Prototype: Bias in the Recall of Information about Children in Divorced Families." *Journal of Marriage and the Family* 53 (February): 59–69.

———. 1993. "Children's Adjustment to Divorce: Theories, Hypotheses, and Empirical Support." *Journal of Marriage and the Family* 55 (February): 23–38.

Anderson, Kristin L. 1997. "Gender, Status and Domestic Violence: An Integration of Feminist and Family Violence Approaches." *Journal of Marriage and the Family* (August): 655–69.

Backhouse, Constance. 1991. *Petticoats and Prejudice: Women and Law in Nineteenth-Century Canada.* Toronto: Women's Press (for The Osgoode Society).

Badgley, Robin F. 1984. *Sexual Offences Against Children in Canada*, vols. 1, 2, and *Summary.* Ottawa: Minister of Supply and Services.

Baxter, Kate, with Eliza Saskamoose, Darlene Little, and Jean. 1995. "Ducking Bullets: Women from Ahtahakoop Cree Nation Work to End Violence." In L. Timmins, ed., *Listening to the Thunder: Advocates Talk about the Battered Women's Movement.* Vancouver: Women's Research Centre.

Best, Joel. 1989. "Dark Figures and Child Victims: Statistical Claims about Missing Children." In Joel Best, ed., *Images of Issues: Typifying Contemporary Social Problems.* New York: Aldine de Gruyter.

Black, Debra. 1998. "Children's Advocates Plan Challenge to Spanking Law." *Toronto Star.* March 4, p. A5.

Canadian Panel on Violence Against Women. 1993. *Changing the Landscape: Ending Violence — Achieving Equality.* Ottawa: Minister of Supply and Services Canada.

Carey, Elaine. 1998a. "Elder Abuse Across Globe Discussed Here." *Toronto Star.* March 2, p. A4.

———. 1998b. "Sharpen Law on Elder Abuse, U.S. Experts Say." *Toronto Star.* March 4, p. A4.

Crook, Farrell. 1998. "Father Sent to Jail After Girl 'Starved.'" *Toronto Star,* July 3, p. B1.

Cutts, Christine. 1996. "A Torres Strait Islander Perspective on Family Violence." In R. Thorpe and J. Irwin, eds., *Women and Violence: Working for Change*. Sydney: Hale & Iremonger.

Danica, Elly. 1988. *Don't: A Woman's Word*. Toronto: McClelland & Stewart.

Darroch, Wendy. 1998a. "Budget Hinders Prosecutors, Inquest Told." *Toronto Star*, May 29, p. B4.

———. 1998b. "Women Trapped by Funding Cuts." *Toronto Star*, June 9, p. B4

DeKeseredy, Walter S., and Linda MacLeod. 1997. *Woman Abuse: A Sociological Story*. Toronto: Harcourt Brace & Company.

Donovan, Kevin, and Moira Welsh. 1998. "Children Still at Risk Unreleased Studies Find." *Toronto Star*, April 28, p. A3.

Duffy, Ann, and Julianne Momirov. 1997. *Family Violence: A Canadian Introduction*. Toronto: James Lorimer.

Dutton, Donald G. 1995. *The Batterer: A Psychological Profile*. New York: Basic Books.

Edleson, Jeffrey L. 1997a. "Children's Witnessing of Adult Domestic Violence." http://www.mincava.umn.edu/papers/witness.htm.

———. 1997b. "The Overlap Between Child Maltreatment and Woman Battering." http://www.mincava.umn.edu/papers/overlap.htm.

Edmonds, Patricia. 1994. "Poll: Abusive Parents Should Lose Children." *USA Today*, April 8, pp. 1A, 8A.

Eggertson, Laura. 1998. "1 in 5 Kids Said Living in Poverty." *Toronto Star*, May 12, p. A7.

Gadd, Jane. 1997. "More Boys Physically Abused than Girls." *Globe and Mail*, July 9, pp. A1, A6.

Garbarino, James. 1977. "The Human Ecology of Child Maltreatment: A Conceptual Model for Research." *Journal of Marriage and the Family* 39 (November): 721–35.

Gelles, Richard J., and Claire Pedrick Cornell. 1990. *Intimate Violence in Families*, 2nd ed. Newbury Park, CA: Sage.

Giles-Sims, Jean. n.d. "The Psychological and Social Impact of Partner Violence." http://www.agnr.umd.edu/users/nnfr/research/pv_ch2.html.

Gilgun, J.F. 1995. "We Shared Something Special: The Moral Discourse of Incest Perpetrators." *Journal of Marriage and the Family* 57: 284–94.

Gillespie, Kerry. 1998. "Kasandra Tragedy Leads to Reforms at Peel CAS." *Toronto Star*, June 24, p. B3.

Gurr, Jane, Louise Mailloux, Diane Kinnon, and Suzanne Doerge. 1996. *Breaking the Links between Poverty and Violence Against Women*. Ottawa: Minister of Supply and Services.

Henderson, Helen. 1998. "Let's Open Our Eyes and Act on Abuse Report." *Toronto Star*, June 27, p. L3.

Hufton, Olwen. 1995. *The Prospect Before Her: A History of Women in Western Europe, 1500–1800*. New York: Alfred A. Knopf.

Infantry, Ashante. 1998. "Fast Action Urged to Curb Wife Abuse." *Toronto Star*, July 19, p. A6.

Johnson, Holly. 1990. "Violent Crime." In C. McKie and K. Thompson, eds., *Canadian Social Trends*. Toronto: Thompson Educational.

———. 1996. *Dangerous Domains: Violence Against Women*. Toronto: Nelson Canada.

Johnson, Michael P. 1995. "Patriarchal Terrorism and Common Couple Violence: Two Forms of Violence Against Women." *Journal of Marriage and the Family* 57/2 (May): 283–94.

Lasch, Christoper. 1977. *Haven in a Heartless World*. New York: Basic Books.

Loseke, Donileen R. 1989. "'Violence' Is 'Violence' … or Is it? The Social Construction of 'Wife Abuse' and Public Policy." In Joel Best, ed., *Images of Issues: Typifying Contemporary Social Problems*. New York: Aldine de Gruyter.

Luxton, Meg. 1988. "Thinking about the Future." In Karen Anderson, ed., *Family Matters*. Scarborough, ON: Nelson Canada.

Maxwell, Gabrielle M. 1994. "Children and Family Violence: The Unnoticed Victims." http://www.mincava.umn.edu/papers/nzreport.htm.

McDonald, Lynn, and Blossom Wigdor. 1995. "Editorial: Taking Stock: Elder Abuse Research in Canada." *Canadian Journal on Aging* 14/2 (Supplement): 1–13.

Messerschmidt, James W. 1993. *Masculinities and Crime: Critique and Reconceptualization of Theory*. Lanham, MD: Rowman & Littlefield.

Miedzian, Myriam. 1991. *Boys Will Be Boys: Breaking the Link between Masculinity and Violence*. New York: Doubleday.

Miller, Leslie J. 1990. "Violent Families and the Rhetoric of Harmony." *British Journal of Sociology* 41/2 (June): 263–88.

Monsebraaten, Laurie. 1998a "Food Aid Doesn't Fill Gap — Study." *Toronto Star,* April 8, p. B1.

———. 1998b. "Older Women Suffering in Silence at Hands of Abusers, Study Says." *Toronto Star,* June 23, p. A9.

———. 1998c. "Spend More to Help Children, National Poll Tells Government." *Toronto Star,* April 10, p. A4.

Murray, Bonnie, and Cathy Welch. 1995. "Attending to Lavender Bruises: A Dialogue on Violence in Lesbian Relationships." In L. Timmins, ed., *Listening to the Thunder: Advocates Talk about the Battered Women's Movement*. Vancouver: Women's Research Centre.

National Council of Welfare. 1998. *Poverty Profile 1996*. Ottawa: Minister of Public Works and Government Services.

Neft, Naomi, and Ann D. Levine. 1997. *Where Women Stand: An International Report on the Status of Women in 140 Countries, 1997–1998*. New York: Random House.

Podnieks, Elizabeth, Karl Pillemer, J. Phillip Nicholson, Thomas Shillington, and Alan Frizzel. 1990. *National Survey on Abuse of the Elderly in Canada*. Toronto: Ryerson Polytechnical Institute.

Prentice, Alison, Paula Bourne, Gail Cuthbert Brandt, Beth Light, Wendy Mitchinson, and Naomi Black. 1988. *Canadian Women: A History*. Toronto: Harcourt Brace Jovanovich.

Priest, Lisa. 1996. "4 Billion Toll of Abuse." *Toronto Star,* August 9, p. A1.

Renzetti, Claire M. 1992. *Violent Betrayal: Partner Abuse in Lesbian Relationships.* Newbury Park: Sage.

Russell, Diana E.H. 1982. *Rape in Marriage.* New York: Macmillan.

Seager, Joni. 1997. *The State of Women in the World Atlas,* 2nd ed. Harmondsworth: Penguin.

Smallwood, Margaret. 1996. "This Violence Is Not Our Way: An Aboriginal Perspective on Domestic Violence." In R. Thorpe and J. Irwin, eds., *Women and Violence: Working for Change.* Sydney: Hale & Iremonger.

Spector, Malcolm, and John I. Kitsuse. 1987. *Constructing Social Problems.* New York: Aldine de Gruyter.

Statistics Canada. 1998. *Family Violence in Canada: A Statistical Profile, 1998.* Ottawa: Minister of Industry. Catalogue no. 85-224-XPE.

Thompson, Linda, and Alexis J. Walker. 1995. "The Place of Feminism in Family Studies." *Journal of Marriage and the Family* 57 (November): 847–65.

Thorne-Finch, Ron. 1992. *Ending the Silence: The Origins and Treatment of Male Violence against Women.* Toronto: University of Toronto Press.

Timmins, Leslie. 1995. *Listening to the Thunder: Advocates Talk about the Battered Women's Movement.* Vancouver: Women's Research Centre.

Toronto Star. 1998a. "The Battle Against Domestic Violence." July 4, p. E2.

———. 1998b. "B.C. Moves to Curb Violence Against Women." April 23, p. B2.

———. 1998c. "Tough New Law Unveiled in Manitoba." May 9, p. A8.

Tower, Cynthia Crosson. 1996. *Understanding Child Abuse and Neglect,* 3rd ed. Boston: Allyn and Bacon.

Trocme, Nico, Debra McPhee, Kwok Kwan Tam, and Tom Hay. 1994. *Ontario Incidence Study of Reported Child Abuse and Neglect.* Toronto: Institute for the Prevention of Child Abuse.

Welsh, Moira, and Kevin Donovan. 1998. "High Praise for New Child Abuse Law." *Toronto Star,* June 14, p. A6.

Wilson, Margo, and Martin Daly. 1994. "Spousal Homicide." *Juristat Service Bulletin,* 14/8: 1–15.

10

▼

CHANGE AND DIVERSITY IN AGING FAMILIES AND INTERGENERATIONAL RELATIONS

ANNE MARTIN-MATTHEWS

LEARNING OBJECTIVES

In this chapter, you will learn that:

- a main source of variability between women and men in later life is that whereas most men live out their old age as married persons, most women spend their last years as widows;
- most of the care and assistance provided to elderly persons is provided by other old people, usually women. Although most of the care provided to elderly persons by their children is provided by daughters, sons are increasingly involved in providing care and assistance across the generations to elderly family members and friends;
- the popular notion of the "**sandwich**" **generation** caught between responsibilities for their children and their elderly parents is largely a myth; very few families in Canada face competing intergenerational demands simultaneously;
- Canada's changing health-care system has significant impact on elderly persons and their families, because reductions in medical and hospital-based services have not been matched by the further development of community-based care;
- immigration policies promoting family reunification have contributed to the ethnic diversity of Canada's elderly population, a substantial minority of whom speak neither English nor French.

INTRODUCTION

As other chapters in this volume well document and discuss, Canada's families are changing. Some would say they are "in decline," others that families are stronger and that, as Canada's health and social "safety nets" weaken, family ties are more important than ever. Some argue that these changes in health and social services in Canada are based on the questionable assumption that

323

families and not the state have the primary role in the care of older persons, a worrisome basis for policy, some believe. One undeniable fact, however, is that Canada's families are aging. With the aging of the population, and the increasing longevity of both women and men, comes a host of structural changes in the size and composition of families, changes in the roles family members play and the dynamics of these roles and relationships, the emergence of new issues in the negotiation of **intergenerational relations**, and increasing diversity in terms of what "family" actually means throughout the life course.

It is important to acknowledge that the heterogeneity and broad diversity of the population of older persons living in Canada is not reflected or acknowledged in much of the terminology we use, especially in such terms as "the elderly." Elders in Canada represent a wide diversity of people, as this chapter documents. Similarly, our language often fails to acknowledge the many ways in which the experiences of aging in families are gendered, and are influenced by socio-economic status class, by location in particular sociocultural contexts, and by geographic and regional differences in the access people have to supportive policies and services.

This chapter examines the changing context of aging and families in Canada, and a selection of the factors that reflect this diversity. The discussion here focusses on the changing demographic context of family ties in later life, including marital-status patterns and socio-economic status in later life, as well as family structures over the life course. The chapter also examines the dynamics of various intergenerational and **intragenerational relations** in later life, including relationships between individuals in couple relationships, between adult children and their elderly parents, sibling relationships, and grandparent–grandchild relationships. A consideration of issues of "caregiving" within the context of families and aging explores the myth of the sandwich generation, the ways in which changing health and social policies are having an impact on older people and their family members, the balance of work and family responsibilities, the issue of payment for care of elderly family members, and statutory obligations across **generations** within families. The chapter ends with a focus on sources of diversity within Canadian families, including gender, ethnicity, and geographical and regional location.

THE CHANGING DEMOGRAPHIC CONTEXT OF FAMILIES IN LATER LIFE: ELDERLY PEOPLE IN CANADA
▼

In order to set the context for considering aging and families, it is necessary to understand the basic characteristics of **population aging** in Canada. At the time of the 1996 census, 12 percent of Canada's population of 30 million people was over the age of 65. The age of 65 is typically used as the criterion for defining the "elderly" population, because this is the age at which persons become eligible for certain age-related pension and income-security benefits. This age has also long been associated with the age of retirement, when people leave the paid labour force. However, very many Canadians now leave full-time employment before the age of 65; it is estimated that, in the 1990s, fully one-third of people who described themselves as "retired" were less than 60 years of age (Statistics Canada, 1997). This transition has become further blurred because many "retired" people continue involvement in the labour force in a part-time or seasonal capacity. Nevertheless, the age of 65 remains, somewhat arbitrarily, as the age at which individuals in the population are defined as having entered "old age."

Overall, Canada's population is much "older" than it was at the turn of the century, although it is still considered young in comparison with many countries in the industrialized world. Canada's proportion of its population over the age of 65 is slightly higher than that of the United States, but well below that of the countries of Western Europe. A century ago only 6 percent of the population of Canada was over the age of 65; by the year 2011, approximately 14 percent of the Canadian population (an estimated 5 million people) will be aged 65 and over (Moore and Rosenberg, 1997). With increases in **life expectancy** and the aging of what is commonly known as the "baby boom generation," the proportion of the population that is over the age of 65 is projected to increase even further, to approximately 25 percent by the year 2031.

Often people think of the population over the age of 65 as one homogeneous group. This is definitely not the case. In fact, census data indicate that approximately 10 percent of people over the age of 65 also have at least one child who is also over the age of 65. In an attempt to reflect one aspect of the heterogeneity of old age, some people distinguish between the "young old" (often those between 65 and 80 years of age) and the "old old" (usually those aged 80 or 85 and older).

It is even difficult to speak of aging in families in Canada, for there is considerable variation in the composition and distribution of the population by region and province; of the ten Canadian provinces and two territories, for example, several have aged populations in excess of 13 percent (Manitoba and Saskatchewan), while others have substantially lower proportions (Alberta, at 9.9 percent; the Yukon and Northwest Territories, each having fewer than 5 percent of their populations over the age of 65) (McPherson, 1998). Thus, the extent to which the increased proportion of elderly persons in the population will have an impact on roles and relationships within families varies across the country.

Since women continue to live longer than men (approximately seven years longer), for the most part the world of elderly people is a world of women. Throughout this chapter, discussions of the patterns and dynamics of families and aging will largely involve discussions of the family relationships of elderly *women*. Where possible, comparisons and contrasts between the family lives of elderly men and women will be considered, but it is important to realize the extent to which the experience of later life, and especially of

---

BOX 10.1
▼
WARNING

by Jenny Joseph

When I am an old woman I shall wear purple
With a red hat which doesn't go, and doesn't suit me.
And I shall spend my pension on brandy and summer gloves
And satin sandals, and say we've got no money for butter.
I shall sit down on the pavement when I'm tired
And gobble up samples in shops and press alarm bells
And run my stick along the public railings
And make up for the sobriety of my youth.
I shall go out in my slippers in the rain
And pick the flowers in other people's gardens
And learn to spit.

You can wear terrible shirts and grow more fat
And eat three pounds of sausages at a go
Or only bread and pickle for a week
And hoard pens and pencils and beermats and things in boxes.

But now we must have clothes that keep us dry
And pay our rent and not swear in the street
And set a good example for the children
We must have friends to dinner and read the papers.

But maybe I ought to practise a little now?
So people who know me are not too shocked and surprised
When suddenly I am old, and start to wear purple.

Source: "Warning," from *Selected Poems*, published by Bloodaxe Books Ltd.
Copyright © Jenny Joseph 1992. (U.S. Distributors: Dufours).

advanced old age, is a largely female experience. Another typical feature of later life is that it is lived as a widow.

MARITAL-STATUS PATTERNS IN LATER LIFE
▼

While the family roles of older persons involve a number of marital statuses, the most typical marital status for women in later life is widowhood. As I have noted elsewhere (Martin Matthews, 1991b), widowhood is both age-related and sex-selective. Table 10.1 illustrates how the percentages of the population who are widowed increase with advancing age. For example, among women, fully 54 percent of those aged 75–79 years are widowed, compared with 29 percent of women aged 65–69 years.

These data also reflect the sex-selective nature of widowhood. In Canada, widows (women whose husbands have died) outnumber widowers (men whose wives have died) by a factor of five to one. We also know that while half of all marriages end with the death of the husband, only one in five ends with the death of the wife. The data in Table 10.2 illustrate this trend very clearly, especially from age 50 onwards. For example, while only 4 percent of men aged

TABLE 10.1
▼
WIDOWED AND DIVORCED POPULATION AGED 65 YEARS AND OVER, BY SEX AND AGE COHORTS, CANADA, 1991

	Widowers		Widows	
	N	%	*N*	%
65–69	30 625	6.8	161 990	28.5
70–74	35 175	10.4	187 900	41.1
75–79	38 630	15.8	195 970	54.4
80–84	33 320	24.2	158 350	67.1
85–89	21 750	35.8	98 540	76.9
90+	12 120	48.5	56 630	82.3

Source: Percentage calculations are from Statistics Canada, *1991 Census* (Catalogue no. 93-310) (Ottawa: Minister of Supply and Services, 1993), Table 5, p. 22. The data on population numbers are from Statistics Canada, *The Nation, 1991 Census of Canada* (Catalogue no. 93-310) (Ottawa: Minister of Supply and Services, 1993), Table 3, p. 32.

TABLE 10.2

▼

WIDOWED POPULATION AGES 15 YEARS AND OVER,
BY SEX AND AGE COHORTS, CANADA, 1971 AND 1991

| | Widowers | | Widows | |
| | Percentage of Age Cohort | | Percentage of Age Cohort | |
	1971	1991	1971	1991
Total, 15+ years	2.5	2.3	9.8	10.4
15–19	0.1	0.0	0.1	0.1
20–24	0.1	0.0	0.3	0.1
25–29	0.2	0.0	0.5	0.2
30–34	0.3	0.1	0.9	0.5
35–39	0.4	0.2	1.6	0.9
40–44	0.7	0.5	2.7	1.7
45–49	1.1	0.8	5.0	3.3
50–54	1.8	1.4	8.8	6.1
55–59	2.9	2.4	14.5	10.8
60–64	4.7	4.2	22.6	18.3
65–69	7.7	6.8	33.0	28.5
70–74	13.1	10.4	46.1	41.1
75–79	20.4	15.8	57.9	54.4
80–84	31.3	24.2	68.8	67.1
85–89	43.5	35.8	76.1	76.9
90+	54.8	48.5	79.3	82.3

Source: Percentage calculations are from Statistics Canada (1976), *Population: Cross-Classifications of Characteristics, 1971 Census of Canada* (Catalogue no. 92-129), Table 1, p. 1–1; and Statistics Canada (1993), *1991 Census* (Catalogue no. 93-310), Table 5, p. 22.

60–64 years are widowed, 18 percent of women in the same age **cohort** are widowed.

There are several reasons for the sex-selective nature of widowhood. These include the differential life expectancy of men and women (today, life expectancy at birth for women is about 81 years, while it is 75 years for men); the fact that women marry men who are on average two or three years older than they are; and also the differences between men and women in their rates of remarriage. Men are not only far less likely to become widowed, but also less likely than are women to remain widowed. Canadian data indicate that 14 percent of widowers and 5 percent of widows remarry. Among the population aged 70 years and older, widowers are nine times more likely than are widows to remarry (Martin Matthews, 1991b).

However, the likelihood of remarriage for widows and widowers has declined by over 40 percent in recent years in Canada. There are several reasons for this. These include societal norms that are increasingly favourable to cohabitation without marriage, as well as economic disincentives to remarriage. These disincentives often involve private pension plans and survivor benefits that some people receive when they are widowed; remarriage is discouraged because these people are financially "punished" by having these benefits discontinue if they remarry. Those who do remarry are generally younger than are the population of widowed persons as a whole: the average age for remarried widowers is 64 years, and, for widows, the comparable figure is 58 years.

In a recent analysis of event history data from the 1990 Canadian Family and Friends Survey, Wu (1995) examined a number of factors that influence the likelihood of remarriage for women and men whose first marriages ended in widowhood. He confirmed some of the earlier findings of large gender differences in rates of remarriage. Moreover, ever-widowed men remarry sooner than do ever-widowed women. Fewer than 6 percent of ever-widowed women, but more than 22 percent of men, have remarried after five years of widowhood. At ten years post-bereavement, 11 percent of women and 35 percent of men will have remarried.[1]

Recent analyses also suggest that the likelihood of widowhood in later life is decreasing (Martin-Matthews, In press b). Reductions in mortality rates of men help explain this trend. In Canada, between 1976 and 1981, there was a 14 percent decline in the death rate for men aged 50 to 54 years (Stone and Fletcher, 1988). The increase in divorce among older people is another explanation. Statistics Canada data report significant increases in the rate of divorce for older men, and even higher percentage increases in the rate of divorce for elderly women (Stone and Frenken, 1988). Table 10.3 illustrates these data as well. This does not reflect the rate at which elderly persons are terminating their marriages, but rather the fact that an increasing number of individuals are entering old age as divorced persons (Stone and Frenken, 1988, p. 39). This rate of divorce does, therefore, have major implications for patterns of widowhood in later life.

The projections are that, with a continuance of currently low rates of marriage and remarriage, about half of all women entering old age in 2025 will not be in any marriage (Martin Matthews, 1991b, In press b). In Canada, in 1971, only 9 percent of persons 30–34 years of age were unmarried; in 1991, 23 percent of this age group was unmarried. The issue is whether many of these individuals will in fact ever marry or enter into a long-term cohabitation relationship. It is entirely possible that as cohorts of younger women

TABLE 10.3

▼

DIVORCED POPULATION AGED 15 YEARS AND OVER, BY SEX AND AGE COHORTS, CANADA, 1971 AND 1991

	Males		Females	
	Percentage of Age Cohort		Percentage of Age Cohort	
	1971	1991	1971	1991
Total, 15+ years	1.0	3.4	1.3	4.9
15–19	0.0	0.0	0.1	0.0
20–24	0.2	0.2	0.5	0.5
25–29	0.9	1.3	1.5	2.4
30–34	1.3	3.1	2.0	4.7
35–39	1.5	4.8	2.1	7.2
40–44	1.6	5.9	2.1	9.0
45–49	1.6	6.4	2.0	9.6
50–54	1.5	6.1	1.9	8.8
55–59	1.5	5.5	1.7	8.0
60–64	1.3	4.7	1.5	6.2
65–69	1.1	3.8	1.1	4.7
70–74	1.0	2.8	0.7	3.2
75–79	0.7	2.2	0.5	2.2
80–84	0.6	1.7	0.4	1.4
85–89	0.5	1.2	0.4	0.9
90+	0.4	1.2	0.3	0.7

Source: Statistics Canada, *Population: Cross-Classifications of Characteristics, 1971 Census of Canada*, vol. 1, part 4 (Catalogue no. 92-729) (Ottawa: Minister of Industry, Trade and Commerce, 1976), Table 1, p. 1–1; Statistics Canada, *The Nation: Age, Sex and Marital Status, 1991 Census of Canada* (Catalogue no. 93-310) (Ottawa: Minister of Supply and Services Canada, 1992), Table 3, p. 32.

grow older and move into old age, widowhood will continue its pattern of decline as *the* normative marital status in later life.

The experience of widowhood in later life is, however, more than a "demographic trend." Some studies of the relative impact of various life events suggest that widowhood is one of the most stressful of life events, surpassed only by the death of a child in its impact (Pearlin, 1980). Widowhood is best understood not only as an event involving the loss of a spouse who in most cases has been a long-time partner, but also as a process of transition over time. This transition begins with the illness of the spouse and proceeds through a period of bereavement, and typically to adaptation and resolution. It is not uncommon, however, for the period of bereavement to be characterized by intense feelings of grief, feelings of meaninglessness, disorganization of one's social world, and identity confusion. But these feelings may not characterize the experience at all. The experience of grief and bereavement is highly diverse, depending on such factors as the nature and duration of the spouse's final illness, the sociocultural context within which the couple lived, their socio-economic status, the nature and extent of the social supports available to the bereaved family members, and the nature of the marital relationship or partnership prior to the death.

For many couples in the past for whom divorce was not an option, and for many today for whom either the stigma of divorce or religious proscriptions against divorce remain strong, widowhood may be the only source of release from an unhappy union. Elsewhere (Martin Matthews, 1991b, In press b), I have noted the issue of what I have termed "ambiguous loss" in relation to the experience of widowhood for some. In my interviews with hundreds of widowed women and men, I have spoken with some who noted the strain of public expectations of grief and mourning for spouses who were especially cruel or mean-spirited and whose "passing was the greatest blessing of my adult life" (Martin-Matthews, In press a). Issues of power and abuse, both within and across generations, are only beginning to be well researched among older people and their families (McDonald and Wigdor, 1995; Neysmith, 1995).

ACCESS TO RESOURCES AND SOCIO-ECONOMIC STATUS IN LATER LIFE
▼

Although the economic circumstances of many elderly persons in Canada are comparatively better today than they were before the introduction this century of old-age security and related pension benefits, there is wide disparity in the level of economic security of old people. Two of the primary factors that produce this inequity of access to economic resources are gender and marital status. Here we discuss how these two factors intersect in relation to the incomes of older persons.

Of those elderly persons who fall below Statistics Canada's low-income cut-offs,[2] the majority are elderly women who are "unattached" (either because they have remained single throughout their lives or, more typically, because they have become widowed or divorced) (McDonald, 1997). Despite some improvements in the economic circumstances of older women in Canada, it remains the case that even today most remain "one man away from poverty" (McDonald, 1997). While poverty is tied to women's transition to "unattached" statuses in later life, it is important to note that later life poverty is not exclusive to them. Among men, levels of poverty in later life are notable among those who have never married.

Of the many life changes that accompany the transition to being an "unattached" person in later life (typically through widowhood, but also through divorce), the transition to poverty, even temporarily, is one that occurs for many women. "The transition from spouse to survivor still holds substantial economic peril" (Burkhauser, Butler, and Holden, 1991, p. 504). For many widowed women, the experience of bereavement precipitates poverty among individuals who have not been poor as a member of a couple (Hurd and Wise, 1987). Many widows have been found to be worse off financially two years after widowhood than before, with the drop in total family income beginning in the year prior to widowhood, when the ill spouse is no longer able to continue working (Hudson, 1984).

It is estimated that 40 percent of widows and more than 25 percent of divorced women fall into poverty for at least some time during the first five years after the end of a marriage (Morgan, 1989). For most widows, the highest risk of becoming poor is in the first period of widowhood (Holden, Burkhauser, and Feaster, 1988). Most longitudinal studies indicate that, for both widowed and divorced women, economic vulnerability is prolonged for at least five years, unless remarriage occurs. This is true despite dramatic increases in labour-force participation and hours worked, especially for those who have experienced separation and divorce (Holden and Smock, 1991).

These data bear testimony to the financial penalties women incur for periods outside paid employment, as in taking time for child rearing. Canada has minimal provision for "opting out" periods in terms of time away from paid labour to care for children, and none for care of other kin; there are no minimum wages for homemaking, and, despite calls to the contrary, no recognition of the labour of caregiving. As well, the recent rise in "non-standard" work — part-time, seasonal, contractual, low-paying — has particularly affected women and typically provides few or no workplace-based financial benefits, such as sick leave or pension benefits. Other factors include the low availability of employer-sponsored pension plans in Canada, and the even lower availability of survivor benefits for women who have lost a spouse (Schellenberg, 1994). Thus women's lower wages, their typical pattern of interrupted labour-force attachment, and the often marginal nature of their paid employment combine to contribute to the poverty that "unattached women," in particular, experience in later life.

However, not all widowed individuals experience the transition to poverty. In terms of economic well-being, less than half of a sample of widowed women reported that their economic circumstances had declined since the loss of their husbands, and only one in five felt that her current status left her with problems in getting along on her current income (O'Bryant and Morgan, 1989). Here again diversity is a characteristic of the experience of socio-economic change associated with marital status change in later life. Thus, while elderly persons in Canada overall are far less likely today to live in poverty than they did several decades ago, structural factors do increase or decrease their chances of being poor. Several of these structural factors reflect the intersection of gender and marital status. For example, elderly women living alone are seven times more likely to be poor than are men living with spouses in their old age. Being male, living as a couple, and having a history of continuous full-time employment reduce the likelihood of poverty in later life (Moore and Rosenberg, 1997).

FAMILY STRUCTURES OVER THE LIFE COURSE
▼

Another demographic change characteristic of aging families today is the structure of family ties over the life course. These structural changes have significant implications for family relationships across generations. Within the dynamics of intergenerational relationships, new roles (such as great-grandparenthood) and responsibilities (such as being an "elderly" child aged 65 years with a very aged parent aged 87 years) have developed over time.

Due to increased longevity, there has been a substantial increase in the duration of family ties across generations. It is now not uncommon for parents and children to share as many as 50 years together. As an illustration, when persons born in 1910 reached their fiftieth birthday in 1960, only 16 percent of them had at least one of their parents still alive. By comparison, when persons born in 1930 reached their fiftieth birthday in 1980, 49 percent of them had at least one of their parents still alive. Projections suggest that when persons born in 1960 reach their fiftieth birthday in 2010, fully 60 percent of them will have at least one of their parents still alive to celebrate the event with them (Gee, 1990).

Other family ties have increased in duration as well. For those who remain married, the duration of the marital tie is now far longer than it has ever been historically. As well, grandparents can typically expect to see one or more of their grandchildren grow to adulthood, and great-grandparent roles are more prevalent than they have ever been. Not only have these roles become more enduring, but in some cases they have assumed different responsibilities as well. For example, because of the increase in the rate of divorce and the poverty of children, among other factors, grandparents now may find themselves in situations requiring that they "parent" their grandchildren, through either ongoing or intermittent custodial relationships (Jendrek, 1993, 1994).

Others find their rights of access to grandchildren or great-grandchildren diminished by separation and divorce in succeeding generations (Kruk, 1995).

Another result of increased longevity, and also of declines in fertility as noted by Gee in this volume, is the trend toward what has been called the "verticalization" of the family or the development of the "bean-pole family." As McPherson (1998, p. 197) describes it, the transition outlined here represents a shift from "the traditional 'pyramid' shape (four to five siblings in a two-to-three-generation family), which prevailed early in the century, to a 'beanpole' shape (four to five generations with zero to two siblings per generation)." Although some sociologists contend that bean-pole families are not as prevalent as is currently supposed (Connidis, 1994; Rosenthal, 1998; Uhlenberg, 1993), these demographic shifts are important and reflect the need to view changes in fertility rates (and their implications for aging families) in historical perspective.

Another change involves the acceleration of rates of "generational turnover" (Hagestad, 1981). This refers to the length of time between the birth of the first and the birth of the last child in families. In the past, when larger families were prevalent, childbearing often extended over 20 or more years of a woman's life. Today, generational turnover is much more rapid, with the duration of childbearing often covering only a few years. Thus, children of the same generation[3] in a family are today far more likely to be chronological-age peers than has been the case in the past.

At the same time, in some families today there is a trend toward what has been called an "age-gapped" structure, with increasing numbers of years between the birth of one generation in a family and the birth of the next (McPherson, 1998). Especially in families where women pursue careers prior to childbearing, it is not uncommon for the gap between generations to be 30 or more years. In the past, this gap was often only about 20 years. Taken together, these structural characteristics contribute to the diversity of families whose members are born in different historical time periods, and thus subject to different social and structural influences. In this way, they have an impact on the nature of the roles and responsibilities of multiple generations of the family over the life course.

FAMILY TIES IN LATER LIFE
▼

Many different types of ties connect family members together over the life course. Only a few of these can be examined here. An important point to remember throughout this section is the extent to which the decisions made or circumstances experienced by one member of the family impact on the lives of other family members and create change for them. As Hagestad (1981) notes, marriage in one generation creates in-laws in another. Parenthood creates grandparenthood and great-grandparenthood. Divorce creates "ex" or "former" relationships that require negotiation. Bereavement creates not only widowhood, but also the loss of a parent or grandparent. The poverty of a single-parent daughter may precipitate her return to her parent's home. Geographic relocation changes the patterns of contact across multiple generations. Although much of the subsequent discussion focusses largely on more dyadic relationships (between spouses or partners, between a parent and an adult child), this is because much of the research on family life in old age has been conducted in this way. The complex interweave of family roles and relationships across the life course remains largely unexplored in the sociology of aging (Bleiszner and Bedford, 1995).

Many of these relationships can be thought of in terms of the extent to which various dimensions of family integration reflect different aspects of "family solidarity" (Bengtson et al., 1985). Bengtson and colleagues (1985) describe six dimensions of solidarity: family structure; associational solidarity (the degree to which members of a lineage are in contact with one another and engage in shared behaviour and common activities); affectual solidarity (the degree of positive sentiment expressed in the intergenerational relationship); consensual solidarity (the degree of consensus or conflict in beliefs or orientations external to the family); functional solidarity (the degree to which financial assistance and service exchanges occur among family members); and normative solidarity (the norms of "familism" held by family members, in terms of expectations of proximity and assistance).

COUPLE RELATIONSHIPS

Among Canadians aged 65 years and over, over half (56 percent) are married, although, as noted earlier, the likelihood of being married decreases precipitously as one ages, especially for women. For most men, the experience of later life involves being married; for most women, the experience of later life involves being married in the early years of old age, and then widowed.

The primary research questions that have guided the study of couple relationships in later life have focussed on how marital roles and marital quality change over time. Especially today, with increasing levels of labour-force participation among older women, and the trend to earlier retirement among older men, couple relationships in later life are increasingly diverse. How couples negotiate the transition to retirement is an important indicator of the level of satisfaction of their later years as a couple. In many cases, retirement from paid employment brings a couple into greater day-to-day proximity than they may have had for many years, requiring adaptations and adjustments that have been characterized as the "What do I do with him 24 hours a day?" syndrome (Keating and Cole, 1980) . Nevertheless, there is evidence that marriages of long duration report quite high levels of marital satisfaction (Connidis, 1994). Certainly, divorce remains relatively uncommon in later life.

While the vast majority of elderly persons, especially those less than 80 years of age, enjoy relatively good health and have comparatively little need for what are called "formal" supports provided by health and social-service agencies, advancing age does bring changes in functional health status and increasing frailty in one or both of them. Thus, the nature of the couple relationship inevitably changes toward the end of the life of at least one of the partners. While much of the literature on "caregiving" focusses on the care of elderly persons by their adult children, in reality most of the assistance provided to elderly persons is provided intragenerationally, that is, by someone of the same generation, usually a spouse. Because, at the end of the life, most women are widowed but most men are married, it is very typical for elderly married women to spend their last years of marriage caring for an increasingly frail spouse.

While providing this care, women may themselves experience health problems. As Gee and Kimball (1987, p. 31) have noted, "Women get sick, but men die." Women are, in fact, more likely than are men to report chronic, ongoing health problems such as high blood pressure and arthritis, and to experience physical limitations. Cognitive impairment in very old age can result from a number of factors, including strokes or drug interactions. More permanent impairment may be associated with dementia, which results from chronic brain damage caused by circulatory problems such as hardening of the cerebrovascular arteries or to disease states in the brain, the most well known of which is Alzheimer's disease (McPherson, 1998). The incidence of dementia is known to increase with age, from 2 percent of those aged 65–74 years, to 11 percent of those aged 75–84 years, and 35 percent of those aged 85 years and older (Canadian Study of Health and Aging, 1994). The symptoms of dementia include cognitive decline and memory loss, disorientation, and loss of emotional abilities leading to inappropriate social behaviour (McPherson, 1998).

Among elderly couples, then, there are many women caring for a very ill partner whose personal characteristics are quite unlike those present before the onset of dementia (O'Connor, 1998). In some cases, illness progresses to the point where one partner can no longer provide the needed care, and one member of the couple is institutionalized (Gladstone, 1995). Thus, some elderly spouses (usually women) continue to live independently in the community while their partners permanently reside in a long-term-care facility, a situation which has been described as "**quasi widowhood**" (Rosenthal and Dawson, 1991; Ross, Rosenthal, and Dawson, 1997) or "married widowhood" (McPherson, 1998).

ADULT CHILD–OLDER PARENT RELATIONSHIPS

Although adult child–older parent relationships have in recent years come to be characterized very much in terms of the "care" the younger generation provides to the older generation (Martin-Matthews, 1998), there is considerable evidence of typically supportive bonds between most older persons and their adult children throughout the life course. Approximately 80 percent of Canadians aged 65 and older have at least one living child; indeed, as noted previously, more than 10 percent of those aged 65 and over have a child who is also over the age of 65 (Rosenthal and Gladstone, 1994). This latter fact highlights the complexity of intergenerational ties and the fallacy of equating family roles (such as being a grandparent or being someone's adult "child") with membership in particular age cohorts.

Despite media images of the abandonment of elderly persons by their adult children (which the media often associate with the rarity of intergenerational households), census data tell us that a majority of older people who have living children live in the same city as at least one of those children, and the vast majority live within a hour's drive (Rosenthal and Gladstone, 1994). Connidis (1989) reports a comparative frequency of contact between older parents and adult children in Canada, with emotional support being the most frequently exchanged type of assistance across households. Indeed, there is consistent research evidence of the flow of aid quite prevalently "down" rather than "up" the generations; the assistance provided by older persons to their family members typically includes help with child care, financial assistance, and advice. The reciprocal exchange of aid across the generations is frequently ignored in analyses that depict older people as passive "recipients" of "care."

It must be noted, however, that the relations between elderly parents and their adult child(ren) are highly gendered. Daughters are far more likely than are sons to maintain ongoing contact with, and to provide a wide variety of assistance to, an older parent. Women play a predominant role as "kin keepers" in maintaining family ties throughout the life course, maintaining communication among family members, continuing family rituals and traditions (Rosenthal, 1985), and playing the role of comforter and confidante as well (Rosenthal, 1987).

As Mandell and Duffy (1995, p. 2) have noted, "gender ideologies are created in the ideologies and practices of family life." The gendered nature of family relations in later life assumes particular importance in this light. For aging and elderly women, gender ideologies get played out in the expectation that women will assume the predominant role in "caring for and caring about" (Aronson, 1994; Baines, Evans, and Neysmith, 1991) family members across generations and across households. For aging and elderly men, gender ideologies play out rather differently in relation to the family ties. Canadian demographic data indicate that, even without divorce, adult children report that, if only their father is alive, they are somewhat less likely to keep in touch with him than they are to keep in touch with their mother if only she is alive, or with both parents (Smith and Dumas, 1994). Widowed and divorced women typically do not reap the economic rewards in later life (as some men do), but as kin keepers, they typically do reap the socio-emotional rewards not as frequently experienced by men in later life.

SIBLING RELATIONSHIPS

Most older people have at least one living sibling. In many respects, the sibling relationship is unique among later-life family ties because of both its long duration and what it represents in terms of shared early-childhood family experiences (Connidis, 1989). Several Canadian studies suggest that sibling ties, frequently having waned throughout young adulthood and midlife, often become quite salient in later life, especially among sisters, and particularly when both are widowed (Connidis, 1989, 1992; Connidis and Davies, 1990; Martin Matthews, 1991b). There is as yet no evidence of a comparable pattern amongst divorced older persons.

One aspect of family life that we expect to be different for elderly persons in the future is the number of sibling ties. Those entering old age in the next 20–30 years (the "baby boomers") will, as a result of the high total fertility rate of the 1950s, have a substantial number of brothers and sisters in comparison with elderly persons today. This is particularly true for those in "later maturity," shortly about to enter "old age." In fact, people now aged 50–64 years have more living siblings than do those aged 30–49 years because large families were more common in the earlier than in the later period (Smith and Dumas, 1994). What does this mean for aging and family life? First, there will, potentially at least, be more kin available to contribute to the care of elderly relatives than is currently the case. Second, the sibling tie is the longest in duration of all family relationships. Given the acceleration of "generational turnover" noted previously, siblings today and in the future will be more likely to share the same historical events and life experiences than has been the case in previous generations.

GRANDPARENT–GRANDCHILD RELATIONSHIPS

The vast majority of older people who have children also have one or more grandchildren. Despite its association with old age, the transition to grandparenthood typically occurs in midlife. Research findings suggest that regular interaction with grandparents usually leaves children with fewer prejudices about old people (McPherson, 1998). For the most part, the grandparent role is seen as one "with minimal rights and obligations" (Rosenthal and Gladstone, 1994), although typically it has a symbolic function in the lineage and dynamics of the family. It primarily involves emotional rather than tangible support. Recently,

---

BOX 10.2
▼
LIFE STORIES OF YUKON NATIVE ELDERS

Mrs. Annie Ned was born sometime during the 1890s, near the old settlement of Hutshi in the southern Yukon Territory. Raised by women who were born in the 1850s or even earlier, it is not surprising that Annie developed a conservative understanding of the "old ways." Mrs. Ned is an extremely competent woman who hunted extensively, both with her husbands and on her own. Her father and second husband were both well-known shamans, or "doctors," and she herself is a remarkably independent woman with a wry sense of humour. Telling stories, she asserts, is how one learns things, and "old style words" are just like learning in school. As one of the last elders, she sees herself as an important teacher. In her own childhood, instructions came directly from "long-time people," who taught with stories. Her recurring theme is that authority to speak about the past comes not from originality, but from accurate repetition, the received wisdom of the elders.

In one of the stories Mrs. Ned tells, entitled "Our *Shagoon*, Our Family History," she reiterates the importance of wisdom passed on through the generations through story telling:

> "Now I'm going to tell a story about long time ago. This is my two grandpas' story, Big Jim's and Hutshi Chief's. I'm telling this story not from myself, but because everybody [old] knows this story. This is not just a story — lots of old people tell it! Just like now they go to school, old time we come to our grandpa. Whoever is old tells it the same way. That's why we put this on paper. I tell what I know."

Source: Julie Cruikshank in collaboration with Angela Sidney, Kitty Smith, and Annie Ned, *Life Lived Like a Story: Life Stories of Three Yukon Elders* (Vancouver: University of British Columbia Press, 1990).

however, the increase in the rate of divorce among Canadian families and in the number of children affected by divorce has seen the emergence of "grandparent rights" groups across the country. Kruk (1995) has identified four circumstances primarily associated with loss of contact between grandparents and grandchildren. These include parental divorce, conflict with both parents, death of adult child, and stepparent adoption following remarriage. Kruk found that grandparents whose child was the non-custodial parent (usually paternal grandparents) are at high risk for contact loss, and adult children-in-law appear to be the primary mediators in the ongoing grandparent–grandchild relationship.

It is important to note here the rather static nature of research in this area, with its focus on older grandparents and younger grandchildren when in fact relationship patterns are more diverse, often involving midlife grandparents with younger grandchildren, older grandparents with adolescent and young-adult grandchildren, and, for the most part, very old great-grandparents with young great-grandchildren.

OTHER FAMILY AND "FAMILY-LIKE" RELATIONSHIPS IN LATER LIFE

The kinds of family relationships described in this chapter are but a few of the relationships to be found within the diversity of Canadian families. Many other kinds of family ties are evident. For example, among the 8 percent of elderly Canadians who have remained single throughout their lives, ties to a broad range of kin (including nieces, nephews, aunts, uncles, and cousins) are common. And, as Rosenthal (1998, p. 10) has recently noted, the increase in birth rates among never-married (ever-single) women means that "in future singlehood will be less likely to be equated with childlessness than is currently the case."[4] There is also evidence that ever-single elderly persons, especially women, have many close ties with an extensive network of friends (Martin Matthews, 1991a). For many, these friendships are often described in "family-like" terms, such as "she's like a sister to me." MacRae (1992) and others have referred to such ties as "fictive kin."

Fictive-kin ties in later life are by no means restricted to those who have remained single throughout their lives. My own research comparing the family ties and social supports of widowed and non-widowed elderly persons in Ontario found that fully 4 percent of the non-widowed and 8 percent of the widowed included at least one friend in their descriptions of their "family" (Martin Matthews, 1991b). In similar research in a small Nova Scotian community, MacRae (1992) found that the majority of elderly persons she interviewed identified at least one person as "fictive kin," with many of these being lifelong friends, and many playing other roles in the family constellation as well, such as "godparent" to the one or more of the elder's children.

One way in which the current cohorts of very elderly persons, the "oldest old," differ from the cohort now entering old age is in their high rate of childlessness. By contrast, those now entering old age are the parents of the baby boomers. Canadian women born in the first two decades of this century had unusually high rates of childlessness and low rates of fertility (Gee and Kimball, 1987). Especially for those women whose one child was a son, it is likely that many of those mothers outlived their child. As a consequence of both these factors, it is likely that substantial proportions of very old people do not have any living children. In fact, my research on caregivers to frail elderly persons receiving home-help services (Martin Matthews, 1993) found that fully 56 percent of the elderly persons interviewed (predominantly women) identified someone other than a child as their primary caregiver, and that 15 percent identified a non-relative as their primary caregiver. While there is some evidence of higher rates of institutionalization among childless and ever-single elderly persons, overall, elderly people without children are not seen to be especially disadvantaged in later life.

A quite neglected research area within the study of families, aging, fictive kin, and "family like" ties is that of gay and lesbian relationships among elderly people. We might speculate that some of the data on the extensive friendship networks and diverse family relationships of "ever-single" or "never-married" elders would include some of this population, but there is little empirical evidence. There is some indication that, for older gay men in particular, high levels of social integration into the gay community provide high levels of supportive relationships and life satisfaction (Dorfman et al., 1995). Lesbian women report similarly high levels of support; there is also some evidence that ties with parents and other family members are more likely to be maintained by lesbian women than by gay men (Dorfman et al., 1995; Dorrell, 1991). However, because much of the literature on these populations is based on individuals with active links to gay and lesbian communities, we cannot yet say that we have a full understanding of how the familial and supportive ties of these individuals differ from those discussed thus far in this chapter.

"CARING FOR" AND "CARING ABOUT" ACROSS THE GENERATIONS
▼

The past decade or so has seen the emergence of "intergenerational caregiving" as a major issue in family dynamics, in gerontological and family research, and on the national policy agenda. When older people become frail and in need of assistance, they typically receive informal and/or formal support. Informal support typically comes from family, but often also from friends and neighbours; as noted previously, the majority of informal support to the elderly is provided by elderly persons themselves, usually spouses, although this "fact" frequently gets lost in the rhetoric of the caregiving debate. Frequently lost, too, in the discussion is the recognition of the reciprocal nature of intergenerational relations even when considerable assistance is provided to the older person; the language of the day is now often couched in terms of "eldercare," a pejorative term implying that the care of an older person is somehow parallel to "child-care" (Martin-Matthews, 1996, 1998). Formal support involves both community-based care (typically allowing an older person to remain in his or her home while receiving assistance from home-care services and other community-based social and health agencies) and institutional-based care. Approximately 12 percent of older Canadians live in some type of long-term-care facility.

THE MYTH OF THE SANDWICH GENERATION

One of the more pervasive of the current misunderstandings of families and aging is that a substantial majority of individuals in midlife are "sandwiched" between the demands of aged parents and dependent children. In fact, where "caregiving" takes place at all, the term "serial caregiving" is now generally understood to be a more appropriate description of the caring responsibilities of most individuals. Typically, caregiving evolves through the life span "in a temporal unfolding rather than providing care to several groups at one time" (Centre on Aging and the Caregivers Association of British Columbia, 1995, pp. 17–18). Analysis of data from the nationally representative sample of the 1990 General Social Survey of Canada suggests that "being caught in the middle" in terms of simultaneously carrying responsibilities to parents and to dependent children is not a typical experience (Rosenthal, Martin-Matthews, and Matthews, 1996). Another version of the "sandwich generation" concept focusses on the combination of care to elderly relatives and engaging in paid employment. Here too, however, Canadian data suggest that this is not a "typical" experience and, even when it does occur, the experience varies widely, as is discussed below.

HEALTH AND SOCIAL POLICIES: CHANGING
THE NATURE OF "CAREGIVING"
▼

Already in this chapter we have identified structural features of Canadian society, particularly the nature of the labour-force attachment of women and their patterns of access to survivor benefits in private pension plans, which create the conditions that affect how gender and marital status intersect in the access old people have to socio-economic resources in later life. We have seen, too, that structural features of families and generations have an influence on the roles, responsibilities, and rights that family members have over the later years of the life course. Health and social policies, and changes to them, also have an impact on aging individuals and families. Elsewhere I have noted how, in comparison with families in many countries of the world, Canadian families benefit enormously from our national medical insurance program, medicare (Martin-Matthews, In press a). Even in the context of changing health-care policy, which will be considered below, it is important to acknowledge the significant degree to which medicare reduces the economic and social burden to families when their members, old or young, become ill. "It is a principle engraved on the Canadian soul: the sick will not face financial ruin" (Janigan, 1995, p. 10). Before considering how changes are affecting the caring role within families across generations and households, it is important to briefly describe the context of the provision of health care in Canada.

In 1991, Canada spent 10 percent of its gross domestic product on health, compared with the U.S. rate of 13 percent (Health and Welfare Canada, 1993). On a per-capita basis, Canada has the second most expensive health-care system in the world, second only to the United States. In fact, Canada spends more on health per capita than any industrialized country that has national health insurance (Chappell, 1994, p. 3).

Throughout much of the 1990s, Canada has been engaged in a thorough review of its federally funded social programs, which includes income security for the elderly. Health-care programs and policies, which fall under the jurisdiction of the provinces through federal transfers of resources, have been very much in flux throughout the period. When the reforms began in the first part of the decade, there was hope that they would in fact benefit the elderly and those who care for them through a channelling of funds away from hospitals and institutions and to more preventative and community-based programs (Béland and Shapiro, 1994). However, as the decade draws to a close, some analysts fear that "reform" has not meant actual system reform, but rather, only cost-cutting (Chappell, 1998).

In efforts at deficit reduction, the federal government has substantially reduced the amount it transfers annually to the provinces for health, post-secondary education, and welfare. Approaches to cost control of the Canadian health-care system vary from province to province, but have several common elements, including caps on payments to individual physicians and the removal of certain products (particular types of medication, for example) and procedures (such as cataract surgery) from the list of insured services. Hospital beds, and in some cases entire hospitals, have been closed in many areas of the country. Overall, throughout the decade,

> administrative consolidation and program integration have given way in most provinces ... to a decentralization of policy and eventually of funding to smaller geographical ... regions. ... [In the process] health care

system policy-makers have chosen to focus almost exclusively on reducing costs to government while deferring questions about alternative programs or services and innovations relative to staffing ratios and mixes of staff. (Havens, 1996, p. 44)

The anticipated extension and strengthening of community care has not occurred in the wake of changes to hospital and medical services (National Advisory Council on Aging [NACA], 1995). The growing need for support agencies "has emerged in a period of relatively slow economic growth, of spending constraint, during a decline in the belief in state intervention. So adaptations to this new reality have been slow in coming" (Underwood and DeMont, 1991, p. 33). As a result, there is evidence of a growing lack of appropriate after-care for patients discharged from hospitals (NACA, 1995). Another negative effect is an increase in the burden of care borne by informal caregivers (usually family members), who already provide about 80 percent of the care needs of older people (Chappell et al., 1986).

These changes in Canadian health-care policy and delivery stand to have substantial impact on Canada's elderly and those who care for them (Martin-Matthews, In press a). Family care is not only recognized as an essential component of care to the elderly, but "indeed has become a cornerstone in the rhetoric of reform for health care in Canada. This recognition comes at a time of perceived fiscal crisis ... [and] ... is being used as part of the argument for re-shaping universal health insurance" (Chappell, 1994). An analysis of public documents reflecting long-term-care policy in Ontario, for example, found that

> governments expect families to provide more care than ever to frail elderly who, increasingly, will remain in the community where ... services and programs will increasingly be under-funded or absent. ... Such an assumption is clearly dangerous for everyone. Older people may be left without adequate sources of support. Or, women may leave paid employment, thereby damaging their own present and future economic situations. (Rosenthal, 1997, p. 18)

THE "COSTS" OF CARING: BALANCING WORK AND FAMILY
▼

What are the consequences or factors associated with involvement in these kinds of roles within the family? Many studies in social gerontology in particular examine the issue of the "costs of caring"; these "costs" may be measured in a number of ways, such as the physical and psychological "burden" of care or the economic costs of care provision, especially in terms of lost, altered, or relinquished labour-force attachment. A recent focus of interest on the part of researchers, policy makers, and human-resources personnel in both the public and private sectors has been on the impact of family members' efforts to combine or balance their responsibilities to their employment and to their families, especially to their elderly relatives. This represents only one way of examining the "costs of caring" across households and generations, and is the issue which we address here.

Statistics Canada data indicate a 100 percent increase in recent decades in absenteeism for personal or family reasons. Some 37 percent of that increase is attributed to time spent caring for an elderly relative (Ontario Women's Directorate, 1991, p. 18). In examining the factors associated with employees' involvement in the provision of care to elderly family members, several Canadian studies have sought to distinguish between shorter-term job costs, longer-term career costs, and personal costs.[5] These costs have been discussed in general elsewhere (Gottlieb, Kelloway, and Fraboni, 1994), by types of care (Martin Matthews and Rosenthal, 1993) and by gender (Martin Matthews and Campbell, 1995), and are only summarized here. For both women and men, the provision of assistance with bathing, feeding, toileting, and dressing of an elderly relative (personal care) is associated with a greater impact than is assistance with shopping, transportation, home and yard maintenance, laundry, and financial arrangements (instrumental care). This pattern holds for virtually all types of job, career, and personal costs.

Once again, the gendered nature of these costs is evident. Women are more likely than men to use sick days in order to meet their family obligations and are more likely to miss work-related social events. Men are generally more likely than women to report interrupted workdays. A major gender difference is evident in relation to promotion or advancement within the hierarchy of the workplace, with women almost twice as likely to report lost opportunities for promotion because of providing family care. Regardless of the type of care provided, women are also significantly more likely than are men to report career costs. However, the long-term consequences associated with not seeking promotion or career advancement are particularly pronounced for women involved in the provision of personal care (Martin Matthews and Campbell, 1995). Clearly the inequities associated with the combination of employment and care to elderly family members (personal care, in particular) "render women less able to be competitive for the best opportunities that society can offer" (McDaniel, 1993, p. 140).

PAYMENT FOR FAMILY CARE: A VIABLE OPTION?
▼

The issue of financial compensation for family members who provide informal care to elderly relatives has been debated for some time in Canada and around the world. The examination of the "payment for care" issue is based on both the recognition that informal (usually family) caregivers play vital roles in caring for and supporting older persons and the acknowledgement that, with reductions in institutional care and the slow pace of development of adequate community support programs, caregivers require special support in carrying out their roles (Keefe and Fancey, 1998). Programs vary in terms of whether or not they involve direct or indirect approaches to financial compensation. Indirect compensation may involve tax relief, pension schemes, or social-security benefits, while direct compensation involves the transfer of money through an allowance, stipend, grant, or voucher system, payable either to the giver or to the receiver of the care (Keefe and Fancey, 1998).

One such program in Canada is the Nova Scotia Home Life Support Program, which financially compensates family members for care of an elderly relative. Financially compensated caregivers tend to be younger females who live in non-urban areas and co-reside with the elderly care recipient. The greater proportion of financially compensated caregivers in non-urban areas is likely influenced by both the limited availability of home-help services and the high rates of unemployment and **underemployment** in these areas; these factors combine to create a surplus pool of labour which is available to provide services to elderly persons in need at very minimal costs (Keefe and Fancey, 1997).

The issues involved in deciding appropriate mechanisms and amounts of financial compensation for the care of an elderly relative are complex. Keefe and Fancey (1998, pp. 4–5) distinguish between the economic and social objectives of such programs, with those driven by social objectives focussing on the "shared value of caring" and designed "to recognize the contribution of informal care and [to] support the informal care system"; programs with economic objectives, on the other hand, view "caring as a commodity" and are designed to "reduce or delay the institutionalization of the person with care needs." Recent calls for the development of a universal home-care program in Canada (National Forum on Health, 1997) speak to the importance of this issue and the growing need in Canada to recognize and facilitate the labour of care to elderly family members.

STATUTORY OBLIGATIONS WITHIN FAMILIES
▼

The legal recognition of the statutory obligations of adult children to elderly parents forms an important backdrop to our consideration of the provision of assistance within families across the generations. Under the Family Law Act in most Canadian provinces, adult children have an obligation to support a parent who can prove need and "who has cared for or provided support for the child" (Snell, 1990; Canadian Press, 1996). While this section of the Family Law Act has existed in various forms since 1921, it has been "rarely ever used" (Carey, 1995, p. A1).

Attempts to enforce filial obligation laws have seldom been an effective means of gaining support for an elderly parent when the support is not given willingly (Snell, 1990). In recent years, however, courts in several provinces have addressed the issue of the limits of the legal obligations between elderly parents and their adult children. A review of these cases (Parsons, 1998) found that, in each decision rendered, certain factors were associated with the award of support from one or more adult children to their parent(s): the parent had to establish that he or she was in financial need; that the adult child(ren) had the financial capacity to provide the needed support; and that the parent had provided adequate care and support to the child when he or she was a "minor." The various judicial interpretations of these cases also reflect a "scale of priorities" that holds "an individual's obligation to support his or her immediate family to be of greater priority than responsibilities to his or her family of origin" (Parsons, 1998, p. 21).

Such cases are of interest and relevance not only in terms of the nature of the judicial decision making in relation to each, but also in terms of societal responses to them. For example, a court ruling ordering three adult children to provide monthly support to their 60-year-old mother was characterized as illustrating that "as the welfare state begins to be restructured or crumble, we may see more jurisdictions calling on these statutory obligations.... Now, the suggestion is that families must once again take on these responsibilities" (Glossop, quoted by Carey, 1995, p. A9). Thus far the pace of submissions for judicial consideration in no way demonstrates such an increase (Parsons, for example, reviewed eight cases from the 1980s and seven from the 1990s). Nevertheless, the perception exists that, as baby boomers age and governments cut back on the social safety net, "going after children could become a way of saving the public purse" (Carey, 1995, p. A1).

DIVERSITY IN FAMILY RELATIONSHIPS IN LATER LIFE
▼

Throughout this chapter, effort has been made to emphasize the diversity of family roles and relationships characteristic of elderly people and their family ties. However, several elements of diversity are especially relevant in this context and warrant specific consideration. These are issues of ethnicity and culture, and of location in particular geographic and regional areas of Canada. Although the gendered nature of family roles and responsibilities has been highlighted throughout this chapter as well, this section will conclude with a focus on the limitations of the "gender lens" typically brought to the study of families and aging.

ETHNICITY AND CULTURAL ISSUES

The diversity of family structures and dynamics in terms of race and ethnicity, and the way in which they intersect with gender, is considered elsewhere in this volume. However, it is important to consider what impact cultural norms involving **filial obligation** and expectations of family members as to appropriate intragenerational and intergenerational roles and responsibilities have on the lives of elderly persons who are members of "minority" ethnic groups. Canada has had an immigration policy of family reunification in recent decades, and this has resulted in an increase in the number of elderly family members from ethnocultural minorities. Approximately 27 percent of Canada's elderly were born outside the country (Norland, 1994), and almost a quarter of the elderly population speaks neither English nor French (McPherson, 1998).

As Canada's aged population becomes increasingly ethnically diverse, the reconsideration of some old assumptions will be required. For example, in the case of elderly widowed women, it has long been our assumption, bolstered by research findings, that daughters are a strong and supportive tie. However, "it is rather ethnocentric for [North] Americans to assume that the mother–daughter tie is inevitably the closest one, since that is not the case for so many societies" (Lopata, 1995, pp. 121–22). Lopata notes that often forgotten is the fact that, throughout much of Asia and the Middle East (countries whose emigrants increasingly come as residents to Canada), it is the son, and not the daughter, who has the closest relationship with the mother. In Indian families, for example, the mother–son tie is known to be one of great love and affection.

Bengtson, Rosenthal, and Burton (1996) note that, in many cases, elderly members of minority ethnic groups may be embedded in large supportive networks. However, little is as yet known as to how pervasive these networks are, both within and across minority groups; the extent to which comparable networks exist for non-ethnic minority elders; and the exact nature of the burdens as well as the benefits incurred for having membership in extended kin networks.

Language barriers, religious and cultural differences, and economic dependency conspire to reduce the access of elderly persons (and the family members who care for them) from ethnocultural minorities to community-based health and social services. Keefe, Rosenthal, and Béland (1996) found that, while ethnicity is related to the amount of intergenerational assistance provided, structural factors such as living arrangements, gender, and age are stronger predictors of the level of assistance than are culturally relevant expectations of filial obligation and ethnic-group identification. Their findings suggest important avenues for further exploration of issues of ethnicity and care of older persons by family members.

GEOGRAPHIC AND REGIONAL LOCATION

Another source of diversity in Canadian families is geographical and regional location. Canadian families differ substantially in their composition and structure from one part of Canada to another — a reality that is masked by references to "the Canadian elderly" and "the Canadian family." The relative proportion of the elderly population varies substantially from one province to another, as has been noted. So, too, does the proportion of the young-adult generation in each of these provinces and regions. Together, these patterns affect not only the opportunity for intergenerational family contact and support, but also the population of employed persons contributing to the resource base upon which services are built and from which public pensions are drawn.

As an illustration, Denton and Spencer (1997) document dramatic changes in the profile of population aging in Newfoundland society. That province currently has the lowest birth rate in Canada and the highest rate of out-migration of young adults. It is projected that these changes will produce a "top-heavy" population structure, quite unlike that of any other province, in terms of the very high proportion of elderly persons in the population. The implications for family life and social policy will be profound in terms of the availability of a wage-earning population base to support the costs of care, and the availability of informal supports for the aged population.

Another source of diversity for Canadian families is the rural–urban nexus. Close to 30 percent of all elderly Canadians reside in the three largest cities in the country: Toronto, Montreal, and Vancouver (Moore and Rosenberg, 1997). However, fully a quarter of all elderly Canadians live in rural areas, defined as areas with fewer than 1000 inhabitants. The highest percentage live in communities of 10 000 or fewer residents. Rural elders typically have limited access to a range of formal support services, despite the fact that rural and small-town Canada have a disproportionate share of our elderly population (Joseph and Martin Matthews, 1994). In many such communities, fully 25 to 30 percent of the population is over the age of 65 years and, not infrequently, over 5 percent of the population is over the age of 80 years (Martin Matthews, 1988). The challenges for service delivery in this context are evident.

The rural aged are no more likely then their urban peers to share a household with other family members, or to include different types of kin in descriptions of their family networks, although they do report higher levels of sibling contact. However, rural environments present particular challenges in later life, in terms of the lack of variety of supportive housing options, the limited range of health and social services, and transportation difficulties.

GENDER ISSUES

As Lopata (1995, p. 116) has recently noted,

> the existence of gender identity as a category in the social structure has led social scientists to use it as a variable in quantitative analyses. Such a conversion of the multiplicity of variation into a single variable ... flattens women (men also, of course) into a single dimension, ignoring their heterogeneity and seeing them as of significance only in contrast to the other gender.

One reason why the full extent and implications of gender comparisons and contrasts are often not well known is reflected in the "lack of visibility of men" in aging families (Bengtson, Rosenthal, and Burton, 1996, p. 267). In many studies, for example, sample sizes are simply not large enough to provide enough males for meaningful analyses of gender differences, controlling for kin relationships.

Nevertheless, men's contribution to the care of elderly family members is often overlooked and is by no means negligible (Creedon, 1995; Phillips and Bernard, 1995). The General Social Survey of Canada found that "over one-third of the population with full-time jobs and with a high level of parent-care responsibility in 1990 consisted of men" (Stone, 1994, p. 11) Men and women are almost equally likely to provide instrumental care, such as shopping and transportation. However, men are only half as likely as women (7 versus 14 percent) to be involved in the provision of the personal care of bathing, feeding, toileting, and dressing (Martin Matthews and Campbell, 1995). There is some suggestion that the predominance of women as carers is a function of the fact that women also predominate among the recipients of care. Certainly, mothers or mothers-in-law are by far the most common recipients of care (Martin Matthews and Rosenthal, 1993), accounting for about three-quarters of those to whom assistance is provided.

Factors that predict the involvement of employed men in caregiving roles to elderly family members have also been examined (Campbell, 1997). For this analysis, the various caring "tasks" that comprise the measure of "family caregiving" were categorized in terms of those that could be deemed "traditionally male" tasks (e.g., yard maintenance), more gender-neutral tasks (e.g., transportation), and typically "non-traditional" tasks for men (e.g., personal care). Although certain factors predict men's involvement independent of the type of task (for example, distance and sibling-network composition, that is, whether the care provider is an "only" child, or has sibling networks of brothers only, or sisters), the gendered nature of the task was important in determining how other factors — such as filial obligation, and parent status, education, and income — influence the provision of care by men (Campbell, 1997).

CONCLUSION
▼

The focus of the discussion thus far in relation to gender has been largely on the issue of gender in terms of the provision of assistance to older persons. Comparatively little is known about older men's family roles and family relationships, especially if those older men are unmarried. Some researchers suggest that, in old age, men may be even more in jeopardy than are women, because family relationships based on parenthood and marriage become more important in later life. "In old age, as employment-based resources become less central and as family relationships based on marriage and parenthood grow in importance, it is males who are at risk" (Goldscheider, 1990, p. 553). While studies of families and aging have yet to find evidence of broad patterns of disadvantage among older men, it is important that the study of diversity and change in intragenerational and intergenerational roles and relationships be inclusive of both men and women in the questions we pose and the findings we study.

SUMMARY
▼

- This chapter has provided an overview of a broad range of issues facing elderly persons and their aging families in Canadian society on the eve of the new millennium. The material presented has documented a variety of structural changes — involving increasing longevity, the duration of intergenerational and intragenerational ties, marital-status patterns, women's labour force participation — and their impact on families.
- These structural changes play out in the dynamics of increasingly diverse relationships between members of couples, between adult children and their aging parents, between generations, and among siblings; they find new expression in fictive-kin ties and the emergence and societal recognition of various "non-traditional" family forms.

- This chapter has also demonstrated the impact of policy changes, especially those involving health and social care, on elderly persons and those who care for them. Other forces that have an impact on the relationship between elderly persons and their families have been considered, such as options involving payment for care and statutory obligations.
- And, finally, the diversity of family forms, structures and dynamics discussed in other chapters in this volume manifest themselves here, too, in the context of families and aging; this chapter has emphasized the extent to which the experience of aging in the context of families varies profoundly as a function of socio-economic status, of ethno-cultural affiliation, of geographical and regional location and gender.

NOTES
▼

1. These figures will be different from those reported above as the figures above note cross-sectional reporting of the number of remarried widows and widowers at any one time, while the data reported by Wu are more useful for our purposes in that they capture the concept of "event history," and the likelihood of an event occurring over the lifetime of the individual.
2. The primary way in which poverty is measured in Canada is Statistics Canada's "low-income cutoff" measure. This measure defines people as living "in poverty" if they spend more than 58.5 percent of their total income on food, clothing, and shelter. The figures are adjusted annually for single individuals, for families of varying sizes, and for residence in rural and urban areas of varying sizes.
3. I am using the term "generation" here to refer to lineage positions in families (such as the "parental" generation or the "child" generation), as it is used by Hagestad (1981) and others. However, this term is used in a variety of ways in the fields of sociology of aging and in social gerontology. Sometimes it describes age groups (people grouped according to their similar ages, usually measured at five-year intervals, e.g., 20- to 24-year-olds). Others use the term to describe age cohorts (people born at particular points in history, e.g., the "baby-boom generation"). Still others use it to describe kinship lineage descent, as I have done. Bengston (1993) calls for conceptual clarity in relation to this term.
4. Rosenthal (1998) reports that among never-married women aged 55–59 in 1991, 13 percent had at least one child, compared with 5 percent of those aged 70 years or older.
5. Examples of job costs include arriving late for work or having to depart early, having to use sick days when they personally were not sick, and using vacation time to attend to family obligations. Examples of career costs are declining or not seeking a promotion, experiencing difficulty with one's manager or supervisor, missing business meetings or training sessions. Examples of personal costs are reducing volunteer work, missing sleep, reducing leisure activities.

CRITICAL THINKING QUESTIONS
▼

1. As increasing proportions of women enter later life outside of marriage, how will this change their experience of old age? How do the circumstances of later life vary for previously married and ever-single persons?

2. For most of this century, the experience of later life has been substantially different for women than for men. How are these differences compounded by being a member of a minority ethnic group, or living in a rural area or within a particular region of the country?

3. Many researchers, and certainly the popular press, make much of the notion of the "sandwich generation." What is fundamentally inaccurate about this image? Why does this myth persist?

4. In what ways have changes in Canadian health and social policy in the past few decades affected the experience of aging for individuals and their families? What kinds of changes might we anticipate in the future?

5. Once adult children and elderly parents no longer share a household, what kinds of obligations, moral and legal, do they have in relation to one another? How might Canadian health and social policy be more supportive of these obligations?

SUGGESTED READING
▼

Sara Arber, and Jay Ginn, eds. 1995. *Connecting Gender and Ageing: Sociological Reflections*. Buckingham, U.K.: Open University Press.
> This book highlights the different social effects of aging on women's and men's roles, relationships, and identity over the life course. The contributors use a feminist perspective to explore the impact of aging on gender roles across a wide range of situations, such as is in the workplace, in retirement, and in marital and other relationships.

Carol Baines, Patricia Evans, and Sheila M. Neysmith, eds. 1991. *Women Caring: Feminist Perspectives on Social Welfare*. Toronto: McClelland & Stewart.
> This book explores the ways in which women's "caring roles" shape the experience of women at different points in the life cycle, and examines the connections between caring and poverty, wife abuse, and child neglect. Grounded within the broad context of social welfare in Canada, it questions how caring can be reformulated so as to support, rather than disadvantage, women in their caring roles.

Ingrid Arnet Connidis. 1989. *Family Ties and Aging*. Toronto: Butterworths/Harcourt Brace.
> This book explores a broad range of the family ties that are part of older adult life, with particular emphasis on intergenerational relationships and sibling ties. Family ties are examined as sources of support and companionship. There is

closing discussion of social policy that emphasizes the important implications of family ties in an aging society.

Ellen M. Gee, and Meredith M. Kimball. 1987. *Women and Aging*. Toronto: Butterworths/Harcourt Brace.

This book addresses the broad range of demographic, social, economic, and policy issues that shape women's experiences of aging. It grounds this analysis in a historical context, and examines women's experiences across the full range of transitions in family life and marital status. Social-policy implications are considered as well.

Jon Hendricks and Carolyn J. Rosenthal, eds. 1993. *The Remainder of Their Days: Domestic Policy and Older Families in the United States and Canada*. New York: Garland.

This book focusses on a comparative, cross-national discussion of social policies in the United States and Canada, especially as they relate to health care. Chapters view family experiences from both Canadian and U.S. perspectives, and examine how these policies shape and affect the lives of older families in both countries.

Anne Martin Matthews. 1991. *Widowhood in Later Life*. Toronto: Butterworths/Harcourt Brace.

This book provides an in-depth examination of the research and policy literature on widowhood. It examines both the process of bereavement and the subsequent reconstruction of one's social world. It also analyzes how the experience of widowhood varies by gender, and by the presence or absence of children, and how it compares with other marital statuses in later life.

REFERENCES
▼

Aronson, Jane. 1994. "Women's Sense of Responsibility for the Care of Old People: 'But who else is going to do it?'" In Victor Marshall and Barry McPherson, eds., *Aging: Canadian Perspectives*. Peterborough, ON: Broadview.

Baines, Carol, Patricia Evans, and Sheila M. Neysmith, eds. 1991. *Women's Caring: Feminist Perspectives on Social Welfare*. Toronto: McClelland & Stewart.

Béland, François, and Evelyn Shapiro. 1994. "Ten Provinces in Search of a Long Term Care Policy." In Victor W. Marshall and Barry D. McPherson, eds., *Aging: Canadian Perspectives*. Peterborough, ON: Broadview.

Bengtson, Vern L. 1993. "Is the 'Contract across Generations' Changing? Effects of Population Aging on Obligations and Expectations across Age Groups." In Vern L. Bengtson and Andrew Achenbaum, eds., *The Changing Contract across Generations*. New York: Aldine de Gruyter.

Bengtson, Vern L., Neal E. Cutler, David J. Mangen, and Victor W. Marshall. 1985. "Generations, Cohorts and Relations beween Age Groups." In Robert H. Binstock and Ethel Shanas, eds., *Handbook of Aging and the Social Sciences,* 2nd ed. New York: Van Nostrand Reinhold.

Bengtson, Vern L., Carolyn J. Rosenthal, and Linda Burton. 1996. "Paradoxes of Families and Aging." In Robert H. Binstock and Linda K. George, eds., *Handbook of Aging and the Social Sciences,* 4th ed. San Diego, CA: Academic Press.

Bleiszner, Rosemary, and Victoria H. Bedford, eds. 1995. *Handbook of Aging and the Family.* Westport, CT: Greenwood Press.

Burkhauser, R.V., J.S. Butler, and K.C. Holden. 1991. "How the Death of a Spouse Affects Economic Well-Being after Retirement: A Hazard Model Approach." *Social Science Quarterly* 72/3: 504–19 .

Campbell, Lori D. 1997. "Sons Who Care: Exploring Men's Involvement in Filial Care." Unpublished Ph.D. dissertation, Department of Family Studies, University of Guelph.

Canadian Press. 1996. "Mother Wins Court Fight for Adult Children to Support Her." *Vancouver Sun,* January 24, p. A5.

Canadian Study of Health and Aging. 1994. "Patterns of Caring for Persons with Dementia in Canada." *Canadian Journal on Aging* 13/4: 470–87.

Carey, Elaine. 1995. "Can Kids Be Forced to Support Parents?" *Toronto Star,* September 17, pp. A1, A9.

Centre on Aging and the Caregivers Association of British Columbia. 1995. *Informal Caregivers to Adults in British Columbia: Joint Report.* Victoria, B.C.: University of Victoria.

Chappell, Neena L. 1994. "Health Care Reform: Will It Be Better or Worse for Families?" Opening Plenary Address, Annual Meetings of the Canadian Association on Gerontology, Winnipeg, October 13.

———. 1998. "Family Caregiving and the Workplace." Keynote presentation at the Conference "Family Caregiving and the Workplace," sponsored by Health Canada, Vancouver, B.C., June 22.

Chappell, Neena L., Laurel A. Strain, and Audrey A. Blandford. 1986. *Aging and Health Care: A Social Perspective.* Toronto: Holt, Rinehart and Winston.

Connidis, Ingrid Arnet. 1989. *Family Ties and Aging.* Toronto: Butterworths/Harcourt Brace.

———. 1992. "Life Transitions and the Adult Sibling Tie: A Qualitative Study." *Journal of Marriage and the Family* 54/4: 972–82.

———. 1994. "Growing Up and Old Together: Some Observations on Families in Later Life." In Victor Marshall and Barry McPherson, eds., *Aging: Canadian Perspectives.* Peterborough, ON: Broadview.

Connidis, Ingrid Arnet, and Lorraine Davies. 1990. "Confidants and Companions in Later Life: The Place of Family and Friends." *Journal of Gerontology: Social Sciences* 45/4: S141–49.

Creedon, Michael A. 1995. "Eldercare and Work Research in the United States." In Judith Phillips, ed., *Working Carers: International Perspectives on Working and Caring for Older People.* Aldershot, U.K.: Avebury.

Denton, Frank T., and Byron G. Spencer. 1997. "Population Aging and the Maintenance of Social Support Systems." *Canadian Journal on Aging* 16/3: 485–98.

Dorfman, R., K. Walters, P. Burke, L. Hardin, T. Karanik, J. Raphael, and E. Silverstein. 1995. "Old, Sad and Alone: The Myth of the Aging Homosexual." *Journal of Gerontological Social Work* 24(1–2): 29–44.

Dorrell, B. 1991. "Being There: A Support Network of Lesbian Women." *Journal of Homosexuality* 20(3–4): 89–98.

Gee, Ellen M. 1990. "Demographic Change and Intergenerational Relations in Canadian Families: Findings and Social Policy Implications." *Canadian Public Policy* 16: 191–99.

Gee, Ellen M., and Meredith M. Kimball. 1987. *Women and Aging*. Toronto: Butterworths/Harcourt Brace.

Gladstone, James. 1995. "The Marital Perceptions of Elderly Persons Living or Having a Spouse Living in a Long-Term Care Institution in Canada." *The Gerontologist* 35/1: 52–60.

Goldscheider, Frances. 1990. "The Aging of the Gender Revolution." *Research on Aging* 12: 531–45.

Gottlieb, Benjamin H., E. Kevin Kelloway, and Marianne Fraboni. 1994. "Aspects of Eldercare that Place Employees at Risk." *The Gerontologist* 34/6: 815–21.

Hagestad, Gunhild O. 1981. "Problems and Promises in the Social Psychology of Intergenerational Relations." In Robert W. Fogel, Elaine Hatfield, Sara B. Kiesler, and Ethel Shanas, eds., *Aging: Stability and Change in the Family*. New York: Academic Press.

Havens, Betty. 1996. "Long Term Care in Five Countries." *Canadian Journal on Aging* 15 (Supplement 1): 1–14.

Health and Welfare Canada. 1993. *Health Expenditures in Canada Fact Sheets*. Ottawa: Planning and Information Branch. February.

Holden, K.C., R.V. Burkhauser, and D.J. Feaster. 1988. "The Timing of Falls into Poverty after Retirement and Widowhood." *Demography* 25/3: 405–14.

Holden, K.C., and P.J. Smock. 1991. "The Economic Costs of Marital Dissolution: Why Do Women Bear a Disproportionate Cost?" *Annual Review of Sociology* 17: 51–78.

Hudson, Cathie Mayes. 1984. "The Transition from Wife to Widow: Short-Term Changes in Economic Well-Being and Labor Force Behavior." Unpublished Ph.D. dissertation, Department of Sociology, Duke University, Durham, North Carolina.

Hurd, Michael D., and David A. Wise. 1987. "The Wealth and Poverty of Widows: Assets Before and After the Husband's Death." National Bureau of Economic Research Working Paper no. 2325. Washington, DC.

Janigan, M. 1995. "A Prescription for Medicare." *Maclean's,* July 31, pp. 10–18.

Jendrek, Margaret. 1993. "Grandparents Who Parent Their Grandchildren: Effects on Lifestyle." *Journal of Marriage and the Family* 55/3: 609–21.

———. 1994. "Grandparents Who Parent Their Grandchildren: Circumstances and Decisions." *The Gerontologist* 34/2: 206–18.

Joseph, Alun E., and Anne Martin Matthews. 1994. "Growing Old in Aging Communities." In Victor Marshall and Barry McPherson, eds., *Aging: Canadian Perspectives*. Peterborough, ON: Broadview.

Keating, Norah D., and Priscilla Cole. 1980. "What Do I Do with Him 24 Hours a Day? Changes in the Housewife Role after Retirement." *The Gerontologist* 20/1: 84–89.

Keefe, Janice M., and Pamela Fancey. 1997. "Financial Compensation or Home Help Services: Examining Differences among Program Recipients." *Canadian Journal on Aging* 1/2: 254–78.

———. 1998. *Financial Compensation versus Community Supports: An Analysis of the Effects on Caregivers and Care Receivers: Final Report.* Ottawa: Health Canada.

Keefe, Janice M., Carolyn J. Rosenthal, and François Béland. 1996. "The Impact of Ethnicity on Helping for Older Relatives: Findings from a Sample of Employed Canadians." Unpublished manuscript. Centre for Gerontology, Mount Saint Vincent University, Halifax, NS.

Kruk, Edward. 1995. "Grandparent–Grandchild Contact Loss: Findings from a Study of 'Grandparent Rights' Members." *Canadian Journal on Aging* 14/4: 737–54.

Lopata, Helena Znaniecka. 1995. "Feminist Perspectives on Social Gerontology." In Rosemary Bleiszner and Victoria H. Bedford, eds., *Handbook of Aging and the Family.* Westport, CT: Greenwood Press.

MacRae, Hazel. 1992. "Fictive Kin as a Component of the Social Networks of Older People." *Research on Aging* 14/2: 226–47.

Mandell, Nancy, and Ann Duffy, eds. 1995. *Canadian Families: Diversity, Conflict and Change.* Toronto: Harcourt Brace.

Martin Matthews, A. 1988. "Aging in Rural Canada." In Eloise Rathbone-McCuan and Betty Havens, eds., *North American Elders: United States and Canada*, Westport, CT: Greenwood Press.

———. 1991a. "The Relationship between Social Support and Morale: Comparisons of the Widowed and Never Married in Later Life." *Canadian Journal of Community Mental Health* 10: 47–63.

———. 1991b. *Widowhood in Later Life.* Toronto: Butterworths/Harcourt Brace.

———. 1993. "Issues in the Examination of the Caregiving Relationship." In Steven H. Zarit, Leonard I. Pearlin, and K. Warner Schaie, eds., *Caregiving Systems: Formal and Informal Helpers.* New York: Lawrence Erlbaum Associates.

Martin-Matthews, Anne. 1996. "Why I Dislike the Term 'Eldercare.'" *Transition* 26/3: 16.

———. 1998. "Intergenerational Caregiving: How 'Apocalyptic' and Dominant Demographies Frame the Questions and Shape the Answers." Presentation at the John K. Friesen Symposium "Apocalyptic Demography and the Intergenerational Challenge," Gerontology Research Centre, Simon Fraser University, Vancouver, B.C., May 14–15.

———. In press a. "Managing Employment and Care of the Frail Elderly." In Viola Lechner and Margaret B. Neal, eds., *Working and Caring for the Elderly: An International Perspective.* New York: Taylor and Francis.

———. In press b. "Widowhood: Dominant Renditions, Changing Demography and Variable Meaning." In Sheila M. Neysmith, ed., *Critical Issues in Social Work with Elderly Persons.* New York: Columbia University Press.

Martin Matthews, Anne, and Lori D. Campbell. 1995. "Gender Roles, Employment and Informal Care." In Sara Arber and Jay Ginn, eds., *Connecting Gender and Ageing: Sociological Reflections*. Buckingham, UK: Open University Press.

Martin Matthews, Anne, and Carolyn J. Rosenthal. 1993. "Balancing Work and Family in an Aging Society: The Canadian Experience." In George L. Maddox and M. Powell Lawton, eds., *Annual Review of Gerontology and Geriatrics: Focus on Kinship, Aging and Social Change*. New York: Springer.

McDaniel, Susan A. 1993. "Caring and Sharing: Demographic Aging, Family and the State." In Jon Hendricks and Carolyn J. Rosenthal, eds., *The Remainder of Their Days: Domestic Policy and Older Families in the United States and Canada*. New York: Garland.

McDonald, Lynn. 1997. *Transitions into Retirement: A Time for Retirement*. Final report, prepared for Human Resources Development Canada, National Welfare Grants Program.

McDonald, Lynn, and Blossom Wigdor. 1995. "Taking Stock: Elder Abuse Research in Canada." *Canadian Journal on Aging* 14/2: 1–6.

McPherson, Barry D. 1998. *Aging as a Social Process,* 3rd ed. Toronto: Harcourt Brace.

Moore, Eric, and Mark Rosenberg. 1997. *Growing Old in Canada: Demographic and Geographic Perspectives*. Ottawa: Statistics Canada.

Morgan, Leslie. 1989. "Economic Well-Being Following Marital Termination." *Journal of Family Issues* 10/1: 86–101.

National Advisory Council on Aging. 1995. *The NACA Position on Community Services in Health Care for Seniors: Progress and Challenges*. Ottawa: Minister of Supply and Services.

National Forum on Health. 1997. *Canada Health Action: Building on the Legacy.* Vol. 1: *Final Report*. Ottawa: Minister of Public Works and Government Services.

Neysmith, Sheila M. 1995. "Power in Relationships of Trust: A Feminist Analysis of Elder Abuse." In Michael Maclean, ed., *Abuse and Neglect of Older Canadians: Strategies for Change*. Toronto: Thompson Educational.

Norland, Joseph. 1994. *Profile of Canada's Seniors*. Ottawa: Statistics Canada.

O'Bryant, Shirley L., and Leslie A. Morgan. 1989. "Financial Experience and Well-Being among Mature Widowed Women." *The Gerontologist* 29/2: 245–51.

O'Connor, Deborah. 1998. "Living with a Memory Impaired Spouse: (Re)cognizing the Experience." Unpublished manuscript, School of Social Work, University of British Columbia, Vancouver, B.C.

Ontario Women's Directorate. 1991. *Work and Family: The Crucial Balance*. Toronto: Ontario Ministry of Community and Social Services.

Parsons, Jeanette. 1998. "Parents Who Sue Their Children for Support: An Examination of Decisions by Canadian Court Judges." Unpublished M.Sc. major paper, Department of Family Relations and Applied Nutrition, University of Guelph, Guelph, ON.

Pearlin, Leonard I. 1980. "The Life Cycle and Life Strains." In H.M. Blalock, Jr., ed., *Sociological Theory and Research: A Critical Approach*. New York: Free Press.

Phillips, Judith, and Miriam Bernard. 1995. "Perspectives on Caring." In Judith Phillips, ed., *Working Carers: International Perspectives on Working and Caring for Older People*. Aldershot, U.K.: Avebury.

Rosenthal, Carolyn J. 1985. "Kinkeeping in the Familial Division of Labor." *Journal of Marriage and the Family* 47: 965–74.

———. 1987. "The Comforter: Providing Personal Advice and Emotional Support to Generations in the Family." *Canadian Journal on Aging* 6/3: 228–39.

———. 1997. "Family Care in Canada in the Context of Social and Demographic Change." *Ageing International* 24/1: 13–31.

———. 1998. "Aging Families: Have Current Changes and Challenges Been 'Oversold'?" Presentation at the John K. Friesen Symposium "Apocalyptic Demography and the Intergenerational Challenge," Gerontology Research Centre, Simon Fraser University, Vancouver, B.C., May 14–15.

Rosenthal, Carolyn J., and Pamela Dawson. 1991. "Wives of Institutionalized Elderly Men: The First Stage of the Transition to Quasi-Widowhood." *Journal of Aging and Health* 3/3: 315–34.

Rosenthal, Carolyn J., and James Gladstone. 1994, "Family Relationships and Support in Later Life." In Victor Marshall and Barry McPherson, eds., *Aging: Canadian Perspectives*. Peterborough, ON: Broadview.

Rosenthal, Carolyn J., Anne Martin-Matthews, and Sarah H. Matthews. 1996. "Caught in the Middle? Occupancy in Multiple Roles and Help to Parents in a National Probability Sample of Canadian Adults." *Journal of Gerontology: Social Sciences* 51 B: S274–83.

Ross, Margaret M., Carolyn J. Rosenthal, and Pamela G. Dawson. 1997. "Spousal Caregiving in the Institutional Setting: Task Performance." *Canadian Journal on Aging* 16/1: 51–69.

Schellenberg, Grant. 1994. *The Road to Retirement: Demographic and Economic Changes in the 90s*. Ottawa: Canada Council on Social Development, Centre for International Statistics.

Smith, G., and J. Dumas. 1994. "The Sandwich Generation: Myths and Reality." In J. Dumas and A. Belanger, eds., *Report on the Demographic Situation in Canada 1994*. Ottawa: Statistics Canada.

Snell, James G. 1990. "Filial Responsibility Laws in Canada: An Historical Study." *Canadian Journal on Aging* 9/3: 268–77.

Statistics Canada. 1997. "Measuring the Age of Retirement." *The Daily*, June 6.

Stone, Leroy. 1994. *Dimensions of Job–Family Tension in Canada*. Ottawa: Statistics Canada.

Stone, Leroy O., and Susan Fletcher. 1988. "Demographic Variations in North America." In Eloise Rathbone-McCuan and Betty Havens, eds., *North American Elders: United States and Canadian Perspectives*. Westport, CT: Greenwood Press.

Stone, Leroy O., and H. Frenken. 1988. *Canada's Seniors*. Catalogue no. 98-121. Ottawa: Minister of Supply and Services.

Underwood, N., and J. DeMont. 1991. "Mid Life Panic." *Maclean's*, August 19, pp. 30–33.

Uhlenberg, Peter. 1993. "Demographic Change and Kin Relationships in Later Life."
    In George L. Maddox and M. Powell Lawton, eds., *Annual Review of Gerontology
    and Geriatrics: Focus on Kinship, Aging and Social Change*. New York: Springer.
Wu, Zheng. 1995. "Remarriage after Widowhood: A Marital History Study of Older
    Canadians." *Canadian Journal on Aging* 14/4: 719–36.

GLOSSARY

absolute poverty: a condition of mere physical survival, most closely approximated by homelessness.

access: legal permission for non-custodial parent to visit his or her child after a divorce.

acculturation: the processes by which new immigrants internalize and adapt to the dominant culture(s) in society.

ADD, or attention deficit disorder: a set of characteristics that tend to cluster together and include difficulty to concentrate and focus on what one is doing, inability to remain on a same task for long, and some disorganization. When hyperactivity is present, the term used is ADHD (attention deficit and hyperactivity disorder). ADD makes it difficult for children to learn in school. Boys are more likely to be afflicted than girls.

agency: the taking of an active role in one's life rather than adopting passivity or helplessness.

assimilation: processes by which a minority member/group loses its own characteristics and becomes like the majority group.

authoritarian parenting: parental behaviours and attitudes that are predominantly controlling and punishing. At the extreme, they can be even harsh and rejecting. The authoritarian approach does not appeal to a child's sense of reasoning or morality. It is a "do-as-I-say-or-you'll-get-smacked" type of upbringing. Authoritarian parents may also be inconsistent: they may threaten to punish, then not follow through with the punishment.

authoritative parenting: combines both warmth and monitoring of children's activities and whereabouts. Authoritative parents make maturity demands on their children. They explain to their children the reasons behind their demands or rules; their method is inductive. Once they have explained the reasons and the consequences, they consistently follow through with enforcement of those rules.

behaviour genetics: Behaviour genetics is a psychological science that focusses on differences and similarities within families in terms of abilities, character traits, and even behaviours. It studies how genes interact with the environment to produce such things as personalities and IQ levels, by comparing children (including adopted children) with parents, and siblings (including identical and fraternal twins) with each other.

bidirectional: describes a theoretical model that studies causality both from A to B and from B to A — for example, from parents to children and from children to parents.

Black Loyalist: Blacks who had been granted freedom in the American colonies for supporting the British.

blaming the victim: holding those whose situation is produced by structural factors beyond their control responsible for their situation in life.

blended family: a family that contains spouses who may have been divorced, widowed, or never married, and with or without children. Within this family unit are various configurations of stepparents and step-/adopted siblings, as well as stepgrandparents/aunts/uncles/cousins.

capitalist: describes societies based on the private ownership of resources, where profit maximization is a prime objective.

census family: a husband and wife (either legally married or in a common-law union), with or without children who are never married, regardless of age; or a lone parent with one or more children who are never married, regardless of age.

child support: the allowance that the court may order a parent (non-custodial/joint-custody parent) to pay for the upkeep of his or her child.

child-support guidelines: a policy implemented by the Canadian government in 1997 to standardize and improve the determination of child-support awards by linking the amount awarded to the income of the payor.

cluttered nest: the phenomenon, increasingly witnessed in the last decade or so, of adult children remaining home to later ages, or of adult children returning home (the latter are sometimes referred to as "boomerang kids").

cohabitation: living together without legal marriage.

cohort: a group of individuals born in the same year (for example, 1970) or within the same period of time (for example, a five- or ten-year period). Sometimes those cohorts whose members have experienced and reacted similarly to significant social, political, or historical events that emerged at particular points in their life cycle come to be characterized in a particular way, such as "baby boomers" or "Generation Xers."

common-law: describes the relationship between a couple living together for a specified period of time without being legally married.

communities of colour: communities that are perceived as non-white in Canada, based on their physical characteristics

comprador: member of a colonized nation who assists colonizers.

compulsory heterosexuality: the belief that people are naturally attracted to the opposite sex and that, therefore, gay and lesbian relations are unnatural or inferior to heterosexual relations.

concealed homelessness: living temporarily with friends or family.

concordance, or concordance rate: a concept, used particularly in comparisons of twins (or of parents with children), that signifies the percentage of occurrences for which both twins have a characteristic that is observable in one of the two twins. For example, we take 100 pairs of monozygotic twins where one twin is known to be schizophrenic and examine the other twin: We may find that in 60 of the pairs, both have schizophrenia. The concordance rate for schizophrenia is then 60 percent.

conduct disorders: generally, children who suffer from conduct or behavioural disorders are "difficult." They frequently and persistently exhibit impulsive, aggressive, confrontational behaviours. Some may steal and lie, while others make incessant demands for attention, have repeated temper tantrums, or are hyperactive, and have a short attention span and a low level of self-control. Some children exhibit all of these behaviours.

confederates: in the context of experimental research, this concept refers to a person who behaves as requested by the researcher in order to test the reactions of those respondents selected to participate in the study.

consensual union: a self-defined co-resident sexual relationship. Terms often used synonymously are "common-law marriage," "living together," and "cohabitation." Most Canadian provinces have a legal definition of common-law marriage, which is more stringent than one based on self-definition.

co-parenting: physical and emotional care of the child shared by both individuals in a relationship even when only one is the "biological" or "adoptive" parent.

correlations: a relationship between two factors or variables, such as poverty and violence, whereby as one increases or decreases, the other also changes. When both change in the same direction (e.g., both increase), this is a positive correlation. A negative correlation exists when one factor increases at the same time that the other decreases, as in the example of an increasing number of hours of television watched by children and the decreasing number of books read. Correlation is a statistical test.

couple: two people who are sexually or intimately together.

Criminal Code: criminal-law texts of Canada.

cult of domesticity: a Victorian ideal that made women responsible for the moral and everyday affairs of the home.

cultural capital: the cultural and financial resources to support a middle-class lifestyle.

culture of poverty: the view that poor families tend to develop fatalistic values and attitudes about their lot in life, devaluing education, career aspirations, and the usual middle-class definitions of success.

custody (of child): the legal right to make decisions about the well-being of the child.

customary marriages: non-traditional but common "marriage" in the fur-trading era, during the 1500s and 1600s in Canada, between Native women and European (mostly French) men.

dead-beat dads: noncustodial fathers who are in arrears in their child-support payments.

deviance model of divorce: a sociological and psychological perspective that tends to view divorce as a social problem.

domestic labour: all unpaid work undertaken by family members to maintain a household, including child care, emotional labour, housework, yard work.

ecological model: the theoretical model popularized by James Garbarino that emphasizes the interplay between violent families and "external" social factors such as the cultural norms surrounding physical discipline of children and the social services that provide support to the family.

endogamy: the practice of marrying within one's own community.

essentialist: describes the explanation of a social phenomenon as natural, biological, or innate.

ethnicity: one's group identity based on common ancestry, language, and religion.

ethnocentrism: viewing and judging the world with one's own ethnic group as a reference point.

exchange/social control theory: the theoretical perspective that approaches family violence in terms of a win–loss calculation. Victimizers employ violence because they can; that is, it achieves their desired goals and does not result in undesired costs. In particular, victimizers achieve control over family members.

familial ideology: the idea that the nuclear-family unit, comprising husband, wife, and their dependent children, is the "normal" and highest form of family.

familialism: the glorification of an idealized nuclear family — a family construed as consisting of a socially and legally recognized heterosexual couple.

family: a social ideal, generally referring to a unit of economic co-operation, typically thought to include only those related by blood, but revised by feminists to include those forming an economically co-operative, residential unit bound by feelings of common ties and strong emotion.

family-based economy: form of economic production wherein the household is a basic unit of the economy and the site for most of the production of goods, services, and income, and their distribution.

family/household: a household that includes a family and unrelated persons residing together.

family law: the legal rules that govern spousal and/or parent–child relationships both during and after the dissolution of a family unit, as well as the relationship between families and the state.

family reunification: a principle in post-1967 immigration policy in Canada that prioritizes the uniting of "family" members.

family violence: the complex array of behaviours — physical, emotional, financial, and sexual — that singly or in combination intentionally result in harm for one or more members of a family group.

family wage: a wage paid to a male worker deemed to be sufficient to provide for wage earners and an economically dependent woman and children.

fathers' rights: the social movement based on the assumption that fathers have lost legal rights as a result of family-law reforms, particularly regarding custody of children.

feminism: a worldview based on the assumptions that, historically, women have occupied a subordinate status relative to men in most societies, and that women must mobilize politically to achieve equality with men; diverse political theories and principles interrogating and advocating social, economic, cultural, and political equality for women.

feminization of poverty: a marked increase in the number of women living in poverty, particularly elderly women and sole-support mothers, that has characterized Canadian society during the late nineteenth and the late twentieth century; the tendency for women to be poor without the support of a man.

filial obligation or piety: a felt need, duty, or moral obligation to honour and care for one's parents in their later years of life.

filles du roi: the poor and orphaned young women sent from Paris in the seventeenth century to become wives of men in the colony of New France.

formal equality: the liberal principle that, regardless of differences (e.g., gender), every citizen is equal under the law and is entitled to the same legal and civil rights and opportunities.

functionalist: describes a view of society as a system of made-up functional parts.

gender behaviour: activities socially typical of males and females.

gender identity: subjective sense of being male or female.

gender roles: socially constructed attitudes and behaviour, usually organized dichotomously as masculinity and femininity, and based on the cultural expectations associated with gender.

generation: kinship lineage positions in families (such as the "parental" generation or the "child" generation). This term is often misused to describe age groups or age cohorts.

get self-sufficient quick: a legal-context orientation primarily directed to those women who have interrupted their employment for marriage and/or child care. This approach assumes that in most current marriages both spouses have careers, and that wives generally have worked fulltime or intermittently throughout the marriage. This orientation, reinforced by judicial indifference to gender-based wage inequities, influences decisions regarding retraining periods for the dependent spouse.

glass ceiling: a structural barrier, invisible to the naked eye, through which those beneath gaze upward at the lifestyle and opportunities of the more privileged above.

heterosexism: a bias that assumes that everyone is heterosexual or that homosexuality is abnormal and/or insignificant.

homophobia: fear and/or disapproval of homosexuality.

household: economic unit of those residing together, with a common economic base.

ideological hegemony: processes by which ruling-class ideas become dominant in society through consensus or coercion.

ideology: a system of beliefs that distorts reality at the same time that it provides justification for the status quo.

intergenerational relations: patterns of interaction with individuals in different generations of the family lineage, either in older generations, such as parents and grandparents, aunts, uncles, or in younger generations, such as children and grandchildren, nieces, and nephews.

intergenerational transmission. *See* social learning.

intragenerational relations: patterns of interaction with individuals who hold similar lineage positions within the family, such as the spouse or partner, brothers and sisters, brothers- and sisters-in-law, cousins.

joint custody: a legal concept based on the assumption that, when parents separate or divorce, they should share legal and/or custodial responsibility for their children. Regardless of residence, both parents have legal rights in decision making regarding the child's welfare, including education and religious upbringing.

life expectancy: the average number of years of life remaining at a given age (e.g., at birth, or at age 65).

lone-parent families: a household in which one parent resides with his or her children.

mating gradient: the phenomenon in which a small difference in age at marriage (husbands are approximately two years older than wives) translates, over time, into a significant economic difference between husband and wife.

matrilineage: ancestry and inheritance through the mother's line.

matrilocal/patrilocal: practice of living with bride/groom's family after marriage.

meritocracy: the belief that all have an equal chance of success and those at the top are those with the most merit.

miscegenation: sexual relations between different racialized groups.

multiculturalism: 1971 Canadian government policy that encourages ethnic/cultural retention.

near poor: families whose standard of living is very close to that of the poor.

neolocal: describes the practice of living with neither the bride nor the groom's family after marriage.

no-fault divorce: a legal concept based on the assumption that terminating a marriage relationship should not be contingent upon one or both spouses each demonstrating that the other

was to blame for the marital breakdown because of adultery, mental or physical cruelty, and so on.

non-agentic: refers to passivity and helplessness; in other words, the opposite of having agency.

non-Status: describes a Native person who is not recognized as "Indian" under the Indian Act for historical reasons, for example, a Native person whose ancestor refused to sign a treaty, or a Native woman who married a non-Native person.

nuclear family: a family structure in which husband and wife reside together with their children.

objective poverty: the prevailing definitions used by bodies whose purpose it is to collect, compile, and report data on poverty within the Canadian population, such as Statistics Canada and the Canadian Council on Social Development.

patriarchal theory of the family: a theoretical viewpoint that sees the male breadwinner/female domestic labourer model as natural, universal, and essential.

patriarchy: institutionalized beliefs and actions in which men dominate women, and where what is considered masculine is more highly valued than what is considered feminine.

patrilocal. *See* matrilocal/patrilocal.

population aging: a demographic phenomenon in which, because of decreased fertility and increased life expectancy, an increasing percentage of the population is made up of older people.

potential homelessness: living on the verge of homelessness.

public/private split: the notion that the world of the family is private, and therefore separate from and uninfluenced by the public world of work and other social institutions.

quasi widowhood: the situation in which one partner in a couple resides permanently in a long-term-care institution while the other continues to reside in the community. Also known as "married widowhood."

quintile: the division of the population into fifths on the basis of wealth.

redefining mothering: refers to the use of eligibility criteria in various welfare-to-work programs in Canada. The definition of "full-time" mothering is based on the age of the child, but this definition often varies from one province to another.

relative poverty: poverty as measured against contemporary standards for "normal" and "wealthy."

romantic love: idealized or sentimental love.

sandwich generation: individuals, usually in midlife, who are "caught" between the simultaneous demands of dependent children and elderly parents or other relatives.

schizophrenic: describes a very severe mental illness characterized by various degrees of distancing or withdrawal from reality as it is perceived by others. Interpersonal difficulties are also present. The more severe forms involve hallucinations (hearing voices and seeing things), delusions, loss of contact with one's bodily needs and external reality, inability to care for oneself, rigid body mannerisms, and inability to initiate or maintain relationships.

secondary data: data collected by persons other than the researcher, often by a statistical agency such as Statistics Canada. They are often used in the study of the family, especially by demographers and quantitative sociologists. Three limitations of secondary data are listed in Chapter 3, Box 3.1.

sexism: the differential valuing of one sex over the other.

single mother on welfare: refers to women who, through marital/common-law separation (or the birth of a child to a never-married woman), find themselves applying and receiving social assistance, and the negative myths that accompany them.

social clock: an internalized time schedule for the "proper" ages at which to experience certain events, such as getting married and having a first child.

social construct: how a society defines an experience or a group of persons. For instance, adolescence is defined by Western societies as a difficult and stormy period. This is a cultural definition of adolescence that does not necessarily apply everywhere. We "construct" and "reconstruct" reality, depending on who and what we are.

social learning/intergenerational transmission: the theoretical perspective in the sociology of family violence that calls attention to the ways in which children growing up in a violent family learn violent roles and, subsequently, may play out the roles of victim or victimizer in their adult families.

social reproduction: the view that social class is reproduced intergenerationally as a result of structural factors such as capitalism and patriarchy.

socialist feminism: feminism that links the liberation of women with the liberation of the working classes.

socialization: refers to the process whereby individuals learn how to think and behave according to the norms of their society and/or of their subgroup. This concept generally refers to children, but the process is lifelong.

state: organized and institutionalized system of power and authority in society, including the government, legal system, police, and military forces.

stereotype: a fixed image about a group.

subjective poverty: how people feel about their standard of poverty.

substantive equality: the principle that, regardless of differences (e.g., gender), every member of a society is entitled to equality or equal outcomes under law and policy.

systemic discrimination: standard policies, procedures, and practices that result in the disadvantaging of a disempowered group.

"The personal is political": a slogan that encapsulates the feminist assumptions that the public/private split is a falsity and that what happens to individual women in the "private" sphere of the family (e.g., abuse) is relevant to all women and of public interest.

underemployment: being employed below one's level of education/training.

Underground Railroad: the route taken into Canada by Blacks escaping slavery in the United States.

unidirectional: describes a theoretical model that considers only one causality path, in this instance generally from parents to children.

vertical intergenerational mobility: the tendency for children to be upwardly or downwardly mobile, vis-à-vis their parents.

working poor: families in which the main breadwinner works at least 49 weeks of the year but who remain poor.

CONTRIBUTOR PROFILES

ANNE-MARIE AMBERT

Anne-Marie Ambert is a professor of sociology at York University. Her most recent books are *Parents, Children and Adolescents: Interactive Relationships and Development in Context* (1997) and *The Web of Poverty: Psychosocial Perspectives* (1998), both published by The Haworth Press, New York. Her current research interests are in the area of the parent–child relationship and the effects of poverty on families and children.

DOROTHY E. CHUNN

Dorothy Chunn is a professor in the School of Criminology and director of the Feminist Institute for Studies in Law and Society at Simon Fraser University. Her publications include *From Punishment to Doing Good: Family Courts and Socialized Justice in Ontario, 1880–1940* (1992) and *Law as a Gendering Practice*, co-edited with Dany Lacombe (forthcoming). Current research projects focus on the regulation of venereal disease in the developing Canadian welfare state and on feminism, law, and social change in Canada since the 1960s.

TANIA DAS GUPTA

Tania Das Gupta is an associate professor in the Department of Sociology at Atkinson College, York University. She also teaches in the Certificate in Anti-Racist Research and Practice (CARRP) based in the department. She has been involved for many years in community activities around issues of racism and sexism. Her research interests include the areas of racism and sexism in workplaces, critical pedagogy, and multiculturalism. Over the past few years, she has been interviewing South Asian homeworkers in Toronto. She is the author of several publications, including *Racism and Paid Work* (1996).

ANN DUFFY

Ann Duffy is a professor in and associate chair of the Department of Sociology at Brock University. She also teaches in the Women's Studies and Labour Studies programs. In 1995, she was awarded an Ontario Confederation of University Faculty Associations Excellence in Teaching Award. Professor Duffy is the co-author of several books on the sociology of work, and has edited a number of books on the sociology of work, Canadian society, and the sociology of the family. She recently co-authored (with Julianne Momirov) the first Canadian text on family violence, entitled *Family Violence: A Canadian Introduction* (1998).

ELLEN M. GEE

Ellen M. Gee is a professor in and chair of the Department of Sociology and Anthropology at Simon Fraser University. She has published extensively in the areas of aging, families, and demography. She has served on the executive of the Canadian Association of Aging and the Canadian Population Society, as a member of the Status of Women Committee of the Canadian Sociology and Anthropology Association, and on the editorial boards of *Journal of Women and Aging* and *Canadian Studies in Population.*

AVIVA GOLDBERG

Aviva Goldberg is a former teacher in the public and private school systems in Toronto. She completed her Master's in Women's Studies in 1997 and is continuing her doctoral studies at York University in the Graduate Program in Women's Studies. Her research interests include contemporary feminist spirituality and the new field of women's ritual studies. She has spoken extensively on Jewish feminist ritual, lesbian voices in faith communities, and lesbian and gay issues. She currently acts as a ritual adviser and facilitator for same-sex and heterosexual life-cycle events.

CAROLYNE A. GORLICK

Carolyne Gorlick is an associate professor of Social Work at King's College, University of Western Ontario. She has just completed a ten-year study of low-income female single-parent families and their children that focusses on economic stress, formal and informal social support, and health and well-being. Publications, conference papers, group and association presentations, and a manuscript have come from this research. Her new research investigates the experiences of participants in "welfare to work" programs across Canada.

LESLEY D. HARMAN

Lesley Harman is an associate professor of Sociology at King's College, University of Western Ontario. She is the author of *The Modern Stranger: On Language and Membership* (1987) and *When a Hostel Becomes Home: Experiences of Women* (1989), as well as book chapters and articles on gender, deviance, social theory, aging, poverty, and women and deviance. She is putting the finishing touches on her third book, an ethnography of women living on islands in the Thousand Islands, and has begun a community study of urban healers.

NANCY MANDELL

Nancy Mandell is an associate professor in Sociology and Women's Studies and past director of the Centre for Feminist Research, School of Women's Studies at York University. Her recent publications include *On Their Own: Making the Transition from School to Work in an Information Era* with Stewart Crysdale and Alan King; a second edition of *Feminist Issues: Race, Class and Sexuality*; an edited collection of essays on Canadian women's lives, *Young Women's Human Rights: Global Challenges*; and chapters and articles on women and violence, poverty, race, human rights, and education. Recent research studies include comparative studies on family violence in Canada and Russia, the implementation of protocols for community–academic research partnerships, the design of inclusive curriculum for the Toronto-based Coalition for Inclusive Curriculum, and a study of Canadian women in their pre-retirement years.

ANNE MARTIN-MATTHEWS

Anne Martin-Matthews is a professor of family studies in the School of Social Work and Family Studies, and associate dean of research and graduate studies in the Faculty of Arts at the University of British Columbia. For thirteen years, she was director of the Gerontology Research Centre at the University of Guelph. Her publications include *Widowhood and Later Life* (1991) and many articles on women's experiences of later life in terms of social support, family roles, work–family balance, and aging in rural environments. A founding member of the Ontario Gerontology Association, she now serves on the board of directors of the Canadian Association on Gerontology. From 1993 to 1996, she was Social Sciences Section Editor for the *Canadian Journal on Aging/La revue canadienne du vieillissment*, and is currently serving as the journal's editor-in-chief (1996–2000).

JULIANNE MOMIROV

Julianne Momirov is completing her Ph.D. in sociology at McMaster University. She has taught at Brock University and is the co-author, with Ann Duffy, of *Family Violence: A Canadian Introduction* (1998). She was the president of the board of directors of a non-profit organization working to open a resource centre for street-involved youth. Among her recent interests are nationalism, violence, and aboriginality and identity.

CAROL-ANNE O'BRIEN

Carol-Anne O'Brien teaches in the Faculty of Social Work at Wilfrid Laurier University. She has been active in Ireland and Canada on lesbian, gay, and bisexual issues. Her research interests include lesbian, gay, and bisexual community development; sexual regulation; and social policy.

INDEX